AF600141

THE CATHOLIC UNIVERSITY OF AMERICA
CANON LAW STUDIES
No. 113

THE EXTRAORDINARY ABSOLUTION FROM CENSURES

AN HISTORICAL SYNOPSIS AND COMMENTARY

A DISSERTATION

Submitted to the Faculty of Canon Law of the Catholic University of America in Partial Fulfillment of the Requirements for the Degree of

DOCTOR OF CANON LAW

BY THE

REV. FRANCIS E. MORIARTY, C.SS.R., J.C.L.
Priest of the Baltimore Province

THE CATHOLIC UNIVERSITY OF AMERICA
WASHINGTON, D. C.
1938

Imprimi Potest:

ANDREAS B. KUHN, C.SS.R.,
Superior Provincialis.
Brooklynii, N. Y., die V Maii, 1938.

Nihil Obstat:

EDUARDUS G. ROELKER, S.T.D., J.C.D.,
Censor Deputatus.
Washingtonii, D. C., die XVIII Maii, 1938.

Imprimatur:

✠ MICHAEL J. CURLEY, D.D.,
Archiepiscopus Baltimorensis.
Baltimorae, Md., die XVIII Maii, 1938.

Printed by
THE PAULIST PRESS
New York, N. Y.

TO

THE MOST HOLY REDEEMER

AND

OUR MOTHER

OF PERPETUAL HELP

TABLE OF CONTENTS

INTRODUCTION

This work concerns the extraordinary absolution from censures, that is, the absolution from censures of penitents in danger of death and in the more urgent cases outside of danger of death, as that absolution is provided for in canons 882, 2252, and 2254 of the Code of Canon Law. It is needless to intimate the value of a knowledge of these canons, for every priest should realize the necessity of preparedness for cases of danger of death, and every confessor should recognize that canon 2254 for the more urgent cases is one which he should know, if not word for word, then at least substantially, whenever he enters the confessional.

The title has been made sufficiently broad to include both reserved and non-reserved censures, for, although almost the entire consideration has been devoted to absolution from censures reserved in the technical sense as developed since the twelfth century and to the old discipline of public penance with its less formal, yet equally effectual, reservation to the bishop, nevertheless there is no intention to exclude the extraordinary absolution from non-reserved censures by those who ordinarily would enjoy no jurisdiction even for such censures. The case in point concerns the absolution from censures in danger of death by priests who, for any reason such as apostasy, or the mere lack of faculties to hear confessions, ordinarily have no power to absolve from non-reserved censures. For this reason the scope of the work could not properly be restricted to reserved censures.

There is no pretension in this dissertation to define the nature of the various censures, except in several unusual cases, nor is there any attempt to explain the causes which diminish or preclude imputability and accordingly excuse from the incurrence of censures. In the entire treatment it has been presupposed that the censure has been contracted and is confessed by the delinquent for the purpose of absolution in danger of death or in one of the more urgent cases.

In the first part of this work an effort has been made to outline the historical development of the legislation on absolution in danger of death and other extraordinary cases, which reached its final form in canons 882, 2252, and 2254 of the Code. In connection with the factors of censure and of absolution in the early Church, it was found necessary to make a study of the evolution of these elements. Further investigation was required for the clearer understanding of early conciliar legislation. Again, public penance, of such great importance in the discipline of the early centuries, proved to be a form of excommunication containing medicinal elements, consequently coming under the early, undeveloped notion of censure. For the better comprehension of the historical section, it has been considered advisable to devote the first chapter to an exposition of these preliminary notions.

In the historical synopsis of the legislation on absolution from censures in danger of death, the complexity and diversity of early legislation on this subject have necessitated, in those articles which cover the period of public penance, a threefold division comprising the actual granting of absolution, the minister of absolution, and the requisites after recovery. The subsequent uniformity and universality of such laws have obviated this necessity in the following periods, in which these features can be treated together without detriment to the clarity of the presentation.

Since public penance involved the release from the *anathema,* or complete excommunication from the Church, and since early legislation on absolution in danger of death seems almost exclusively devoted to the subject of public penance, it has been considered sufficient to trace the discipline on absolution in the early centuries through legislation on public penance, rather than to delve into the study of other ecclesiastical penalties. With the stabilization of the scope of censure, limiting it to excommunication, suspension, and interdict, a broader view is possible at a single glance, in the consideration of specific provisions for the absolution from all censures in danger of death.

Since the time of the Decretals the legislation on absolution in danger of death has been closely interwoven with that on absolution in other extraordinary cases, but it has been considered advisable to give a separate treatment to each of these sets of evolving norms, to avoid confusion of details in legislation which appeared shortly before the Code. This method has entailed not a few repetitions, but this may be compensated by greater simplicity and clarity in the distinct discussion of these matters.

It will be noticed in the historical section that in some places, for the sake of greater adequacy of the outline, references have been made to various sources and writings which have a merely confirmatory value for points already established; but it is to be remarked that in several instances the confirmatory evidence serves the purpose of indicating a continuance of an identical discipline over an extended period of time. Again, in the footnotes frequently the substance of legislation and occasionally that of historical commentary has been quoted, not simply to support the contentions of the present writer, but to reflect the actual development as depicted in sources and writings which may not be available to the average reader. The frequent reference to the work of Morinus on the sacrament of Penance regarding matters pertaining to the first thirteen centuries may find some justification in a statement of Schulte (*Geschichte der Quellen,* III, Part I, p. 593) concerning that work and another by the same author on the sacrament of Orders: *"Beide liefern das bis dahin reichste historische Material für diese Gegenstände."*

In the second part of the dissertation, consisting of a commentary on the present legislation, it has been found imperative to divide the matter into two sections, one on the absolution from censures in danger of death, the other on absolution in the more urgent cases; otherwise, the advantage of consecutive numbering of the chapters would have become a source of confusion.

It would have been preferable in the commentary on canons 882 and 2252, to devote one chapter to the absolution, as in canon 882, and another to the requisites after recovery, as in canon 2252. However, the material on recourse after absolution in danger of death was too unwieldly to admit of such a division, but demanded a special chapter, consequently necessitating a separate chapter on the mandates.

The nature of canon 2254 has compelled an unproportionate division, for each paragraph of this canon calls for treatment in a separate chapter, but the great preponderance of material is to be found in canon 2254, § 1, with the result that the consideration has suffered a serious lack of balance. But any other method of handling the material would have led to hopeless confusion.

As in the historical section, so in the commentary on the present legislation there is very much in common between the provisions for absolution in danger of death and the norms for absolution in the more urgent cases. The inevitable result, consequently, is the recurring appearance of almost identical material under slightly differing aspects. The only alternative to the repetition of lengthy discussions has been a substantial restatement of conclusions with cross-references to the development of arguments, and this alternative has required acceptance lest the material go beyond all bounds. In an effort to mitigate the reader's unwelcome burden of searching from place to place for sections in which particular points are professedly discussed, the cross-references have been indicated as clearly and as accurately as possible.

It is the impression of the writer, as it may have been the impression of others who have devoted themselves to such specialized works, that there must be few canons in the Code which have led to such divergency of opinion as the three canons considered in this dissertation, especially canon 2254. In the historical section the main difficulty was the proper understanding of the nature of public penance and its place in the evolving discipline on absolution in danger of death. But in the commentary on the present legislation the major task has been to sift and weigh conflicting opinions, to evaluate arguments, to determine the existence or non-existence of objective doubt, and to arrive at practical conclusions in the presence of controversy. At times the views of eminent authors have been rejected, but the writer disclaims all presumptousness in his efforts to reach satisfactory solutions and professes nothing but the highest respect for those whose opinions he has in places disregarded. Due deference has been expressed regarding the contingency of authoritative decisions on doubtful points, but in no other wise does the writer retract or retrench from what he has set down as the result of diligent application to this particular subject.

The chief aim of this work, after canonical truth, has been clarity. Some of the questions involve inherent difficulty and obscurity, and their presentation will require close reading. Others appear insoluble in the present state of the legislation, and can be settled only on the principles of the Code regarding doubtful matters. Unanimous approval of the opinions adduced in the course of these pages can hardly be expected, for viewpoints on the interpretation of questionable positive law are not to be harnessed into consent; but it is trusted that the reasoning processes, even if not convincing to others, will at least be evident, and that the conclusions, even though repudiated by some, will not suffer from ambiguity.

The writer takes pleasure in discharging a debt of gratitude by expressing his appreciation to his Very Reverend Provincial, Andrew B. Kuhn, C.SS.R., for the opportunity of advanced studies in Canon Law; to the faculty of the School of Canon Law of the Catholic University for their cordial, painstaking and illuminating instruction and advice; to his family and relatives, and to many confreres and friends, for a keen interest and for many aids in the preparation of this work; to the librarians of the Catholic University for their genial and capable assistance; finally, and above all, to Those to whom this dissertation is dedicated, for encouragement and strength of another order.

Part I
HISTORICAL SYNOPSIS

CHAPTER I

PRELIMINARY NOTIONS

ARTICLE I. THE DEVELOPMENT OF THE CONCEPT OF CENSURE

THE term "censure" can be traced as far back as the days of the Roman Republic. Most probably in the year 443 B. C. the office of censor was established, and it was in connection with this office that the word *censura* came into use. One of the duties of the censors was to exercise vigilance over the morals of the people, and to punish all acts in public or private life that might militate against the material or moral integrity of the State. When such matters were brought before the censors, they passed judgment on them, and, if they found the accused citizen guilty, they inflicted a punishment on him. This penalty consisted mainly in the degradation of the citizen, whether from a place in the senate, or from the rank of knighthood, or from a tribe of higher standing and greater political power to one of lower status. From a political and financial point of view, there was nothing more serious than such a removal from the list of senators or from the ranks of the knights. This penalty was recorded next to the name of the citizen in the registers of the census, with a note indicating the reason for which he was degraded.[1] At first the term *censura* was applied to the office of the censor, but later it was transferred not only to the sentence he pronounced, but also to the penalty he inflicted.[2] It was in this last sense of "censure," as referring to a penalty, that it was taken over by the

[1] *Cf.* Daremberg-Saglio, "Censor," *Dictionnaire des Antiquités Grecques et Romaines* (Paris, 1873), I, 995-997; "Censore," *Enciclopedia Italiana* (Milan: Treccani, 1929—), IX, 739-741.

[2] *Cf.* "Censura," *Thesaurus Linguae Latinae* (Lipsiae, 1904—), III, 803-806; Suarez, *De Censuris in Communi,* Opera Omnia, vol. XXIII (Parisiis, 1866), disp. I, sec. 1, n. 2; Reiffenstuel, *Jus Canonicum Universum* (Parisiis, 1864-1870), lib. V, tit. 39, n. 2; Schmalzgrueber, *Jus Ecclesiasticum Universum* (Romae, 1843-1845), lib. V, tit. 39, n. 1; Cappello, *Tractatus Canonico-Moralis de Censuris* (3. ed., Taurinorum Augustae: Marietti, 1933), n. 1, nota 1.

Church and employed to designate ecclesiastical punishments and corrections.[3]

As early as the time of St. Cyprian (+ 258) [4] *censura* was used in the Church in the general meaning of an ecclesiastical punishment.[5] In the same sense [6] it was used by Pope St. Felix III in the year 488,[7] by the Council of Lerida in 546,[8] by Pope St. Gregory I in 601,[9] by the eleventh Council of Toledo in 675,[10] and by Pope St. Nicholas I (858-867).[11] At some time between 1198 and 1205, Pope Innocent III declared that, when the term "censure" was used, it was to be understood as referring to excommunication, suspension, and interdict.[12] Since the time of the Decretals this term has become one of the common elements of penal law.

Although the term "censure" came early into usage in the Church, it was slow in attaining the precise meaning attached to it today, as a spiritual penalty with primary medicinal purpose, from which the penitent is to be absolved when, and only when, his contumacy has ceased.[13] It seems that this exact meaning was unknown not only to such outstanding writers of the eleventh century as Burchard of Worms and Ives of Chartres, but also to Gratian, Peter Lombard, and Hugh of St. Victor of the twelfth century.[14] Even the declaration of Innocent III, mentioned above,[15] only settled

[3] *Cf.* Reiffenstuel, *loc. cit.;* Cappello, *loc. cit.*

[4] *Ep. 62, ad Pomponium—MPL,* IV, 370.

[5] *Cf.* "Censura," *Thesaurus Linguae Latinae,* III, 805, linea 75.

[6] Richter, *Lehrbuch des katholischen und evangelischen Kirchenrechts* (8. ed., Leipzig, 1886), p. 774, note 2.

[7] *Cf.* c. 118, D. IV, *de cons.*

[8] *Cf.* c. 38, C. XII, q. 2.

[9] *Cf.* c. 13, D. XII.

[10] *Cf.* c. 7, D. LVI.

[11] *Cf.* c. 10, C. II, q. 1.

[12] C. 20, X, *de verborum significatione,* V, 40.

[13] *Cf.* canons 2241, § 1; 2248, § 2.

[14] Morinus, *Commentarius Historicus de Disciplina in Administratione Sacramenti Poenitentiae Tredecim Primis Seculis in Ecclesia Occidentali, et huc usque in Orientali Observata* (Parisiis, 1651), lib. V, cap. 25, num. 12.

[15] *Cf.* above, note 12.

the scope of censure and did not define its concept.[16] This has been denied, and the assertion made [17] that the concept of censure has been clear since the time of Hostiensis (+ 1271), later quoted by Panormitanus (+ 1453). But it seems that Hostiensis, speaking of excommunication,[18] and basing his remark on a statement by St. Augustine,[19] only approaches the general notion of censure, while Panormitanus [20] is obscure in indicating the distinction between medicinal and vindictive penalties. This distinction became clearer toward the end of the fifteenth century, but it was only in the next century that the definite and ultimate concept of censure was fully evolved. [21] Especially is this true since the time of Suarez (1548-1617), who introduces an extensive and precise treatment by defining a censure as "poena spiritualis et medicinalis, privans usu aliquorum spiritualium bonorum, per ecclesiasticam potestatem ita imposita, ut per eamdem ordinarie absolvi possit."[22] At least from the time of Suarez, canonists have been clear on the nature of censure, as is evident from their works.[23] It is in line with this evolution of the

[16] Wernz, *Ius Decretalium* (Romae et Prati, 1906-1913), VI, 149; Hinschius, *System des katholischen Kirchenrechts* (Berlin, 1869-1897), V, 126, note 1.

[17] Hollweck, *Die kirchlichen Strafgesetze* (Mainz, 1899), § 22, note 1.

[18] ". . . Cum haec sententia [excommunicationis] sit poena contumacium et rebellium, ab initio medicinalis."—*Summa Aurea* (Venetiis, 1570), lib. V, *de sententia excommunicationis*, n. 1.

[19] ". . . Quamvis haec prohibitio [a communione] nondum sit mortalis, sed medicinalis . . ."—*Cf.* c. 18, C. II, q. 1.

[20] "[C. 20, V, *de verborum significatione*, V, 40] non comprehendit in se depositionem vel degradationem, quia illae poenae sunt multum odiosae, et istae de quibus in textu sunt favorabiles, et in animarum medicinam inductae. Unde facimus strictam interpretationem maxime, quia secundum communem consuetudinem ecclesiae fere semper contumaces compescuntur remediis, de quibus hic."—*Commentaria in Quinque Libros Decretalium* (Venetiis, 1588), lib. V, *de verborum significatione*, cap. 20.

[21] Hinschius, *Kirchenrecht*, V, 641.

[22] *De Censuris*, disp. I, sec. 1, n. 5.

[23] *Cf.* Reiffenstuel, lib. V, tit. 39, nn. 1-46; Schmalzgrueber, lib. V, tit. 39, nn. 1-111; Wernz, *Ius Decret.*, VI, 150. For a brief summary of the development of the notion of censure, *cf.* Chelodi, *Ius Poenale* (Tridenti, 1925), pp. 36, 37; Cappello, *De Censuris*, n. 1, nota 1; Coronata, *Institutiones Iuris Canonici* (Taurini, Italia: Marietti, 1928-1936), IV, 146, 147.

nature of censure that the term is used in this work, with no attempt to force ancient ecclesiastical penalties under the specific category of censure as finally determined.

Article II. The Nature of Public Penance

From the beginning the Church has inflicted penalties directly concerned with the improvement of the sinner.[24] It has been disputed whether the major excommunication, or *anathema,* in the earliest times was a purely vindictive penalty,[25] or whether it has always been intended only for the improvement of the sinner,[26] but it seems rather to have combined both elements.[27] However this may be, among the penalties directed toward the improvement of the sinner must be considered public penances, modified forms of excommunication, for these were at least partially medicinal not only in the early centuries,[28] but throughout the time of their existence.[29]

Public penance originated in the earliest ages of the Church,[30] but its duration in the East varied from that in the West.

In both the East and the West for the first four centuries, public penance was imposed for all grave sins, whether public or occult.[31]

[24] Probst, *Kirchliche Disciplin in den drei ersten christlichen Jahrhunderten* (Tübingen, 1873), p. 385.

[25] Hinschius, *Kirchenrecht,* V, 127.

[26] Kober, *Der Kirchenbann* (Tübingen, 1863), pp. 23-27.

[27] Probst, *Kirchl. Disciplin,* pp. 399-401.

[28] Hinschius, *Kirchenrecht,* IV, 696, 747; Schmitz, *Die Bussbücher und die Bussdisciplin der Kirche* (Mainz, 1883), p. 19.

[29] *Cf.* Hollweck, *Kirchl. Strafgesetze,* § 22, note 5, § 94, note 5; Hyland, *Excommunication, Its Nature, Historical Development and Effects,* The Catholic University of America, Canon Law Studies, n. 49 (Washington: The Catholic University of America, 1928), pp. 27, 28.

[30] Morinus, *De Admin. Sacr. Poenit.,* L. V, cc. 1, 2; L. V, c. 25, n. 1.

[31] *Cf.* Morinus, *op. cit.,* L. V, cc. 8-14; Rauschen, *Eucharist and Penance in the First Six Centuries of the Church,* authorized transl. from 2. German ed. (St. Louis, 1913), p. 196; Vacandard, "Les Origines de la Confession Sacramentelle," *Etudes de Critique et d'Histoire Religieuse,* 2me série (3. ed., Paris, 1914), p. 100; Batiffol, "Les Origines de la Pénitence," *Etudes d'Histoire et de Théologie Positive,* 1re série (4. ed., Paris, 1906), I, 200;

Toward the end of the fourth century, probably in the year 391, it began to disappear in the East when Nectarius, Patriarch of Constantinople, issued a decree abolishing it.[82] The disappearance of public penance in the East seems to have become complete about the year 500.[83]

In the West public penance continued for a much longer time. The discipline of public penance for both public and occult grave sins seems to have endured till about the year 700.[84] About that time there began the practice of imposing public penance for public grave sins only, and private penance for occult sins, a practice which was universal in the Western Church by about the year 730.[85] This discipline remained almost unchanged for nearly four hundred years,[86] and during this period there was still a large number of public penitents.[87] Due to various causes,[88] immediately after the eleventh century the penitential discipline began to relax very

Teetaert, *La Confession aux Laiques dans l'Eglise Latine depuis le VIIIe jusqu'au XIVe Siècle,* Universitas Catholica Lovaniensis, Dissertationes ad gradum magistri in Facultate Theologica consequendum conscriptae, Series II, Tomus 17 (Wetteren, Bruges, Paris: De Meester, Beyaert, Gabalda, 1926), pp. 4, 5.

[82] *Cf.* Morinus, *De Admin. Sacr. Poenit.*, L. VI, c. 22; Rauschen, *op. cit.*, pp. 196, 210; Pignataro, *De Disciplina Poenitentiali Priorum Ecclesiae Saeculorum Commentarius* (Romae, 1904), pp. 89, 90.

[83] Rauschen, *op. cit.*, p. 212.

[84] Morinus, *De Admin. Sacr. Poenit.*, L. VI, c. 27, n. 1. However, it appears that at least in some places the practice of permitting private penance for grave sins arose at an earlier date, for in a work ascribed to Gennadius (c. 492) the following is found: " . . . quem mortalia crimina post baptismum commissa premunt, hortor prius publica poenitentia satisfacere, et ita sacerdotis judicio reconciliatum communioni sociari . . . Sed et secreta satisfactione solvi mortalia crimina non negamus . . . "—*De Ecclesiasticis Dogmatibus*, cap. 53—*MPL*, LVIII, 994. *Cf.* Pignataro, *De Discipl. Poenit.*, pp. 61, 62, 85.

[85] Morinus, *op. cit.*, L. VII, c. 1, n. 1; Teetaert, *Confession aux Laiques*, pp. 20, 21.

[86] Morinus, *op. cit.*, L. VI, c. 27, n. 2.

[87] Morinus, *op. cit.*, L. VII, c. 2, n. 4.

[88] For a discussion of these causes, *cf.* Morinus, *op. cit.*, L. X, cc. 16-23; Teetaert, *Confession aux Laiques*, pp. 22, 23; Pignataro, *De Discipl. Poenit.*, p. 93.

rapidly,[39] and at some time shortly after the year 1100 public penance disappeared in the West.[40]

At the time of its broadest development, public penance consisted of four grades or "stations." These grades, starting with the highest, were called *consistentia, substratio, auditio,* and *fletus.*[41] It is unnecessary to outline the types of sinners comprised under each grade, the place each group occupied inside or outside the churches, the ritual prayers and impositions of hands prescribed for various penitents, or the actual works of penance.[42] The purpose here is merely to show the different degrees in which the penitents of the various grades were separated from participation in the life of the Church.

The penitents in the grade of *consistentia,* namely the *consistentes,* were deprived of the reception of the Eucharist and of the privilege of offering their gifts during the Mass. The *substrati,* besides being denied the Eucharist and a share of the offering, were cut off from the public prayers of the Church. To the above inhibitions was added, for the *audientes,* the privation of those prayers said by individual members of the clergy and laity over the kneeling *substrati* and catechumens, and attendance at Mass was limited to its first part. Finally, the *flentes* were not only subject to the foregoing elements of removal from the life of the Church, but were also forbidden even to enter a church.[43]

It may be noted, in passing, that it was not necessary to proceed from one grade to the one immediately higher—for example, the

[39] Morinus, *op. cit.,* L. X, c. 16, nn. 1, 2.

[40] Morinus, *op. cit.,* L. VII, c. 7, n. 1; Rauschen, *Eucharist and Penance,* p. 213.

[41] For an extensive consideration of each of these grades in the order mentioned, *cf.* Morinus, *op. cit.,* L. VI, cc. 17, 18; cc. 6-8; cc. 3-5; c. 2.

[42] For these, *cf.* Morinus, *loc. cit.*; Hinschius, *Kirchenrecht,* IV, 715-726; Frank, *Die Bussdisciplin der Kirche von den Apostelzeiten bis zum siebenten Jahrhundert* (Mainz, 1867), pp. 555-650; Hyland, *Excommunication,* pp. 28, 29.

[43] *Cf.* Morinus, *De Admin. Sacr. Poenit.,* L. VI, c. 25, n. 13; L. VI, c. 26, n. 18; L. IV, c. 3, n. 10; Rauschen, *Eucharist and Penance,* p. 202; Van Espen, *Scripta Omnia* (Lovanii, 1753), II, 379; Pignataro, *De Discipl. Poenit.,* pp. 86-89.

penitent might pass directly from *fletus* to *substratio*.[44] It was in the *substratio* that the properly so-called works of penance were performed, and it was likewise in this grade that the largest part of the time prescribed for public penance was spent.[45]

From the consideration of the elements of separation from the communion of the faithful involved in the different grades, it is evident that public penance was a form of excommunication. Although this type of excommunication is unknown today, a vestige of it is found in the *excommunicatio minor,* mentioned both before [46] and in [47] the Decretals of Gregory IX. Public penitents, however, were still members of the Church, for their separation was only partial, to a greater or less degree; the complete expulsion from the Church was the *anathema,* later known as the *excommunicatio maior,* which was never a public penance.[48]

That public penance was a form of excommunication is also seen from various testimonies.[49] Such is that of St. Augustine in his Epistle to Seleuciana, in which he writes: "Agunt etiam homines poenitentiam, si post Baptismum ita peccaverint, ut *excommunicari* et postea reconciliari mereantur: sicut in omnibus Ecclesiis illi qui proprie *poenitentes* appellantur." [50] It is clear that the penitential canons and the writings of the Fathers referred to the grades of public penance as an excommunication, especially in the use of such expressions as *communione privetur*.[51] In the earlier centuries of the

[44] *Cf.* Morinus, *op. cit.,* L. VI, c. 19.

[45] *Cf.* Morinus, *op. cit.,* L. VI, c. 6, n. 4; L. VI, c. 11, n. 1; L. VI, c. 8, n. 2.

[46] "Est autem triplex excommunicatio, una quae separat a perceptione corporis Christi, altera . . . "—Bernardus Papiensis, *Summa Decretalium* (ed. Laspeyres, Ratisbonae, 1860), lib. V, tit. 34, *de sent. excom. et absol.,* § 2.

[47] *Cf.* c. 59, X, *de sententia excommunicationis,* V, 39; c. 2, X, *de exceptionibus,* II, 25; c. 10, X, *de clerico excommunicato, deposito vel interdicto ministrante,* V, 27.

[48] *Cf.* Morinus, *De Admin. Sacr. Poenit.,* L. V, c. 26, n. 18; L. IV, c. 2, n. 3; L. IV, c. 3, n. 1; Van Espen, *Tractatus Historico-Canonicus de Censuris Ecclesiasticis* (Lovanii, 1753), pp. 8, 9; Hyland, *Excommunication,* pp. 22-25, 27-29; Pignataro, *De Discipl. Poenit.,* pp. 94-97.

[49] For a consideration of these, *cf.* Morinus, *op. cit.,* L. IV, cc. 2-7.

[50] *Ep. 265,* n. 7—*MPL,* XXXIII, 1088.

[51] *Cf.* Morinus, *De Admin. Sacr. Poenit.,* L. IV, c. 3, n. 1; Van Espen, *Tract. de Censuris,* p. 6.

Church, when the term "excommunication" or equivalent expressions were used without qualification, they were accepted as referring to the minor excommunications; only when the penalty was designated as *anathema* or *excommunicatio mortalis* was it understood as the major excommunication or complete expulsion from the Church. This practice appears to have obtained until, with the growing use of the major excommunication, it was determined in the Decretals of Gregory IX that the major excommunication was intended when the simple word "excommunication" was used.[52] Even the sole privation of the Eucharist, which was common to all the grades of public penance, but was practically the only element of the highest grade, was a form of excommunication, although the very slightest.[53] Consequently, it appears necessary to accept the conclusion that the public penances were forms of excommunication, and, specifically, not as types of the major excommunication, but as varying forms of the minor excommunication.[54]

From the fact that public penance was an excommunication, the implication cannot necessarily be drawn that it was also a censure, for the clear distinction between medicinal and vindictive penalties was slow in reaching its full development.[55] It would be absurd to contend that public penance was a pure censure, but, despite the claim that it was entirely vindictive,[56] it seems to have contained

[52] C. 59, X, *de sententia excommunicationis*, V, 39; *cf.* Van Espen, *Tract. de Censuris*, p. 7; Gonzalez Tellez, *Commentaria Perpetua in Singulos Textus Quinque Librorum Decretalium Gregorii IX* (Lugduni, 1715), lib. V, tit. 39, cap. 59.

[53] Morinus, *De Admin. Sacr. Poenit.*, L. VI, c. 17, n. 7; Van Espen, *op. cit.*, pp. 5b, 6a, 7b; Suarez, *De Censuris*, disp. XXIV, sec. 1, n. 6; Pignataro, *De Discipl. Poenit.*, p. 19.

[54] *Cf.* Morinus, *op. cit.*, L. VI, c. 25, n. 13; Van Espen, *Scripta Omnia*, II, 380; *Idem*, *Tract. de Censuris*, p. 6a; Suarez, *loc. cit.*; Richter, *Kirchenrecht*, pp. 776, 777; Phillips-Vering, *Compendium Iuris Ecclesiastici* (1. Latin version from 3. German ed., Ratisbonae, 1875), p. 366; Pignataro, *De Discipl. Poenit.*, pp. 68, 73.

[55] *Cf.* Hinschius, *Kirchenrecht*, V, 125, 126, 641.

[56] Meurer, "Die rechtliche Natur der Pönitenzen der katholischen Kirche in historischer Entwicklung," *AKKR*, XLIX (1883), 180-187.

such medicinal elements as would warrant its consideration as a foreshadowing of censure in its later precise sense.[57]

One of the most striking features of public penance was its unusual duration, which was expressed as extending over a definite number of years or to the end of one's life. This is seen throughout the penitential canons [58] and the penitential books.[59] At first glance this creates the impression that these penances were of purely vindictive character. But most important is the consideration that, from the very beginning of the Church throughout the entire period of public penance, the bishops and their vicars were allowed to curtail or remit canonical penances inflicted for sins, whenever the penitents' ardor of conversion or zeal in performing the penances appeared to justify it.[60] The time a penitent spent in the various grades of penance depended not only on the gravity of the crime he had committed, but also on the diligence and ardor of his penance.[61] Thus, it depended to a large extent on the spirit of contrition and humiliation shown in the lower grades of *fletus* and *auditio* as to how soon the penitent would be admitted to the higher grade of *substratio*.[62] At times it also happened that persons guilty of serious crimes, who voluntarily confessed them to the bishop and showed great sorrow, were exempted from the lower grades of public penance and were admitted immediately to the highest grade, the *consistentia*.[63]

[57] *Cf.* Morinus, *De Admin. Sacr. Poenit.*, L. V, c. 26, nn. 18, 19; Hollweck, *Kirchl. Strafgesetze*, § 22, note 5c, § 94, note 5; Pignataro, *De Discipl. Poenit.*, pp. 80, 94, 95, 137, 142.

[58] *E. g.*, Council of Elvira (305), c. 5—Mansi, II, 6; Council of Nice (325), c. 12—Mansi, II, 956; Council of Ancyra (314), cc. 4-8, 19-24—Mansi, II, 523-528.

[59] *E. g.*, those attributed to Theodore, Egbert of York, etc., as in Schmitz, *Bussbücher*, pp. 524-550, 573-587, etc.

[60] Morinus, *De Admin. Sacr. Poenit.*, L. VI, c. 25, n. 8.

[61] Morinus, *op. cit.*, L. VI, c. 2, n. 15; Vacandard, "Origines de la Confession," *Etudes de Critique*, 2me série, p. 117.

[62] *Cf.* Council of Nice (325), c. 12—Mansi, II, 956; Council of Ancyra (314), cc. 5, 7—Mansi, II, 523, 524. *Cf.* Morinus, *op. cit.*, L. VI, c. 5, n. 5; L. IX, c. 6; L. X, c. 16, n. 3.

[63] Morinus, *op. cit.*, L. VI, c. 18, nn. 3, 5.

Besides, the ancient Fathers throughout their works referred to the various penances as "medicines," and to the ministers of absolution as "physicians of the soul," [64] also, especially St. Augustine,[65] designating the minor excommunication of the public penance as *medicinalis*. The contention that such terms were used solely in the sense that the penalty would lead to one's improvement, if not disregarded,[66] does not seem to be sufficiently strong to command assent, for these expressions, as used by popes,[67] Fathers, and councils, may as easily have contemplated the purpose of the penalty as its actual effect. At no time, whether in the past or in the present, has a censure, no matter how medicinal its purpose, produced a medicinal effect if it was repudiated, and this may well be the meaning intended in such expressions as that of Pope Innocent IV.[68] The first Council of Tours (461), determining a major excommunication for one who would withdraw from public penance and return to sin, inflicted it primarily for the improvement of the sinner,[69] and it seems that a slighter penalty of partial separation from the communion of the faithful would hardly be imposed for a purely vindictive purpose.

Especially during the period from 700 to 1100, public penance was considered chiefly as a medicine, and the sinner as one who was sick[70] as can be seen, for example, from the preface to the book *Corrector et Medicus* of Burchard of Worms on Penance.[71]

[64] *Cf.* Morinus, *op. cit.*, L. VII, c. 21, n. 7; L. III, c. 12, n. 24.

[65] *Sermo 351*, n. 10—*MPL*, XXXIX, 1546; quoted above, note 19.

[66] Hinschius, *Kirchenrecht*, V, 126, note 2.

[67] *E.g.*, Innocent IV: "Quum medicinalis sit excommunicatio, non mortalis, disciplinans, non eradicans, dum tamen is, in quem lata fuerit, non contemnat . . ."—C. 1, *de sententia excommunicationis, suspensionis et interdicti*, V, 11, in VI°.

[68] *Cf.* the preceding note.

[69] C. 8: ". . . a communione ecclesiae, vel a convivio fidelium extraneus habeatur, quo facilius et *ipse compunctionem per hanc confusionem accipiat*, et alii ejus terreantur exemplo."—Mansi, VII, 946. *Cf.* Morinus, *De Admin. Sacr. Poenit.*, L. VI, c. 20, n. 5.

[70] Morinus, *De Admin. Sacr. Poenit.*, L. VII, c. 6, n. 1.

[71] *MPL*, CXL, 949.

It seems, therefore, that public penance contained medicinal elements that would justify its consideration in an investigation into the evolving notion of censure, and, specifically in this work, in a study of the Church's discipline regarding absolution from censures in extraordinary cases.[72] That it was not a censure in the completely developed sense of the term is fully admitted; but that, taken in general, it was a purely vindictive penalty, is just as fully denied.

Article III. The General Development of Absolution From Censures

The term "*absolutio*," though found occasionally in the writings of Tertullian,[73] was rarely used in the early ages of the Church.[74] To signify absolution, the words ordinarily used were *reconciliatio*, *communio*, *pax*, and *venia*.[75] As will be seen, these expressions referred primarily to the remission of sins, but from this fact much can be inferred regarding the partial or complete absolution from the excommunication of the public penances, for the remission of sins was ordinarily granted only after certain requirements of public penance had been fulfilled.[76]

There was no special formula of absolution from the minor excommunication of the public penances, but the penitent was released from the greater degree of separation from the communion of the faithful by the fact of his formal admission into a higher

[72] Much attention is here given to public penance because early legislation on absolution in danger of death seems exclusively concerned with public penance during the time of its existence. Regarding the development of excommunication, *cf.* Hyland, *Excommunication, Its Nature, Historical Development and Effects*, The Catholic University of America, Canon Law Studies, n. 49 (Washington: The Catholic University of America, 1928), pp. 11-34; for the development of suspension, *cf.* Rainer, *Suspension of Clerics*, The Catholic University of America, Canon Law Studies, n. 111 (Washington: The Catholic University of America, 1937), pp. 1-33; for the development of interdict, *cf.* Conran, *The Interdict*, The Catholic University of America, Canon Law Studies, n. 56 (Washington: The Catholic University of America, 1930), pp. 10-50.

[73] *Cf.* Morinus, *De Admin. Sacr. Poenit.*, L. VIII, c. 1, n. 2.

[74] Van Espen, *Tract. de Censuris*, p. 57b.

[75] Morinus, *loc. cit.*; Van Espen, *loc. cit.*

[76] *Cf.* Teetaert, *Confession aux Laiques*, pp. 6, 22.

grade of penance. In other words, the formal and ritual admission into the higher grade implied and effected the termination of those more extensive elements of exclusion from the communion of the faithful entailed in the lower grades. In the same way, in the early ages the only form of absolution from the *anathema,* or complete separation from the Church, was the admission of the person to the lowest grade of public penance, for, from being an outcast from the Church, he was now accepted as a member of the Church, in which he could gradually attain to full participation. As the union with the Church was increased by successive releases from the *anathema* and the grades of penance, the degree of excommunication was diminished, until at last the sinner was again a partaker of all the rights and privileges of the faithful.[77]

Before the time of Novatian, who lived in the third century, it seems that public penance was not divided into grades, and the remission of sins was granted only after the entire penance was completed. To this remission of sins was immediately joined the right to receive the Eucharist. Shortly after Novatian the grades of penance appeared, and it seems that according to this discipline the absolution from sins was granted at the completion of the *substratio,* so that those in the highest grade, the *consistentes,* were already absolved from their sins but were not yet allowed to receive the Eucharist.[78] Consequently, before Novatian, when the penitent was absolved from his sins, he was also admitted to full membership in the Church, being no longer affected by partial separation involved in the public penance. After Novatian, the penitent at the time of absolution from his sins was in almost full communion with the Church, being deprived only of the reception of the Eucharist, and this privation ceased when he completed the *consistentia.* So it happens that, from statements in the canons and penitential books concerning the remission of sins, justified inferences can be drawn regarding the liberation from the minor excommunication of public

[77] *Cf.* Morinus, *De Admin. Sacr. Poenit.,* L. I, c. 10, n. 13; L. VI, c. 5, n. 2; Probst, *Kirchl. Disciplin,* pp. 406, 407; Hollweck, *Kirchl. Strafgesetze,* § 22, note 5b; Hinschius, *Kirchenrecht,* IV, 695.

[78] *Cf.* Morinus, *op. cit.,* L. I, c. 10, n. 13; L. VI, c. 21, n. 1.

penance.[79] It is true that, also after Novatian, in certain cases such as in some laws on absolution of public penitents in danger of death, full reconciliation with the Church was directly granted, including the absolution from sins and the permission to receive the Eucharist. Whether the reconciliation was complete, or whether it was only partial to the extent that the sins were remitted but not the *excommunicatio levissima*[80] involved in the privation of the Eucharist, can be judged only by a study of the terms used with reference to absolution.

Briefly, before Novatian, such terms as *reconciliatio, communio,* and *pax* meant full reconciliation with the Church, including, therefore, the right to receive the Eucharist.[81] After Novatian, when such terms were used with reference to public penance, if they stood alone and without qualification, they signified only the absolution from sins and not the granting of the Eucharist, the full reconciliation being expressed by such terms as *reconciliatio absolutissima, communio cum reconciliatoria manus impositione, communio legitima, admissio ad altarium,* or *participatio boni et perfecti*.[82] It seems that there is an exception to this general rule in the fact that *pax,* as used by St. Cyprian[83] and the Council of Elvira (305),[84] included both the absolution from sins and the granting of the Eucharist.[85]

The knowledge of these terms is essential for an inquiry into the Church's practice regarding absolution in danger of death. Terms that are obscure and confusing can be disregarded, and the investigation confined to those laws containing terms of clearer and more precise meaning. Without this knowledge it would be impossible to draw any conclusions with regard to absolution from public penance, which for so many centuries occupied such a prominent place in the penitential discipline of the Church.

[79] *Cf.* Morinus, *op. cit.*, L. IX, c. 3, n. 27; L. I, c. 10, n. 13.

[80] *Cf.* Morinus, *op. cit.*, L. VI, c. 17, n. 7.

[81] *Cf.* Morinus, *op. cit.*, L. IV, c. 21, n. 1.

[82] *Cf.* Morinus, *op. cit.*, L. VI, c. 21, nn. 5-11.

[83] *E. g., cf.* below, Chapter II, notes 15, 32.

[84] *Cf.* cc. 47, 61—Mansi, II, 13, 15, 16.

[85] *Cf.* Morinus, *De Admin. Sacr. Poenit.*, L. VIII, c. 23, n. 8; Pignataro, *De Discipl. Poenit.*, p. 119.

Public penance, during its existence of four centuries in the Eastern Church and eleven centuries in the Western Church, possessed a sacramental character, that is, it was a constituent part, with confession and absolution, of the sacrament of Penance. Consequently, the same one who absolved from sins also absolved from the excommunication of the public penance.[86] In the earliest times it was the bishop, together with his council of priests, who granted the absolution. Later, probably about the third century, the bishops or their special delegates granted it.[87] About the beginning of the twelfth century, when the last vestiges of public penance were disappearing, there grew the general practice of confining the absolution from sins to the internal or penitential forum, and the absolution from excommunication and other ecclesiastical penalties to the external or jurisdictional forum. About this time not only the bishop, but also the archdeacon and the *officialis* appointed by either the bishop or the archdeacon, absolved from censures.[88]

Since the time of the Decretals the broad outlines of the doctrine on absolution from censures have remained substantially the same. Subsequent developments through legislation, ecclesiastical practice, and deductions by canonists from the common law, have been mainly concerned rather with the specification of details than with changes in the general notions. Thus, the three censures, excommunication, suspension, and interdict,[89] are removed only by absolution.[90] A censure *ab homine* is absolved only by the one who in-

[86] *Cf.* Morinus, *op. cit.*, L. I, c. 10, nn. 11-14; L. I, c. 9, n. 6; L. VIII, c. 23, n. 7; L. VI, c. 25, n. 1; Van Espen, *Tract. de Censuris*, p. 15.

[87] *Cf.* Morinus, *op. cit.*, L. I, c. 10, nn. 1, 12; Vacandard, "Origines de la Confession," *Etudes de Critique*, 2me série, p. 123. It may be noted here that the term *sacerdos*, when found in use before the fifth century, almost always refers only to the bishop (Vacandard, *op. cit.*, p. 61), and it was only from the sixth century that it was commonly used to designate the priest (Batiffol, "Origines de la Pénitence," *Etudes d'Histoire*, 1re série, I, 145).

[88] *Cf.* Morinus, *op. cit.*, L. I, c. 9, n. 6; L. I, c. 10, n. 11; Van Espen, *Tract. de Censuris*, p. 16; Fournier, *Les Officialités au Moyen Age* (Paris, 1880), pp. 1-24, 82, 134-136.

[89] C. 20, X, *de verborum significatione*, V, 40.

[90] *Cf.* cc. 23, 28, 38, X, *de sententia excommunicationis*, V, 39; c. 11, X, *de officio iudicis ordinarii*, I, 31; c. 1, X, *de regulis iuris*, V, 41; c. 11, X, *de*

flicted it, his successor, competent superior, or delegate.[91] A non-reserved *a iure* censure is absolved by anyone possessing jurisdiction in the external forum, and by those included under the term *proprius* sacerdos.[92] Finally, a reserved *a iure* censure is absolved by the one to whom it is reserved, or by his successor, superior, or delegate.[93]

From the beginning of the Church special delegations of power have been granted for absolution in danger of death and, at least from the time of the Decretals, for other extraordinary cases, as will be seen in the following chapters.

constitutionibus, I, 2; c. 25, X, *de appellationibus, recusationibus, et relationibus,* II, 28; cc. 15, 30, X, *de sententia excommunicationis,* V, 39; cap. unic., *de maioritate et obedientia,* I, 17, in VI°; cc. 7, 20, *de sententia excommunicationis, suspensionis et interdicti,* V, 11, in VI°. *Cf.* Suarez, *De Censuris,* disp. VII, sec. 1, nn. 2-14; Reiffenstuel, lib. V, tit. 39, n. 240; Schmalzgrueber, lib. V, tit. 39, nn. 107-111; Kober, *Kirchenbann,* pp. 447 ff.; Wernz, *Ius Decret.,* VI, 176, 177.

[91] *Cf.* cc. 8, 11, X, *de officio iudicis ordinarii,* I, 31; c. 1, X, *de regulis iuris,* V, 41; c. 26, X, *de officio et potestate iudicis delegati,* I, 29; cap. unic., *de maioritate et obedientia,* I, 17, in VI°; Reg. 68, R. J., in VI°. *Cf.* Suarez, *op. cit.,* disp. VII, sec. 2; Reiffenstuel, lib. V, tit. 39, nn. 242-244; Schmalzgrueber, lib. V, tit. 39, nn. 85-94; Van Espen, *Tract. de Censuris,* pp. 60, 61; Kober, *op. cit.,* pp. 458 ff.; Wernz, *op. cit.,* VI, 179, 180.

[92] *Cf.* cc. 23, 29, X, *de sententia excommunicationis,* V, 39. *Cf.* Suarez, *op. cit.,* disp. VII, secc. 3, 4; Reiffenstuel, lib. V, tit. 39, nn. 246, 247; Schmalzgrueber, lib. V, tit. 39, nn. 95, 96; Van Espen, *op. cit.,* pp. 61, 62; Wernz, *op. cit.,* VI, 180.

[93] *Cf.* c. 29, X, *de sententia excommunicationis,* V, 39. *Cf.* Suarez, *op. cit.,* disp. VII, sec. 5; Reiffenstuel, lib. V, tit. 39, n. 249; Schmalzgrueber, lib. V, tit. 39, n. 97; Van Espen, *op. cit.,* p. 62; Wernz, *op. cit.,* VI, 180-182.

CHAPTER II

ABSOLUTION FROM CENSURES IN DANGER OF DEATH

ARTICLE I. FROM THE EARLIEST TIMES TO THE MIDDLE OF THE FOURTH CENTURY

A. Absolution

THE Church has always been maternally solicitous about the spiritual welfare of her children, and has from the very beginning been especially concerned to provide spiritual aid in the hour of death. Testimonies regarding the practice of the Church in the earliest centuries with reference to the dying are not numerous, but are sufficient to delineate the general outlines of the discipline.

Before this matter is approached, it may be well to recall important points indicated in the preceding chapter, namely, that such expressions as *communio, viaticum,* and *venia* in the usage of the early Church signified reconciliation, that is, primarily absolution from sins,[1] and that absolution of the sins of public penitents involved the remission of all or part of the minor excommunication contained in public penance.[2]

Concerning those sinners who, while in good health, had undertaken public penance and were consequently among the ranks of the

[1] *Cf.* above, p. 15. *Cf.* also Poschmann, *Die abendländische Kirchenbusse im frühen Mittelalter,* Breslauer Studien zur historischen Theologie, Band XVI, (Breslau: Müller & Seiffert, 1930), p. 207; Galtier, *De Paenitentia,* (Parisiis, 1923), n. 301. This is not admitted by those who oppose the opinion that the Church refused absolution to any class of dying sinners in the early centuries. Their interpretation of such terms as *communio* varies (*e. g., cf.* Pignataro, *De Discipl. Poenit.,* pp. 105, 119, 125, 126), at one time as meaning a canonical remission only of the excommunication, at other times as referring to the Eucharist, in a manner which suggests an arbitrary adaptation of the meaning in an effort to meet very serious objections to their view.

[2] *Cf.* above, p. 14.

penitents, it was the practice of the Church in the first centuries, as well as during the whole period of public penance, to grant reconciliation in danger of death.[3] This is indicated by the first Council of Nice (325) in canon 13,[4] which, from its context, refers to penitents,[5] and in using the phrase *ultimo et maxime necessario viatico* signifies the absolution from sins.[6] This discipline toward dying penitents, designated by the Council of Nice as the "ancient law," is seen also in canons of the Council of Elvira (305),[7] the Council of Ancyra (314),[8] and the Council of Neocaesarea (314).[9]

Even if the penitents became unconscious and could not indicate in any way their desire for reconciliation, absolution was granted to them because of the state they had assumed,[10] in accordance with the notion later expressed by such axioms as *"Sat petit qui bene vivit"* and *"Nulli poenitentiam agenti denegandus est poenitentiae fructus,"* namely reconciliation.[11]

Another class consisted of those who, although guilty of grave sins, had never apostatized and had never been expelled from the Church, but had never undertaken public penance, asking for penance and reconciliation only when overtaken by dangerous illness.

[3] *Cf.* Morinus, *De Admin. Sacr. Poenit.*, L. X, c. 5; L. X, c. 1, n. 3.

[4] "De his qui ad exitum veniunt, etiam nunc *lex antiqua regularisque* servabitur; ita ut *si quis egreditur e corpore,* ultimo et maxime necessario *viatico minime privetur* . . ."—Mansi, II, 681.

[5] *Cf.* Morinus, *De Admin. Sacr. Poenit.*, L. X, c. 3, n. 2; L. X, c. 14, n. 5.

[6] *Cf.* Morinus, *op. cit.*, L. VI, c. 21, n. 6.

[7] *E.g.*, c. 5: " . . . Quod si infra tempora constituta fuerit infirmata, accipiat communionem"; c. 9: " . . . si duxerit [alterum maritum], non prius accipiat communionem, nisi quem reliquerit, prius de saeculo exierit; nisi forte necessitas infirmitatis dare compulerit"; *cf.* also cc. 13, 32, 37, 42, 61, 69, 71—Mansi, II, 6-17.

[8] C. 6: " . . . Quod si alicui horum [qui suscepti sint ad poenitentiam] quodlibet mortis periculum aut ex aegritudine, aut ex qualibet causa immineat, his communio propter viaticum suum non negabitur."—Mansi, II, 530; *cf.* also c. 22—Mansi, II, 534.

[9] C. 2: " . . . Verumtamen in exitu, propter misericordiam, . . . fructum poenitentiae consequatur."—Mansi, II, 543.

[10] *Cf.* Morinus, *De Admin. Sacr. Poenit.*, L. X, c. 5, nn. 2-8.

[11] *Cf.* Morinus, *op. cit.*, L. X, c. 10, n. 3; L. X, c. 5, n. 6.

It seems clear that penance and absolution were granted to this class of sinners if they asked for them during their sickness.[12] If they became unconscious before the arrival of the priest, but evidence could be given of their desire for reconciliation, it seems that it was granted,[13] but this is uncertain, and definite norms for such cases appeared only at a later date, as will be seen.

Finally, a third class comprised those who had apostatized or who had been expelled from the Church, but had never embraced public penance, and asked for penance and reconciliation only when in danger of death. The practice of the Church with regard to this class sets off this period as distinctly different from all others in the history of ecclesiastical discipline with reference to the dying. For the Church in the early centuries refused absolution to these apostates and excommunicates, distrusting the sincerity of their conversion and preferring to leave them to the judgment and mercy of God.[14] This discipline is clearly shown in an epistle of St. Cyprian, written in the year 252.[15] It is also evident from the Council of Elvira (305), which excluded eighteen classes of sinners from absolution in danger of

[12] *Cf.* Morinus, *op. cit.*, L. X, c. 4, n. 2.

[13] *Cf.* Morinus, *op. cit.*, L. X, c. 4, n. 3.

[14] *Cf.* Morinus, *op. cit.*, L. X, c. 1, nn. 3, 5; Rauschen, *Eucharist and Penance*, pp. 207, 208, note 49; Lea, *A History of Auricular Confession and Indulgences in the Latin Church* (Philadelphia, 1896), I, 60. *Cf.* also Galtier, *De Paenitentia*, n. 250. Some authors (*e.g.*, Cappello, *De Poenitentia* [2. ed., Taurinorum Augustae: Marietti, 1929], nn. 68-71; Pignataro, *De Discipl. Poenit.*, pp. 100-126) have denied the fact that absolution was refused in the early Church to certain sinners, but the evidence against this opinion is very strong, and it seems that the question should concern the extent of this practice rather than its existence. It is to be noted that the issue does not refer to the Church's power to absolve, nor to its realization of that power, but to its actual practice. For a discussion of the matter, besides the above authors, *cf.* Galtier, *op. cit.*, nn. 300-304, 250.

[15] *Ep. 52, ad Antonianum*, n. 23: " . . . Poenitentiam non agentes, nec dolorem delictorum suorum toto corde et manifesta lamentationis suae professione testantes, *prohibendos omnino censuimus a spe communicationis et pacis*, si in infirmitate atque in periculo coeperint deprecari; quia rogare illos non delicti poenitentia sed mortis urgentis admonitio compellit, nec dignus est in morte accipere solatium qui se non cogitavit esse moriturum."—*MPL*, III, 789, 790; IV, 345.

death,[16] as is seen in various canons by the use of such expressions as *"nec in fine eum communionem accipere."* [17] Other testimonies to this same practice are found in the first Council of Arles (314) [18] and in a reference by Pope St. Innocent I in the year 405 to the former severe discipline.[19]

Again, attention is called to the fact that in the use of the words *communio* and *viaticum,* absolution from sins, not the Eucharist, is meant, not only by St. Cyprian and the Council of Arles,[20] but also by the Council of Elvira [21] and Pope St. Innocent,[22] for such was the general usage in those centuries.[23] Otherwise the cogency of these testimonies with reference to the absolution from sins and the involved remission of the minor excommunication of public penance, will be utterly misunderstood and unappreciated. However, it may be recalled that, before the time of Novatian, the absolution from sins brought with it the right to the reception of the Eucharist.[24]

As is evidenced by the epistle of Pope St. Innocent, it was the practice in the early centuries to impose penance upon dying apos-

[16] *Cf.* Vacandard, "Origines de la Confession," *Etudes de Critique,* 2me série, p. 75; Rauschen, *Eucharist and Penance,* p. 177.

[17] *Cf.* cc. 1-3, 6-8, 10, 12, etc.—Mansi, II, 5-8.

[18] C. 22: "De his qui apostatant, et nunquam ad Ecclesiam repraesentant ne quidem poenitentiam agere quaerunt, et postea infirmitate arrepti petunt communionem: placuit *eis non dandam communionem* nisi revaluerint, et egerint dignos fructus poenitentiae."—Mansi, II, 473.

[19] *Ep. 6, ad Exsuperium,* nn. 5, 6: "Hoc quaesitum est, quid de his observari oporteat, qui post baptismum omni tempore incontinentiae voluptatibus dediti, in extremo fine vitae suae poenitentiam simul et reconciliationem communionis exposcunt. De his observatio prior, durior; posterior, interveniente misericordia, inclinatior. Nam consuetudo prior tenuit, ut concederetur poenitentia, sed *communio negaretur.* Nam cum illis temporibus crebrae persecutiones essent, ne communionis concessa facilitas homines de reconciliatione securos non revocaret a lapsu, merito *negata communio est;* concessa poenitentia, ne totum penitus negaretur: et duriorem remissionem fecit temporis ratio . . . "—*MPL,* XX, 498.

[20] *Cf.* Morinus, *De Admin. Sacr. Poenit.,* L. X, c. 1, n. 6.

[21] *Cf.* Morinus, *op. cit.,* L. X, c. 14, n. 2.

[22] *Cf.* Morinus, *op. cit.,* L. X, c. 1, n. 10.

[23] *Cf.* above, p. 15; also above, in the present chapter, note 1.

[24] *Cf.* above, p. 14.

tates and excommunicates, but not to grant them reconciliation. It seems that this practice of imposing penance was not adopted by the Council of Elvira, but the influence of this council was not very widespread, extending only to its own province and certain churches of Africa.[25] Apparently the general practice of almost the entire Western Church was that indicated by Pope St. Innocent, which was probably exercised by St. Cyprian and the Council of Arles, though neither makes express mention of it.[26] The purpose of this imposition of penance seems to have been to release the sinner from the major excommunication, or *anathema*, and thus admit him to partial communion with the faithful, to assist him by the prayers and impositions of hands accompanying the admission to penance, and to grant him the right, in case of recovery, to fulfill his penance and ultimately attain to full participation in the life of the Church.[27]

The refusal of absolution to dying apostates and excommunicates lasted during the period of the persecutions and, as has been seen, was still in force at the time of the first Council of Arles (314), celebrated during the time of the Emperor Constantine the Great. It seems that this practice very probably continued in a large part of the Western Church throughout at least the whole time of Constantine (+ 337),[28] and then gradually fell into desuetude, disappearing about the middle of the fourth century.[29]

B. The Minister of Absolution

Regarding the minister of absolution to those in danger of death during this period, the bishop by reason of his office could grant

[25] *Cf.* Morinus, *De Admin. Sacr. Poenit.*, L. X, c. 2, nn. 1, 4.

[26] *Cf.* Morinus, *op. cit.*, L. X, c. 1, n. 8; L. X, c. 3, n. 4.

[27] *Cf.* Morinus, *op. cit.*, L. X, c. 2, n. 3. Cappello (*De Poenitentia*, n. 71) considers that the *poenitentia*, mentioned by Pope St. Innocent as granted to the dying sinners in the original discipline, refers to sacramental absolution, *i. e.*, absolution in the internal forum, while the *communio* denied to these sinners signifies the full reconciliation, *i. e.*, absolution in both fora; the distinction is excellent, but it seems to be based on a discipline far more advanced than that in question, and to all appearances it does not concur with historical facts.

[28] *Cf.* Morinus, *op. cit.*, L. X, c. 1, n. 9.

[29] Rauschen, *Eucharist and Penance*, p. 207.

reconciliation, and also the priest, with delegated powers from the bishop.[30] This is seen in a fragment of a decree attributed to Pope St. Evaristus of the early second century.[31]

For the absolution of those *lapsi* who possessed letters from the martyrs, St. Cyprian granted power not only to his priests but also to the deacons, as appears from epistles to his clergy.[32] Similarly, the Council of Elvira (305) bears witness in this period to the practice of absolution of the dying by priests or deacons.[33]

C. The Requisites After Recovery

To complete the consideration of the discipline concerning the dying, it will be necessary to mention briefly the practice with reference to those who received absolution in danger of death but subsequently recovered from their illness.

[30] *Cf.* Morinus, *De Admin. Sacr. Poenit.*, L. I, c. 10, n. 1; Vacandard, "Origines de la Confession," *Etudes de Critique*, 2me série, p. 110.

[31] The entire fragment consists of these words: "Ut presbyteri de occultis peccatis jussione episcopi poenitentes reconcilient et, sicut supra scripsimus, infirmantes absolvant et communicent."— Jaffé, *Regesta Pontificum Romanorum ab condita Ecclesia ad annum post Christum natum MCXCVIII* (2. ed., Lipsiae, 1881), n. 23; *cf.* also *MPG*, V, 1057, 1058; Mansi, I, 632; c. 4, C. XXVI, q. 6.

[32] *Ep. 12, ad clerum:* " . . . Occurrendum puto fratribus nostris, ut qui libellos a martyribus acceperunt, . . . si incommodo aliquo et infirmitatis periculo occupati fuerint, non expectata praesentia nostra, *apud presbyterum quencumque* praesentem, *vel,* si presbyter repertus non fuerit, et urgere exitus coeperit, *apud diaconum* quoque exomologesin facere delicti sui possint, ut manu eis in poenitentiam imposita veniant ad Dominum cum pace . . . "—*MPL*, IV, 259.

Ep. 13, ad clerum: "Cyprianus *presbyteris et diaconibus* fratribus salutem. . . . Qui libellum a martyribus acceperunt, . . . si premi infirmitate aliqua et periculo coeperint, exomologesi facta et manu eis *a vobis* imposita, cum pace a martyribus sibi promissa ad Dominum remittantur."—*MPL*, IV, 260, 261. *Cf.* Morinus, *De Admin. Sacr. Poenit.*, L. VIII, c. 23; Vacandard, "Origines de la Confession," *Etudes de Critique*, 2me série, pp. 63-65; Rauschen, *Eucharist and Penance*, pp. 194, 195.

[33] C. 32: "Apud presbyterum, si quis gravi lapsu in ruinam mortis inciderit, placuit agere poenitentiam non debere, sed potius apud episcopum: cogente tamen infirmitate necesse est *presbyterum* communionem praestare debere, et *diaconum*, si ei jusserit sacerdos."—Mansi, II, 11.

For about the first three hundred years it seems that such persons, after recovery, were immediately accepted as members in full communion with the faithful, with no obligation to continue the penance that was interrupted by their infirmity, or to perform the penance imposed on them only at the time of their reconciliation.[34] This conclusion appears plausible from a letter of St. Cyprian to Antonianus, who inclined toward the rigoristic doctrines of Novatian, and whom St. Cyprian was trying to reclaim. In this letter the Saint defends the practice of reconciling those in infirmity, and the whole point of dispute seems to be the fact that, if such persons recovered from their illness, they were no longer subject to the obligations of penance.[35] Again, it is worthy of note that the Council of Elvira, with all its rigor in excluding many sinners from the benefit of absolution in illness, and in deferring the reconciliation of many others till their last hour, made no provision for the performance of penance by those who recovered after being reconciled in danger of death. It seems that such an omission would hardly have occurred if it had been the practice to oblige such persons to resume works of penance after their recovery.[36]

However, shortly after this time, a change took place. Penances became more severe and also longer in duration, and it happened at times that penitents would simulate a grave illness to obtain reconciliation and escape the penances.[37] To discourage this and to maintain the integrity of the penitential discipline, gradually obli-

[34] *Cf.* Morinus, *De Admin. Sacr. Poenit.*, L. X, c. 14, nn. 1-4.

[35] *Ep. 52, ad Antonianum*, n. 13: "Si qui [lapsi] enim infirmitatibus occupantur, illis, sicut placuit, in periculo subvenitur. Postea tamen quam subventum est, et periclitantibus pax data est, offocari [suffocari?] a nobis non possunt aut opprimi, aut vi et manu nostra in exitum mortis urgeri, ut quoniam morientibus pax datur, necesse sit mori eos qui acceperint pacem, cum magis in hoc indicium divinae pietatis et paternae lenitatis appareat, quod qui pignus vitae in data pace percipiunt, hic quoque ad vitam percepta pace teneantur. Et idcirco si, accepta pace, commeatus a Deo datur, nemo hoc debet in sacerdotibus criminari, cum semel placuerit fratribus in periculo subveniri."—*MPL*, III, 779, 780. *Cf.* Morinus, *op. cit.*, L. X, c. 14, n. 1; Pignataro, *De Discipl. Poenit.*, pp. 102, 103.

[36] *Cf.* Morinus, *op. cit.*, L. X, c. 14, n. 2.

[37] *Cf.* Morinus, *op. cit.*, L. X, c. 14, n. 4.

gations began to be imposed on those who regained health after reconciliation in danger of death. At first, the obligation was slight, for, as is seen from the first Council of Nice (325),[38] the penitent returned only to the grade of *consistentia,* in which he was deprived of the Eucharist, but was subject to no works of penance.

Severer practices in this regard soon came into existence, as will be seen in the treatment of the following period.

Article II. From the Middle of the Fourth Century to the *Decretum Gratiani*

A. Absolution

After the middle of the fourth century, there began the discipline with relation to the dying which has continued till the present. This milder discipline of granting absolution to all dying persons, whether or not they were excommunicated, or whether they asked for reconciliation for the first time when actually in sickness, is described by Pope St. Innocent I.[39] In his use of the terms *communio* and *venia,* there can be hardly any doubt that the pope referred to the absolution of penitents from sins rather than to the reception of the Eucharist.[40]

[38] C. 13: "... Quod si desperatus, et consecutus communionem, oblationisque particeps factus, iterum convaluerit, sit inter eos qui *communionem orationis tantummodo* consequuntur."—Mansi, II, 681. *Cf.* Morinus, *op. cit.,* L. X, c. 14, n. 5. Those who enjoyed the *communio orationis tantum* were the penitents in the highest grade of public penance, namely, the *consistentes.*

[39] *Ep. 6, ad Exsuperium,* n. 6: " . . . De his observatio prior, durior; posterior, interveniente misericordia, inclinatior . . . Postquam Dominus noster pacem Ecclesiis suis reddidit, jam depulso terrore, *communionem dari abeuntibus placuit,* . . . quasi viaticum profecturis, et ne Novatiani haeretici, negantis veniam, asperitatem et duritiem sequi videamur. *Tribuetur* ergo cum poenitentia extrema *communio*: ut homines hujusmodi vel in supremis suis, permittente Salvatore nostro, a perpetuo exitio vindicentur."—*MPL,* XX, 498, 499. Compare above, in the present chapter, note 19. *Cf.* also Denzinger-Bannwart, *Enchiridion Symbolorum Definitionum et Declarationum de Rebus Fidei et Morum* (16. et 17. ed., Friburgi Brisgoviae: Herder, 1928), n. 95.

[40] *Cf.* Morinus, *De Admin. Sacr. Poenit.,* L. X, c. 1, n. 10; Batiffol, "Origines de la Pénitence," *Etudes d'Histoire,* 1re série, I, 161.

It seems that this discipline was in force in Carthage by at least the year 390,[41] but apparently some diversity of practice still existed when, as indicated above, Exsuperius, Bishop of Toulouse, asked Pope St. Innocent I for the settlement of this question in the year 405.[42]

In the year 428 Pope St. Celestine I, in a famous epistle included in nearly all the later collections, decried the practice of denying penance to dying sinners, and commanded that the remedy be granted them to free them from their sins.[43] From this epistle it seems clear that the former severe practice concerned not merely the denial of the Eucharist, but the refusal of absolution.

Again, the first Council of Orange (441) made precise provisions for the reconciliation of the dying.[44]

The practice of granting absolution to the dying, even if unconscious, as long as someone could testify to their desire to receive penance, is shown in an epistle of Pope St. Leo the Great, written in 452 and cited in all the later collections.[45]

[41] *Cf.* second Council of Carthage (390), c. 4: "Si *quisquam* in periculo fuerit constitutus, et se reconciliari divinis altaribus petierit, si episcopus absens fuerit, debet utique presbyter consulere episcopum, et sic periclitantem ejus praecepto reconciliare."—Mansi, III, 693.

[42] *Cf.* Morinus, *De Admin. Sacr. Poenit.*, L, X, c. 1, n. 9. *Cf.* above, in the present chapter, notes 19, 39.

[43] *Ep. 4, ad Episcopos Provinciae Viennensis et Narbonensis,* cap. 2: "Agnovimus poenitentiam morientibus denegari, nec illorum desideriis annui, qui obitus sui tempore hoc animae suae cupiunt remedio subveniri. Horremus, fateor, tantae impietatis aliquem reperiri, ut de Dei pietate desperet: quasi non possit ad se quovis tempore concurrenti succurrere, et periclitantem sub onere peccatorum hominem pondere, quo se ille expediri desiderat, liberare. . . . *Quovis tempore non est deneganda poenitentia postulanti,* cum illi se obliget judici cui occulta omnia noverit revelari."—*MPL,* L, 431, 432; Denzinger-Bannwart, *Enchir. Symbol.*, n. 111.

[44] C. 3: "Qui recedunt de corpore, poenitentia accepta, placuit sine reconciliatoria manus impositione eis communicari; quod morientis sufficit consolationi . . . "—Mansi, VI, 436.

[45] *Ep. 108, ad Theodorum,* capp. 4, 5: "His autem qui in tempore necessitatis et in periculi urgentis instantia praesidium poenitentiae et mox reconciliationis implorant, nec satisfactio interdicenda est, *nec reconciliatio deneganda*: quia misericordiae Dei nec mensuras possumus ponere, nec tempora definire. . . . Talium necessitati ita auxiliandum est, ut et *actio* illis *poenitentiae, et com-*

In a canon ascribed to the fourth Council of Carthage (398), but actually belonging to the collection of the *Statuta Ecclesiae Antiqua* of the late fifth or early sixth century,[46] there is found a similar provision for the absolution of the unconscious dying.[47]

Thus it became the practice to grant absolution to all dying sinners who showed the proper dispositions, and later evidences in this regard only repeat and confirm this practice. Such a repetition is found in the eleventh Council of Toledo (675), which quoted the above-mentioned epistle of Pope St. Leo and provided that penance be imposed and reconciliation granted immediately to those in danger of death.[48]

During the following centuries, the continuation of this practice is seen in an examination of the penitential books and collections. Although canons are included which defer the reconciliation of penitents to the hour of death, it is apparent from both the penitentials and the collections that it was not the custom to refuse absolution to any class of dying sinners.

Among the penitentials, indications of the discipline in relation to the dying are found in those ascribed to St. Cummian (+ c.

munionis gratia, si eam *etiam amisso vocis officio,* per indicia integri sensus postulant, *non negetur.* At si aliqua vi aegritudinis ita fuerint aggravati, ut, quod paulo ante poscebant, sub praesentia sacerdotis significare non valeant, testimonia eis fidelium circumstantium prodesse debebunt, ut simul et poenitentiae et reconciliationis beneficium consequantur."—*MPL,* LIV, 1012-1014; c. 10, C. XXVI, q. 6; *cf.* also Denzinger-Bannwart, *Enchir. Symbol.,* nn. 146, 147. *Cf.* Morinus, *De Admin. Sacr. Poenit.,* L. X, c. 4, nn. 2, 3; Rauschen, *Eucharist and Penance,* p. 208.

[46] *Cf.* Hefele-Leclercq, *Histoire des Conciles* (Paris, 1908-1921), II, 102-108; Van Hove, *Prolegomena ad Codicem Iuris Canonici* (Mechliniae-Romae: Dessain, 1928), n. 131.

[47] C. 76: "Is qui poenitentiam in infirmitate petit, si casu, dum ad eum sacerdos invitatus venit, oppressus infirmitate obmutuerit, vel in phrenesim versus fuerit, dent testimonium qui eum audierunt, et accipiat poenitentiam. Et si continuo creditur moriturus, reconciliatur per manus impositionem, et infundatur ori ejus eucharistia . . . "—Mansi, III, 957.

[48] C. 12: "Qui poenitentiam in mortis agit periculo, non diutine a reconciliationis gratia referendus: sed si praeceptum mortis urget periculum, poenitentia per manus impositionem accepta, *statim ei reconciliatio adhibenda est.* . . . Juxta papae Leonis edictum: His qui . . . nec reconciliatio deneganda . . . "—Mansi, XI, 144.

661),[49] Halitgar, Bishop of Cambrai from 817 to 831,[50] and Rhabanus Maurus, Bishop of Mainz from 847 to 855.[51] Since this work is here concerned, not with private penance, but with public penance as a form of excommunication, relevant material is not found in the famous English penitentials, such as those attributed to Theodore (+ 690), St. Bede (+ 755), and Egbert of York (+ 767), for public penance was not in usage at that time in England or Ireland.[52] However, further references to the reconciliation of dying penitents are found in several penitentials of the eighth century.[53]

Among the earlier systematic collections, the reconciliation of the dying is mentioned in the collection of Cresconius of the seventh century[54] and in the *Collectio Isidoriana,* probably also of the seventh century.[55]

In the later collections, evidences of the same discipline are found in a work of Regino of Prüm, written about the year 906,[56] in the collection of Burchard of Worms, compiled about the year 1012,[57] and in that of St. Ivo of Chartres, written between 1090 and 1095.[58] Finally, the greatest of the private collections, the *Decretum Gratiani,* although published after the disappearance of public penance,

[49] *Liber de Mensura Poenitentiarum,* cap. 14—*MPL,* LXXXVII, 997, 998.

[50] *De Vitiis et Virtutibus et de Ordine Poenitentium,* lib. III, capp. 2, 3, 10, 13—*MPL,* CV, 677-680.

[51] *Poenitentium Liber,* capp. 35, 36, 38—*MPL,* CXII, 1422, 1423.

[52] *Cf. Theodori Poenitentiale,* cap. 14—*MPL,* XCIX, 936; *Sancti Egberti Poenitentiale,* lib. I, pars 2, cap. 12—*MPL,* LXXXIX, 414, 415. *Cf.* also Rauschen, *Eucharist and Penance,* p. 194; Lea, *History of Auricular Confession,* II, 73, 74.

[53] *Cf. Poenitentiale Valicellanum II,* cc. 28, 32—Schmitz, *Bussbücher,* pp. 361, 363; *Poenitentiale Casinense,* c. 56—*op. cit.,* p. 412.

[54] *Concordia Canonum,* cc. 79, 220—*MPL,* LXXXVIII, 873, 874, 914, 915.

[55] *Liber Canonum,* lib. II, tit. 15-18; lib. III, tit. 30—*MPL,* LXXXIV, 49-51, 59.

[56] *Libellus de Ecclesiasticis Disciplinis,* lib. I, cc. 106-113—*MPL,* CXXXII, 212, 213.

[57] *Liber Decretorum,* lib. XVIII, cc. 1, 3-18, 21-24—*MPL,* CXL, 937-944.

[58] *Decretum,* pars XV, cc. 8-11, 17, 22, 26, 28-40, 43, 44, 71, 84, 143—*MPL,* CLXI, 858-891.

referred to the former discipline regarding public penance and absolution in danger of death.[59]

Thus it is seen that in this period, from the middle of the fourth century, or at least from the time of Pope St. Innocent I in the early fifth century, it became an increasingly common, and gradually the universal, practice to grant reconciliation to all sinners, whether excommunicates, penitents, or non-penitents, seeking absolution in danger of death.

B. *The Minister of Absolution*

The minister of absolution to the dying was the same in this period, namely, from the middle of the fourth century to the *Decretum Gratiani*, as in the previous one. Although the bishop alone possessed the power to reconcile penitents publicly, and the priest was expressly forbidden to do so,[60] or to bless penitents in the church,[61] nevertheless the priest, with the permission of the bishop, was empowered to grant absolution to those in danger of death. This is evident from councils of Carthage, namely the second (390) [62] and third (397),[63] and especially from a letter written by Pope Felix III (483-493) to all the bishops.[64] It is also clear from the denunciation of priests who would refuse reconciliation to the dying, expressed by Pope St. Julius I (337-352)[65] and copied in many of the later collections.[66]

[59] *Cf.* cc. 4-14, C. XXVI, q. 6.

[60] *Cf.* second Council of Carthage (390), c. 3—Mansi, III, 693; c. 1, C. XXVI, q. 6.

[61] *Cf.* Council of Agde (506), c. 44—Mansi, VIII, 332; c. 3, C. XXVI, q. 6.

[62] C. 4—*cf.* above, in the present chapter, note 41.

[63] C. 32: " . . . ut presbyteri inconsulto Episcopo non reconcilient poenitentes, nisi absentia Episcopi et necessitate cogente."—Mansi, III, 885.

[64] *Ep. 7, ad universos Episcopos:* " . . . Quod si, ut pote mortales, intra metas praescripti temporis coeperit vitae finis urgere, subveniendum est imploranti, et seu ab episcopo qui poenitentiam dederit, seu ab alio, qui tamen datam esse probaverit, aut similiter *a presbytero* viaticum abeunti de saeculo non negetur."—*MPL,* LVIII, 926.

[65] "Si presbyter poenitentiam morientibus abnegaverit, reus erit animarum . . . "—*MPL,* VIII, 968; also indicated by Jaffé, *Regesta,* n. 198.

[66] *Cf.* footnote to c. 12, C. XXVI, q. 6 in the Richter-Friedberg edition of the *Decretum Gratiani.*

Regarding the power of deacons to absolve, it seems that, despite the assertion of St. Ambrose that priests alone have the power to bind and loose, deacons were permitted to grant reconciliation in some places, not only during this period, but even as late as the thirteenth century.[67]

C. *The Requisites After Recovery*

As has been seen in the consideration of the preceding period, the first Council of Nice determined that penitents who recovered health after being reconciled in danger of death should return to the highest grade of public penance, the *consistentia*.[68] A more severe practice was prescribed by St. Gregory of Nyssa (+ 398), who stated that those who allowed themselves to be rebaptized and were absolved in danger of death should, upon recovering, return to that grade of penance in which they were at the time of their reconciliation.[69]

Similarly, in the year 441 the first Council of Orange declared that penitents who were absolved in danger of death and later recovered, should complete the time of their penance and only thereupon be admitted to the reception of the Eucharist.[70] This same prescription was repeated a short time later by the second Council

[67] *Cf.* Rauschen, *Eucharist and Penance*, pp. 194, 195; Poschmann, *Kirchenbusse im frühen Mittelalter*, pp. 201, 202. For a discussion of the question whether or not, according to St. Albert the Great, absolution granted by laymen in cases of necessity was sacramental, *cf.* Teetaert, *Confession aux Laiques*, pp. 310-321, 481.

[68] *Cf.* above, in the present chapter, note 38.

[69] *Ep. canonica ad Letoium*, can. 5: " . . . Si quis autem non expleto tempore a canonibus praestituto vita excedat, . . . non viatico vacuus . . . mittatur. Sin autem, postquam sacramenti particeps fuerit, rursus ad vitam reversus sit: *statutum tempus expectet, in illo gradu existens in quo erat ante communionem* illi ex necessitate datam."—*MPG*, XLV, 231. *Cf.* Morinus, *De Admin. Sacr. Poenit.*, L. X, c. 14, n. 7.

[70] C. 3: "Qui recedunt de corpore, . . . placuit . . . eis communicari. . . . Quod si supervixerint, stent in ordine poenitentium et ostensis necessariis poenitentiae fructibus, legitimam communionem cum reconciliatoria manus impositione percipiant."—Mansi, VI, 437; *cf.* above, in the present chapter, note 44. *Cf.* Morinus, *op. cit.*, L. X, c. 14, n. 9. For the meaning of *communio legitima*, *cf.* above, p. 15.

of Arles, which is divergently designated as having been held in the year 443 or in the year 452.[71]

However, Pope Felix III, writing to all the bishops toward the end of the fifth century, renewed the prescriptions of the first Council of Nice, determining the return of convalescent penitents to the grade of *consistentia*.[72] On the other hand, the *Statuta Ecclesiae Antiqua,* perhaps slightly later than Pope Felix, reflect a more severe practice similar to that of St. Gregory of Nyssa.[73]

The stricter practice was adopted in the year 517 by the Council of Epaon,[74] and again in the year 658 in a frequently quoted canon of the Council of Nantes.[75]

During the remaining duration of the discipline of public penance, up to the twelfth century, although the collections[76] include both the more lenient regulation of Nice and the more rigorous provision such as that of Nantes, the stricter practice was the one commonly in use.[77]

The general practice of this period was to demand the performance of penance after recovery. However, this affected only

[71] C. 28—Mansi, VII, 882. *Cf.* Morinus, *loc. cit.*

[72] *Ep. 7, ad universos Episcopos:* " . . . Quod si ante praefinitum tempus desperatus a medicis, aut evidentibus mortis pressus indiciis, recepta quisquam communionis gratia convalescit; servemus in eo quod Nicaeni canones ordinaverunt, ut habeatur inter eos *qui in oratione sola communicant,* donec impleatur temporis eidem praestitutum."—*MPL,* LVIII, 926. The only penitents who enjoyed the *communio orationis* were the *consistentes.*

[73] C. 76: " . . . Si supervixerit, . . . subdatur statutis poenitentiae legibus, quamdiu sacerdos, qui poenitentiam dedit, probaverit."—Mansi, III, 957. Compare above, in the present chapter, note 47. *Cf.* Morinus, *De Admin. Sacr. Poenit.,* L. X, c. 14, n. 8.

[74] C. 36—Mansi, VIII, 563.

[75] C. 5: "Infirmus, qui necessitate mortis urgente confitetur peccata sua, sub ea conditione a sacerdote reconcilietur, ut si ei dominus vitam donaverit, sanitatemque reddiderit, secundum qualitatem delicti omnimodis poeniteat."—Mansi, XVIII, 167, 168; XI, 61, 62. *Cf.* Morinus, *De Admin. Sacr. Poenit.,* L. X, c. 14, n. 12.

[76] *E. g.,* Burchard of Worms, *Liber Decretorum,* lib. XVIII, cc. 3, 6, 10, 17—*MPL,* CXL, 938-942; St. Ivo of Chartres, *Decretum,* pars XV, cc. 8, 28, 31, 39—*MPL,* CLXI, 858-866.

[77] *Cf.* Morinus, *De Admin. Sacr. Poenit.,* L. X, c. 14, nn. 11-14.

those sinners who were guilty of crimes for which canonical penance was prescribed. Those who were already performing penance at the time of the absolution in danger of death completed it after their recovery, while those who received the penance only while actually in sickness fulfilled the entire penance after their restoration to health. At some times and in some places the remainder of the penance was performed in the grade of *consistentia,* according to the Nicene prescription or according to the discretion of the bishop, but the predominant practice seems to have been that the penance would be resumed and continued in the same way as if it had not been interrupted by the infirmity.

Article III. From the *Decretum Gratiani* to the Council of Trent

At the time when the *Decretum Gratiani* appeared, toward the middle of the twelfth century, public penance was perhaps entirely obsolete, and legislation on absolution was concerned chiefly with excommunication. The discipline of reservation was now in force,[78] and this began to occupy a prominent place in such legislation, for provisions had to be made for cases in which the guilty party could not approach that ecclesiastical authority to whom the absolution was reserved.

The *Decretum Gratiani* cannot be passed without mention of a canon it borrowed from the second Council of the Lateran (1139)—a canon which became the subject of much subsequent legislation—namely, the famous decree *"Si quis suadente diabolo."* [79] However, although this law offers a provision for absolution in danger of death, and similar laws are found in the *Antiquae Compilationes*

[78] *Cf.* below, p. 45.

[79] "Si quis suadente diabolo huius sacrilegii vitium incurrerit, quod in clericum vel monachum violentas manus iniecerit, anathematis vinculo subiaceat, et nullus episcoporum illum presumat absolvere, *nisi mortis urgente periculo,* donec apostolico conspectui presentetur, et eius mandatum suscipiat."—C. 29, C. XVII, q. 4. Second Council of the Lateran, c. 15—Mansi, XXI, 530. This canon is also found at an earlier date, in the Council of Rheims (1131), c. 13—Mansi, XXI, 461.

which followed the *Decretum*,[80] the study of the discipline concerning absolution in danger of death during this period may well be begun with the Decretals of Gregory IX, which incorporated this previous legislation. In this period, in contrast to the preceding ones, authentic, uniform and universal legislation came into being, a fact which greatly simplifies the study of the discipline.

The Decretals contained in the collection of Gregory IX provided that a person who had incurred the reserved excommunication for maliciously striking a cleric could, under certain conditions, be absolved in danger of death.[81] This absolution could be granted by the bishop,[82] and apparently, although it is not clear, by a priest,[83]

[80] *E. g., Compilatio I,* lib. V, tit. 34, c. 6; *Compilatio II,* lib. V, tit. 18, cc. 1, 15—Augustinus, *Antiquae Collectiones Decretalium* (Parisiis, 1621), pp. 83, 122, 123; Friedberg, *Quinque Compilationes Antiquae* (Lipsiae, 1882), pp. 63, 102, 103.

[81] "Non dubium est vobis, sicut credimus, vel incertum, quod hi, qui violentas manus in clericos vel canonicos, aut cuiuslibet religionis conversos iniiciunt, ex constitutione concilii sententiam excommunicationis incurrunt, nec *nisi in articulo mortis* sine Romano Pontifice absolutionis possunt beneficium impetrare."—C. 5, X, *de sententia excommunicationis,* V, 39.

" . . . Is, qui asserit, se in canonem latae sententiae incidisse, non aliter, quam per sedem apostolicam vel eius legatum absolutionis potest beneficium obtinere, *nisi forte in mortis sit articulo constitutus,* vel paupertate . . . "—C. 26, X, *de sententia excommunicationis,* V, 39.

"Quamvis incidens in canonem latae sententiae propter violentam manuum iniectionem iuxta proprias facultates eis satisfaciat, quibus iniurias irrogavit: non tamen taliter, quam per sedem apostolicam vel eius legatum absolutionis potest beneficium obtinere, *nisi imminente mortis articulo,* infirmitate . . ."—C. 58, X, *de sententia excommunicationis,* V, 39.

[82] " . . . Fraternitas tua . . . postulavit de his, qui violentas manus in clericos aliqua temeritate iniiciunt, nec eis suppetunt facultates, ut ad sedem apostolicam valeant laborare, quomodo his scilicet possit salubriter provideri. . . . Duximus respondendum, quod . . . , licet ad apostolicam sedem non veniant, *ab episcopis* valeant salutis remedium accipere . . . Si vero huiusmodi *infirmitatis tempore timore mortis* beneficium fuerit absolutionis indultum, . . . iniungatur eisdem, ut, postquam sanitati fuerint restituti, ad Romanam ecclesiam vel eius legatum accedant . . . "—C. 13, X, *de sententia excommunicationis,* V, 39.

[83] " . . . Requisivit a nobis fraternitas tua, utrum is, qui se confitetur in latae sententiae canonem incidisse, nec ad hoc potest induci, ut ad sedem apostolicam veniat absolvendus, ab episcopo vel etiam *a simplici presbytero*

on condition that the guilty party would offer satisfaction to the injured cleric according to his means [84] and bind himself under oath to present himself to the Holy See or its legate, in case of recovery, to accept its mandate.[85] However, if the person absolved in danger of death were a woman or an adolescent, or if the person labored under a perpetual impediment which would prevent his going to Rome or its legate, for example, if he were permanently crippled, then this obligation of recourse did not bind, for even outside of danger of death he or she could be absolved without this obligation of appearing before the Holy See.[86]

Such is the law on absolution in danger of death as found in the Decretals of Gregory IX. It is true that it considers only the one excommunication incurred for maliciously striking a cleric, although Hostiensis lists thirty-three *ipso facto* excommunications determined in these Decretals,[87] of which seven were reserved to the pope.[88] However, interpreters such as Abbas Martinus, who lived at about the time of Hostiensis (+ 1271), considered that this legislation

absolutionis beneficium possit vel debeat promereri . . . Duximus respondendum, quod is, qui asserit, se in canonem latae sententiae incidisse, non aliter, quam per sedem apostolicam vel eius legatum absolutionis potest beneficium obtinere, *nisi forte in mortis sit articulo constitutus,* vel paupertate . . . "—C. 26, X, *de sententia excommunicationis,* V, 39.

[84] " . . . ab episcopis valeant salutis remedium accipere, . . . *satisfacto iuxta facultates* his, quibus per eos constiterit iniurias irrogatas . . . "—C. 13, X, *de sententia excommunicationis,* V, 39. *Cf.* also c. 58, X, *de sententia excommunicationis,* V, 39, as above, in the present chapter, note 81.

[85] " . . . Si vero huiusmodi infirmitatis tempore timore mortis beneficium fuerit absolutionis indultum, *iuramento praestito* iniungatur eisdem, ut, postquam sanitati fuerint restituti, *ad Romanam ecclesiam vel eius legatum accedant, mandatum apostolicum super talibus recepturi.*"—C. 13, X, *de sententia excommunicationis,* V, 39.

" . . . Ceterum quibusdam praedictorum, videlicet qui temporali impedimento laborant, exceptis pueris, *sub debito iuramenti,* quod secundum ecclesiae formam praestare tenentur, consuevit iniungi, *ut impedimento cessante ad apostolicam sedem accedant, mandatum ipsius humiliter suscepturi.*"—C. 58, X, *de sententia excommunicationis,* V, 39.

[86] *Cf.* cc. 6, 60, 58, X, *de sententia excommunicationis,* V, 39; *cf.* below, pp. 46-48.

[87] *Summa Aurea* (Venetiis, 1570), lib. V, *de sent. excom.,* n. 3.

[88] Hostiensis, *op. cit.,* lib. V, *de sent. excom.,* n. 12, § In supradictis casibus.

applied to all excommunications, and that absolution could be given in danger of death by any priest, unless he himself was an excommunicate, a heretic, or a schismatic.[89] The *glossa ordinaria* of Bernardus Parmensis de Botone (+ 1263) also admitted this power to the priest, but restricted it to cases of extreme necessity.[90]

Regarding the meaning of the phrase *articulus mortis* as used in the Decretals, it was considered to refer not merely to the actual moment before death, but to danger of death in a broader sense.[91]

Finally, there is the question whether the excommunication was reincurred by one who was obliged to go to Rome after his recovery, but failed to do so when the opportunity presented itself. Some interpreters held that it was reincurred, but the apparently more common opinion, supported by the better-known writers, denied this.[92]

The next step in the development of the legislation on absolu-

[89] "Excommunicatus *quacunque excommunicatione* potest absolvi in articulo mortis *a quolibet sacerdote,* dummodo haereticus non sit, schismaticus, vel excommunicatus, quia tales suspensi sunt, secundum se, et quo ad alios, ideoque ad eos non est recurrendum."—Excerpt from work of Abbas F. Martinus, included as an annotation in *Summa Aurea* of Hostiensis (edit. 1570) within lib. V, *de sent. excom.,* n. 12, § Si vero.

[90] *Cf. glossa* to *licet dioecesano* of c. 11, X, *de sententia excommunicationis,* V, 39: "Numquid et presbytero? Respondeo, *in summa necessitate licet, alias non,* nisi hoc faceret de mandato episcopi, quia episcopus hanc absolutionem bene potest committere."

[91] *Cf. glossa* to c. 26, X, *de sententia excommunicationis,* V, 39, with reference to the word *articulo* [*mortis*]: "Alias, periculo, ut in codice Barbatiae." *Cf.* also the interpretation of Abbas Martinus, in an annotation in the *Summa Aurea* of Hostiensis (as above, in the present chapter, note 89): "Periculum autem mortis secundum jurisperitos potest dici, cum quis positus est in obsidione, vel transferat, et est in naufragii periculo: ubi enim statim in mari navigat quis, in mortis periculo esse dici solet. Similiter ubi aggreditur bellum. In his igitur casibus et similibus potest a quocunque et a quolibet absolvi peccato." *Cf.* also Hostiensis, *Commentaria in Quinque Decretalium Libros* (Venetiis, 1581), lib. V, *de sent. excom.,* c. 26, n. 1.

[92] *Cf. glossa* of Bernardus Parmensis de Botone to *suscepturus* of c. 11, X, *de sententia excommunicationis,* V, 39: "Non dicit absolvendus, quia iam erat absolutus, quia obligatio semel extincta non reviviscit . . . Quidam dicunt quod opportunitate recepta recidunt in excommunicationem, quod non placet. Quod si non fecerit, tamquam periurus habebitur, et posset compelli ut iuramentum servet." *Cf.* also below, in the present chapter, note 96.

tion in danger of death is found in the *Liber Sextus* of Boniface VIII. In the following single law Pope Boniface completely summarized the previous legislation on absolution in danger of death and other extraordinary cases in a manner similar to many respects to the present law of the Code.

> Eos, qui a sententia canonis vel hominis, quum ad illum, a quo alias de iure fuerant absolvendi, nequeunt *propter imminentis mortis articulum aut aliud impedimentum legitimum* pro absolutionis beneficio habere recursum, ab alio absolvuntur, si, cessante postea periculo vel impedimento huiusmodi, se illi, a quo his cessantibus absolvi debebant, quam cito commode poterunt, contempserint praesentare, mandatum ipsius super illis, pro quibus excommunicati fuerant, humiliter recepturi et satisfacturi, prout iustitia suadebit, decernimus, (ne sic censurae illudant ecclesiasticae), in eandem sententiam recidere ipso iure. . . .[93]

According to this law a person could be absolved from any reserved excommunication in danger of death, but, if he should recover, he was obliged to make satisfaction to the injured party, and also, under pain of relapsing into the same excommunication, to present himself to the one by whom he ordinarily should have been absolved, in order to receive and fulfill his mandate. The explanation of this text is clearly seen in a commentary upon it, written by Dominicus de Sancto Geminiano (+ c. 1436), indicating the complete power of the priest to absolve in danger of death.[94]

This law of Boniface VIII was reaffirmed by Pope Clement V,

[93] C. 22, *de sententia excommunicationis, suspensionis et interdicti,* V, 11, in VI°.

[94] "Nota primo quod constitutus in periculo mortis potest absolvi a sententia canonis vel hominis, et a simplici sacerdote: etiam si absolutio sit reservata Romano Pontifici. Nam in reservatis Apostolicae sedi excipitur periculum mortis. Et in periculo mortis potest quis absolvi a simplici sacerdote a quacunque excommunicatione . . . Nota insuper quod quandoque sententia canonis et hominis aequiperantur. Nota ultimo quod absolutio facta ab excommunicatione per illum qui non est iudex propter periculum imminens, non est apta durare perpetuo, sed tantum limitatur ad tempus impedimenti."—In the *Casus* preceding the *glossae* to c. 22, *de sententia excommunicationis, suspensionis et interdicti,* V, 11, in VI°.

who mentioned the same elements—the absolution in danger of death, and the obligation, under pain of reincurring the excommunication, of presenting oneself to the pope as soon as convenient after recovery.

> . . . Sane, si quis in aliquo casuum praedictorum fuerit ab excommunicationis sententia in mortis articulo absolutus, nisi, postquam pristinae restitutus fuerit sanitati, quam cito commode poterit, conspectui Romani Pontificis se praesentare curaverit, eius mandatum humiliter recepturus, prout iustitia suadebit: in eandem excommunicationis sententiam reincidat ipso facto.[95]

During the rest of this period up to the Council of Trent, further indications of the discipline are found in the doctrinal interpretations of the canonists in their commentaries on the Decretals of Gregory IX and the *Liber Sextus* of Boniface VIII.

In the *glossa ordinaria* to the *Liber Sextus* is noted the fact that the new law brought about a change regarding the canonical effect when a person absolved in danger of death failed to fulfill his oath to present himself, after recovery, to the Hoy See for its mandate. Previously, the better opinion had held that such a one did not, by reason of his negligence, relapse by law into the excommunication.[96] On this same point Joannes Andreae († 1348) referred to the discipline before Boniface VIII, asserting that, previous to the *Liber Sextus,* a person who failed to have recourse for the mandate after his recovery might reincur the excommunication, but only through a *sententia hominis,* whereas in the new law he relapsed into it *ipso iure.* He also quoted Joannes Monachus († 1313) in support of the opinion that, under pain of reincurring the excommunication, the person after recovery was not only obliged to fulfill his oath to have recourse to the proper superior, but

[95] C. 1, *de poenis,* V, 8, in Clem.

[96] *Cf. glossa* to *decernimus* of c. 22, *de sententia excommunicationis, suspensionis et interdicti,* V, 11, in VI°: "Non dicit 'declaramus,' et sic suo tempore vera fuit opinio Goffredi, Bernardi Parmensis, et Hostiensis (another *glossa* adds Joannes Monachus), qui dicebant eum non recidere. Dicebat tamen Hostiensis hoc praetextu multi illudunt censurae, unde providendum esset. Modo igitur est provisum." *Cf.* also above, in the present chapter, note 92.

also had to comply with the terms of the mandate imposed upon him.[97]

Although during this period the apparently all-embracing phraseology of the law of Boniface VIII was not extended to all excommunications for extraordinary cases outside of danger of death, as will be seen in the following chapter,[98] nevertheless, that there was no reservation in danger of death, and that consequently a person could be absolved by a priest from any excommunication, whether *a iure* or *ab homine,* is clear from the writings not only of Joannes Andreae,[99] but also of Bellamera (+ c. 1392),[100] Abbas Panormitanus (+ 1435),[101] and Dominicus de Sancto Geminiano (+ c. 1436).[102]

The phrase "danger of death" was not confined to the danger arising from serious sickness, but was interpreted as including other cases which involved the risk of one's life. Such are the interpretations of Joannes Andreae [103] and Abbas Panormitanus.[104]

Such, then, is the discipline of this period regarding absolution in danger of death, determined especially by the Decretals of Gregory IX and the *Liber Sextus* of Boniface VIII, and illustrated by the interpretations of canonical writers. The authentic and universal character of the laws afforded uniformity of practice,

[97] *Novella Commentaria in Sex Decretalium Libros* (Venetiis, 1581), lib. VI, *de sent. excom.*, c. 22, n. 1.

[98] *Cf.* below, pp. 50, 51.

[99] Lib. V, *de sent. excom.*, c. 58, n. 2; c. 13, n. 2.

[100] *Cf.* excerpt from his work as subjoined to Abbas Panormitanus' *Commentaria in Quinque Libros Decretalium*, lib. V, *de sent. excom.*, c. 58.

[101] *Loc. cit.*

[102] *Cf.* above, in the present chapter, note 94.

[103] "[*Periculo*] aliter quam per infirmitatem per id, quod sequitur, ut si capitalem hostem timet, vel est obsessus, vel est in manibus praedonis, vel tyranni, vel navigaturus est periculoso navigio, vel patitur naufragium, vel iturus per loca periculosa, vel obsidet alium in loco, in quo proiiciuntur frequenter machinae et balistae."—Lib. V, *de sent. excom.*, c. 26, n. 2.

[104] "Potest quis esse in periculo mortis absque tamen infirmitate, ut quia est obsessus in aliqua arce et tunc verisimiliter potest timere mortem, vel est in alio loco periculoso ubi exercetur pestifera ars sagittariorum, vel forte vult navigare."—Lib. V, *de sent. excom.*, c. 26, n. 1.

without, however, eliminating questions of details on which commentators came to disagree.

Article IV. From the Council of Trent to the Code

The Council of Trent occasioned no departure from the law of the Decretals of Gregory IX and of the *Liber Sextus* of Boniface VIII. Rather, in granting full power to all priests to absolve in danger of death, it crystallized the preceding legislation in the oft-quoted text:

> Verumtamen pie admodum, ne hac ipsa occasione aliquis pereat, in eadem Ecclesia Dei custoditum semper fuit, ut nulla sit reservatio in articulo mortis: atque ideo omnes sacerdotes quoslibet poenitentes a quibusvis peccatis, et censuris absolvere possunt.[105]

It is true that the council omitted mention of the obligation of recourse after recovery, confining its decree to the consideration of the confessor's power to absolve, but, as will be indicated presently, the obligation of recourse remained the same as in the law of the *Liber Sextus.*

Provisions for absolution in danger of death are found also in the famous *Bullae Coenae.* These bulls, directed against heretics and apostates, and remaining the same except for slight additions by successive popes, originated probably about the beginning of the fourteenth century,[106] and, although their promulgation was discontinued by Clement XIV at his accession to the papacy in 1769, they retained their force until the appearance of the constitution "*Apostolicae Sedis*" in 1869.[107] Since these bulls remained substantially the same, differing only in the augmentation of the twenty classes of excommunicated persons according to the circumstances of the times, the provision of any one of them for absolution may be considered as the provision of practically all. Such a norm is found in the *Bulla Coenae* promulgated by Clement

[105] Sess. XIV, *de poenitentia,* c. 7.

[106] *Cf.* Cappello, *De Censuris,* n. 8.

[107] *Cf.* Pennacchi, *Commentaria in Constitutionem Apostolicae Sedis* (Romae, 1883), I, 67.

X in 1671, which provided that the persons excommunicated by reason of the bull could be absolved in danger of death, but only if they promised to obey the mandates of the Church and to make due satisfaction.[108]

That the discipline on absolution in danger of death remained the same from the Council of Trent to the constitution *"Apostolicae Sedis"* is evident from the repetition of the same refrain by the canonical writers: in danger of death, any priest can absolve from any censure, provided the dying person binds himself, in case of his recovery, to make satisfaction and to have recourse to the proper superior for his mandates.[109] It may be mentioned that Reiffenstuel expressed as the common opinion one which had not always been admitted, namely, that in danger of death absolution could be given by any priest, whether he was a simple priest, an apostate, degraded, excommunicated, or irregular, as long as no approved priest was present.[110] He also asserted that a simple

[108] "Caeterum a praedictis sententiis nullus per alium quam per Romanum Pontificem, *nisi in mortis articulo constitutus,* nec etiam tunc, nisi de stando Ecclesiae mandatis, et satisfaciendo cautione praestita, absolvi possit . . ."—Clement X, bulla *"Pastoralis Romani Pontificis,"* 26 Martii 1671, § 22—*Bullarum Diplomatum et Privilegiorum Sanctorum Romanorum Pontificum Taurinensis Editio* (Augustae Taurinorum, 1857-1872), XVIII, 180, 181. *Cf.* also Julius II, bulla *"Consueverunt Romani Pontifices,"* 1 Martii 1511, § 13—*op. cit.*, V, 492; Paul V, bulla *"Pastoralis Romani Pontificis,"* 8 Aprilis 1610, § 22—*op. cit.*, XI, 622; Alexander VII, bulla *"Pastoralis Romani Pontificis,"* 13 Aprilis 1656, n. 21—*op. cit.*, XVI, 147.

[109] *Cf.* Barbosa, *Collectanea Doctorum in Jus Pontificium Universum* (Lugduni, 1716), lib. V, tit. 39, c. 11, n. 5; *ibid.*, c. 26, n. 3; lib. VI, tit. 11, c. 22, n. 3; Pirhing, *Jus Canonicum Nova Methodo Explicatum* (Dilingae, 1674-1678), lib. V, tit. 39, nn. 76, 78, 81; Reiffenstuel, lib. V, tit. 39, n. 254; lib. V, tit. 7, nn. 407-413; Leurenius, *Forum Ecclesiasticum, in quo Jus Canonicum Universum Explanatur* (Venetiis, 1729), lib. V, tit. 39, q. 69, n. 3; Schmalzgrueber, lib. V, tit. 39, nn. 97, 245, 260; Pichler, *Jus Canonicum secundum Quinque Decretalium Titulos Explicatum* (Ravennae, 1741), lib. V, tit. 39, § I, n. 14; Böckhn, *Commentarius in Jus Canonicum Universum* (Salisburgi, 1776), lib. V, tit. 39, n. 54; St. Alphonsus Liguori, *Theologia Moralis* (ed. Gaudé, Romae, 1905-1912), lib. VI, n. 561.

[110] Lib. V, tit. 7, nn. 408, 409. *Cf.* also Ferraris, *Prompta Bibliotheca* (ed. Migne, Parisiis, 1863), "Absolvere," Art. I, n. 48; St. Alphonsus Liguori, *op. cit.*, lib. VI, n. 560 (*cf.* note *b* by Gaudé).

priest could grant the absolution even in the presence of an approved priest,[111] but this was rejected by some authors as less probable, because opposed to the common opinion, [112] or was admitted only for certain very unusual cases.[113]

The broad sense of "danger of death" was held as the common opinion, namely, that the *articulus mortis* also included the *probabile periculum mortis.*[114]

The constitution *"Apostolicae Sedis,"* reorganizing the entire legislation on *latae sententiae* censures, provided for the absolution, in danger of death, of those censures reserved *speciali modo* to the pope, affirming the obligation of recourse for the Church's mandates in case of recovery.[115]

After the appearance of this constitution various doubts arose on some points, and these were sent to the Holy Office for solution. That in cases of danger of death the priest need not apply to the

[111] Lib. V, tit. 7, n. 409. This view was subsequently confirmed by the Holy Office, on July 29, 1891, as follows: "Non sunt inquietandi qui tenent validam esse absolutionem in articulo mortis concessam a sacerdote non adprobato, etiam quando facile advocari seu adesse potuisset sacerdos adprobatus; et qui tenent validam esse absolutionem in eodem articulo mortis concessam a peccatis reservatis, sive simpliciter sive cum censura, per sacerdotem non habentem iurisdictionem in reservata, etiamsi advocari seu adesse facile potuisset sacerdos habens praedictam iurisdictionem."—*Fontes,* n. 1141; *ASS,* XXIX (1896-1897), 574.

[112] *Cf.* Ferraris, *Prompta Bibliotheca,* "Absolvere," Art. I, n. 51.

[113] *Cf.* St. Alphonsus Liguori, *Theol. Mor.,* lib. VI, nn. 562, 563.

[114] *Cf.* Reiffenstuel, lib. V, tit. 7, n. 407; Ferraris, *Prompta Bibliotheca,* "Absolvere," Art. I, nn. 49, 50; St. Alphonsus Liguori, *Theol. Mor.,* lib. VI, nn. 560, 561; Kober, *Kirchenbann,* p. 461.

[115] Pius IX, const. *"Apostolicae Sedis,"* 12 Octobris 1869, § I, n. 12: "A quibus omnibus excommunicationibus huc usque recensitis absolutionem Romano Pontifici pro tempore speciali modo reservatam esse et reservari . . . declaramus. . . . Absolvere autem praesumentes sine debita facultate, etiam quovis praetextu, excommunicationis vinculo Romano Pontifici reservatae innodatos se sciant, *dummodo non agatur de mortis articulo,* in quo tamen firma sit quoad absolutos obligatio standi mandatis Ecclesiae, si convaluerint."—*Fontes,* n. 552. It should be noted that in the pre-Code legislation on censures there were no censures reserved *specialissimo modo* by the law, though this term was used by some authors; the *speciali modo* reservation was the strictest form mentioned in the law.

Holy See for faculties to absolve from reserved censures was taken for granted,[116] but divergent views appeared regarding the obligation of the absolved person to have recourse after recovery.[117] This question of the person's obligation of recourse for the mandates was presented to the Holy Office, which replied that this obligation, in so far as it concerned those absolved in danger of death, bound only those who had been absolved from a censure reserved *speciali modo* to the pope, and that recourse must take place according to the manner prescribed in the decree of June 23, 1886, referring evidently to the method of recourse at least by a letter written by the confessor, and probably to the designation of a month as also the time-limit for recourse after recovery.[118]

A further question appeared on the obligation of recourse by a person after recovery, namely, whether this obligation bound

[116] *Cf.* S. C. S. Off., 23 Iunii 1886, q. 2. Since the response to this second question has an important bearing on the method of recourse later prescribed for persons recovering health after being absolved from reserved censures in danger of death, it is here quoted in that part which is relevant.

"2. . . . Utrum recurrendum sit, saltem per litteras ad Eñum Card. Poenitentiarium pro omnibus casibus Papae reservatis, nisi Episcopus habeat speciale indultum, praeterquam in articulo mortis, ad obtinendam absolvendi facultatem.

"Resp. Ad 2. Affirmative; at in casibus vere urgentioribus, . . . dari posse absolutionem, . . . a censuris etiam speciali modo Summo Pontifici reservatis, sub poena tamen reincidentiae in easdem censuras, nisi saltem infra mensem per epistolam et per medium confessarii recurrat ad S. Sedem."—*Fontes,* n. 1102. For the complete text of this response, *cf.* below, p. 56.

[117] *Cf.* Vecchiotti, *Institutiones Canonicae* (16. ed., Augustae Taurinorum, 1875), II, 342.

[118] "3. Utrum auctores moderni post Const. *Apostolicae Sedis* (contra ius commune, cap. *Eos qui 22, De sent. excomm.,* in VI, V, 11; cap. *Ea noscitur* 59, X, V, 39; et contra Rituale Romanum, *De Poenit.,* tit. III, c. 1, n. 23) recte doceant, ei qui in articulo mortis a quolibet confessario a quibusvis censuris quomodocumque reservatis absolutus fuerit, tunc solummodo imponendam esse obligationem se sistendi Superiori recuperata valetudine, si agatur de absolutione a censuris *speciali modo* Papae reservatis; an huiusmodi recursus ad Superiorem etiam necessarius sit in absolutione a censuris simpliciter Summo Pontifici reservatis?

"Resp. Ad 3. Affirmative ad primam partem, negative ad secundam partem, iuxta resolutionem fer. IV, 23 Iunii 1886.—SSñus approbavit."—S. C. S. Off., 17 Iunii 1891—*Fontes,* n. 1137. For the response of June 23, 1886, *cf.* above, in the present chapter, note 116.

under pain of reincurrence of the censure. The doubt arose from the fact that the constitution "*Apostolicae Sedis,*" while affirming the obligation, omitted mention of the fact that it bound under penalty of relapse into the censure.[119] This question was submitted to the Holy Office, which replied that this obligation did bind *sub poena reincidentiae* and defined the meaning of the words "*standi mandatis Ecclesiae.*" [120]

Other questions were submitted to, and answered by, the Holy Office regarding the obligation of recourse after recovery, but their solution was substantially contained in the previous responses of June 17, 1891 and August 19, 1891, so no further light was shed on this point.[121]

The law on absolution from censures in danger of death was now clear, as is seen from the unanimity of the authors in their treatment of this subject.[122] According to the common opinion, the phrase "danger of death" was considered to include such cases as those of soldiers about to enter war, persons embarking on a long voyage, women in child-birth, and persons threatened with approaching insanity.[123] This broad interpretation was supported

[119] *Cf.* above, in the present chapter, note 115.

[120] "1. An obligatio standi mandatis Ecclesiae, a Bulla *Apostolicae Sedis* imposita, sit sub poena reincidentiae vel non.

"2. An obligatio standi mandatis Ecclesiae, in sensu Bullae *Apostolicae Sedis,* idem sonat ac obligatio se sistendi coram S. Pontifice, vel an ab illa debeat distingui.

"Resp. Ad. 1. Affirmative ad primam; negative ad secundam partem.

"Ad 2. Obligationem *Standi mandatis Ecclesiae* importare onus sive per se sive per confessarium, recurrendi ad S. Pontificem, eiusque mandatis obediendi, vel novam absolutionem petendi ab habente facultatem absolvendi a censuris S. Pontifici speciali modo reservatis."—S. C. S. Off., litt. 19 Augusti 1891—*Fontes,* n. 1143.

[121] *Cf.* S. C. S. Off., 13 Ianuarii 1892, ad 6—*Fontes,* n. 1147; 30 Martii 1892, ad 1-4—*Fontes,* n. 1151. For the responses of June 17, 1891, and August 19, 1891, *cf.* above, in the present chapter, notes 118, 120.

[122] *Cf.* Konings-Putzer, *Commentarium in Facultates Apostolicas* (4. ed., Neo-Eboraci, 1897), n. 143; Makée, *Institutiones Juris Ecclesiastici tum Publici tum Privati* (Romae, 1897), nn. 1186, 1189; Hollweck, *Kirchl. Strafgesetze,* § 36; Wernz, *Ius Decret.,* VI, 181.

[123] *Cf.* Makée, *op. cit.,* n. 1186; Konings-Putzer, *loc. cit.*; D'Annibale,

by a declaration of the Sacred Penitentiary on May 29, 1915, stating that soldiers, by the fact of their being mobilized, can be regarded as being in danger of death and can be absolved by any priest.[124]

It was at this time that the Church was preparing the new codification of its laws. Concerning absolution in danger of death, the method of recourse was clear from the responses of the Holy Office, but the introduction of the *specialissimo modo* reservation called for a modification, and *ab homine* censures, in accordance with the law of Boniface VIII, were included under the obligation of recourse. However, it may be said in general that the Church, in forming its new legislation on absolution from censures in danger of death, had only to look back upon the tradition of centuries for the extent of the confessor's power to absolve, to glance over the prescriptions of the few preceding decades for the details of recourse, to adjust several matters in conformity with the realignment of penal legislation, and, after condensing these elements, it had its canons 882 and 2252 of the new Code.

Summula Theologiae Moralis (5. ed., Romae, 1908), I, n. 38; Friedle, "Ueber die Absolutio a Censuris in articulo mortis," *AKKR*, XXX (1873), 185.

[124] *AAS*, VII (1915), 282.

CHAPTER III

ABSOLUTION FROM CENSURES IN EXTRAORDINARY CASES OUTSIDE OF DANGER OF DEATH

Article I. From the Second Lateran Council to the Council of Trent

Although the element of necessity was mentioned in an obscure manner in the early Church as warranting absolution from public penance before its due time,[1] this necessity appears to have been that of imminent death, and the present legislation on the more urgent cases seems properly an outgrowth of the discipline of reservation.

About the ninth century there arose the custom of sending penitents to Rome for absolution from certain crimes, such as homicide and the malicious striking of a cleric, but this practice grew to such tremendous proportions that steps were taken in the eleventh century to curtail it.[2] It seems that it was during the eleventh century that superiors began to reserve to themselves the absolution from certain sins and censures.[3] The first general law of this kind,[4] reserving absolution to the pope, was established in the following century by the second Lateran Council (1139) in the well-known canon concerning the malicious striking of a cleric.

> Si quis suadente diabolo hujus sacrilegii reatum incurrit, quod in clericum vel monachum violentas manus injecerit, anathematis vinculo subjaceat, et nullus episcoporum illum

[1] *Cf.* third Council of Carthage (397), c. 32—Mansi, III, 885—*cf.* above, Chapter II, note 63; Pope St. Leo I, *Ep. 108, ad Theodorum*, capp. 4, 5—*MPL*, LIV, 1012-1014—*cf.* above, Chapter II, note 45.

[2] *Cf.* Dargin, *Reserved Cases According to the Code of Canon Law*, The Catholic University of America, Canon Law Studies, n. 20 (Washington: The Catholic University of America, 1924), p. 9; Morinus, *De Admin. Sacr. Poenit.*, L. VII, c. 16, nn. 4-8.

[3] *Cf.* Van Espen, *Tract. de Censuris*, p. 62a.

[4] *Cf.* Schmalzgrueber, lib. V, tit. 39, n. 216.

> presumat absolvere, nisi mortis urgente periculo, donec apostolico conspectui presentetur, et ejus mandatum suscipiat.[5]

Before long it was realized that this obligation of going to Rome for absolution would cause more harm than good, not only in cases of danger of death, which had been provided for at the very outset, but also in other circumstances; so exemptions were made for certain classes of persons, who could be absolved by their bishop.

Among those excommunicated for maliciously striking a cleric, the obligation of a journey to Rome for absolution was eliminated by Pope Alexander III (1158-1181) for guilty clerics below the age of puberty, monks, public officials, also those clerics who, in exercising the order of *ostiariatus,* struck other clerics, unless it were a case of serious injury; likewise, women in general, and others who were not *sui iuris,* and also those for whom, because of enmity or other reasons, the journey would be dangerous.[6] Pope Clement III (1187-1191) added to this list by excusing from the obligation those guilty of only a slight injury to a cleric, also the poor, invalids, old men, and all others who would be prevented for any canonical reason from going to Rome.[7] Although women were already excused, this same pope granted an explicit exemption to nuns; he also explained the conditions under which servants were to be excepted from the obligation of going to Rome.[8] Pope Honorius III (1216-1227) extended this exemption to the Hospitallers of St. John of Jerusalem, except in the case of a very serious injury.[9] Finally, Pope Gregory IX (1227-1234) renewed these exemptions

[5] C. 15—Mansi, XXI, 530; *cf.* c. 29, C. XVII, q. 4.

[6] *Cf. Compilatio I,* lib. V, tit. 34, cc. 2, 3, 4, 7, 16—Augustinus, *Antiquae Collectiones Decretalium,* pp. 83, 84; Friedberg, *Quinque Compilationes Antiquae,* pp. 63, 64.

[7] *Cf. Compilatio II,* lib. V, tit. 18, cc. 1, 6, 15—Augustinus, *op. cit.,* pp. 123, 124; Friedberg, *op. cit.,* pp. 102, 103.

[8] *Cf. Compilatio III,* lib. V, tit. 21, cc. 6, 11—Augustinus, *op. cit.,* p. 226; Friedberg, *op. cit.,* p. 133.

[9] *Cf. Compilatio V,* lib. V, tit. 18, c. 1—Friedberg, *op. cit.,* p. 185.

by incorporating them in his authentic collection of decretals,[10] promulgated in the year 1234, making a résumé of their provisions in one law, and determining that those absolved by reason of a temporary impediment would have to present themselves to the Holy See for its mandate when the impediment ceased.[11] However, boys under the age of puberty were excused from this obligation of recourse, even though at some later date they might be able to make the journey, and even if they asked for absolution from the bishop only after reaching puberty.[12]

This, then, is the law of the Decretals on absolution in extraordinary cases from reserved censures, or, more correctly, from a reserved censure—a discipline which remained almost unchanged, as will be seen, until a short time before the new Code of Canon Law.

Before the interpretation of this legislation by canonists is considered, it may be expedient to mention the law on absolution in extraordinary cases as expressed by Pope Boniface VIII (1294-1303). In his authentic collection, promulgated in the year 1298 and derogating from the Decretals of Gregory IX only in so far as the provisions of the latter could not be reconciled with those of the *Liber Sextus*, he decreed that those who were absolved, because of danger of death or some other legitimate impediment, from a censure reserved *a iure* or *ab homine* by someone other than the one by whom they ordinarily should have been absolved, would relapse into the same censure, if they did not present them-

[10] *Cf.* cc. 1-3, 6, 11, 13, 17, 26, 33, 37, 50, X, *de sententia excommunicationis*, V, 39.

[11] "Quamvis incidens in canonem latae sententiae propter violentam manuum iniectionem iuxta proprias facultates eis satisfaciat, quibus iniurias irrogavit: non tamen taliter [aliter?], quam per sedem apostolicam vel eius legatum absolutionis potest beneficium obtinere; nisi imminente mortis articulo, infirmitate, inimicitia aut inopia, puerili vel senili aetate, fragilitate sexus seu alia corporis impotentia, sive quolibet impedimento canonico retrahatur, quo minus Romanum Pontificem possit adire, vel nisi iuris beneficio a labore huiusmodi excusetur. Ceterum quibusdam praedictorum, videlicet qui temporali impedimento laborant, exceptis pueris, sub debito iuramenti, quod secundum ecclesiae formam praestare tenentur, consuevit iniungi, ut impedimento cessante ad apostolicam sedem accedant, mandatum ipsius humiliter suscepturi."—C. 58, X, *de sententia excommunicationis*, V, 39.

[12] *Cf.* cc. 58, 60, X, *de sententia excommunicationis*, V, 39.

selves to the proper superior for his mandate after the impediment ceased.[13]

Certain points in the legislation were clarified by the glossators and commentators. For example, Joannes Andreae considered as "old men" those above the age of fifty, for it was probable that a journey to Rome would be sufficiently dangerous for them that they should be excused from undertaking it.[14] The law concerning women was interpreted as referring only to married women, but a custom extended this to widows and unmarried women.[15] Among the poor, those were obliged to go to Rome who were sufficiently strong and who would not be ashamed to beg on the way; [16] otherwise they were excused. Invalids were exempted only when their sickness was dangerous or of long duration.[17] The boys excused from the journey were those who, though of sufficiently developed mind for the incurrence of an excommunication, were under fourteen years of age.[18] The general excusing cause expressed by such phrases as *aliud impedimentum legitimum* or *quodlibet impedimentum canonicum* was interpreted in the broadest sense, as any reason for which a person would be unable to endure the effort required for a journey to Rome.[19]

Persons absolved because of a temporary impediment preventing their going to Rome for absolution, were obliged to bind themselves under oath that they would appear personally before the

[13] C. 22, *de sententia excommunicationis, suspensionis et interdicti*, V, 11, in VI°; *cf.* above, p. 36.

[14] Lib. V, *de sent. excom.*, c. 58, n. 1; lib. II, *ut lite non contestata*, c. 5, n. 6.

[15] *Cf.* Hostiensis, *Commentaria*, lib. V, *de sent. excom.*, c. 6, n. 1; Joannes Andreae, lib. V, *de sent. excom.*, c. 6, n. 1; Panormitanus, lib. V, *de sent. excom.*, c. 13, prooemium.

[16] *Cf. glossa* to *pauperes* in c. 13, X, *de sententia excommunicationis*, V, 39; also Hostiensis, *Commentaria*, lib. V, *de sent. excom.*, c. 26, n. 1.

[17] *Cf.* Hostiensis, *op. cit.*, lib. V, *de sent. excom.*, c. 26, n. 2.

[18] *Cf.* the *casus* and the *glossa* to *pueris* in c. 60, X, *de sententia excommunicationis*, V, 39.

[19] *Cf.* Hostiensis, *Commentaria*, lib. V, *de sent. excom.*, c. 58, n. 1; Panormitanus, lib. V, *de sent. excom.*, c. 26, n. 1.

pope or his legate after the impediment ceased.[20] Women, however, simply by reason of their sex and without any additional cause, could be absolved by their bishop,[21] and, since they were considered to be perpetually impeded from going to Rome, they were not subject to this obligation. Likewise, boys, because of the imperfectly developed age at which they committed their crime, were exempted from this obligation, even if they asked for absolution only after reaching puberty.[22] Strangely, a *glossa* included old men and those laboring under a permanent disability as being only temporarily impeded,[23] but Hostiensis [24] and Joannes Andreae [25] rejected this interpretation, except for the case in which a passing legate would become accessible to such classes of persons.

If, after the cessation of an impediment, a person failed to make the recourse as he had sworn to do, canonists before the time of the *Liber Sextus* were divided on the question whether he reincurred the excommunication. Some held the affirmative opinion, but Hostiensis,[26] Bernardus Parmensis de Botone [27] and others denied this, and this latter opinion seems to have been the correct one at that time.[28] However, in the *Liber Sextus* Pope Boniface VIII changed this by decreeing explicitly that in such a case the excommunication was reincurred,[29] and the question was definitely settled.

[20] *Cf.* c. 58, X, *de sententia excommunicationis,* V, 39, as above, in the present chapter, note 11; c. 22, *de sententia excommunicationis, suspensionis et interdicti,* V, 11, in VI°, as above, p. 36.

[21] C. 6, X, *de sententia excommunicationis,* V, 39.

[22] *Cf.* cc. 58, 60, X, *de sententia excommunicationis,* V, 39.

[23] *Cf. glossa* to *quibusdam praedictorum* in c. 58, X, *de sententia excommunicationis,* V, 39.

[24] *Commentaria,* lib. V, *de sent. excom.,* c. 26, n. 3; *ibid.,* c. 58, n. 1.

[25] Lib. V, *de sent. excom.,* c. 26, n. 4.

[26] *Commentaria,* lib. V, *de sent. excom.,* c. 11, nn. 2-4.

[27] In *glossa* to *suscepturus* in c. 11, X, *de sententia excommunicationis,* V, 39; quoted above, Chapter II, note 92.

[28] *Cf. glossa* to *decernimus* in c. 22, *de sententia excommunicationis, suspensionis et interdicti,* V, 11, in VI°; quoted above, Chapter II, note 96.

[29] C. 22, *de sententia excommunicationis, suspensionis et interdicti,* V, 11, in VI°; quoted above, p. 36. *Cf.* also *glossa* to *decernimus* of this text, as indicated in the preceding note

Concerning the power to absolve, it seems that during this period it was restricted to the bishop or abbot according to the case, and was allowed to a priest only in extreme necessity or by reason of delegation from the bishop.[80] As will be seen, this power to absolve in cases of impediments preventing a journey to the Holy See was later extended to priests in circumstances in which the impeded persons were also unable to approach the bishop for absolution.

It is interesting to trace the development of canonical opinion on the question whether this legislation on impeding causes applied to all *latae sententiae* censures reserved to the pope or only to the single excommunication inflicted for the malicious striking of a cleric. Before this is discussed, it may be noted again that the Decretals of Gregory IX established thirty-three *latae sententiae* censures,[81] seven of which were reserved to the pope,[82] and the *Liber Sextus* constituted thirty-two, of which sixteen were reserved to the pope.[83] Although one law in the Decretals of Gregory IX speaks in general of a *canon latae sententiae*,[84] and the same underlying reason seems to be present for all reserved censures, Hostiensis [85] and Abbas Martinus,[86] both writing before the time of the *Liber Sextus*, limited these exemptions to the one case of the malicious striking of a cleric. Joannes Andreae, in commenting on the Decretals,[87] embraced the opinion of Hostiensis, but later, in his commentary on the *Liber Sextus*,[88] he admitted that this new law seemed contrary to the opinion he had previously expressed. How-

[80] *Cf. glossa* to *licet dioecesano* in c. 11, X, *de sententia excommunicationis*, V, 39; quoted above, Chapter II, note 90. *Cf.* also Hostiensis, *Commentaria*, lib. V, *de sent. excom.*, c. 11, n. 1; Joannes Andreae, lib. V, *de sent. excom.*, c. 11, n. 5; Panormitanus, lib. V, *de sent. excom.*, c. 11, n. 1.

[81] *Cf.* Hostiensis, *Summa Aurea*, lib. V, *de sent. excom.*, n. 3.

[82] *Cf.* Hostiensis, *op. cit.*, lib. V, *de sent. excom.*, n. 12, § In supradictis.

[83] *Cf. glossae* to c. 22, *de sententia excommunicationis, suspensionis et interdicti*, V, 11, in VI°.

[84] C. 26, X, *de sententia excommunicationis*, V, 39.

[85] *Summa Aurea*, lib. V, *de sent. excom.*, n. 4, § Secunda regula; also as quoted by Joannes Andreae, lib. V, *de sent. excom.*, c. 58, n. 2.

[86] *Cf.* excerpt from his writings included as an annotation in Hostiensis, *op. cit.*, lib. V, *de sent. excom.*, n. 12, § Si vero.

[87] Lib. V, *de sent. excom.*, c. 58, n. 2.

[88] Lib. VI, *de sent. excom.*, c. 22, prooemium.

ever, Abbas Panormitanus (+ 1435), who lived a century after Joannes Andreae, asserted that it was the common opinion of the doctors that this legislation referred only to the one excommunication incurred for the malicious striking of a cleric.[39] Consequently, it seems that this latter opinion was the one generally held during this period, and that the broader interpretation gained a foothold only in the next period.

Article II. From the Council of Trent to the Constitution *"Apostolicae Sedis"*

The Council of Trent ordained that, outside of danger of death, priests had no power in reserved cases, but could only persuade the penitents to approach the proper superiors for absolution.[40] Likewise, the *Bullae Coenae*[41] restricted absolution from their reserved excommunications to the case of penitents in danger of death.[42] However, the previous legislation on absolution in extraordinary cases outside of danger of death remained in force, although for a time authors were uncertain whether or not the excommunications of the *Bullae Coenae* could be included under these norms.[43]

The causes excusing from the obligation to obtain absolution from the proper superior were the same in this period as in the previous one, and were expressed in the verse:

[39] Lib. V, *de sent. excom.*, c. 58, n. 3.

[40] " . . . Custoditum semper fuit, ut nulla sit reservatio in articulo mortis: . . . extra quem articulum sacerdotes cum nihil possint in casibus reservatis, id unum poenitentibus persuadere nitantur, ut ad superiores, et legitimos iudices pro beneficio absolutionis accedant."—Sess. XIV, *de poenitentia*, c. 7. *Cf.* above, p. 39.

[41] *Cf.* above, p. 39.

[42] "Ceterum a praedictis sententiis nullus per alium quam per Romanum Pontificem, nisi in mortis articulo constitutus, . . . absolvi possit, etiam praetextu quarumvis facultatum . . . "—Clement X, bulla *"Pastoralis Romani Pontificis,"* 26 Martii 1671, § 22—*Bullarum Diplomatum et Privilegiorum Sanctorum Romanorum Pontificum Taurinensis Editio*, XVIII, 180, 181. *Cf.* above, Chapter II, note 108.

[43] *Cf.* Reiffenstuel, lib. V, tit. 7, nn. 371-377; St. Alphonsus Liguori, *Theol. Mor.*, lib. VII, n. 84.

Regula, mors, sexus, hostis, puer, officialis,
Deliciosus, inops, aegerque, senesque, sodalis,
Janitor, adstrictus, dubius, causae, levis ictus,
Debilis: absolvi sine summa Sede merentur.

It may be useful to explain some of the less evident words of this verse. *Regula* refers to monks; *mors* means danger of death; *sexus* signifies women; *deliciosus* includes those of such delicate constitution that they were unable to go to Rome; *sodalis* refers to clerics living in community; an *adstrictus* is one who is not *sui iuris*; *dubius* concerns one who was uncertain whether or not he had struck a cleric, but whom general rumor accused of doing so, and who could be absolved *ad cautelam* by the bishop; *causae* is the general term embracing other legitimate reasons for inability to approach the proper superior; *levis ictus* refers to the case of a very slight injury to a cleric.[44]

Ever since the time of the Decretals of Gregory IX these impediments had been divided into two classes, temporary and perpetual. However, at the time of St. Alphonsus Liguori (+ 1787) more definite norms existed. This author divided the impediments into those which were perpetual, those of long duration, and those of brief duration. Perpetual impediments were those which lasted for one's lifetime, for an indefinite period, or for at least five years. Such impediments were considered to affect members of a family who were not *sui iuris,* monks, old men (at least sixty years of age), servants, the poor, prisoners, invalids afflicted with an infirmity of long duration, those responsible for the care of a family or a public office, nuns and all women, boys below the age of puberty, soldiers, seminarians, and those who for fear of grave spiritual or physical harm to themselves or their families would be unable for at least five years to go to Rome. An impediment of long duration was considered to be one which lasted at least six months, and one which extended over a shorter period than six months was regarded as an impediment of brief duration.

According to this division, St. Alphonsus considered that those laboring under an impediment of brief duration could not be ab-

[44] *Cf.* Reiffenstuel, lib. V, tit. 7, nn. 378-388; Ferraris, *Prompta Bibliotheca,* "Absolvere," Art. I, nn. 8-25.

solved from a reserved censure by anyone but the one to whom it was reserved, unless there was a necessity to celebrate Mass or receive Communion, namely, to avoid scandal or infamy. Those affected by an impediment of long duration could be absolved from the reserved censure by someone other than the proper superior, but under the obligation of having recourse to that superior after the cessation of the impediment. Those perpetually impeded could be absolved by an inferior without this obligation.[45]

Important during this period is the gradually more and more general acceptance of the view that the legislation providing for the absolution of those impeded from going to Rome applied not only to the single case of the malicious striking of a cleric, but to all *latae sententiae* censures. Thesaurus (+ 1655), departing from the former common opinion, and claiming to express the opinion of all the doctors, interpreted this legislation as extending to all reserved excommunications, but excluded suspensions and interdicts.[46] However, Pirhing (+ 1679) adhered to the common opinion of the previous period, and maintained that the legislation referred only to the single excommunication for the malicious striking of a cleric.[47] But apparently all the later better-known authors asserted that the norms concerning those impeded from going to Rome applied at least to all censures reserved *a iure*.[48]

In these cases the bishop had power to absolve, but whether or not priests had the same power was a disputed question. Regarding this point it may be briefly said that the more common opinion before the time of St. Alphonsus denied to priests the power to absolve in such cases, but St. Alphonsus [49] sponsored the view, held as cer-

[45] St. Alphonsus Liguori, *Theol. Mor.*, lib. VII, nn. 86, 88. For a compendious treatment of this matter, *cf.* Cappello, *De Censuris*, nn. 134, 135.

[46] *De Poenis Ecclesiasticis Praxis Absoluta et Universalis* (ed. Giraldi, Romae, 1831), p. 34b.

[47] Lib. V, tit. 39, n. 81.

[48] *Cf.* Reiffenstuel, lib. V, tit. 39, nn. 249-254; lib. V, tit. 7, nn. 373, 374; Schmalzgrueber, lib. V, tit. 39, n. 97, sec. 5; Pichler, lib. V, tit. 39, § 1, n. 14; Ferraris, *Prompta Bibliotheca*, "Absolvere," Art. I, n. 6; St. Alphonsus Liguori, *Theol. Mor.*, lib. VII, n. 84; Böckhn, lib. V, tit. 39, n. 54; also other authors cited by these in support of this opinion.

[49] *Theol. Mor.*, lib. VII, n. 92.

tain by Reiffenstuel,[50] that any approved confessor could absolve from reserved censures those persons who were impeded from approaching both the pope and their bishop. However, both these authors opposed the opinion that any confessor could absolve when the persons were not prevented from reaching their bishop.[51]

Another question discussed during this period was whether or not the bishop, or, by way of devolved right, the approved confessor, could absolve from reserved censures in extraordinary cases if the person could write to the Sacred Penitentiary for absolution. Thesaurus [52] maintained that, according to the more acceptable opinion, bishops could not absolve in such cases, but, although the practice of writing to the Holy See was becoming more general,[53] the common opinion at the time of St. Alphonsus, which this doctor held as the more probable opinion,[54] asserted that the bishops did have the power to absolve in such cases, for the obligation of the penitent to write to the Holy See was nowhere contained in the law. It is this opinion, as held by St. Alphonsus and others, which seems to have been confirmed by a response of the Holy Office on July 18, 1860.[55] However, if such a confirmation was actually intended, the Holy Office later reversed its stand on this question, as will be seen in the consideration of the following period.

[50] Lib. V, tit. 7, n. 397.

[51] Reiffenstuel, lib. V, tit. 7, nn. 395, 396; St. Alphonsus Liguori, *Theol. Mor.*, lib. VII, n. 92.

[52] *De Poenis Ecclesiasticis*, pp. 34, 35.

[53] *Cf.* Giraldi, *Expositio Juris Pontificii Juxta Recentiorem Ecclesiae Disciplinam* (Romae, 1769), Pars I, sec. 919 (II, 758).

[54] *Theol. Mor.*, lib. VII, n. 89. St. Alphonsus has been incorrectly cited by some authors (*e.g.*, Lega, *De Delictis et Poenis*, n. 146; Ayrinhac-Lydon, *Penal Legislation*, n. 99, 100) as supporting the opposite opinion; he admitted it as probable, but held that the other opinion was more probable.

[55] "2. An impediti adire Romam in persona, teneantur adire saltem per epistolam, aut procuratorem ad absolutionem a casibus Sedi Apostolicae reservatis impetrandam.

"Resp. Ad 2. Consulat probatos auctores, inter quos Sanctum Alphonsum de Ligorio . . . "—mentioned in Vecchiotti, *Instit. Can.*, II, 344; also in Konings, *Theologia Moralis* (5. ed., Neo Eboraci, 1882), I, p. lxxxi. This is not the same response as that of the Holy Office on the same date and on similar matter, as in *Fontes*, n. 962.

It seems, then, that the general opinion on absolution in extraordinary cases at the end of this period was as follows. If a person is impeded from going to the proper superior for absolution, he can be absolved by the bishop from at least all censures reserved *a iure,* and if he cannot approach the bishop, he can be absolved by any approved confessor. However, if the impediment is not perpetual, he must bind himself under oath to present himself, as soon as he can conveniently do so after the cessation of the impediment, to the superior by whom he ordinarily should have been absolved; otherwise, he relapses into the same censure. He may, but he is not obliged to, write to the Holy See for absolution if he cannot appear personally.

Article III. From the Constitution "*Apostolicae Sedis*" to the Code

The constitution "*Apostolicae Sedis,*" reorganizing the entire matter on *latae sententiae* censures, raised doubts whether or not the previous doctrine on absolution from reserved censures in extraordinary cases outside of danger of death could still be followed, but authors maintained, with some hesitancy, that the old discipline had not been changed by the constitution.[56]

However, before long, questions on doubtful points were submitted to the Holy Office, and the responses by this Congregation practically revolutionized the discipline on absolution in extraordinary cases outside of danger of death. Formerly, the basic reason for the power granted to an inferior to absolve in certain cases from censures reserved to a superior was the inability of the penitent to appear personally before the superior. But the practice of sending by letter to the Holy See for absolution had been growing, and the facility and safety of correspondence had developed to a very large extent. Consequently, the fundamental reason of the former discipline was no longer valid, for presence in person could be easily and safely supplanted by means of the moral presence by letter. It

[56] *Cf.* Pennacchi, *Comment. in Const. Apos. Sedis,* I, 439-450; Grandclaude, *Jus Canonicum juxta Ordinem Decretalium* (Parisiis, 1883), III, 580, 583; Smith, *Elements of Ecclesiastical Law* (6. ed., New York, 1887), I, n. 682.

was this change which led to the complete recasting of the legislation on absolution in extraordinary cases.

The new discipline was first expressed by the Holy Office on June 23, 1886. Apparently not a few canonists were uncertain whether, after the constitution "*Apostolicae Sedis,*" the former method of dealing with reserved censures could still be followed. Questions to this effect were submitted to the Holy Office, which, in the following momentous decree, declared that the old discipline was abrogated, and that the new method should consist in this: that in more urgent cases, to prevent the danger of grave scandal or infamy, the confessor could absolve from any censure reserved to the pope on condition that, under pain of reincurrence of the censure, the penitent would have recourse to the Holy See within a month, at least by letter and through the agency of the confessor. The decree is as follows:

> 1. Utrum tuto adhuc teneri possit sententia docens ad Episcopum aut ad quemlibet sacerdotem approbatum devolvi absolutionem casuum et censurarum etiam speciali modo Papae reservatorum, quando poenitens versatur in impossibilitate personaliter adeundi S. Sedem.
>
> 2. Quatenus negative: utrum recurrendum sit, saltem per litteras ad Emum Card. Poenitentiarium pro omnibus casibus Papae reservatis, nisi Episcopus habeat speciale indultum, praeterquam in articulo mortis, ad obtinendam absolvendi facultatem.
>
> Resp. Ad 1. Attenta praxi S. Poenitentiariae, praesertim ab edita Constitutione Apostolica sac. mem. Pii PP. IX quae incipit *Apostolicae Sedis, Negative.*
>
> Ad 2. Affirmative; at *in casibus vere urgentioribus, in quibus absolutio differri nequeat absque periculo gravis scandali vel infamiae,* super quo confessariorum conscientia oneratur, *dari posse absolutionem, iniunctis de iure iniungendis, a censuris etiam speciali modo Summo Pontifici reservatis, sub poena tamen reincidentiae in easdem censuras, nisi saltem infra mensem per epistolam et per medium confessarii recurrat ad S. Sedem.* Facto verbo cum SSmo.—SSmus approbavit.[57]

[57] S. C. S. Off., 23 Iunii 1886—*Fontes*, n. 1102.

Doubts persisted as to whether persons perpetually impeded from going to Rome were to be excluded from the advantages of the previous discipline, and further questions were submitted to the Holy Office. On June 17, 1891, the Holy Office, including in full the above response of June 23, 1886, declared that the old discipline applied also to the perpetually impeded, and that the penalty of reincurrence of the censure affected not only penitents absolved from censures *speciali modo* reserved to the pope, but also those absolved from censures *simpliciter* reserved. After a statement of the complete decree of June 23, 1886, the response continues:

> Quum vero inter doctores de hisce responsis dubia fuerint exorta, S. Congregationi Inquisitionis sequentia ad resolvendum proponuntur.
>
> 1. Utrum responsum ad primum valeat etiam pro casu quando poenitens fuerit *perpetuo* impeditus personaliter Romam proficisci.
>
> 2. Utrum responsi ad secundum clausula "sub poena tamen reincidentiae in easdem censuras etc." referatur solummodo ad absolutionem a censuris et casibus *speciali modo* S. P. reservatis, an etiam ad absolutionem a censuris et casibus simpliciter Papae reservatis.
>
> Resp. Ad 1. Affirmative.
>
> Ad 2. Negative ad primam partem; affirmative ad secundam partem.
>
> . . . —SSm̃us approbavit.[58]

It should be remembered that, although authors writing shortly before the Code[59] used the term *specialissimo modo reservata* with reference to the case of absolving one's accomplice *in peccato turpi*, which had been excluded by the Holy Office[60] from the general faculties granted to bishops for absolution from reserved censures, the strictest form of reservation contained in the law was the *speciali modo* reservation.[61]

[58] S. C. S. Off., 17 Iunii 1891—*Fontes*, n. 1137.

[59] *E. g.*, Makée, *Instit. Juris Eccles.*, n. 1187; Wernz, *Ius Decret.*, VI, n. 175, 1.

[60] *Cf.* S. C. S. Off., decr. 27 Iunii 1866—*Fontes*, n. 995; 4 Aprilis 1871—*Fontes*, n. 1017.

[61] *Cf.* Konings-Putzer, *Comment. in Facult. Apos.*, Appendix, p. 463, n. 13.

Some authors,[62] writing before the above-mentioned decrees of the Holy Office, had taught that, in cases of impediments of brief duration, an inferior could absolve only indirectly from the reserved censure, that is, he would declare that, because of the necessity to avoid scandal or infamy, he would absolve from the sins, and the person could celebrate Mass or receive Communion, but the censure would remain unabsolved until the proper superior could be approached. The question whether this opinion applied to the decree of June 23, 1886, was sent to the Holy Office, which, in the following response of August 19, 1891, replied that this opinion did not apply.

> 3. An absolutio data in casibus urgentioribus, a censuris etiam speciali modo S. Pontifici reservatis, in sensu decreti S. Officii (23 Iun. 1886) sit directa, vel tantum indirecta.
>
> Resp. Ad 3. Affirmative ad primam; negative ad secundam partem.[63]

It seems that canonists must have found it hard to believe that the former discipline was no longer in force, for the Holy Office, repeating its previous response on the direct character of the absolution granted in the more urgent cases, replied on March 30, 1892, that the new discipline was obligatory, and that the old practice could no longer be followed.

> 5. An decretum S. Officii 23-30 Iunii 1886 obliget ita, ut praxis ante hoc decretum servata non sit deinceps toleranda?
>
> 6. An absolutio in casibus urgentioribus, virtute decreti praelaudati data, directa sit vel indirecta?
>
> Resp. Ad 5. Decretum diei 23 Iunii 1886 omnino obligare, praximque contrariam tolerandam non esse.
>
> Ad 6. Affirmative ad primam partem; negative ad secundam.[64]

[62] *E. g.*, Grandclaude, *Jus Can.*, III, 583.

[63] S. C. S. Off., litt. 19 Augusti 1891—*Fontes*, n. 1143.

[64] S. C. S. Off., 30 Martii 1892—*Fontes*, n. 1151.

The next doubt, which evoked a most generous concession, is best seen in the wording of the decree of the Holy Office of June 16, 1897. The import of the decree is that, even when there is no danger of scandal or infamy, the confessor can absolve in the case in which it is very hard for the penitent to remain in sin during the interval necessary for the confessor to obtain the proper faculty for absolution from reserved censures. Prefacing its response with the statement that, according to the decree of June 23, 1886, any confessor can absolve from reserved censures in the more urgent cases to prevent scandal or infamy, the Holy Office continues:

> . . . Dubium tamen oritur pro casu, quo nec scandalum nec infamia est in absolutionis dilatione, sed poenitens censuris papalibus innodatus in mortali diu permanere debet, nempe per tempus requisitum ad petitionem et concessionem facultatis absolvendi a reservatis; praesertim quum theologi cum S. Alphonso de Ligorio ut quid durissimum habeant pro aliquo per unam vel alteram diem in mortali culpa permanere. Hinc post decretum 23 Iunii 1886, deficiente hac in quaestione theologorum solutione, quaeritur:
>
> 1. Utrum *in casu quo nec infamia, nec scandalum est in absolutionis dilatione, sed durum valde est pro poenitente in gravi peccato permanere* per tempus necessarium ad petitionem et concessionem facultatis absolvendi a reservatis, *simplici confessario liceat* a censuris S. Pontifici reservatis directe *absolvere,* iniunctis de iure iniungendis, sub poena tamen reincidentiae in easdem censuras, nisi saltem infra mensem per epistolam et per medium confessarii absolutus recurrat ad S. Sedem:
>
> 2. Et quatenus negative . . .
>
> Resp. Ad 1. *Affirmative,* facto verbo cum SSmo.
>
> Ad 2. Provisum in primo.—SSmus adprobavit.[65]

A further concession was granted by the Holy Father through a decree of the Holy Office of November 9, 1898, with reference to those cases in which neither the confessor nor the penitent is able to have recourse by letter to the Holy See. In such cases it was determined that the absolution could be granted without the obligation of recourse by letter. The decree reads as follows:

[65] S. C. S. Off., 16 Iunii 1897—*Fontes,* n. 1187.

1. Utrum decretum S. R. et U. Inquisitionis, datum sub die 23 Iunii 1886, intelligendum sit tantum de iis, qui *corporaliter* S. Sedem adire nequeunt; vel etiam de iis, qui *ne per litteras quidem per se, neque confessarium,* ad S. Sedem recurrere valent.

2. Et quatenus decretum praedictum extendi debeat etiam ad eos, qui ne per litteras quidem ad S. Sedem recurrere valent, quomodo se gerere debeat confessarius.

Resp. Ad 1. et 2. Quando neque confessarius neque poenitens epistolam ad S. Poenitentiariam mittere possunt, et durum sit poenitenti adire alium confessarium, *in hoc casu liceat confessario poenitentem absolvere,* etiam a casibus S. Sedi reservatis, *absque onere mittendi epistolam,* facto verbo cum SSmo.—SSmus adprobavit et confirmavit.[66]

From the benefit of the last-mentioned decree was excluded the case of a priest who had absolved his accomplice *in peccato turpi,* and who found it very difficult to confess this to a priest in his own region, and so had gone to a confessor in another place, to which his means did not allow him to return. The Holy Office, on June 7, 1899,[67] replied that this case was not included in the provisions for absolution without recourse as in its decree of November 9, 1898.

The doctrine on absolution in the more urgent cases was further developed by a response of the Holy Office, on September 5, 1900, to the question whether the inability to write to the Holy See had to affect both the penitent and the confessor, or whether it was sufficient if the penitent could not write, could not return to the confessor by whom he was absolved, and would find it difficult to go to another confessor. It was decided that the latter set of circumstances was sufficient to excuse from the obligation of recourse by letter. The decree begins with the above response of November 9, 1898, and proposes and answers the following question:

An ut onus epistolam mittendi cesset, scribendi impedimentum adstringere debet confessarium simul et poenitentem; *vel sufficiat,* sicuti aliqui interpretati sunt, *quod poenitens scribendi impar, eidem confessario a quo*

[66] S. C. S. Off., 9 Novembris 1898—*Fontes,* n. 1207.

[67] S. C. S. Off., 7 Iunii 1899—*Fontes,* n. 1224.

vi decret. 1886 et 1897 *absolutus fuerit, se praesentare nequeat, et ipsi durum sit alium confessarium adire;* licet confessarius absolvens, pro poenitente, epistolam ad S. Sedem mittere posset.

Resp. Negative ad primam partem; Affirmative ad secundam.—SSm̃us adprobavit.[68]

Finally, questions were asked as to whether the prescribed recourse by letter to the Holy See could be made to a bishop with faculties to absolve from reserved censures, or to his vicar-general, or to a priest with habitually subdelegated faculties. The Holy Office on December 19, 1900, making mention of the provisions of the original decree of June 23, 1886, and speaking of the quinquennial faculties by which bishops were empowered to absolve from certain reserved censures, published the following response, determining that the recourse could be made to the bishop or vicar-general possessing the proper faculties, but not to the subdelegated priest.

1. *Utrum sufficiat* in casu absolutionis, ut supra, concessae *recursus ad Episcopum facultate absolvendi instructum;* et quatenus affirmative:

2. *Utrum sufficiat etiam* in casu eodem *recursus ad Vicarium generalem* Episcopi, tamquam ad Ordinarium facultatum episcopalium absolvendi de iure participem.

3. *Utrum generatim sufficiat recursus ad quemlibet sacerdotem habitualiter subdelegatum* ab Ordinario ad absolvendum ab his papalibus reservatis, a quibus poenitens fuerit accidentaliter, ut supra, vi decreti S. Officii 1886 absolutus.

Resp. Ad 1. et 2. *Affirmative,* facto verbo cum Sanctissimo.

Ad 3. *Negative.*—SSm̃us resolutionem Em̃orum ac Rm̃orum Patrum ratam habuit et confirmavit.[69]

[68] S. C. S. Off., 5 Septembris 1900—*Fontes,* n. 1247.

[69] S. C. S. Off., 19 Decembris 1900—*Fontes,* n. 1249. A further decree of the Holy Office, on September 6, 1909 (*Fontes,* n. 1288), with reference to the original decree of June 23, 1886, applied these same norms to cases of occult irregularities arising from the violation of censures, but this is not directly concerned with the absolution from censures, and it was subsequently incorporated, not in canon 2254, but in canon 990.

Thus, by this series of responses made by the Holy Office, the Church, departing from the practice that had existed for six and a half centuries with regard to absolution from reserved censures in extraordinary cases, established an entirely new discipline within little more than thirty years before the promulgation of the new Code. Certain features of the old discipline were retained, such as the *ipso facto* reincurrence of the censure for failure to have recourse within the proper time, but the former underlying element of physical inability to appear before the proper superior was replaced by the moral factors of necessity to avoid scandal or infamy and of difficulty to remain in mortal sin. Although some questions were open to dispute,[70] nevertheless, so complete were the provisions of the Holy Office on this matter of absolution from reserved censures in more urgent cases that, with only slight changes and additions, they were ready to be embodied in the new Code.

To show the similarity of the decrees of the Holy Office and the present legislation, the main features of the decrees may be summarized in the following manner.

The old practice is abrogated, and the new discipline is introduced, by which any confessor can absolve from all censures reserved in any way to the pope in the more urgent cases, namely, to preclude the danger of grave scandal or infamy, on condition that the penitent, under pain of relapsing into the censure, have recourse to the Holy See by letter and through the agency of the confessor within a month after his absolution (June 23, 1886). The penalty of reincurrence of the censure applies not only to censures reserved *speciali modo*, as in the case of absolution in danger of death, but also to those reserved *simpliciter* to the pope (June 17, 1891). Another urgent case which warrants the granting of absolution is the hardship of remaining in mortal sin until the proper faculty can be obtained by the confessor—and theologians with St. Alphonsus have said that for some persons it is most difficult to remain in such a state even for one or the other day (June 16,

[70] *E. g.*, whether in the more urgent cases an approved confessor could absolve from censures reserved to the bishop by particular law; *cf.* Wernz, *Ius Decret.*, VI, 180, nota 161. D'Annibale (*Summula Theol. Mor.*, I, n. 349) held that it was more probable that such censures could be absolved.

1897). When neither the confessor nor the penitent can write to the Sacred Penitentiary, and it is difficult for the penitent to go to another confessor, he can be absolved without the burden of recourse (November 9, 1898). However, the case of absolving one's accomplice *in peccato turpi* is not to be included in this provision (June 7, 1899). To be freed from the obligation of recourse, it is sufficient that the penitent is incapable of writing to the Holy See, that he cannot see the confessor again, and that he finds it difficult to go to another confessor (September 5, 1900). The prescribed recourse can be made to the bishop or vicar-general when they have faculties for the reserved censure from which the penitent has been absolved, but it cannot be made to a priest with habitually subdelegated faculties (December 19, 1900).

This summary indicates in brief the legislation of the Holy Office on absolution in the more urgent cases. Add to this the provision which the Holy Office had made on August 19, 1891 [71] for those recovering health after being absolved, in danger of death, from censures reserved *speciali modo* to the pope, namely, that they must either have recourse to the Holy See for its mandates, or receive a new absolution from a confessor with the faculty to absolve from these censures without the subsequent obligation of recourse.

Finally, when these decrees are condensed, slightly clarified and specified, and extended to include all *latae sententiae* censures reserved to any superior, there appears canon 2254 of the new Code.

[71] *Cf.* above, Chapter II, note 120, ad 2.

HISTORICAL SUMMARY

As with all matters of ecclesiastical discipline, the penal legislation in its rudimentary form in the early Church did not possess that precision of character and completeness of detail which only the working of many minds in the passing centuries has brought to it. There was no clear-cut distinction between medicinal and vindictive penalties, for the punishments combined both elements to a greater or less degree. Prominent among the ecclesiastical penalties were the public penances, which, in partially separating the sinner from the communion of the faithful, were a form of excommunication and which were, though not exclusively, at least to a large extent medicinal in character. Consequently, they can be regarded as a type of minor excommunication and a form of censure. These public penances were the only means of release from the *anathema,* which meant complete expulsion from the Church, and the penitent, by ascending in the grades of penance in which the admission to a higher grade was the automatic absolution from the lower, gradually attained to full participation in the life of the Church, being absolved from his sins and allowed to partake of the Eucharist.

Since the public penances were imposed for specific periods of time, in contrast to an essential element of the later notion of censure, provisions were made in the earliest ages for absolution of the penitent from this form of partial excommunication when he was in danger of death.

With the single exception that during the first three and a half centuries absolution was apparently refused to one class of sinners because of their presumed lack of proper dispositions, namely, apostates and excommunicates who sought reconciliation only when actually in serious illness, the Church has always granted absolution in danger of death, unless the lack of dispositions was evident in the particular case. This absolution was granted by the bishop, or, with his permission, by any priest, and in some places this power was granted even to deacons.

These features remained the same throughout the duration of public penance, that is, till about the twelfth century. However, in the matter of obligations of absolved persons after recovery from danger of death changes took place. For almost the first three centuries no obligation was imposed after recovery, and the absolved person remained in full communion with the faithful. After this time, however, at first the penitent was obliged to complete the time of his penance in the highest grade, in which he was deprived only of the Eucharist, but soon the predominant practice demanded that the absolved person continue his penance in exactly the same way as if he had not been absolved.

The discipline of reservation, by which the absolution from certain sins and censures could be obtained only from the pope, succeeded that of public penance in the twelfth century, and it in turn called for provisions not only for cases of danger of death, but for other extraordinary cases in which penitents were unable to go to Rome for absolution.

According to the law of the Decretals and the *Liber Sextus,* a person in danger of death could be absolved from any censure by any priest in good standing. Likewise, those impeded from going personally to Rome, such as women, old men, and invalids, could be absolved by the bishop or a delegated priest, but the common opinion at the time restricted this to the one excommunication inflicted for the malicious striking of a cleric, although there were other censures reserved to the pope. In all cases, a person laboring under a temporary impediment was obliged under oath to have recourse to the Holy See after the cessation of the impediment, and after the *Liber Sextus* this obligation bound under penalty of reincurrence of the censure. Later the legislation on extraordinary cases outside of danger of death was interpreted in a broader sense, at first as extending to all reserved excommunications, and then to all reserved censures. This discipline remained in force till the second half of the nineteenth century.

In 1869 the constitution *"Apostolicae Sedis"* established a twofold reservation to the pope, *simpliciter* and *speciali modo.* A response of the Holy Office declared that the obligation of recourse to the Holy See after recovery from danger of death applied only to persons absolved from censures reserved *speciali modo,* but that this obligation bound under penalty of reincurrence of the censure.

However, in place of this recourse, the person could obtain a new absolution from a confessor with the delegated faculty to absolve from the reserved censure.

In 1886 the discipline on absolution in extraordinary cases outside of danger of death underwent a complete change by a decree of the Holy Office. As late as 1860 the Holy Office, in a reference to the view held by approved authors, had apparently confirmed the opinion that persons who were impeded from appearing personally before the pope were not obliged to write to the Holy See for absolution; but in 1886 it made clear its acceptance of the opposite opinion and, in affirming the obligation to write for absolution, provided entirely new norms for extraordinary cases. In a series of responses it determined that persons could be absolved by any approved confessor from reserved censures in more urgent cases, namely, to avoid grave scandal or infamy, or to escape the hardship of remaining in mortal sin until the confessor could obtain the proper faculties. However, under pain of reincurring the censure, no matter in what way it was reserved to the pope, the person had to have recourse to the Holy See at least by a letter written by the confessor, unless he would not see the confessor again, was personally unable to write to the Holy See, and would find it hard to go to another confessor. This recourse could also be made to a bishop or vicar-general with the proper faculties to absolve from reserved censures.

Regarding legislation on absolution in danger of death, it was the traditional discipline as specified by the constitution "*Apostolicae Sedis*" and by responses of the Holy Office, which was incorporated into canons 882 and 2252 of the new Code. On absolution from reserved censures in the more urgent cases, it was the series of decrees and responses of the Holy Office from the year 1886 which provided the norms embodied in canon 2254.

Part II
CANONICAL COMMENTARY

SECTION I

ABSOLUTION FROM CENSURES IN DANGER OF DEATH

CHAPTER IV

THE ABSOLUTION IN DANGER OF DEATH

Canon 882. In periculo mortis omnes sacerdotes, licet ad confessiones non approbati, valide et licite absolvunt quoslibet poenitentes a quibusvis peccatis aut censuris, quantumvis reservatis et notoriis, etiamsi praesens sit sacerdos approbatus, salvo praescripto can. 884, 2252.

Article I. Danger of Death

Prior to the Code, canonical legislation on absolution in danger of death always employed the phrase *articulus mortis* to signify that situation of approaching death in which the most extensive faculties were enjoyed by priests for the absolution of the dying. Strictly, this phrase has always, as at the present,[1] been understood to mean that condition in which death is imminent and physically certain. Yet, in the laws on absolution in danger of death, *articulus mortis,* as has been seen, has constantly been interpreted in a broad sense as equivalent to *periculum mortis.* This broad interpretation has been accepted by the Code, which eliminated the technically stricter terminology of the old law and, in canons 882 and 2252 on absolution in danger of death, substituted the phrase which more accurately fits the time-honored concept, namely, *periculum mortis.*

[1] *Cf.* Salucci, *Il Diritto Penale secondo il Codice di Diritto Canonico* (Subiaco: Tipografia dei Monasteri, 1926-1930), I, 217; Cipollini, *De Censuris Latae Sententiae Iuxta Codicem Iuris Canonici* (Taurini: Marietti, 1925), p. 51.

Danger of death is that which arises from a hazardous condition or situation in which it is truly and seriously probable that a person may either survive or die as the result of it. The danger may arise from intrinsic causes, such as sickness, a wound, difficult childbirth, or extreme old age, or from extrinsic causes, as impending or actual war, a dangerous journey or voyage, a surgical operation (supposing that the danger is not already present intrinsically), or capital punishment. In an equivalent sense, a person is considered to be in danger of death if he is in serious danger of falling into perpetual insanity or is in such circumstances that he will probably never again have an opportunity of making his confession.[2]

For danger of death it is sufficient that the danger be truly probable, and it not necessary that it be certain, or most probable, or imminent.[3] In general it may be said that the danger is probable when such is the nature of the cause, whether intrinsic or extrinsic, that death follows from it, not rarely and *per accidens*, but frequently and *per se*.[4] When it is asserted that the danger need not be imminent, it seems that this must be understood in the sense that

[2] The notion of danger of death, as expressed by nearly all authors, is borrowed from D'Annibale, *Summula Theologiae Moralis* (5. ed., Romae, 1908), I, n. 38, and is as follows: "Heic admonendi sumus, duo haec, *mortis articulum*, et *periculum mortis*, in iure Canonico, et apud Nostros, idem plerumque, et praesertim cum agitur de sacramentis administrandis, vel recipiendis, significare: significant autem illud rerum discrimen, in quo, cum quis constitutus est, ipsum, et superesse, et occumbere posse, utrumque est vere graviterque probabile; sive periculum immineat ab *intrinseco*, ut puta ex morbo, vulnere inflicto, partu difficili, extrema senecta; sive ab *extrinseco* immineat, velut ex bello, navigatione vel itinere periculoso, etc. Hoc amplius; si quis versetur in periculo incidendi in perpetuam amentiam, vel in ea rerum conditione versetur, ut deinceps copiam confessarii probabiliter non amplius sit habiturus, perinde habetur ac si versaretur in periculo mortis." *Cf.* Coronata, *Institutiones Iuris Canonici* (Taurini: Marietti, 1928-1936), IV, 174; Cappello, *Tractatus Canonico-Moralis de Censuris iuxta Codicem Iuris Canonici* (3. ed., Taurinorum Augustae: Marietti, 1933), n. 114, 1; Cerato, *Censurae Vigentes Ipso Facto A Codice Iuris Canonici Excerptae* (2. ed., Patavii: Typis Seminarii, 1921), p. 40; Salucci, *Diritto Penale*, I, 217, 218.

[3] Cappello, *De Censuris*, n. 114, 1.

[4] Cipollini, *De Censuris*, p. 51.

death need not be actually impending. However, if a probable or even certain danger is clearly remote, it would appear that *per se* such a danger would not be sufficient for the use of the faculties of canon 882. As an example of an intrinsic cause of such a danger, take the earliest stages of some protracted disease which ordinarily results in eventual death, such as cancer of a vital organ. Although it may be probable or morally certain that the person will not recover from the malady but will die as the result of it, if it is clear that the person will not be in any actual danger of dying from it for a long time (and such may be the case for years), then the person could not be absolved by reason of canon 882, but the danger must be judged in the same way as for any other illness. Similarly, among the extrinsic causes, the danger may be certain but clearly remote, for example, in the case of a sentence of capital punishment which is passed now but is not to be executed until some definite time in the distant future. *Per se,* such a danger would not be sufficient for absolution at the present. In other cases, however, the danger arising from either intrinsic or extrinsic causes may not be clearly proximate, but is probable in the sense that it may appear unexpectedly at any time. This is verified in cases of serious illness, of extreme old age, of those about to enter war, and the like. Relative to this point are the faculties granted by a decree of the Sacred Penitentiary,[5] which permitted approved confessors, acting as army chaplains, to grant absolution from all sins and censures, *iniunctis de iure iniungendis,* to all those engaged in battle, and to all attached to the army in any capacity and living in the camps. Similarly, a response of the Sacred Penitentiary[6] declared that every soldier in a state of mobilization can *ipso facto* be regarded as in danger of death and can be absolved by any priest. This seems to refer, however, only to mobilization for war that is actually being waged or that is imminent.[7]

Danger of death is sufficiently verified if it is morally and subjectively judged to be present. If the priest who acts as confessor

[5] 25 Maii, 1915—*AAS,* VII (1915), 281.

[6] 18 Martii, 1912; 29 Maii, 1915—*AAS,* VII (1915), 282.

[7] Aertnys-Damen, *Theologia Moralis* (11. ed., Taurinorum Augustae: Marietti, 1928), II, n. 361, 1.

has a positive doubt whether or not the penitent is in danger of death, he can licitly and validly absolve, as is evident from canon 209.[8] Even if it subsequently becomes evident that the danger of death was actually and objectively not present at the time of the absolution, although the doubt concerning its presence had arisen from a prudent judgment, the absolution was certainly valid.[9] Similarly, if no notion of doubt entered, but an erroneous judgment was made in good faith concerning the danger of death, the absolution was valid and licit, unless the penitent falsely pretended to be in danger of death. In this latter case, the absolution would be invalid, and, on the part of the penitent, illicit.[10]

As is indicated in the foregoing statements, the circumstance of danger of death, at least as prudently judged to be present, is necessary for both the valid and the licit use of the faculties of canon 882. It is true that this conclusion, as regards the validity of the absolution, cannot be unmistakably deduced from the express wording of canon 882.[11] That the words *"valide et licite absolvunt"* of canon 882 do not clearly and necessarily imply the converse in the absence of danger of death, namely, that the absolution would be both illicit and invalid, may be seen from the series of doubts and responses concerning the similar wording *"confessio . . . valida et licita"* of canon 522.[12] However, it is evident that the general

[8] Canon 209: "In errore communi aut in dubio positivo et probabili sive iuris sive facti, iurisdictionem supplet Ecclesia pro foro tum externo tum interno."

[9] *Cf.* Cappello, *De Censuris*, n. 118, 12; Coronata, *Instit. Iuris Can.*, IV, 174, 175; Vermeersch-Creusen, *Epitome Iuris Canonici* (3. ed., Mechliniae et Romae: Dessain, 1928), III, n. 452, 1; Rossi, "De sacerdotibus qui matrimonium etiam civile tantum contrahere praesumpserint quoad absolutionem a censura de qua in can. 2388, § 1," *Perfice Munus*, XII (1937), 17. It may be noted here that this series of articles by Rossi has a far broader scope than its title indicates, including detailed discussions of the ordinary and extraordinary absolution from censures.

[10] *Cf.* Cappello, *loc. cit.;* Coronata, *loc. cit.;* Rossi, *loc. cit.;* Galtier, "De ignorantia et errore in censurarum specialissimo modo reservatarum absolutione," *Periodica*, XVII (1928), 62*.

[11] *Cf.* canons 11 and 15.

[12] For a unified summary of these responses, *cf.* Bouscaren, *Canon Law Digest* (Milwaukee: Bruce, 1934, 1937), I, 295-297; II, 63.

delegation of faculties in canon 882 is given for the particular circumstance of danger of death; that outside of this danger, the norms of canon 2253 must be used for ordinary cases, and of canon 2254 for the more urgent cases; that if the condition of danger of death is not present, the priest does not possess the faculties granted for danger of death; and consequently, any absolution given simply by reason of the faculties of canon 882, which are not possessed in the case supposed, would be invalid, for it would not be a legitimate absolution as required by canon 2248, § 1. This necessity of danger of death for the valid use of the faculties of canon 882 is admitted by all authors who consider the question.[13]

Article II. The Absolution in Danger of Death

A. The Minister of Absolution

The provision of canon 882 for the minister of absolution to those in danger of death could hardly have been expressed in more general terms. Whoever has been validly ordained to the priesthood, no matter how unbecomingly he may have subsequently fulfilled his sacred office, can validly and licitly grant absolution in danger of death, with the single exception of canon 884 regarding licitness. Therefore, not only any priest in good standing, even without faculties to hear confessions, but also any priest who has become an apostate, a heretic, or a schismatic, who has been reduced to the lay state, or who has been suspended, interdicted, excommunicated, deposed, degraded, or subjected to any ecclesiastical penalty or irregularity whatsoever, is nevertheless a capable minister of valid and licit absolution in this situation.[14]

This obtains, according to canon 882, even if an approved priest

[13] *E. g.*, Cappello, *De Censuris*, n. 118, 12; Coronata, *Instit. Iuris Can.*, IV, 174, 175; Rossi, "De sacerdotibus . . .," *Perfice Munus*, XII (1937), 17.

[14] *Cf.* Cappello, *Tractatus Canonico-Moralis de Sacramentis*, Vol. II, Pars I—*De Poenitentia* (2. ed., Taurinorum Augustae: Marietti, 1929), n. 408, 3; Augustine, *A Commentary on the New Code of Canon Law*, Vol. IV—*On the Sacraments and Sacramentals* (3. ed., St. Louis: Herder, 1925), pp. 287, 288; Kelly, *The Jurisdiction of the Confessor* (New York: Benziger, 1929), pp. 92, 93; Marc-Gestermann-Raus, *Institutiones Morales Alphonsianae* (19. ed., Lugduni: Vitte, 1934), n. 1760, 2.

is present.[15] Cipollini,[16] however, maintains that an heretical, schismatical, or excommunicated priest, or a priest who has been the accomplice of the penitent *in peccato turpi,* would validly but illicitly absolve in the presence of any other priest, even a *sacerdos simplex,* who could hear the confession without danger of scandal or infamy and would not refuse to do so. Regarding the priest-accomplice, there is no doubt that the absolution in the presence of another priest, though valid, would be illicit if contrary to the conditions of canons 884 and 2367, § 1, under which such absolution is permitted. This is the single exception in which licit absolution has been excluded by the legislator, and it has been expressly mentioned in canon 882 in the phrase *"salvo praescripto can. 884."* Canon 884 states that the absolution by a priest of his accomplice *in peccato turpi* is invalid except in danger of death, and that even in danger of death it is illicit outside of the case of necessity.[17] If any priest other than the priest-accomplice can hear the confession of the dying person, without danger of grave infamy to the two accomplices or of scandal to others, and the penitent does not refuse to confess to this other priest, then the case of necessity is not considered to be present; and a priest absolving his accomplice *in peccato turpi* from the sin of complicity in such circumstances would grant an absolution that is valid, but gravely illicit. Through his commission of such a sin he incurs the *latae sententiae specialissimo modo* reserved excommunication for *absolutio complicis.*[18]

[15] *Cf.* S. C. S. Officii, 29 Iulii, 1891—*ASS,* XXIX (1896-1897), 574; quoted above, Chapter II, note 111; note, however, that this response refers only to the validity of the absolution.

[16] *De Censuris,* p. 51.

[17] Canon 884: "Absolutio complicis in peccato turpi invalida est, praeterquam in mortis periculo; et etiam in periculo mortis, extra casum necessitatis, est ex parte confessarii illicita ad normam constitutionum apostolicarum et nominatim constitutionis Benedicti XIV *Sacramentum Poenitentiae,* 1 Iun., 1741."

[18] Canon 2367, § 1: "Absolvens vel fingens absolvere complicem in peccato turpi incurrit ipso facto in excommunicationem specialissimo modo Sedi Apostolicae reservatam; idque etiam in mortis articulo, si alius sacerdos, licet non approbatus ad confessiones, sine gravi aliqua exoritura infamia et scandalo, possit excipere morientis confessionem, excepto casu quo moribundus recuset alii confiteri."

However, when an excommunicated, heretical, or schismatical priest is the minister of absolution in danger of death, it seems that a different conclusion must be maintained regarding the licitness of the absolution. It is true that any excommunicated priest is forbidden to administer the sacraments, but this prohibition is limited by explicit exceptions.[19] One of these exceptions is this—that the faithful in danger of death can licitly ask for sacramental absolution from excommunicates, even *vitandi* or other excommunicates after a condemnatory or declaratory sentence, the absolution to be given *"ad normam can. 882, 2252."* Apparently then, if the absolution is given according to the norm of canon 882, the excommunicated priest, even if he is a *vitandus* or if a judicial sentence has been passed, validly and licitly absolves even in the presence of an approved priest. This licitness of the absolution in the presence of an approved priest is confirmed by the distinction in the provision for the penitent in danger of death, namely, that the penitent can licitly ask sacramental absolution from the excommunicated priest, *and also, if no other minister is present, the other sacraments and sacramentals.*[20] The conclusion, then, is that an excommunicated priest, even *vitandus* or *post sententiam,* can validly and licitly absolve the faithful in danger of death, whether an approved priest is present or not, and the same applies to priests under suspension or personal interdict.[21]

[19] Canon 2261, § 1: "Prohibetur excommunicatus licite Sacramenta et Sacramentalia conficere et ministrare, salvis exceptionibus quae sequuntur."

[20] Canon 2261, § 3: "Sed ab excommunicatis vitandis necnon ab aliis excommunicatis, postquam intercessit sententia condemnatoria aut declaratoria, fideles in solo mortis periculo possunt petere tum absolutionem sacramentalem ad normam can. 882, 2252, tum etiam, si alii desint ministri, cetera Sacramenta et Sacramentalia."

[21] *Cf.* canons 2261, § 3; 2275, n. 2; 2284. *Cf.* Cappello, *De Poenitentia,* n. 409, 7; Coronata, *Instit. Iuris Can.*, IV, 175; Cerato, *Censurae Vigentes,* p. 40; Cavigioli, *De Censuris Latae Sententiae Quae In Codice Juris Canonici Continentur Commentariolum* (Torino: Libreria Editrice Internazionale, 1918), n. 56; Augustine, *Commentary,* IV, 287, 288; Rossi, "De sacerdotibus . . .," *Perfice Munus,* XII (1937), 17; Genicot-Salsmans, *Institutiones Theologiae Moralis* (11. ed., Bruxellis: Dewit, 1927), II, n. 332, 3. De Meester (*Juris Canonici et Juris Canonico-Civilis Compendium* [Brugis: Desclée, 1921-1928],

When a priest is a public apostate, a heretic, or a schismatic, he may nevertheless validly and licitly absolve a person in danger of death.[22] However, under certain circumstances it may be illicit for the penitent to ask for absolution from such a priest. This question will be treated under the following heading.

It has been said that if a priest without faculties to hear confessions would grant absolution in danger of death when an approved priest was present, "he would seem to commit a light sin, at any rate, by violating the order of preference demanded by natural equity." [23] This is not at all evident. It attaches a note of inherent illicitness to any use of canon 882 by a priest without faculties in the presence of an approved priest. But the canon simply says that the absolution in such a case is both valid and licit. Whatever may have been the purpose of the legislator in formulating this canon, whether it was to provide most carefully for the salvation of souls by precluding any hesitation or doubt of action on the part of the minister because of a question of illicitness, or whether there was any other reason that prompted the concession, the canon as it stands clearly indicates that the absolution is not only valid, but also licit.[24] Consequently, any illicitness in the use of the faculties of canon 882 will not arise *per se,* from the nature of the case, but rather *per accidens;* for example, if absolution were given in a noticeable manner before bystanders by a priest who is a public apostate, or by one dressed as a layman, when the absolution could be given by another priest without such danger.

The faculties of canon 882 can be used even if recourse to a

III, Pars II, 180) makes an excessive requirement in the statement: ". . . omnis sacerdos, etiam intrusus, haereticus, schismaticus, excommunicatus vitandus, deficiente alio, valide absolvit"; likewise Vermeersch-Creusen (*Epitome,* II, n. 152, nota 1).

[22] *Cf.* Cappello, *De Poenitentia,* n. 408, 3, n. 409, 9; Augustine, *Commentary,* IV, 287, 288.

[23] Kelly, *Jurisdiction of the Confessor,* p. 93.

[24] Kelly later, in "Faculties of Absolving and Dispensing in Danger of Death," *Ecclesiastical Review,* LXXXV (1931), 257, revised his wording to read: ". . . he would seem to commit at most a light sin . . ."

competent superior for faculties to absolve can be made easily.[25] The reason is that in danger of death the Church grants jurisdiction for the particular case to any and all priests who do not already possess jurisdiction,[26] and that in harmony with the provision of the Council of Trent,[27] all reservation ceases in danger of death. However, it has been suggested by De Meester [28] that it would be advisable, in cases in which the obligation of recourse will affect the penitent after recovery, to allow a priest with the proper faculties to absolve if he is present, rather than that the absolution be given by one without such faculties. But the supposition is hardly practical, for it will be extremely rare that a priest will have faculties to absolve from *ab homine* censures, from censures reserved *specialissimo modo,* or from the specific case of canon 2388, § 1, which has been reserved exclusively to the Sacred Penitentiary, and these are the only cases in which recourse is prescribed after recovery from danger of death.

Although the Code in general refers only to the Latin Church,[29] nevertheless there seems to be no doubt that the faculties of canon 882 can also be used by validly ordained priests of the Oriental rites, for without question this canon concerns the good of souls, and in such cases, according to the principles of Canon Law and theology, no distinction is to be made between Catholics of the Latin and the Oriental rites.[30]

In canons 882 and 2252 there is no mention of the phrase *"iniunctis de iure iniungendis,"* such as is found in canon 2254, § 3.

[25] Cappello, *De Censuris,* n. 114, 2; Cerato, *Censurae Vigentes,* p. 40; Reintjes, *De Absolutione Censurae,* Dissertatio ad obtinendum gradum Doctoratus in Facultate Juris Canonici in Pontificio Collegio "Angelico" de Urbe Elaborata, 1925, p. 20; Rossi, "De sacerdotibus . . . ," *Perfice Munus,* XII (1937), 18.

[26] *Cf.* Cerato, *Censurae Vigentes,* p. 40; Marc-Gestermann-Raus, *Instit. Mor. Alph.,* n. 1760.

[27] Sess. XIV, *de poenit.,* c. 7; *cf.* above, p. 39.

[28] *Compendium,* III, P. II, 180.

[29] Canon 1.

[30] Cappello, *De Censuris,* n. 132, 1.

However, De Meester [81] supplies this phrase, and Cipollini [82] asserts that, if the exception is to be made, it cannot affect those things which by natural or positive divine law must be enjoined. It seems that the confessor, in granting absolution in danger of death, can omit those injunctions which proceed purely from ecclesiastical law; he should impose a penance, proportionate to the ability of the penitent, for the sin and also for the censure in those cases which do not entail the obligation of recourse; and he must demand, as far as is possible, the requirements of the natural or positive divine law, such as reparation of scandal, satisfaction to an injured party for harm inflicted, or the restoration of ill-gotten goods. If the penitent is absolved from a notorious censure, he will be obliged, after recovery from danger of death, to observe it in the external forum in all matters which may cause scandal, and he may be forced to give satisfaction for the censure in this forum.[83] Likewise, if he has been absolved from a censure for which recourse is prescribed after recovery, the injunctions of the ecclesiastical law and the penance for the censure will be provided for in the mandates which he will receive.

There is a certain order which the confessor must observe in some cases in absolving from sins and censures. If, in a case of danger of death, there is an excommunication or a personal interdict, it must be absolved before the sins, since these two types of censure prevent the licit reception of the sacraments; and though the absolution of the sins before these censures would be valid, for the confessor has the faculty to absolve, the deliberate inversion of the proper order in absolving would be gravely illicit.[84] However, if a suspension is present, it may be absolved either before or after the sins, for suspension does not impede the licit reception of the sacraments.[85]

[81] *Compendium*, III, P. II, 180.

[82] *De Censuris*, p. 52.

[83] *Cf.* canon 2251. *Cf.* Cipollini, *loc. cit.*

[84] *Cf.* canons 2246, § 3; 2250, § 2; 2260, § 1; 2275, n. 2. *Cf.* Cappello, *De Censuris*, nn. 106, 107, 147, 465; Cerato, *Censurae Vigentes*, p. 33; Aertnys-Damen, *Theol. Mor.*, II, nn. 329, 3°, 997, 1004.

[85] *Cf.* canons 2250, § 1; 2278, § 1. *Cf.* Coronata, *Instit. Iuris Can.*, IV, 171; Cerato, *loc. cit.*

Before any further progress is made in the consideration of canon 882, it will be advisable to dispose of the phrase "*salvo praescripto can. . . . 2252.*" This concerns the obligation of recourse to a competent superior when a person recovers health after being absolved, in danger of death, from an *ab homine* censure or a censure reserved *specialissimo modo* to the Holy See. This obligation of recourse, together with the recently added case under canon 2388, § 1, which is now included under the same obligation, will be discussed in some detail in the following chapter.

B. *The Penitent*

Any penitent in danger of death is a capable subject of sacramental absolution, for, according to canon 882, in danger of death all priests "*valide et licite absolvunt quoslibet poenitentes . . . , salvo praescripto can. 884. . .*" This is the general statement to be drawn from canon 882. But it must be borne in mind that the person in danger of death must be a "penitent"; in other words, he must be possessed of the proper dispositions.[36] Throughout this work it is assumed that nothing is wanting on the part of the penitent's dispositions, but this matter of dispositions calls for special attention in the present instance. For in cases of danger of death any baptized person, Catholic or non-Catholic, can be absolved as long as the proper dispositions are present. But it is evident that the required dispositions will vary, depending on whether the dying penitent is conscious or unconscious, and whether he is a Catholic or a non-Catholic, and the confessor must be acquainted with these requisites if he is to act with any sense of assurance in unusual cases.

The first supposition to be considered concerns the case in which the person in danger of death is conscious. If he is a Catholic, he must have the dispositions ordinarily required for any confession, namely, contrition and the purpose of amendment. If he has been

[36] *Cf.* Cocchi, *Commentarium in Codicem Iuris Canonici* (Taurinorum Augustae: Marietti, 1922-1930)—Liber V, *De Delictis et Poenis* (2. ed., 1928), p. 121.

leading an evil life, however, he should not be absolved until he has promised to change his life and to give due satisfaction, as far as may be possible in the event of his recovery, for the scandal he has caused. If the person is a heretic or a schismatic, even in good faith and even if he asks for absolution, he is not to be absolved unless he rejects his errors and becomes reconciled to the Church.[37] Even if death is impending, he may not be absolved unless he rejects his errors and makes a profession of faith in the best manner possible.[38] But if, because of circumstances, such a dying person cannot be instructed about the true Church, the confessor should urge him to make an act of perfect contrition, and it seems that, if there is no danger of scandal, the confessor can leave him in good faith and absolve him, provided that the penitent admits the validity and usefulness of confession.[39]

The second supposition concerns the case in which the person in danger of death is already unconscious. If, before lapsing into unconsciousness, the person manifested sorrow for his sins and a desire for confession, he is to be absolved, but the absolution should be conditional whenever there is doubt about his dispositions. In cases in which it is not evident but can be presumed with probability that a baptized person, before losing consciousness, possessed contrition and manifested the desire for confession, he can be absolved, but conditionally. These dispositions can be prudently presumed not only in persons who have lived a Christian life, but at times even in those who have led an evil life, and in schismatics and also in many heretics who do not belong to a sect which rejects the

[37] Canon 731, § 2.

[38] "1. An schismaticis materialibus in mortis articulo constitutis, *bona fide sive absolutionem sive extremam unctionem petentibus,* ea sacramenta conferri possint sine abiuratione errorum.

"R. Ad 1. *Negative,* sed requiri, ut, meliori quo fieri possit modo, errores reiiciant et professionem fidei faciant."—S. C. S. Off., 17 Maii 1916; quoted by Cappello, *De Poenitentia,* n. 238.

[39] *Cf.* Marc-Gestermann-Raus, *Instit. Mor. Alph.,* n. 1853; Wouters, *Manuale Theologiae Moralis* (Brugis: Beyaert, 1932, 1933), II, n. 478, II, b; Vermeersch, *Theologiae Moralis Principia, Responsa, Consilia* (2. ed., Brugis: Beyaert, 1926-1928), III, nn. 196, 599.

Sacrament of Penance.[40] If there is doubt whether a dying non-Catholic, who is unconscious, admits or rejects confession, he can be absolved conditionally, provided that all danger of scandal is removed.[41]

Another consideration may be briefly added, namely, the case in which the penitent has already died. Because of the distinction between apparent and real death, it may be said that one who is seemingly dead after a long illness may be absolved within a half-hour after apparent death; one who has in outward appearance died suddenly, while previously enjoying good health, can be absolved within an hour and a half, or even two or three hours, after apparent death. Whether or not this absolution can be given will also depend on the same norms which have just been expressed regarding the presumed dispositions of unconscious persons in danger of death; but the absolution is always conditional, because of the uncertainty whether the person actually possesses life.[42]

The question has arisen whether a Catholic in danger of death is allowed to ask for a validly ordained heretical or schismatical priest, to obtain absolution from him. He is permitted to do so under certain conditions, namely, provided that no scandal will be given, that no Catholic priest can be secured, that there is no danger of perversion, and that it is at least probable that such a priest will administer absolution according to the rite of the

[40] "2. An schismaticis in mortis articulo sensibus destitutis absolutio et extrema unctio conferri possint.

"R. Ad 2. Sub conditione *affirmative,* praesertim si ex adiunctis coniicere liceat, eos implicite saltem errores suos reiicere, remoto tamen efficaciter scandalo, manifestando scilicet adstantibus, Ecclesiam supponere eos in ultimo momento ad unitatem rediise."—S. C. S. Off., 17 Maii, 1916; quoted by Cappello, *De Poenitentia,* n. 237. On this entire consideration, *cf.* Marc-Gestermann-Raus, *Instit. Mor. Alph.,* n. 1854; Aertnys-Damen, *Theol. Mor.,* II, nn. 336, 337.

[41] Marc-Gestermann-Raus, *op. cit.,* n. 1854, 2, c, nota 1; Wouters, *Theol. Mor.,* II, n. 478, Coroll. I.

[42] *Cf.* Marc-Gestermann-Raus, *op. cit.,* n. 1855, II; Aertnys-Damen, *Theol. Mor.,* II, n. 338. The above considerations pertain more directly to the field of moral theology, and more extensive treatments of these points will be found in the works of moralists. *Cf.* also King, *The Administration of the Sacraments to Dying Non-Catholics,* The Catholic University of

Church.[43] Therefore, it is illicit for a penitent in danger of death to ask for absolution from an heretical or schismatical priest if a Catholic priest can be obtained to whom the penitent can make his confession without great repugnance; for, outside of the case of necessity, there is a grave prohibition against *communicatio in sacris* with a heretic or schismatic, and besides, there may be danger of scandal or perversion, from the fact that others of the faithful may consider such an absolution as a testimony of the penitent's belief in false doctrines, or that the heretical or schismatical priest may attempt to induce the penitent to join his sect.[44] Because of this danger of perversion in the case in which only an heretical or schismatical priest can be obtained, some authors[45] consider that in practice it would be better for the dying person to make an act of perfect contrition and commit himself to the mercy of God, rather than expose himself to such danger.

Concerning the phrase *"salvo praescripto can. 884"* in canon 882, this refers to the case of *absolutio complicis in peccato turpi* and involves a restriction which affects the confessor rather than the penitent. It has been treated under the preceding heading on the minister of absolution.

C. *Nature and Form of the Absolution*

As has been remarked in the course of the preceding discussion, the absolution is absolute or conditional according to the character,

America, Canon Law Studies, n. 23 (Washington: The Catholic University of America, 1924), pp. 82-91.

[43] "6. In pericolo di morte, mancando un sacerdote cattolico, si può cercare l'assoluzione da un sacerdote scismatico?

"R. Ad 6. Licere, dummodo tamen et aliis fidelibus non praebeatur scandalum, nec sit alius sacerdos catholicus, nec sit periculum ut fidelis ab haeretico pervertatur, et tandem probabiliter credatur sacerdotem haereticum administraturum hoc sacramentum secundum ritus Ecclesiae."—S. C. S. Off., 30 Iunii, 7 Iulii, 1864—*Fontes*, n. 978.

[44] *Cf.* Cappello, *De Poenitentia*, n. 409, 9; Genicot-Salsmans, *Instit. Theol. Mor.*, II, nn. 130, 332; Marc-Gestermann-Raus, *Instit. Mor. Alph.*, n. 1760, 2; Vermeersch-Creusen, *Epitome*, II, n. 152, nota 1.

[45] *E. g.*, Noldin-Schmitt, *De Sacramentis* (19. ed., Oeniponte: Rauch, 1929), n. 43, 3, b.

condition, and dispositions of the person in danger of death. This applies to the manner in which the confessor grants the absolution. Apart from this, when a censure is absolved which involves subsequent recourse *sub poena reincidentiae,* the absolution is an *absolutio ad reincidentiam,* and such an absolution is commonly regarded as an absolution with a resolutive condition.[46] However, this notion of the resolutive condition must be correctly understood. The *absolutio ad reincidentiam* has its complete effect immediately in remitting the censure, and this particular censure is utterly and irrevocably removed. If a prescribed recourse is not properly fulfilled, the resolutive condition does not destroy the previous absolution, but the effect of that absolution is equivalently nullified with regard to the censure, for, as will be seen more fully in another place,[47] a censure is reincurred which, although it is numerically different from the absolved censure and consequently is not simply the former censure revived, is specifically the same as the previous censure. But it must be noted that the *absolutio ad reincidentiam* does not affect the confessor in his manner of granting absolution. For *per se* the confessor absolves absolutely; the absolution produces an immediate effect in removing sins and censures; and the condition arises from the law itself, namely, if the prescribed recourse is culpably omitted, the same kind of censure is reincurred by reason of the law and not by reason of the confessor.[48]

If the confession is sacrilegious and consequently the absolution does not effect the forgiveness of the penitent's sins, nevertheless this

[46] D'Annibale, *Summula Theol. Mor.,* I, n. 354; Lega, *De Delictis et Poenis* (2. ed., Romae, 1910), n. 138; Cappello, *De Censuris,* nn. 94, 95; Coronata, *Instit. Iuris Can.,* IV, 140; Vermeersch-Creusen, *Epitome,* III, n. 447, 3; Sole, *De Delictis et Poenis* (Romae: Pustet, 1920), n. 152, 3; De Meester, *Compendium,* III, P. II, 162; Cocchi, *Commentarium,* lib. V, p. 88; Cerato, *Censurae Vigentes,* p. 38; Salucci, *Diritto Penale,* I, 176; Blat, *Commentarium Textus Codicis Iuris Canonici* (Romae: Collegio "Angelico," 1921-1924)—Liber V, *De Delictis et Poenis* (1924), p. 86.

[47] *Cf.* below, Chapter V, Article VI, p. 124.

[48] *Cf.* Cerato, *Censurae Vigentes,* pp. 37, 38, 291, 292; Cappello, *De Censuris,* n. 95.

absolution given in the sacramental forum does avail for the remission of the censures.[49]

The form of absolution is that ordinarily used for the Sacrament of Penance, namely, "*Misereatur . . . , Indulgentiam . . . , Dominus noster . . . , Passio . . .*" When any grave necessity urges, the short form may be used: "*Ego te absolvo ab omnibus censuris et peccatis, in nomine Patris, et Filii,* ✠ *et Spiritus Sancti. Amen.*" These forms provide that the censures are absolved before the sins, and the use of them binds at least *sub levi*.[50]

D. Object of the Absolution

Provided that a person in danger of death is baptized and has the proper dispositions, there is no sin or censure from which he cannot be absolved, for, according to canon 882, any penitent in danger of death can be absolved "*a quibusvis peccatis aut censuris, quantumvis reservatis et notoriis.*" The censure may be single or multiple; occult, public, or notorious; it may be excommunication, suspension, or interdict, whether *latae sententiae* or *ferendae sententiae, ab homine* or *a iure*, previous or subsequent to a declaratory or condemnatory sentence; it may be reserved to the ordinary, to the Holy See, even *specialissimo modo*, or personally to the pope.[51] Whatever kind of censure it may be, it can be absolved.[52]

The question has been raised whether the censure of suspension, since it does not impede the licit reception of the sacraments, can be absolved in danger of death. Genicot-Salsmans [53] and Jone [54] claim that it cannot be absolved by reason of the faculties of canon 882.

[49] *Cf.* D'Annibale, *Summula Theol. Mor.*, I, n. 336, nota 13; Coronata, *Instit. Iuris Can.*, IV, 143, 170, 171; Vermeersch, *Theol. Mor.*, III, n. 475.

[50] Canon 2250, § 3. *Cf.* Cappello, *De Censuris*, nn. 99, 100.

[51] Concerning the censures reserved personally to the pope, *cf.* below, Chapter VII, Article III, A, 6, p. 178.

[52] Canon 882. *Cf.* Cappello, *De Poenitentia*, n. 408, 4; *Idem, De Censuris*, n. 114, 3; Rossi, "De sacerdotibus . . . ," *Perfice Munus*, XII (1937), 17, 18.

[53] *Instit. Theol. Mor.*, II, n. 332.

[54] "Die Absolutionsvollmachten in Todesgefahr," *TPQ*, LXXIX (1926), 16.

However, the words of the canon provide for the absolution of all censures without restriction, and the opinion allowing the absolution of the censure of suspension in danger of death is without doubt sufficiently strong to be followed in practice. It is held by nearly all the recent authors, who either expressly include this censure [55] or simply apply the faculties for danger of death to all censures without distinction.[56]

Though it is beyond the scope of this work, which professedly treats only of the extraordinary absolution from censures, the question may be asked whether vindictive penalties or irregularities can be dispensed in danger of death. No special provision is made in the Code for such dispensation in danger of death, and it seems that only the norms given for the remission of vindictive penalties and irregularities in urgent cases, where the danger of scandal or infamy is present, may be applied in so far as they may be verified in danger of death.[57] Since irregularities only prevent the reception or the exercise of ecclesiastical orders, the case in which dispensation in danger of death will be of any use is extremely rare. It is conceivable when the danger of death arises from an extrinsic cause; for example, a military chaplain, about to set out for war, is laboring under an occult irregularity which will prevent his saying Mass, with the consequent probability that his reputation will suffer. In such a case, if the ordinary cannot be reached, any confessor can dispense from the irregularity so that the priest may exercise his orders, provided that it has not been brought to the judicial forum,

[55] *E. g.*, Cappello, *De Poenitentia*, n. 408, 4, nota 3; Marc-Gestermann-Raus, *Instit. Mor. Alph.*, n. 1760, 3; Kelly, *Jurisdiction of the Confessor*, pp. 94, 95; Rainer, *Suspension of Clerics*, The Catholic University of America, Canon Law Studies, n. 111 (Washington: The Catholic University of America, 1937), p. 213.

[56] *E. g.*, De Meester, *Compendium*, III, P. II, 180, 181; Cipollini, *De Censuris*, p. 51; Salucci, *Diritto Penale*, I, 218; Augustine, *Commentary*, IV, 288; Ayrinhac-Lydon, *Penal Legislation in the New Code of Canon Law* (new, revised edition, New York: Benziger, 1936), n. 94.

[57] Canons 2290; 990. *Cf.* Rainer, *Suspension of Clerics*, pp. 232-234; Kelly, *Jurisdiction of the Confessor*, pp. 95, 96; Jone, "Die Absolutionsvollmachten in Todesgefahr," *TPQ*, LXXIX (1926), 15.

or provided that it is not the irregularity contracted because of voluntary homicide or effectual abortion, or because of co-operation in either of these two crimes.[58] To take the same example and to suppose that the chaplain has incurred a vindictive penalty rather than an irregularity, if it was *latae sententiae* and no declaratory sentence has been pronounced, he is not bound to observe the penalty in the case given, as long as the penalty is not notorious.[59] Similarly, in the same case, if the *latae sententiae* vindictive penalty is occult and there is danger of scandal or infamy from the observance of it, as may happen if it is a vindictive suspension, then the confessor can suspend the obligation of observing the penalty or can dispense from it according to the norms of canon 2290. However, it is readily seen that there will be very few cases in which dispensation from vindictive penalties and irregularities can or need be given in danger of death. In brief, it may be said that if the conditions concerning the remission of vindictive penalties and irregularities in urgent cases are verified in a case of danger of death, there is no reason why the norms should not be applied in danger of death.

Before the next subject is taken up, it may be useful to advert to a particular case which may cause some confessors to hesitate before granting absolution in danger of death. The case concerns a priest who, having contracted the excommunication of canon 2388, § 1, because of an attempted marriage, is prevented by very serious reasons from leaving the woman in the event of his recovery, but must continue to live with her, and sincerely promises to observe perfect chastity in the future. The marriage, of course, cannot be convalidated.[60] But absolution can be given to the priest in these circumstances, and as will be seen, there is a subsequent obligation of recourse if he recovers from the danger of death.[61]

[58] Canons 990, § 2; 985, n. 4.

[59] Canon 2232, § 1.

[60] *Cf.* canon 1043.

[61] *Cf.* S. Poenit., decr. 18 Aprilis, 1936—*AAS,* XXVIII (1936), 242, 243; decl. 4 Maii, 1937—*AAS,* XXIX (1937), 283, 284. The obligation of recourse in this case is treated below, Chapter V, Article III, B, p. 110. A detailed discussion of the case itself will be found in Chapter X, Article IV, p. 279.

E. *Forum of the Absolution*

The absolution granted in danger of death by reason of canon 882 is given in the sacramental forum, and it produces its effect only for the internal forum and not for the external forum.[62]

Since censures, like delicts, can be occult, public, or notorious,[63] the manner in which a person may act upon recovery after absolution in danger of death will vary according to the character of the censure absolved. If the censure was occult, and, according to the practice of the Sacred Penitentiary, it may be occult by reason of the persons, the place, or the time,[64] then the person may act in the external forum as completely absolved, since there is no danger of scandal. But if the censure was public, the person may perform only those acts in the external forum which will not give rise to scandal, and, if his absolution in the internal forum cannot be proved or at least legitimately presumed, he can be obliged by superiors to observe the censure in the external forum until he obtains absolution in this forum.[65]

If the censure was notorious, it seems that for practical purposes it may be examined to see whether it is at present public or occult. If it is notorious with notoriety of fact, there is no doubt that it is also public.[66] But if it is solely notorious with notoriety of law,

[62] "D. An absolutio in periculo mortis secundum canonem 882 limitetur ad forum internum, an extendatur etiam ad forum externum.

"R. *Affirmative* ad primam partem, *negative* ad secundam."—Pont. Comm., 28 Decembris, 1927, II—*AAS*, XX (1928), 61. *Cf.* Roberti, "De Absolutione in Periculo Mortis," *Apollinaris*, I (1928), 102, 103; [Vermeersch?], "Annotationes—De absolutione in periculo mortis," *Periodica*, XVII (1928), 41, 42.

[63] Cappello, *De Censuris*, n. 5; Rossi, "De sacerdotibus . . .," *Perfice Munus*, XI (1936), 534, nota 1.

[64] Rossi, *ibid.*, p. 532, nota 2.

[65] *Cf.* canon 2251.

[66] *Cf.* canon 2197, nn. 1, 3. Coronata (*Instit. Iuris Can.*, IV, 15, nota 4) distinguishes between *notitia publica* and *divulgatio* and considers that there can be a case in which a censure that is notorious with notoriety of fact is not public; but it seems that a censure that is *publice nota* is also *divulgata*, and that a censure that is notorious with notoriety of fact is always public; the converse, of course, is not necessarily true.

because a declaratory or condemnatory sentence has been passed or because the delinquent has made a juridical confession,[67] then it may be *de facto* occult, if the sentence or the confession has not been, and will not be, brought to the public attention.[68] In this latter case, it appears that a person can act as absolved in the external forum according to the norm of canon 2251, which lays down a precaution against scandal, and scandal will not be given in this case. However, the superior can demand the observance of the censure in the external forum until the absolution in the internal forum has been proved or legitimately presumed, or, this failing, until absolution has been obtained in the external forum.[69]

Finally, it may be noted that, when a cleric in sacred orders, absolved in the internal forum from an occult censure, acts in the external forum by performing a function pertaining to the power of orders, as he is permitted to do in accordance with the rule of canon 2251, he does not contract the irregularity of canon 985, n. 7, even if the censure should subsequently become known, for he is not to be considered as violating the censure.[70]

[67] Canon 2197, n. 2.

[68] *Cf.* Coronata, *Instit. Iuris Can.*, IV, 18, 19.

[69] These notions will have more frequent application when absolution has been given according to canon 2254, and will be treated more fully in their consideration under that canon. *Cf.* below, Chapter VII, Article II, D, p. 160; Article III, A, 3, 4, 5, p. 169 ff.

[70] *Cf.* Cappello, *De Censuris*, n. 98, 7.

CHAPTER V

THE RECOURSE

Canon 2252. Qui in periculo mortis constituti, a sacerdote, specialis facultatis experte, receperunt absolutionem ab aliqua censura ab homine vel a censura specialissimo modo Sedi Apostolicae reservata, tenentur, postquam convaluerint, obligatione recurrendi, sub poena reincidentiae, ad illum qui censuram tulit, si agatur de censura ab homine; ad S. Poenitentiariam vel ad Episcopum aliumve facultate praeditum, ad normam can. 2254, § 1, si de censura a iure; eorumque mandatis parendi.

Article I. Nature of the Obligation

Appended to canon 882, which grants the faculties for absolution in danger of death, is the phrase *"salvo praescripto can. . . . 2252."* Canon 2252 prescribes that, when anyone was absolved in danger of death from an *ab homine* censure or a censure reserved *specialissimo modo* to the Holy See by a confessor not enjoying any special faculty, he must have recourse to a competent authority after his recovery from danger of death.

First of all, it is necessary to indicate who is a *"sacerdos specialis facultatis expers,"* for upon this depends whether or not the obligation of recourse exists. Canon 882 does not contain a special faculty such as is contemplated in canon 2252.[1] Therefore, any priest who has no faculty outside of danger of death to absolve from censures reserved *specialissimo modo* to the Holy See or from the *ab homine* censure confessed by the penitent, is a priest not possessing a special faculty for these censures. Since it will be extremely rare that a

[1] Coronata, *Instit. Iuris Can.*, IV, 176.

priest will have special faculties for such censures, the obligation of recourse in these cases will practically always be present. Whether or not the obligation may cease under certain conditions is a different question, which will be treated in its own place.[2]

What is this recourse which must be made? The terms *recursus* and *recurrere* are used in a very confusing manner by some authors,[3] signifying at one time the petition addressed to a competent superior for the grant of faculties to absolve, at another the approach to a specially authorized confessor for absolution as in canon 2254, § 2, and again the communication with a competent authority, by personal approach or by letter, to obtain his *mandata,* or instructions, after the absolution has been granted. The recourse prescribed in canon 2252 is neither a petition for faculties nor a quest for absolution from a specially authorized confessor, but is a communication with the proper superior for his mandates after absolution has been given by a confessor, whether this communication is effected by letter or by personal appearance before the superior.

The obligation of recourse arises from the law, yet canon 2252, unlike canon 2254, § 1,[4] does not explicitly demand that the confessor impose this obligation upon the penitent or inform him of it. It is generally agreed that *per se* the confessor is not bound to impose this obligation on the penitent in danger of death, but that it is left to his prudence to inform the penitent or remain silent about the obligation.[5]

There are various reasons why the legislator refrained from requiring absolutely that the confessor impose the obligation of recourse on a penitent in danger of death, such as: the tenderness of the Church toward the dying; the fear that the imposition of the obligation of recourse might be an occasion of spiritual or temporal harm to the penitent; the fear that the confessor might impose the

[2] *Cf.* below, in the present chapter, Article V, p. 118.

[3] *E. g.,* Creusen, *Epitome,* III, nn. 452, 454.

[4] Canon 2254, § 1: " . . . absolvere potest, iniuncto onere recurrendi . . ."

[5] *Cf.* Cerato, *Censurae Vigentes,* p. 42; Cappello, *De Censuris,* n. 116; Coronata, *Instit. Iuris Can.,* IV, 175; Cipollini, *De Censuris,* p. 52; Salucci, *Diritto Penale,* I, 219; De Meester, *Compendium,* III, P. II, 181; Vermeersch-Creusen, *Epitome,* III, n. 452, 3.

obligation when it would more prudently be omitted, and thus deprive a dying person of his tranquillity of soul, so important at such a time; and the uselessness of imposing the obligation in many cases, namely, when it is foreseen that the penitent will certainly succumb to the danger of death.

However, although the confessor is not bound by reason of the law, at times he can and should impose the obligation of recourse. It may be said that, if the penitent is actually dying, the confessor should refrain from informing him about the obligation of recourse; if the confessor prudently fears that the information will disturb the penitent, or at least doubts whether it will be of benefit to the penitent, he may omit it; if he foresees that the imposition of the obligation will certainly be to the advantage of the penitent, he should inform the penitent of this obligation of recourse.[6]

It does not appear correct to say that *per accidens* the confessor may be bound to impose the obligation of recourse in most cases, giving as a reason for this statement that otherwise the penitent, at least if he is a layman, will never know of the obligation.[7] It may be presumed that, if the penitent is a priest, he will know of the obligation of recourse without being informed, but whether he is a priest or a layman, it seems that the confessor should follow the norms which have just been mentioned.

That the obligation of recourse binds under grave sin is beyond question,[8] and if it is deliberately neglected without sufficient cause beyond the time allotted for it, it entails the reincurrence of a new censure of the same species as the one which was absolved.

Article II. Recourse After Absolution from *Ab Homine* Censures

A. *The Ab Homine Problem*

Before the conclusion is presented which will be adduced concern-

[6] *Cf.* Cerato, *loc. cit.;* Cappello, *loc. cit.;* De Meester, *loc. cit.*

[7] *Cf.* Kelly, *Jurisdiction of the Confessor,* p. 97; *Idem,* "Faculties of Absolving and Dispensing in Danger of Death," *Ecclesiastical Review,* LXXXV (1931), 260.

[8] Cappello, *De Censuris,* n. 127.

ing the question of recourse after recovery from danger of death when an *ab homine* censure has been absolved, it will be expedient, as an anticipation of objections, to explain some notions about the *ab homine* censure and its reservation. It is obvious that the matter of reservation of censures is of the highest importance in the consideration of the absolution from censures, and in this work the question of the reservation of the *ab homine* censure has a very practical bearing not only with regard to the recourse after absolution in danger of death but also with reference to absolution in the more urgent cases. Consequently, it calls for more than a mere cursory treatment.

Because of the complicated nature of the material about to be discussed, it seems advisable, in order to eliminate the possibility of confusion, to draw attention to the fact that there are three points to be considered under the two headings of the present article, namely: 1. when a *latae sententiae* censure is attached to a particular precept, and consequently is incurred *ipso facto* upon the violation of the precept, is such a censure an *ab homine* censure, or is it not; 2. if it is an *ab homine* censure, is it or is it not reserved; 3. if it is an *ab homine* censure but is not reserved, is there any necessity for recourse after recovery when such a censure has been absolved in a case of danger of death? Since the difficulty revolves about the second point, regarding the question of the reservation or non-reservation of the *latae sententiae* censure attached to a particular precept, the material unfortunately does not readily permit of the treatment of the three points in the order given, and careful scrutiny will be required for the recognition of each point as it appears. All three points will appear under the present heading, in which an attempt will be made to delineate the *status quaestionis;* likewise, all will be discussed under the following heading, in which practical conclusions will be deduced from this involved matter. It may be helpful to emphasize what should be clear from the treatment in the following pages, namely, that the problem considered here is not concerned with any form of *ferendae sententiae* censure, whether proceeding from a particular precept, or proceeding from the law but inflicted by a condemnatory sentence; but it is concerned with the *latae sententiae* censure attached to a particular precept, that is, a censure which is threatened in a particular precept in such a way that it is incurred *ipso facto* through the violation of the precept.

Evidently the recourse of canon 2252 is prescribed when a *reserved* censure has been absolved, whether reserved *specialissimo modo* by law to the Holy See, or reserved *ab homine*; [9] for any confessor, whether his faculties proceed from approbation or from canon 882, can absolve in the sacramental forum from censures which are not reserved or which are doubtfully reserved,[10] and since no special faculty is needed for the absolution of such censures, the recourse required by canon 2252 would not apply. When a non-reserved censure is absolved in ordinary circumstances by one without any special faculty, there is no need of recourse, and there seems to be no reason to suppose that a stricter practice is prescribed when a non-reserved censure or a doubtfully reserved censure is absolved in danger of death. The recourse of canon 2252 is attached only to censures reserved *specialissimo modo* to the Holy See and to *ab homine* censures. Concerning censures reserved *specialissimo modo* to the Holy See, to say that they are reserved is to state the obvious. Consequently, there is no difficulty in that regard. But can there be any case in which an *ab homine* censure is not reserved, or are all *ab homine* censures reserved?

The difficulty arises from canon 2245, which, in its second paragraph, affirms that an *ab homine* censure is reserved to the one who inflicted it or pronounced a judicial sentence, or to his competent superior, successor, or delegate; while in its fourth paragraph the same canon states that a *latae sententiae* censure is not reserved unless the reservation is expressly mentioned in the law or precept, and in a doubt of law or of fact the reservation does not bind.

The point of controversy is this: when a censure is both *ab*

[9] *Cf.* Collison, *Non Omnis Censura Ab Homine Est Reservata,* Dissertatio ad Gradum Doctoris in Facultate Iuris Canonici Consequendum Scripta apud Pontificium Institutum Angelicum, Romae, 1935 (typis impressa, Lovanii: Bibliotheca S. Alphonsi, 1936), pp. 70, 71; Wouters, *Man. Theol. Mor.,* II, n. 865, 3, c, nota: "Si absolutus a censura ab homine reservata . . ."

[10] Canons 2253, n. 1; 2245, § 4. *Cf.* Collison, *loc. cit.;* Cerato, *Censurae Vigentes,* p. 29.

homine and *latae sententiae*, and no express mention is made of reservation, is the censure reserved according to canon 2245, § 2, or not reserved according to canon 2245, § 4? In other words, when a censure is attached to a particular precept in such a way that the censure is incurred *ipso facto* by the commission of the thing prohibited in the precept, or by the omission of the thing commanded, is this censure reserved when the reservation is not explicitly stated in the precept? For example, a bishop says to one of his priests: "You must stay away from that place, and if you go there again, you are *ipso facto* suspended"; or "You must leave that parish from which you have been legitimately removed, and if you do not leave it within three days, you are *ipso facto* suspended." (It is such a censure which is meant here when the terms "*latae sententiae ab homine* censure" or "*latae sententiae* censure through a particular precept" are used.) In the supposition that the priest has actually incurred such a censure, is it reserved? And, what is specifically the question here, if the priest has been absolved from such a censure in danger of death, must recourse be made to the bishop after recovery?

Before the solutions attempted by various authors on this problem are advanced, the general notions of the Code on the *latae sententiae* penalty and the *ab homine* penalty must be indicated.

A *latae sententiae* penalty (medicinal or vindictive), according to canon 2217, is a determined (*i. e.*, specific) penalty so attached to a law or precept that it is incurred by the very fact that the delict is committed. This appears to be unquestionably clear, with a possibility of doubt arising only from an uncertainty whether the terms used in a particular case are equivalent to *ipso facto*.[11] Yet in an opinion which he held in 1919, apparently relinquished in 1920, and resumed in 1925 and 1933, Cappello makes a distinction and asserts that a *latae sententiae* penalty is one so attached to a law or a *general precept* that it is incurred *ipso facto* by the commission of the delict.[12] But Cappello himself gives an example that

[11] *Cf.* canon 2217, § 1, n. 2, § 2.

[12] *De Censuris iuxta Codicem Iuris Canonici* (Augustae Taurinorum: Marietti, 1919), n. 2, 3°; "De Absolutione a Censuris 'ab Homine,'" *NRT*, XLVII (1920), 525-527; *De Censuris* (2. ed., 1925; 3. ed., 1933), n. 4, 3°:

manifestly includes reference to a *latae sententiae* penalty attached to a particular precept.[13]

There seems to be absolutely no reason to assert that a bishop, in imposing a particular precept, is restricted to *ferendae sententiae* penalties, and that he cannot attach a censure to the particular precept in such a way that it is incurred *ipso facto* when the delict is committed, without any need of a judicial sentence. No distinction is made in canon 2217, § 1, n. 2, between a general and a particular precept, nor is this distinction made in canon 2220, § 1, which simply states that those who enjoy the power to make laws or impose precepts can attach penalties to the law or precept.[14] Consequently, there seems to be no justification for the implication that a *latae sententiae* penalty cannot be attached to a particular precept.

According to canon 2217, § 1, n. 3, an *ab homine* penalty is one which is inflicted by way of a particular precept or by a judicial condemnatory sentence, even if the penalty is stated in the law; and consequently when a *ferendae sententiae* penalty is attached to the law, before the condemnatory sentence it is *a iure tantum,* but after the sentence it is both *a iure* and *ab homine,* but is considered as *ab homine.*[15] The text of the law offers difficulties not only in itself, but far more so when it is compared with other canons. First,

"Vocantur *latae sententiae* quae ita sunt additae legi vel praecepto generali ut incurrantur *ipso facto* delicti commissi, quin opus sit sententia auctoritatis ecclesiasticae."

[13] *De Censuris* (ed. 1925 et 1933), n. 34, 2: "Itaque si Episcopus v. g. velit in clericum concubinarium censuris animadvertere, debet prius illi intimare, ut intra definitum tempus concubinam dimittat sub poena ex. gr. suspensionis, vel *ipso facto incurrendae* vel in eum irrogandae." *Cf.* also *op. cit.*, n. 75, 7, on the question of declaring a censure inflicted *ad modum praecepti particularis.*

[14] Canon 2220, § 1: "Qui pollent potestate leges ferendi vel praecepta imponendi, possunt quoque legi vel praecepto poenas adnectere: . . ."

[15] Canon 2217, § 1, n. 3: "(Poena dicitur) *A iure,* si poena determinata in ipsa lege statuatur, sive latae sententiae sit sive ferendae; *ab homine,* si feratur per modum praecepti peculiaris vel per sententiam iudicialem condemnatoriam, etsi in iure statuta; quare poena ferendae sententiae, legi addita, ante sententiam condemnatoriam est *a iure tantum,* postea *a iure* simul et *ab homine,* sed consideratur tanquam *ab homine.*"

in canon 2217, § 1, n. 3, there is not an adequate distinction, since there is no single *ratio distinctionis* for the division of penalties into *a iure* and *ab homine;* for the definition of *a iure* penalties is based on the manner in which the penalties are *constituted, or established,* while the definition of *ab homine* penalties is dependent on the manner in which the penalties are *inflicted.* The legislator foresaw the possibility of a doubt regarding these two definitions, namely, in the case in which a *ferendae sententiae* penalty is constituted by the law but is inflicted by a condemnatory sentence, for such a penalty would be embraced by both definitions. So he immediately settled the doubt by adding, as the second part of the same number, the explanation that such a penalty, though after its infliction it is both *a iure* and *ab homine,* is to be considered as *ab homine.* This explanation is not restricted to the definition of *ab homine* penalties in this canon, but clarifies all that precedes it in the first part of canon 2217, § 1, n. 3, and therefore the clause *"quare poena ferendae sententiae . . . "* is not to be regarded as an indication that an *ab homine* penalty can be only *ferendae sententiae.*[16]

Secondly, difficulties arise from the comparison of canon 2217 with other canons. For instance, canons 2244 and 2245 seem to consider *ab homine* censures and *latae sententiae* censures as two distinct and opposed categories; while canon 2254, granting the power to absolve from all *latae sententiae* censures, does not make the same explicit provision as does canon 2252 for the recourse after absolution from an *ab homine* censure.

From all this the question arises—can a *latae sententiae* censure be also *ab homine,* or *vice versa,* can an *ab homine* censure be *latae sententiae?* Or, what amounts to the same thing—when a *latae sententiae* censure is attached to a particular precept, is it *ab homine, a iure,* or neither?

The vast majority of canonists [17] maintain the existence of the

[16] This question is considered in more detail in the course of the following pages, under the discussion of the phrase *"per modum praecepti peculiaris"* of canon 2217, § 1, n. 3, with reference to the opinion of Michiels and Roberti on the nature of *ab homine* penalties.

[17] *E. g.,* Coronata, *Instit. Iuris Can.,* IV, 78; Vermeersch-Creusen, *Epitome,* III, n. 406; Cipollini, *De Censuris,* p. 7; Sole, *De Delictis et Poenis,* n. 70;

latae sententiae ab homine censure, which is the *latae sententiae* censure attached to a particular precept. No one asserts that such a censure is *a iure,* but Michiels [18] claims that it is neither purely *ab homine* nor *a iure,* but *"tamquam a iure"*; and Roberti,[19] holding the same opinion, explains it as a censure *"per praeceptum ad instar legis."*

From a practical standpoint, the most important question arising from this problem is that of the reservation of a *latae sententiae* censure attached to a particular precept. Is it reserved as an *ab homine* censure by canon 2245, § 2, or is it *per se* not reserved according to canon 2245, § 4? The explanations offered by various authors in an effort to answer this question will be outlined, after the puzzling text of canon 2245 has been quoted.

> Canon 2245. § 1. Censurae aliae sunt *reservatae,* aliae *non reservatae.*
>
> § 2. Censura *ab homine* est reservata ei qui censuram inflixit aut sententiam tulit, eiusve Superiori competenti, vel successori aut delegato; ex censuris vero *a iure* reservatis aliae sunt reservatae *Ordinario,* aliae *Apostolicae Sedi.*
>
> § 3. E reservatis Apostolicae Sedi aliae sunt *reservatae simpliciter,* aliae *speciali modo,* aliae *specialissimo modo.*
>
> § 4. Censura latae sententiae non est reservata, nisi in lege vel praecepto id expresse dicatur; et in dubio sive iuris sive facti reservatio non urget.

1. Creusen [20] has consistently offered a tentative solution which was adopted by Cappello [21] with the utmost conviction in 1925, and

Salucci, *Diritto Penale,* I, 198, nota 1; De Meester, *Compendium,* III, P. II, 141, 169; Ayrinhac-Lydon, *Penal Legislation,* n. 35, d.

[18] "De reservatione censurae latae sententiae praecepto peculiari adnexae," *ETL,* IV (1927), 192.

[19] "An censura latae sententiae per praeceptum constituta sit reservata," *Apollinaris,* VI (1933), 342.

[20] "De Reservatione Censurae Praecepto Latae," *Jus Pontificium,* IV (1924), 26-29; *Epitome* (3. ed., 1927, 1928), III, n. 406; "La réserve des censures 'ab homine,'" *NRT,* LV (1928), 436.

[21] *De Censuris* (ed. 1925 et 1933), n. 68.

was also accepted by others.[22] It is this: from the context, § 4 of canon 2245 refers to censures *a iure,* and the term *"praecepto"* should be interpreted as referring, not to a particular precept, but to a general precept, since this is equivalent to a law. But it is generally admitted, even by Creusen,[23] that the Code nowhere speaks of a general precept. At times it refers specifically to a particular precept,[24] and again it speaks simply of a *"praeceptum."*[25] That the term *"praecepto"* in canon 2245, § 4, is to be understood solely of the general precept and exclusive of the particular precept seems to do violence to the text, for the normal method of interpretation would suggest that it refers to both the general and the particular precept, or at least to the particular precept.[26] Again, it should be remembered that Cappello, one of the most ardent proponents of this opinion, limits *latae sententiae* penalties to a law or a general precept and ignores the *latae sententiae* penalty as attached to a particular precept.[27] Therefore, when he says that "censurae *ab homine,* scil. actu inflictae per praeceptum particulare vel per iudicialem sententiam, sunt semper reservatae,"[28] this should be understood only of *ferendae sententiae* censures, the reservation of which no one denies.

2. Sole[29] claimed that the *latae sententiae ab homine* censure

[22] *E.g.,* Blat, *Commentarium,* lib. V, p. 101; Cocchi, *Commentarium,* lib. V, p. 108 (but *cf.* also pp. 112, 113); De Meester, *Compendium,* III, P. II, 170; Kinane, "The Reservation of Censures 'Latae Sententiae' Imposed by a Particular Precept," *Irish Eccles. Record,* XL (1932), 533, 534.

[23] *Epitome,* III, n. 406.

[24] *E.g., cf.* canons 2217, § 1, n. 3; 2225; 24.

[25] *E.g., cf.* canons 2217, § 1, n. 2; 2220, § 1; 2226, § 1; 2242, § 2; 2243.

[26] *Cf.* Michiels, "De reserv. censurae l. s. . . . ," *ETL,* IV (1927), 185; Roberti, "An censura l. s. . . . ," *Apollinaris,* VI (1933), 344, 346; Salucci, *Diritto Penale,* I, 199, in nota; Collison, *Non Omnis Censura Ab Homine Est Reservata,* pp. 74-76; Rainer, *Suspension of Clerics,* p. 54.

[27] *Cf.* above, in the present chapter, note 12.

[28] *De Censuris* (3. ed., 1933), n. 68.

[29] *De Delictis et Poenis,* n. 173, 2: "Censura latae sententiae, sive sit a iure, sive ab homine per praeceptum, nisi expresse dicatur in lege vel praecepto, non est reservata, can. 2245, § 4. Ratio quae datur pro censuris a iure

is to be included under canon 2245, § 4, and that consequently such a censure is not reserved unless the reservation is expressly stated in the precept. Practically the same opinion as this one of Sole was suggested in 1920 by Cappello,[30] namely, that when a censure is attached to a particular precept as *incurrenda,* without any actual infliction, it is *per se* not reserved; but if a censure attached to a particular precept is *actu irrogata,* it is reserved. However, this seems to be the same distinction between *latae sententiae* and *ferendae sententiae ab homine* censures as found in the correct interpretation of Sole's opinion. But the view of Sole is open to the objection that it implies a contradiction between § 2 and § 4 of canon 2245 regarding the reservation or non-reservation of the *latae sententiae ab homine* censure. Coronata [31] admits the contradiction, says there is a doubt of law, applies the provisions of canon 2245, § 4, concerning a doubt of law on reservation and of canon 2246, § 2, for the restrictive interpretation of reservation, and concludes that the *latae sententiae ab homine* censure can be considered as *per se* not reserved.

3. Collison,[32] writing an entire dissertation on this point, and defending the opinion of Sole, attempts to explain away the contra-

in cap. 29, X, *de sententia excommunicationis,* V, 39, est 'quia tamen conditor canonis eius absolutionem sibi specialiter non retinuit, eo ipso concessisse videtur facultatem aliis relaxandi.' Et haec regula tradita ab Innocentio III in praedicto capite pro censuris a iure, *nunc in novo Codice,* can. 2245, § 4, valet etiam pro censura ab homine lata per praeceptum." This final clause has been interpreted by Cappello (*De Censuris,* ed. 1933, n. 68, nota 4) and Raus (*Institutiones Canonicae,* 2. ed., Lugduni: Vitte, 1931, p. 697, nota 1) as including *ferendae sententiae* censures inflicted by a particular precept, and has been rejected; but it seems evident from the context that Sole is speaking only of the *censura latae sententiae,* and it has been properly understood as such by Roberti ("An censura l. s. . . . ," *Apollinaris,* VI, 1933, 347), Coronata (*Instit. Iuris Can.,* IV, 163, nota 2), and Collison (*Non Omnis Censura Ab Homine Est Reservata,* p. 72). Besides, it is hardly possible that Sole or any other canonist would adduce canon 2245, § 4, as a reason for the non-reservation of any variety of *ferendae sententiae* censure!

[30] "De absolutione a censuris 'ab homine' ac de metu relate ad censuras," *NRT,* XLVII (1920), 525-527. *Cf.* also Raus, *Instit. Can.,* p. 697, nota 1.

[31] *Instit. Iuris Can.,* IV, 162, 163.

[32] *Non Omnis Censura Ab Homine Est Reservata,* pp. 66, 67.

diction by asserting that canon 2245, § 2, does not say that *all ab homine* censures are reserved, but is to be understood as meaning that, *if* an *ab homine* censure is reserved, it is reserved to those mentioned in the canon. He claims that when an *ab homine* censure is reserved, the reservation arises from canon 2236, § 1, and that canon 2245, § 2, simply states the persons by whom a *reserved ab homine* censure can be absolved, while canon 2247, § 2, merely indicates the extent of the reservation *when* the *ab homine* censure is *reserved*. He would interpret canon 2245, § 2, as "Censura ab homine, *si sit reservata,* est reservata ei qui . . . " But it is not easy to admit this interpretation of canon 2245, for the canon, stating that some censures are reserved and others not reserved, seems to speak in a universal sense in both § 2 and § 4—namely, that every *ab homine* censure is reserved, and that no *latae sententiae* censure is reserved unless the reservation is expressly mentioned. The sense of canon 2245, § 2, seems rather to be—"Censura ab homine est reservata, et reservatur ei qui . . . "

4. Salucci,[83] reasoning in the opposite direction from Creusen, has offered the following explanation, which is reducible to the opinion of Sole. Canon 2245, § 4, refers to all *latae sententiae* censures, whether *a iure* or *ab homine,* as is evident from the use of the terms "*lege vel praecepto,*" and it is entirely out of place to interpret the "*praecepto*" as meaning only a general precept. Consequently, from the context canon 2245, § 2, refers to all *ferendae sententiae* censures, whether *a iure* or *ab homine,* for, according to canon 2217, § 1, n. 3, the *ferendae sententiae* censure *a iure* is *ab homine* after its infliction. Therefore, Salucci concludes, no *latae sententiae* censure is *per se* reserved, which he considers proper, since such a censure is more odious than a *ferendae sententiae* censure.[84] But the opinion of Salucci is likewise not immune to objection, for Salucci restricts the *ab homine* censure of canon 2245, § 2, to *ferendae sententiae* censures, which restriction is not made in the canon. Besides, if the *latae sententiae* censure *ab homine* is expressly reserved in the precept, as in § 4, it would apparently be subject to the norm

[83] *Diritto Penale,* I, 198-200, in nota.

[84] *Cf.* canon 2217, § 2, for the presumption of law in this matter.

of § 2 as to the persons who can ordinarily absolve from it, which produces a rather strange commingling of the two paragraphs. Moreover, the Code nowhere distinguishes between reserved and non-reserved *ab homine* censures, but seems to presume that the *ab homine* censure is reserved.[85]

5. Finally, Michiels [86] and Roberti [87] attempted to solve the problem by asserting that a *latae sententiae* censure attached to a particular precept is not *ab homine,* but "*tamquam a iure,*" and is *per se* not reserved, according to the norm of canon 2245, § 4. An excellent distinction was made between a *praeceptum ad instar legis,* constituting a penalty in the manner of a penal law, and a *praeceptum ad instar sententiae,* or the extra-judicial decree corresponding to a condemnatory sentence, by which a penalty is inflicted.[88] Then the conclusion was drawn that, when the Code uses the term "*praeceptum,*" it refers to the *praeceptum ad instar legis;* when it uses the phrase "*per modum praecepti,*" it means the *praeceptum ad instar sententiae.* Consequently, when a *latae sententiae* censure is threatened by a *praeceptum ad instar legis,* and therefore can be incurred without any actual infliction by a *praeceptum ad instar sententiae,* it is not *ab homine,* but *tamquam a iure.* Again, it was asserted that a *latae sententiae* penalty is "incurred," but not really "inflicted," and that the "*feratur*" of canon 2217, § 1, n. 3, refers only to a *ferendae sententiae* penalty inflicted by a particular precept *ad instar sententiae,* consistently with the penalty inflicted by a condemnatory sentence, which can be only *ferendae sententiae.*[89] Further arguments were adduced from the opposition of *ab homine* and *latae sententiae* censures in canons 2244 and 2245, and from the assimilation of laws and precepts in canon 2195, § 2.

However, the argument of Michiels concerning the assimilation of laws and precepts, as drawn from canon 2195, § 2, seems woefully

[85] *E. g., cf.* canons 2252; 2253, n. 2; 2247, § 2.

[86] "De reservatione censurae latae sententiae praecepto peculiari adnexae," *ETL,* IV (1927), 180-194, 613-619.

[87] "An censura latae sententiae per praeceptum constituta sit reservata," *Apollinaris,* VI (1933), 341-348.

[88] *Cf.* Roberti, *op. cit.,* pp. 342, 345; Michiels, *op. cit.,* pp. 191, 193, 194.

[89] *Cf.* Michiels, *op. cit.,* pp. 190-194; Roberti, *op. cit.,* pp. 341, 342.

weak, for the legislator is apparently considering only the *violations* of laws and precepts as similar; and even if this canon is applied to the laws and precepts themselves, its clause *"nisi ex adiunctis aliud appareat"* seems to be verified in canon 2217, § 1, n. 3, where a dissimilarity is indicated by reference to the *law* under *a iure* penalties and to the *particular precept* under *ab homine* penalties. Besides, the contention that *latae sententiae* censures are "incurred" but not "inflicted" seems to be utterly destitute of any probatory value, for the Code itself uses the term "inflict" in connection with *latae sententiae* censures.[40] It is not denied that *latae sententiae* penalties are commonly considered from the side of the delinquent, and are said to be "incurred,"[41] but that this usage as a consequence excludes the correlative infliction on the part of the superior cannot be admitted. When does the infliction of a *latae sententiae* take place? The infliction is established in the precept and is based on a suspensive condition—"Do not go to that place; if you do, you are *ipso facto* suspended"; when the condition is verified, the infliction becomes effective, corresponding on the part of the superior to the incurrence of the penalty on the part of the culprit.

Concerning the use of the phrase *"per modum praecepti"* as referring only to the *praeceptum ad instar sententiae,* the following may be said. When the Code speaks of the nature of precepts, of

[40] Canon 2241, § 2: "Censurae, praesertim *latae sententiae,* maxime excommunicatio, *ne infligantur,* nisi sobrie et magna cum circumspectione." Also, would canon 2220, § 2 mean that a vicar-general with a special mandate can inflict only *ferendae sententiae* penalties, since *latae sententiae* penalties cannot be "inflicted"? And would canon 2236, § 1, for the same reason, refer only to *ferendae sententiae* penalties, since the remission is granted by him "qui poenam *tulit*"? Again, in canon 2225 it is said: " . . . si poena latae vel ferendae sententiae inflicta sit ad modum praecepti particularis, . . ."; but Michiels ("De reserv. censurae l. s. . . . ," *ETL,* IV, 1927, p. 191, nota 23) claims that the *"inflicta sit,"* with reference to the *"poena latae sententiae,"* means *"comminetur"*; and Coronata (*Instit. Iuris Can.,* IV, 77) interprets it as *"declaretur."* But it is not readily admissible that the single word *"inflicta"* is to be understood in a double sense, namely, as *"irrogetur"* when referred to *ferendae sententiae* penalties, and as either *"comminetur"* or *"declaretur"* when referred to *latae sententiae* penalties, for neither the threat nor the declaration of a *latae sententiae* penalty is by any means an infliction.

[41] *Cf.* canon 2242, § 2.

attaching penalties to precepts, of threatening penalties by precepts, of the transgression of precepts, of reservation by precepts, it uses the term "*praeceptum*"; [42] but when it speaks of the infliction of penalties by precepts, its style is to express the infliction as, not "*per praeceptum,*" but consistently "*per modum praecepti*" or "*ad modum praecepti.*" [43] When this locution, "*per modum praecepti,*" is used, it cannot be presumed to apply only to the infliction of a *ferendae sententiae* penalty by a *praeceptum ad instar sententiae,* but it also refers to the infliction of a *latae sententiae* penalty by means of the *praeceptum ad instar legis*—that is, unless the context clearly shows that only the *ferendae sententiae* penalty can be included.[44]

Consequently, it seems clear that the words "*feratur per modum praecepti peculiaris*" of canon 2217, § 1, n. 3, cannot be restricted to the *ferendae sententiae* penalty, but that the *latae sententiae* penalty inflicted by reason of a particular precept, both before and after it is incurred, must also be considered as an *ab homine* penalty. As a result of this, the question regarding the reservation or non-reservation of a *latae sententiae* censure attached to a particular precept has not been solved by the opinion of Michiels and Roberti.[45]

[42] *Cf.* canons 24; 2310; 2220, § 1; 2243, § 2; 2242, § 2; 2245, § 4.

[43] *Cf.* canons 1933, § 4; 2217, § 1, n. 3; 2225; 2243, § 1.

[44] *Cf.* canon 1933, § 4.

[45] More particular attention has been given to this view of Michiels and Roberti than to the other opinions because of the question, to be treated immediately, whether their arguments are sufficiently strong to create a *dubium iuris* concerning the nature of the *latae sententiae* censure attached to a particular precept. If it is not *ab homine,* the recourse of canon 2252 is not necessary for such a censure, whether it is reserved or not. The question will also arise in the treatment of absolution according to canon 2254. Full justice could not be done to the arguments of Michiels and Roberti in this brief summary, and the reader is referred to their articles as cited above; objections to their view are considered briefly by Vermeersch-Creusen (*Epitome,* III, n. 406), and at length by Collison (*Non Omnis Censura Ab Homine Est Reservata,* pp. 79-89) and Kinane ("The Reservation of Censures 'Latae Sententiae' Imposed by a Particular Precept," *Irish Eccles. Record,* XL [1932], 528-534).

B. Practical Conclusions

From the foregoing consideration of the sources of the difficulty in the Code and the various solutions proposed, it seems unquestionably evident that objectively there is a *dubium iuris* regarding the reservation of the *latae sententiae* censure attached to a particular precept—a doubt arising not only from internal reasons in the text of the law, but also from the weight of external authority provided by the authors who maintain that such a censure is not reserved.[46] It is admitted that the opinion of Creusen, affirming the reservation, appears more probable from its conformity with provisions of the Code for absolution from *ab homine* censures; nevertheless the doubt remains, and this doubt will not be satisfactorily solved until the present law on reservation is either revised or authentically interpreted by the Holy See.

But how is this doubt to be settled in practice? Creusen,[47] in 1924, insisted that canon 6, n. 4, be invoked, and that the *latae sententiae ab homine* censure be regarded as reserved in the light of the old law. But in 1928 he admitted,[48] in view of the authority of the canonists who maintain that the old law is uncertain or that the old law was modified by the Code, and granting the intrinsic value

[46] Among these authors are: Sole, *De Delictis et Poenis,* n. 173, 2; Coronata, *Instit. Iuris Can.*, IV, 162, 163; Salucci, *Diritto Penale,* I, 198-200, in nota; Collison, *Non Omnis Censura Ab Homine Est Reservata, passim;* Wouters, *Man. Theol. Mor.*, II, n. 863, iii, 1, nota 1 (p. 725); Raus, *Instit. Can.*, p. 697, nota 1; Ayrinhac-Lydon, *Penal Legislation,* n. 86; Reintjes, *De Absolutione Censurae,* pp. 13, 14; "Il Codice di Diritto Canonico—Riassunto e Dilucidazioni," *Il Monitore Ecclesiastico,* serie IV, vol. IV (1922), 147. Michiels cannot be listed here in support of this opinion, for he claims ("De reserv. censurae l. s . . .," *ETL,* IV [1927], 184) that if the *latae sententiae* penalty attached to a particular precept is *ab homine,* it is reserved. However, Roberti ("An censura l. s. . . .," *Apollinaris,* VI [1933], 341-348) and Rainer (*Suspension of Clerics,* pp. 49-56), who hold the same opinion as Michiels on the nature of this censure, do not expressly affirm the reservation if this type of censure must be considered as *ab homine,* but both maintain the existence of a *dubium iuris* in canon 2245.

[47] "De Reservatione Censurae Praecepto Latae," *Jus Pontificium,* IV (1924), 29.

[48] "La réserve des censures 'ab homine,'" *NRT,* LV (1928), 444.

of arguments brought against his opinion, that the reservation of the *latae sententiae ab homine* censure can be considered with a safe conscience as doubtful in law and consequently as non-existent, as long as the reservation is not expressly mentioned in the precept. But apart from this, it seems proper to arrive at the same conclusion by using the provision of the very canon which causes the difficulty, namely, canon 2245, § 4—"*in dubio sive iuris sive facti reservatio non urget*"; and also canon 2219, § 1—"*in poenis benignior est interpretatio facienda.*"[49] Therefore, unless and until the contrary is authoritatively determined, the *latae sententiae* censure attached to a particular precept, when it is not expressly reserved in the precept, can safely be regarded as *not reserved.*

Before the conclusion can be stated regarding recourse after absolution from *ab homine* censures in danger of death, one more practical question must be settled. Does the opinion of Michiels and Roberti, as outlined above, create a *dubium iuris* concerning the nature of the *latae sententiae* censure attached to a particular precept? For if such a censure is not *ab homine*, but *tamquam a iure*, then whether it is reserved or not, it does not come under the obligation of recourse in canon 2252 for the simple reason that it is neither *ab homine* nor *specialissimo modo* reserved to the Holy See.

With all due respect to these authors and to those who have em-

[49] *Cf.* Coronata, *Instit. Iuris Can.*, IV, 162, 163; Roberti, "An censura l. s. . . .," *Apollinaris*, VI (1933), 348; Michiels, "De reserv. censurae l. s. . . .," *ETL*, IV (1927), 619; Reintjes, *De Absolutione Censurae*, pp. 14, 15. Reintjes (*loc. cit.*), denies the prevalence of canon 6, n. 4 over the special norms of interpretation for penal law, for "*generi per speciem derogatur*" (Reg. 34, R. J., in VI°). Michiels (*loc. cit.*), says that canon 6, n. 4 is never to be applied in matters of penal law or matters connected with penal law, but that canon 6, n. 5, is to be used, so that all penalties or penal ordinances in force before the Code are to be considered as abrogated "quotiescumque non certo constat eas fuisse in Codice retentas." *Cf.* also Neuberger, *Canon 6, or The Relation of the Codex Juris Canonici to Preceding Legislation*, The Catholic University of America, Canon Law Studies, n. 44 (Washington: The Catholic University of America, 1927), p. 50: "It seems the entire fifth book follows the prescription of Canon 6, n. 5. All accessories follow their principal; therefore, all legislation which is an integral part of penalties is governed by Canon 6, n. 5."

braced their opinion, it is here considered with Creusen [50] that that opinion is very uncertain. For, besides the objections which may be brought against their arguments,[51] their view logically leads to such an anomalous conclusion as this, that a *latae sententiae* censure attached to a particular precept, when expressly reserved in the precept, would fall under the norms of reserved censures *a iure*, so that the reservation would not oblige outside the territory of the superior, even if he expressly said "and I reserve this censure to myself"; [52] it presumes that the legislator was either unaware of this kind of censure or failed to classify it in canon 2217, § 1, n. 3; and it is opposed not only to the common opinion of authors who considered this point before the Code,[53] but also to the almost unanimous consent of authors who have written since the Code.[54] Consequently, it is not admitted here that there is sufficient ground for a *dubium iuris*, but it is maintained that the *latae sententiae* censure *per praeceptum particulare* is an *ab homine* censure.

Finally, the conclusion may now be reached concerning the obligation of recourse after recovery when an *ab homine* censure has been absolved in danger of death. But first, a point that has been

[50] *Epitome*, III, n. 406. *Cf.* also Collison, *Non Omnis Censura Ab Homine Est Reservata*, pp. 79-89; Kinane, "The Reservation of Censures 'Latae Sententiae' Imposed by a Particular Precept," *Irish Eccles. Record*, XL (1932), 528-534.

[51] *Cf.* the preceding heading of this article, opinion n. 5.

[52] *Cf.* canon 2247, § 2.

[53] *E. g.*, Lehmkuhl, *Theologia Moralis* (10. ed., Friburgi Brisgoviae, 1902), II, n. 863, 4: "Censurae 'ab homine' feruntur aut *per modum mandati*, aut *per modum sententiae*. Priores imitantur censuras latae sententiae, siquidem Superior aliquid praecipit vel prohibet, ita ut inobediens ipso facto poenam incurrat; per modum sententiae censura fertur, quando, criminis perpetrati nondum plane praeteriti inquisitione facta, Superior reum pro culpa punit." *Cf.* also Lega, *De Delictis et Poenis* (2. ed., Romae, 1910), n. 84: "Poena vel *a iure* vel *ab homine* lata subdividitur in poenam *fer. sententiae* et *lat. sententiae*." *Ibid.*, n. 111: "Explorati enim iuris est, censuras *ab homine*, esse aut *l.* aut *f. s.*" *Ibid.*, n. 130, 3: "Sententia praeterea *ab homine* dicitur, quum ab Ordinario loci seu a *iudice ipso*, sua auctoritate, editur particularis censura sive haec incurratur *ipso facto*, sive sit *ferendae s.* ob transgressionem alicuius legis aut praecepti."

[54] *Cf.* above, in the present chapter, note 17.

mentioned may be briefly repeated—namely, it seems logical to suppose that, if there is no necessity of recourse when a non-reserved *latae sententiae ab homine* censure is absolved outside of danger of death, there is likewise no reason for the necessity of such recourse when the same censure has been absolved in danger of death. It may well be objected that canon 2252 does not distinguish between reserved and non-reserved *ab homine* censures, and that consequently the distinction should not be made. Neither is this distinction made in other canons.[55] That is why the opinion of Creusen, supposing that every *ab homine* censure is reserved, although it is open to a serious intrinsic objection, seems more probable. But that there is a *dubium iuris* in this matter seems almost incontrovertible, and the principles of interpretation for penal law indicate that the doubt is to be settled on the side of leniency. Therefore, a distinction becomes necessary in treating those canons which deal with the *ab homine* censure. When the *latae sententiae ab homine* censure is not expressly reserved, it seems that it can be absolved in the sacramental forum by any confessor, without any obligation of recourse, by reason of canon 2253, n. 1, which is worded broadly enough to include this censure.[56]

Consequently, the following opinion is offered regarding the obligation of recourse after recovery from danger of death when an *ab homine* censure has been absolved by one without any special faculty. The obligation of recourse binds when:

1. any *ferendae sententiae* censure was inflicted, either by way of a particular precept or by a condemnatory sentence;

[55] *E.g.*, canons 2245, § 2; 2247, §§ 2, 3; 2253, n. 2.

[56] Canon 2253: "Extra mortis periculum possunt absolvere:

"1. A censura non reservata, in foro sacramentali quilibet confessarius . . . " *Cf.* Sole, *De Delictis et Poenis*, nn. 190, 191; Salucci, *Diritto Penale*, I, 223; Collison, *Non Omnis Censura Ab Homine Est Reservata*, pp. 71, 72; Reintjes, *De Absolutione Censurae*, p. 25; *cf.* also Coronata, *Instit. Iuris Can.*, IV, 163, on the general notions on absolution in cases of doubtful reservation. It may be remarked that, if every *ab homine* censure were reserved, canon 2253 would be more properly and more clearly divided into the absolution from: 1. *censura ab homine; 2. censura a jure non reservata;* 3. *censura a jure reservata.*

2. a *latae sententiae* censure attached to a particular precept was incurred, and in the precept the superior had expressly reserved the absolution to himself.

In other words, and perhaps more simply—whenever an *ab homine* censure has been absolved in danger of death, the penitent after recovery is *per se* always obliged to have recourse, except when the *ab homine* censure was attached to a particular precept as *latae sententiae* and the superior did not expressly reserve its absolution to himself.[57]

Article III. Recourse After Absolution from *A Iure* Censures

A. *Censures Reserved Specialissimo Modo*

There is little difficulty in the question of the particular censures which involve the obligation of recourse after recovery when absolution was given in danger of death from a censure reserved *specialissimo modo* to the Holy See.

According to the Code, there are only four censures reserved *specialissimo modo* to the Holy See, and these are incurred by:

1. those who throw away the Consecrated Species, or take them or retain them for an evil purpose—canon 2320;
2. those who lay violent hands on the person of the Roman Pontiff—canon 2343, § 1;
3. confessors who absolve or pretend to absolve an accomplice *in peccato turpi*—canon 2367;

[57] *Cf.* Wouters, *Man. Theol. Mor.*, II, n. 865, 3, c, nota (p. 729) with II, n. 863, III, 1, nota 1 (p. 725); Collison, *op. cit.*, pp. 70, 71. It may be recalled that the opinion of Michiels and Roberti (*cf.* opinion n. 5 under heading A of the present article) would logically lead to a broader conclusion than that stated here, for if the *latae sententiae* censure attached to a particular precept were not *ab homine*, then, whether it were expressly reserved or not, it would not come under the obligation of recourse, since it would be neither *ab homine* nor reserved *specialissimo modo* to the Holy See.

4. confessors who dare to violate directly the seal of confession—canon 2369, § 1.

Therefore, when absolution has been given in danger of death from any or all of these censures, the penitent is bound after recovery by the obligation of recourse.

However, in this connection there are also other censures which are included under the obligation of recourse. These are the censures which are reserved personally to the pope, for they are considered as equivalent to censures reserved *specialissimo modo* to the Holy See,[58] and consequently involve the obligation of recourse after recovery from danger of death.[59]

In brief, the censures reserved personally to the pope are as follows:

1. the excommunications attached to delicts in the election of the Roman Pontiff; [60]
2. the excommunication for violation of the secret of the Holy Office; [61]
3. the excommunication for violation of the secret of the Sacred Congregation of Rites by anyone who performs some function in causes of beatification or canonization.[62]

[58] Cappello, *De Censuris,* n. 207; Cavigioli, *De Censuris,* n. 80. *Cf.* also Coronata, *Instit. Iuris Can.,* IV, 162, 344; Ayrinhac-Lydon, *Penal Legislation,* pp. 326, 327.

[59] Cappello, *op. cit.,* n. 115, 4.

[60] *Cf.* canon 2330; Pius X, const. *"Vacante Sede Apostolica,"* 25 Decembris 1904, n. 51. *Cf.* Cappello, *De Censuris,* nn. 66, 207, 565-578; Coronata, *Instit. Iuris Can.,* IV, 344-349; Cipollini, *De Censuris,* pp. 237-254.

[61] *Cf.* canon 243, § 2; Ordo Servandus in Sacris Congregationibus, Tribunalibus, Officiis Romanae Curiae, Pars II, Cap. VII, Art. II, n. 4, Art. VII, n. 2—*AAS,* I (1908), 82, 83, 98; S. C. Consist., 25 Aprilis, 1917—*AAS,* IX (1917), 232, 233. *Cf.* also Cappello, *De Censuris,* n. 207; Coronata, *Instit. Iuris Can.,* IV, 162.

[62] *Cf.* canon 2037, §§ 1, 3; S. R. C., decr. 15 Octobris, 1678, § 1, n. 3, §§ 3, 4—*Fontes,* n. 5626. *Cf.* Cappello, *loc. cit.* These three types of censures reserved personally to the pope will be treated more fully under canon 2254; *cf.* below, Chapter VII, Article III, A, 6, p. 178.

These, then, are the censures reserved *specialissimo modo* which are embraced under the obligation of recourse in canon 2252. But besides these and reserved *ab homine* censures, there are two other special cases which entail the obligation of recourse after recovery when absolution has been given in danger of death. These two cases are considered under the following heading.

B. Special Cases Involving Recourse

Within the past two years the Sacred Penitentiary has issued a decree [63] and a declaration [64] concerning the absolution of priests who, having attempted civil marriage, are prevented by very grave reasons from ceasing to dwell in the same house with their accomplices, but promise to observe absolute and perfect chastity in the future, and wish to be absolved and receive the sacraments as laymen.[65] The declaration confines itself to an explicit exclusion of this case from the faculties of canon 2254, so it is the decree to which one must look concerning the norms for danger of death. According to the decree, in the above case absolution can be given in danger of death, but, although the censure remains reserved *simpliciter* to the Holy See as in canon 2388, § 1, nevertheless after recovery from danger of death there is an obligation of recourse in the same way as for censures reserved *specialissimo modo* to the Holy See.

It is to be noted that the case specified in this decree concerns only diocesan or religious clerics:

1. who have been ordained to the priesthood;
2. who have dared to attempt marriage, even only a civil marriage; *and*
3. who intend, because of most grave reasons, to continue living under the same roof with their accomplice in the manner of brother and sister.

[63] S. Poenit., decr. 18 Aprilis, 1936—*AAS*, XXVIII (1936), 242, 243.

[64] S. Poenit., declar. 4 Maii, 1937—*AAS*, XXIX (1937), 283, 284.

[65] This case has been mentioned briefly above, Chapter IV, Article II, D, p. 86; it is treated at length in Chapter X, Article IV, p. 279 ff.

All three of these elements must be found in a case before it becomes subject to the reservation stated in the decree; if any one of the three is lacking, this reservation does not bind.[66] Consequently, if the penitent who was absolved in danger of death is a priest, but either or both of the other conditions are not verified; or if the absolved penitent is any of the other persons mentioned in canon 2388, § 1; then there is no obligation of recourse after recovery from danger of death, for the case is not embraced in the decree, and it is not affected by the obligation as in canon 2252, since the censure is reserved, not *specialissimo modo,* but *simpliciter,* to the Holy See.

For the sake of completeness, although the matter does not concern censures, it may be mentioned that there is one reserved sin for which the obligation of recourse is binding after recovery, when absolution has been given in danger of death. This reserved sin consists in this, that a confessor grants sacramental absolution to anyone who belongs to *"L'Action Française"* and who refuses to withdraw from it when warned to do so. It is the confessor who commits this sin by giving absolution to an obstinate adherent of this movement, and the sin is reserved to the Holy See in such a way that, if absolution is given to such a priest in danger of death or in any other circumstances, there is an obligation of recourse to the Sacred Penitentiary after recovery, under pain of incurring an excommunication reserved *speciali modo* to the Holy See.[67]

[66] *Cf.* Rossi, "S. Poenit. Apos., Decretum 18 Aprilis, 1936—Annotationes," *Apollinaris,* IX (1936), 587, 588; *Idem,* "De sacerdotibus qui matrimonium etiam civile tantum contrahere praesumpserint quoad absolutionem a censura de qua in can. 2388, § 1," *Perfice Munus,* XII (1937), 404; Lopez, "De reconciliatione sacerdotis, qui matrimonium attentare praesumpsit," *Periodica,* XXVI (1937), 505, 506.

[67] S. Poenit., decr. 16 Novembris, 1928: " . . . Sacra Poenitentiaria statuit ac decernit peccatum confessariorum sacramentaliter absolventium quos quomodocumque noverint factioni 'L'Action Française' actu adhaerentes quique ab ipsis, uti tenentur, moniti, ab ea se retrahere renuant, Sanctae Apostolicae Sedi reservari. Huius reservationis ea vis est ut in illis quoque casibus, in quibus iuxta canonicas dispositiones quaevis reservatio cessat, onus adhuc remaneat praedictis sacerdotibus ad S. Poenitentiariam recurrendi, sub poena excommunicationis specialiter Sanctae Sedi reservatae, intra mensem a die

To recapitulate this whole matter on the censures and the sin which involve the obligation of recourse after recovery from danger of death, it may be said that the obligation binds when the penitent has been absolved from:

1. any *ferendae sententiae* censure;
2. any *latae sententiae ab homine* censure that was expressly reserved in the particular precept;
3. any of the four censures reserved *specialissimo modo* to the Holy See;
4. any of the excommunications contracted because of delicts in the election of the Roman Pontiff;
5. an excommunication for the violation of the secret of the Holy Office;
6. an excommunication for the violation of secrecy in causes of beatification or canonization;
7. the excommunication contracted, according to canon 2388, § 1, by a priest who attempted marriage and intends, because of very grave reasons, to continue living with his accomplice in the manner of brother and sister;
8. the reserved sin committed by a confessor who deliberately absolved any obstinate adherent of *"L'Action Française."*

Article IV. Elements of Recourse

A. Remissive Statement

As will be readily seen from the character of the elements in the foregoing enumeration, the obligation of recourse after recovery from danger of death will be comparatively rare. Partly for this reason, but mainly because this recourse in many respects is *"ad normam can. 2254, § 1,"* the detailed treatment of this matter will be deferred until its consideration under canon 2254.[68] At that place

obtentae sacramentalis absolutionis, vel postquam convaluerint si aegroti, et standi eius mandatis."—*AAS,* XX (1928), 398, 399.

[68] *Cf.* below, Chapter VII, Article IV, p. 195 ff.

there will be found a discussion of such factors as the persons by whom and to whom the recourse is to be made, the time allowed for the recourse, and the manner in which the recourse is made. However, there are several points regarding these matters which call for explicit mention here, as being proper to, or of more probable application in, the recourse after absolution in danger of death.

B. Recourse—To Whom

Regarding the recourse to be made after recovery from danger of death when an *ab homine* censure was absolved, canon 2252 prescribes that it be made *"ad illum qui censuram tulit."* However, it seems that this is not to be restricted to him alone who inflicted the censure, but that the recourse may be made also to those others who, by virtue of canon 2245, § 2, are capable of granting absolution from an *ab homine* censure, namely, the competent superior of the one who inflicted the censure, or the latter's successor or delegate.[69] However, it may quite probably happen that the superior will not accept the recourse, but will transmit it to the one who inflicted the censure so that he, with his exact knowledge of the particular case, may give more fitting instructions in his mandates. Again, it is to be noted that a judge who applies a *ferendae sententiae* censure is *per se* incapable of remitting it.[70] Although recourse has not as its purpose the grant of absolution, nevertheless the only one who is competent to accept the recourse and to give the mandates is one who has the power to absolve from the censure concerned. Therefore, a judge cannot receive the recourse and give the mandates, unless he is at the same time the ordinary who established the censure, or his superior or successor, or unless he possesses a delegated faculty to absolve from the censure.

If the censure absolved in danger of death was reserved *specialissimo modo* to the Holy See, the recourse, even though the penitent

[69] *Cf.* Cappello, *De Censuris,* n. 115, 4; Coronata, *Instit. Iuris Can.,* IV, 176; De Meester, *Compendium,* III, P. II, 182, nota 1; contrary to Cerato, *Censurae Vigentes,* p. 41.

[70] Canon 2366, § 3.

be an Oriental,[71] is to be directed *"ad S. Poenitentiariam vel ad Episcopum aliumve facultate praeditum."* Cerato [72] maintains that the *"aliumve facultate praeditum"* must be interpreted as referring to some *superior* enjoying the proper faculty, basing his opinion on a pre-Code response of the Holy Office.[73] But this response was given in connection with the absolution in more urgent cases and has been incorporated in canon 2254, § 1, which, unlike canon 2252, speaks of *"aliumve Superiorem praeditum facultate."* So, theoretically, Cappello [74] and Coronata [75] are correct in saying that the recourse can be made to any confessor who possesses the proper faculty. But the question will be hardly of any practical value, for the confessor, to receive such recourse, would have to possess the faculty to absolve from censures reserved *specialissimo modo* to the Holy See, and it is the present practice of the Sacred Penitentiary not to grant these faculties.[76] Even the bishop is not competent to receive the recourse and give the mandates in cases of censures reserved *specialissimo modo* to the Holy See, unless he has the proper faculties to absolve from these censures,[77] and it will be rare that

[71] "Cum postulatum fuerit 'utrum ad ea quae forum internum, etiam non sacramentale, respiciunt, de quibus in can. 258 Codicis iuris canonici, fideles ad Ecclesias rituum orientalium pertinentes recurrere debeant ad Sacram Poenitentiariam Apostolicam,' Sacra haec Congregatio, collatis consiliis cum Emo D. Card. Poenitentiario Maiore, respondendum censuit *Affirmative*. . . . " —S. C. pro Eccl. Or., 26 Iulii, 1930—*AAS*, XXII (1930), 394.

[72] *Censurae Vigentes*, p. 41.

[73] S. C. S. Off., 19 Decembris, 1900—*Fontes*, n. 1249; *cf.* above, p. 61.

[74] *De Censuris*, n. 115, 4.

[75] *Instit. Iuris Can.*, IV, 176.

[76] *Cf.* Rossi, "De sacerdotibus . . . ," *Perfice Munus*, XII (1937), 87.

[77] "Utrum in canone 2252, quo statuitur obligatio recurrendi *ad S. Poenitentiariam vel ad Episcopum aliumve facultate praeditum*, etc., verba illa *facultate praeditum* restringenda sint ad vocabulum *aliumve*; an etiam pertinere dicenda sint ad aliud vocabulum *Episcopum*, ita ut Episcopus qui non sit facultate praeditus, mandata dare nequeat.

"Resp. Negative ad 1am partem, affirmative ad 2am, seu Episcopum mandata dare non posse, nisi facultatem habeat a iure vel ex Sedis Apostolicae concessione."—Pont. Comm., 12 Novembris, 1922, VIII—*AAS*, XIV (1922), 663.

he will have such faculties.[78] But since it is possible that such a faculty may be possessed by the bishop or the Apostolic Delegate for one or the other case, it may be best for the confessor to have recourse to the Sacred Penitentiary through his bishop or the Apostolic Delegate,[79] provided, of course, that there would be no danger of the violation of the seal of confession.

C. *Recourse—When*

According to canon 2252, the prescribed recourse binds the penitents *postquam convaluerint*. A person may be said to be thoroughly recovered from the danger of death when he has regained his full strength and has resumed his ordinary course of life; [80] or, if the danger of death arose from some extrinsic cause, then the *postquam convaluerint* would have its equivalent in the cessation of the extrinsic cause of danger.[81]

Must the obligation of recourse be fulfilled immediately after the complete convalescence or the cessation of external danger? It is the practically universal opinion of the authors that the recourse is to be made within a month after convalescence or the passing of the external danger of death. The only point on which they are divided in this regard is whether the *"intra mensem"* may be drawn directly from the wording of canon 2252, as being included in the phrase *"ad normam can. 2254, § 1,"* or whether it arises, according to canon 20, from a clear analogy with canon 2254. Some [82] find it in the wording *"ad normam can. 2254, § 1,"* in canon 2252;

[78] *Cf.* Ayrinhac-Lydon, *Penal Legislation*, nn. 94, 104; Vermeersch-Creusen, *Epitome*, III, n. 452, 4.

[79] *Cf.* Kelly, *Jurisdiction of the Confessor*, pp. 174, 175.

[80] *Cf.* Cipollini, *De Censuris*, p. 53; Ayrinhac-Lydon, *Penal Legislation*, n. 94.

[81] *Cf.* Vermeersch-Creusen, *Epitome*, III, n. 452, 5; Rossi, "De sacerdotibus . . . ," *Perfice Munus*, XII (1937), 87.

[82] *E. g.*, Vermeersch-Creusen, *loc. cit.*; Coronata, *Instit. Iuris Can.*, IV, 176; De Meester, *Compendium*, III, P. II, 181; Blat, *Commentarium*, lib. V, p. 111; Raus, *Instit. Can.*, p. 698.

others [83] do not include it in this phrase, but deduce it from an analogy with canon 2254; while others [84] simply state that the time allowed is one month, without indicating the basis of their opinion. It seems that the *intra mensem* may well be drawn from the *"ad normam can. 2254, § 1,"* not only for the censures reserved *specialissimo modo* to the Holy See, but also, despite the fact that the clause is so deeply entrenched between semi-colons, for *ab homine* censures, since the recourse for the latter is certainly according to the norm of canon 2254, § 1, in as far as it may be made *per epistolam et per confessarium.* But whether the month allowed is from canon 2252 or from analogy, the important point is that the time within which the recourse may be made is a month.

There appears to be some discrepancy in canonical writings as to how this month is to be computed, namely, whether it begins on the day of complete convalescence [85] or on the day on which the penitent becomes aware of the obligation of recourse.[86] However, the question seems to offer no difficulty, but is to be settled by a combination of these two elements.[87] Therefore, if the penitent when fully recovered knows of the obligation of recourse, then the month allowed for recourse begins. Since the *tempus a quo* is explicitly mentioned as the time of recovery, the first day in the computation of the month will be the day of such recovery, if the recovery is considered to have been complete at the beginning of the day; but the first day in the computation will be the day after such recovery, if the convalescence is regarded as having become complete only at some time during the day; and the month will be computed as it is

[83] *E. g.*, Cappello, *De Censuris*, n. 115, 7; Cocchi, *Commentarium*, lib. V, p. 122; Rossi, *loc. cit.;* Reintjes, *De Absolutione Censurae*, p. 23; *cf.* also Cipollini, *De Censuris*, pp. 52, 53.

[84] *E. g.*, Cerato, *Censurae Vigentes*, p. 41; Salucci, *Diritto Penale*, I, 219; Cavigioli, *De Censuris*, n. 56; Ayrinhac-Lydon, *Penal Legislation*, n. 94.

[85] *Cf.* Coronata, *Instit. Iuris Can.*, IV, 175; Vermeersch-Creusen, *Epitome*, III, n. 452, 5; De Meester, *Compendium*, III, P. II, 181; Cavigioli, *De Censuris*, n. 56.

[86] *Cf.* Blat, *Commentarium*, lib. V, p. 111.

[87] *Cf.* Cappello, *De Censuris*, n. 116, 9; Cerato, *Censurae Vigentes*, p. 41; Ayrinhac-Lydon, *Penal Legislation*, n. 94; Rossi, "De sacerdotibus . . . ," *Perfice Munus*, XII (1937), 87 with nota 2.

in the calendar.[88] However, this computation is to be understood in the sense that, if within the month any day occurs during which there is no substantial opportunity for making recourse, such a day is not counted, and for every such day the original month is prolonged by an additional day of twenty-four hours from midnight to midnight.[89]

When the penitent after recovery does not know of the obligation of recourse, the month will begin when he becomes aware of it, and the first day in the computation will be the day following his realization of the obligation. But technically it amounts to the same thing to say that the obligation of recourse is to be fulfilled within a month after recovery, for this month is *tempus utile*,[90] and consequently the time will not be computed as long as the penitent is ignorant of the obligation, but will begin when he becomes aware of it.[91]

It is sufficient that the recourse be *begun* within the month, and therefore the penitent is not bound to take action in time for the mandates to be actually in his hands before the month has elapsed.[92]

The month allowed for recourse is *ad urgendam obligationem*, so that if the recourse for any reason cannot be made within that time, the obligation still remains,[93] and it continues to bind until the penitent has either fulfilled it or has reincurred the censure for

[88] *Cf.* canon 34, § 3.

[89] *Cf.* canon 32, § 1.

[90] *Cf.* Coronata, *Instit. Iuris Can.*, IV, 181; Vermeersch-Creusen. *Epitome*, III, n. 454, 3; Cipollini, *De Censuris*, p. 53; Blat, *Commentarium*, lib. V, p. 117; Cocchi, *Commentarium*, lib. V, p. 124; Kelly, *Jurisdiction of the Confessor*, p. 173; Rainer, *Suspension of Clerics*, pp. 216, 217. Most of these writers are considering the words *intra mensem* of canon 2254, § 1, but the same notion applies to the time for recourse in canon 2252.

[91] Canon 35: "Tempus *utile* illud intelligitur quod pro exercitio aut prosecutione sui iuris ita alicui competit ut ignoranti aut agere non valenti non currat . . . "

[92] *Cf.* Coronata, *Instit. Iuris Can.*, IV, 176; Jone, "Die Absolutionsvollmachten in Todesgefahr," *TPQ*, LXXIX (1926), 20.

[93] Vermeersch-Creusen, *Epitome*, III, n. 454, 3; Cocchi, *Commentarium*, lib. V, p. 124; Reintjes, *De Absolutione Censurae*, p. 34; Augustine, *Commentary*—Vol. VIII, *Penal Code* (2. ed., St. Louis: Herder, 1924), p. 160, note 90.

culpably failing to make the recourse within a month of unimpeded time.[94]

Article V. The Cessation of the Obligation of Recourse

The most evident and perhaps the most common manner in which the recourse prescribed by canon 2252 will cease, will be through the death of the penitent who was absolved in danger of death. However, if the penitent recovers from the danger of death, there are also ways in which the burden of recourse, which would otherwise be obligatory, does not bind or ceases to bind, and it is these which are to be considered under the following headings.

A. The Application of Canon 2254, § 2

In the more urgent cases, as will be seen, when a penitent has been absolved from a reserved censure with the obligation of recourse, he may relieve himself of this burden by going to another confessor with a special faculty for that censure, confessing again the sin and the censure from which he was absolved, and receiving a new absolution and the mandates from the confessor.[95] In this way the obligation of recourse, which was already binding, entirely ceases.

The question has arisen whether this same procedure can be followed by a penitent who has been absolved in danger of death from an *ab homine* censure or a censure reserved *specialissimo modo* to the Holy See, and who has accordingly become subject to the obligation of recourse after recovery. Although canon 2252 makes no provision for this norm, it is agreed by all authors who treat the question that, from analogy, canon 2254, § 2, can be used by the penitent, since the same reason exists for its use after absolution in danger of death as after absolution in the more urgent cases, and

[94] *Cf.* the similar discussion on this matter under canon 2254, § 1, in Chapter VII, Article IV, D, p. 205, ff. Regarding the possibility of the cessation of the obligation of recourse through ignorance of it, *cf.* below, in the present chapter, the following article, C, D, p. 121, ff.

[95] *Cf.* below, Chapter VIII, for a detailed explanation of canon 2254, § 2.

since a favor granted to those bound by a stricter law should also be permitted to those bound by the more lenient law for absolution in danger of death.[96]

However, a practical note is struck by Rossi,[97] who says that, although in theory canon 2254, § 2, can be applied to canon 2252, in practice it will be useless, for no confessor will be found who possesses the faculties to absolve from *ab homine* censures or censures reserved *specialissimo modo* to the Holy See. Very likely this is true of the censures reserved *specialissimo modo*, but it may happen that some confessor has delegated faculties from his ordinary to absolve from *ab homine* censures reserved to him. If the latter case should be verified, then a penitent after recovery from danger of death could go to such a confessor according to the norm of canon 2254, § 2, confess again the sin and the *ab homine* censure, and be released from the obligation of recourse to the ordinary.

B. *The Application of Canon 2254, § 3*

Strictly conceived, the use of canon 2254, § 3, is not a provision for the "cessation" of the obligation of recourse, for the confessor absolves without imposing the obligation of recourse, and since the obligation does not arise, it consequently cannot be said to cease.[98] So the application of canon 2254, § 3, would more properly be called an "elimination" of recourse. But in a broader sense, it is another method by which a person who would ordinarily be bound by the obligation of recourse may escape that obligation, and it is here treated as such.

Can the provision of canon 2254, § 3, be applied to canon 2252? There is no reference in the latter canon to such a provision, but from

[96] *Cf.* Cappello, *De Censuris*, n. 118, 13; Coronata, *Instit. Iuris Can.*, IV, 175; Cerato, *Censurae Vigentes*, p. 42; Salucci, *Diritto Penale*, I, 219; Kelly, *Jurisdiction of the Confessor*, p. 99; Ferreres, *Institutiones Canonicae* (2. ed., Barcinone: Subirana, 1920), II, n. 1007; Pruemmer, *Manuale Theologiae Moralis* (4. et 5. ed., Friburgi Brisgoviae: Herder, 1928), III, n. 494; Reintjes, *De Absolutione Censurae*, p. 22.

[97] "De sacerdotibus . . . ," *Perfice Munus*, XII (1937), 87, 88.

[98] *Cf.* below, Chapter IX, for a detailed consideration of canon 2254, § 3.

analogy of law it is admitted by all authors who consider the point, that except for the censure contracted through *absolutio complicis in peccato turpi,* a confessor who foresees that recourse after recovery from danger of death will be morally impossible for the penitent, can absolve him, without the obligation of recourse, from either *ab homine* censures or censures reserved *specialissimo modo* to the Holy See, imposing instead a penance and satisfaction which must be performed under pain of reincurrence of the same kind of censure.[99] This penance and satisfaction may be enjoined in such a way that the penitent will be bound to perform them only after he has recovered from the danger of death.[100]

A point for practical consideration arises in connection with the application of canon 2254, § 3, to canon 2252. In canon 2254 the recourse obliges within a month after the absolution; in canon 2252 it obliges within a month after recovery. How, then, is the confessor to judge concerning the moral impossibility of recourse when he is absolving in danger of death? Is it sufficient if he foresees that the recourse will be morally impossible within a month after the absolution, because, for example, he sees that the penitent, if he does convalesce, will not regain full health for more than a month? Or is it necessary that the recourse be foreseen as morally impossible within a month after the actual recovery?

Most of the authors who treat the general question of applying canon 2254, § 3, to canon 2252 are not clear on this specific point. However, the following observations may be made and a conclusion drawn from them. If § 3 of canon 2254 were transferred bodily to canon 2252 so as to become part of the latter canon, the *"hic recursus"* could refer to nothing but the recourse within a month after

[99] *Cf.* Cappello, *De Censuris,* n. 117; Coronata, *Instit. Iuris Can.,* IV, 176; Cocchi, *Commentarium,* lib. V, p. 123; De Meester, *Compendium,* III, P. II, 181; Ferreres, *Instit. Can.,* II, n. 1007; Ayrinhac-Lydon, *Penal Legislation,* n. 94; Rainer, *Suspension of Clerics,* pp. 212, 213; Rossi, "De sacerdotibus . . . ," *Perfice Munus,* XII (1937), 88; Kelly, *Jurisdiction of the Confessor,* p. 98; *Idem,* "Faculties of Absolving and Dispensing in Danger of Death," *Eccles. Review,* LXXXV (1931), 261; [*Idem?*], "Faculties of Confessor in Case of Danger of Death," *Eccles. Review,* XCI (1934), 411-413.

[100] *Cf.* Rossi, *loc. cit.;* Kelly, *Jurisdiction of the Confessor,* pp. 98, 99.

recovery. Besides, if the penitent in danger of death could be absolved without the obligation of recourse whenever the recourse was foreseen as morally impossible within a month after the absolution, this exceptional method for the more urgent cases would become practically the ordinary method of acting in cases of absolution in danger of death, for it will not be common that a penitent will regain full health within a month after the absolution in danger of death. Consequently, it would seem to be overdrawing the analogy to say that the penitent can be absolved without the obligation of recourse whenever it is seen that recourse will be morally impossible within a month after the absolution, and therefore it appears that canon 2254, § 3, can be applied only when the recourse is foreseen as morally impossible within a month after recovery from danger of death.[101] However, this conclusion is not to be accepted in so restrictive a sense as to exclude this method of acting when it is foreseen that the penitent will never completely recuperate.

C. *Subsequent Impossibility of Recourse*

In canon 2252 it is to be understood, as is expressed in canon 2254, § 1, that the prescribed recourse must be made *si id fieri possit sine gravi incommodo.*[102] This case it not to be confused with that which has just been considered, namely, the application of canon 2254, § 3, to canon 2252. That case concerns the situation in which the confessor foresees that recourse will be morally impossible, absolves the penitent without the obligation of recourse, and imposes a special penance and a satisfaction to be performed under pain of reincurring the censure. The present case under discussion is that in which the confessor has absolved without using the provision of canon 2254, § 3, and has either imposed the obligation of recourse on the penitent, or the latter has become aware of

[101] *Cf.* Kelly, *loc. cit.*; [*Idem?*], "Faculties of Confessor in Danger of Death," *Eccles. Review*, XCI (1934), 412, 413; Rainer, *Suspension of Clerics*, pp. 212, 213.

[102] As to what constitutes a grave inconvenience excusing from the obligation of recourse, *cf.* the discussion under canon 2254, § 1, in Chapter VII, Article IV, F, p. 279.

the obligation in some other manner. Therefore, in this case the obligation of recourse is present, but, in the supposition, it cannot be fulfilled because of some grave inconvenience, and consequently the obligation is suspended until the excusing cause of grave inconvenience disappears.[103]

Since it may happen that the grave inconvenience, suspending the obligation of recourse, will persist over an extended period of time, the question arises as to whether the obligation of recourse in such circumstances may ultimately cease. Cerato [104] maintains that, if this excusing cause preventing recourse lasts for a long time, the obligation of recourse ceases. Cappello,[105] citing this opinion of Cerato, refers it to the case in which the penitent becomes aware of the obligation of recourse only after a long time, rejects the view as improbable, and says that the most that can be admitted is that the obligation would cease after a very long time. Coronata [106] considers the same case as Cappello, asserts that the obligation of recourse remains, even if the knowledge of it comes to the penitent only after a long time, and then mentions the opinion of Cappello without approval or disapproval.

Two different cases thus become confused with each other, the first case concerning the penitent who is prevented from fulfilling the obligation of recourse because of a grave inconvenience, and the second case regarding the penitent who learns of the obligation only at some remote time after his recovery from danger of death. However, it seems that both cases may be settled in the same way, and that, excepting the case of *absolutio complicis,* the opinion tentatively suggested by Cappello may be admitted, namely, that the obligation of recourse in such circumstances would cease after a *very long time.* It is true that there is no basis in the law for such a conclusion, but it would appear to be justified by equity and by

[103] *Cf.* Cerato, *Censurae Vigentes,* pp. 41, 42; Cipollini, *De Censuris,* pp. 45, 48; Cappello, *De Censuris,* n. 128, 11; Reintjes, *De Absolutione Censurae,* p. 23.

[104] *Loc. cit.; cf.* also Reintjes, *loc. cit.*

[105] *De Censuris,* n. 116, 9.

[106] *Instit. Iuris Can.,* IV, 175.

the fact that the continuance of the obligation for an indefinite number of years in these cases would be apparently excessive and opposed to the benign attitude of the legislator in matters of penal law.

The very practical question may be asked: "How long is a very long time?" As has been seen in the consideration of the old law on absolution from censures in extraordinary cases outside of danger of death,[107] causes which prevented the penitent from going to the proper superior for absolution were divided into impediments of brief duration, impediments of long duration, and perpetual impediments. Impediments of brief duration were considered to be those which lasted for less than six months; impediments of long duration, those which extended from six months to five years; and perpetual impediments, those which lasted for one's lifetime, for an indefinite length of time, or for at least five years. This old discipline has indeed been completely supplanted by the present discipline, but there seems to be no reason why the practical norms of the old canonists on the relative length of time may not still be used where they can be applied. In the present instance, the "very long time" would correspond to the norm given for perpetual impediments in the old law.

Therefore, the final conclusion on this point may be stated as follows: with the exception of the censure inflicted for *absolutio complicis,* if the penitent has been ignorant of the obligation of recourse for at least five years, the obligation may be regarded as having ceased; if the penitent has been prevented from fulfilling the obligation of recourse for at least five years, or if it is foreseen, after the penitent has been absolved with the obligation of recourse, that this excusing cause of grave inconvenience will last for five years, for an indefinite period (not clearly less than five years), or for life, the obligation may be considered as not binding.

D. Ignorance of the Obligation

This point, as has just been mentioned, is properly distinct from the subsequent impossibility of fulfilling the obligation of recourse

[107] *Cf.* above, Chapter III, Article II, p. 52.

because of grave inconvenience, but the two considerations have been so closely conjoined in their discussion by authors that they have been treated simultaneously under the preceding heading. It will suffice here to restate the above conclusion, namely, that except with reference to the censure of canon 2367, if the ignorance of the obligation of recourse has existed for a *very long time* after recovery from danger of death, that is, for at least five years, it would seem justifiable to say that the obligation has ceased.

Article VI. The Sanction Attached to the Obligation of Recourse

In canon 2252 it is declared that the obligation of recourse binds *sub poena reincidentiae.* In other words, if the prescribed recourse, when obligatory, is not properly performed, the penitent falls back into the same kind of censure from which he was absolved in danger of death. If the censure was *ab homine,* the censure which is reincurred in also *ab homine;* if it was reserved *specialissimo modo* to the Holy See, the new censure is similarly reserved. If it was any other kind of censure, there is no reincurrence, for the *poena reincidentiae* is attached to the obligation of recourse after absolution given in danger of death from *ab homine* censures and censures reserved *specialissimo modo,* and no recourse is prescribed after absolution from any other censures in danger of death.[108]

The law states that a censure, remitted by absolution, does not revive except in the case in which an obligation, imposed under pain of the reincurrence of the censure, is not fulfilled.[109] This is verified in canon 2252 with regard to the obligation of recourse, and therefore it appears that the absolved censure revives if the recourse is not made. It is true that the penitent falls back into

[108] *Cf.* above, Chapter V, Article III, B, p. 112, for a summary of the censures included under the terms "*ab homine*" and "reserved *specialissimo modo*." It is for these that the obligation of recourse *sub poena reincidentiae* is prescribed.

[109] Canon 2248, § 3: "Censura, per absolutionem sublata, non reviviscit, nisi in casu quo onus impositum sub poena reincidentiae impletum non fuerit."

a censure, but the notion that the censure "revives" is commonly interpreted in the sense that a *new* censure of the same species is incurred.[110] Therefore, if a penitent was absolved in danger of death from an *ab homine* censure and after recovery culpably fails to have recourse, he incurs a new *ab homine* censure by reason of the law; if the censure was reserved *specialissimo modo,* the new censure is also reserved in the same way. In other words, the new censure is numerically distinct from the absolved censure, which was completely taken away, but it is of the same species.

If the penitent assumes the obligation of recourse personally and fails by his own fault to fulfill it within a month, it is clear that he reincurs the same kind of censure. If the confessor applied canon 2254, § 3, in absolving in danger of death and accordingly imposed a penance and satisfaction, it is likewise clear that, if the penitent culpably fails to perform the penance and satisfaction within the time specified by the confessor, while knowing them to be obligatory *sub poena reincidentiae,* he falls back into the same kind of censure.[111]

However, when the confessor undertakes the recourse, the question of reincidence is not settled so easily. It is admitted that the

[110] D'Annibale, *Summula Theol. Mor.,* I, n. 354; Cappello, *De Censuris,* n. 95; Coronata, *Instit. Iuris Can.,* IV, 140, 141; Cipollini, *De Censuris,* pp. 33, 34; Cocchi, *Commentarium,* lib. V, pp. 115, 116; Ayrinhac-Lydon, *Penal Legislation,* n. 89, c; Reintjes, *De Absolutione Censurae,* p. 9; Cerato, *Censurae Vigentes,* p. 38; Sole, *De Delictis et Poenis,* n. 152, 3; Kelly, *Jurisdiction of the Confessor,* p. 173; Rainer, *Suspension of Clerics,* p. 217; Rossi, "De sacerdotibus . . . ," *Perfice Munus,* XI (1936), 531; Noldin-Schönegger, *De Censuris* (ed. 20 et 21, Oeniponte: Rauch, 1928), n. 28, e.

[111] Coronata (*Instit. Iuris Can.,* IV, 176) has slipped into an error in citing various authors (Arregui, Vermeersch-Creusen, Salucci, Chelodi) for the opinion that, in the last case stated, the penitent would not reincur a censure for failure to perform the penance and satisfaction. These authors deny or at least express doubt as to whether or not the obedience to the mandates in canons 2252 and 2254, § 1, obliges *sub poena reincidentiae;* but none of them denies or doubts the reincurrence of the same kind of censure for culpable neglect of the penance and satisfaction as in canon 2254, § 3, the wording of which is so clear as to leave no room for doubt. Cappello (*De Censuris,* n. 117, 10) has apparently made the same mistake in citing Chelodi in this regard.

recourse need only be *begun* within a month after the recovery of the penitent, even though the response may not arrive for a considerable time after that.[112] Again, it is generally held that, when the confessor has undertaken to send for the mandates, the penitent must, *sub poena reincidentiae,* return to him to receive the mandates sent to the confessor by the superior to whom recourse was made.[113] However, this latter opinion has been called into question by Raus,[114] who says that it is not certain that the penitent who culpably fails to return to the confessor for the mandates reincurs the censure. He claims that this return pertains rather to the *standi mandatis* than to the *onus recurrendi,* since to obey the mandates, one must learn what they are, and to learn what they are, he must return to the confessor. But this reasoning is not very compelling, for one might add—"and to learn what they are, he must write personally or through the confessor to the superior;" and thus what is certainly recourse would be included under the phrase *standi mandatis.* It seems that the *standi mandatis* means

[112] *Cf.* Coronata, *Instit. Iuris Can.,* IV, 176; Jone, "Die Absolutionsvollmachten in Todesgefahr," *TPQ,* LXXIX (1926), 20; Roberti, *De Delictis et Poenis,* I, Pars I, n. 318 (pp. 364, 365), as quoted by Raus, "Der Zusatz 'sub poena reincidentiae' beim kirchenrechtlichen Rekurs gemäss can. 2254, § 1," *TPQ,* LXXXIX (1936), 126, 127.

[113] *Cf.* Arregui, *Summarium Theologiae Moralis* (10. ed., Bilbao, 1927), n. 617, 2, 3; Vermeersch, *Theol. Mor.,* III, n. 476, 1; Noldin, *De Sacramentis,* n. 368, 2, 3; Cappello, *De Poenitentia,* n. 588; Pruemmer, *Man. Theol. Mor.,* III, 304, 307, 308; *Idem,* "Der kirchenrechtlich vorgeschriebene Rekurs bei der Absolution von Reservatfällen," *TPQ,* LXXVIII (1925), 767; Jone, "Die Absolutionsvollmachten in Todesgefahr," *TPQ,* LXXIX (1926), 239; Genicot-Salsmans, *Instit. Theol. Mor.,* II, n. 574, 3, b. Besides, all authors who maintain that both the obligation of recourse and the obligation of obedience to the mandates are *sub poena reincidentiae* must necessarily, if only implicitly, hold that the penitent is bound, under the same penalty, to return to the confessor for the mandates.

[114] "Der Zusatz 'sub poena reincidentiae' . . .," *TPQ,* LXXXIX (1936), 126, 127. He quotes Chrétien, *De Poenitentia,* p. 90 ff., for a clear statement denying that the return of the penitent to the confessor is *sub poena reincidentiae;* he also quotes Roberti, *De Delictis et Poenis,* I, Pars I, n. 318 (pp. 364, 365), in excerpts which are not entirely convincing as support of this opinion.

nothing more nor less than *mandatis parendi*, that is, obedience to mandates which have been received through recourse, and that the common opinion on this point is the only true opinion, namely, that the penitent who does not return to the confessor for the mandates, when recourse is being made through the confessor, falls back into the same kind of censure; for, although the recourse is begun when the confessor writes to the superior, it is completed only when the penitent receives the mandates, and it must be complete to fulfill the requirements of the law.[115]

Suppose, then, that a penitent, absolved in danger of death from a censure reserved *specialissimo modo* to the Holy See, goes to the confessor three weeks after recovery and asks him to write the letter of recourse, and the confessor agrees to do so. When is the penitent bound, under pain of reincurring the same kind of censure, to return to the confessor to accept the mandates from the Holy See? In the case as given, it is evident that the mandates cannot arrive, nor the recourse be completed, within a month after the recovery of the penitent. How, then, is the time to be determined within which the penitent must return for the mandates or fall back into the same kind of censure? Certainly this cannot be left to the penitent's judgment, but it seems that the confessor would have to decide on a reasonable time within which the mandates can be safely expected, and then impose on the penitent the obligation of returning to him at that time under pain of reincurring the same kind of censure as that from which he was absolved.

It would be different if, for example, immediately after the recovery of the penitent, the confessor made recourse to the local ordinary for the case of an *ab homine* censure. He could urge the penitent to return to him within one or two weeks to receive the mandates, but he could not impose this upon the penitent *sub poena reincidentiae*, for the law allows the penitent a month.

It must be understood that reincidence, or reincurrence of the same kind of censure, takes place only if there is grave culpability

[115] It may be noted that Cappello (*De Poenitentia*, n. 588), maintains that if the penitent cannot return to the confessor without great inconvenience, the recourse can be regarded as morally impossible and no longer obligatory.

on the part of the penitent in failing to make the recourse or to return to the confessor for the mandates, for there is a new censure, and consequently there must be a new delict, external, grave, consummated, and joined with contumacy.[116] Therefore, any cause which would excuse from the incurrence of a censure, such as ignorance, fear, inadvertence, or forgetfulness, would likewise excuse from the penalty of reincidence attached to the obligation of recourse.[117]

[116] *Cf.* canons 2242, § 1; 2228. *Cf.* Cappello, *De Censuris*, n. 95, 8, ñ. 115, 6; Sole, *De Delictis et Poenis*, n. 152, 3; Noldin-Schönegger, *De Censuris*, n. 28, e; Rossi, "De sacerdotibus . . . ," *Perfice Munus*, XI (1936), 531.

[117] *Cf.* canons 2199-2206; 2229. *Cf.* Cappello, *De Censuris*, n. 127; Chelodi, *Ius Poenale et Ordo Procedendi in Iudiciis Criminalibus* (Tridenti, 1925), p. 41; Blat, *Commentarium*, lib. V, p. 116; Cerato, *Censurae Vigentes*, pp. 38, 41. A discussion of the circumstances in which the penitent is bound by, or released from, the obligation of recourse will be found under canon 2254, § 1, in Chapter VII, Article IV, A, p. 195; upon this, as is evident, will depend to a large extent whether or not the omission of recourse involves the reincurrence of a censure.

CHAPTER VI

THE MANDATES

ARTICLE I. NATURE OF THE MANDATES

THE *mandata,* here called the "mandates," must at the very outset be properly understood. The mandates are not a concession of faculties for absolution, for this is not the purpose of the recourse either in canon 2252 or in canon 2254, § 1. The absolution has already been given, and recourse is made to receive a rescript which will contain the orders and instructions which the superior requires the penitent to observe. In the rescript the superior ordinarily provides for the *iniunctis de iure iniungendis,* and it is for this reason that this clause is not included in canons 2252 and 2254, § 1, while it is expressly stated in canon 2254, § 3, according to which the recourse is not made. Likewise, the superior imposes a penance and satisfaction proportionate to the gravity of the crime. The things enjoined by the superior, together with the penance and satisfaction, comprise the *mandata,* or mandates.

The rescript sent by the Sacred Penitentiary is sometimes *in forma gratiosa,* namely, when the penitent himself makes the recourse and asks for the rescript in this form so that it will not need an executor.[1] But ordinarily the rescript will be *in forma commissoria necessaria,*[2] for it is in this manner that the rescript is sent when the recourse has been undertaken by the confessor.

When the rescript containing the mandates of the Sacred Peni-

[1] *Cf.* De Meester, *Compendium,* III, P. II, 186: "Sic, quando absolvitur poenitens qui iterum non occurret, v. gr., tempore missionis, sufficit ab eo exigere promissionem scribendi ad S. Poenitentiariam aut ad Superiorem, quin confessarius ipse scribat. Immo, si iisdem in adjunctis poenitens praeterea aegre accederet ad *alium* confessarium, ipse scribat petendo, addita ratione, ut S. Poenitentiaria sibi provideat per rescriptum *in forma gratiosa* ad se transmittendum, ita ut jam non requiratur interventus confessarii vel confessio sacramentalis ad rescriptum executioni mandandum: sufficiet hoc in casu ut poenitens rescriptum cognoscat." *Cf.* also Coronata, *Instit. Iuris Can.,* IV, 182, nota 1.

[2] For the notion of rescripts and their execution, *cf.* canons 36-62.

tentiary is directed to the confessor, it is contained in a double envelope. The confessor opens the outside envelope addressed to him, and within it finds another envelope which contains the rescript. He does not open this sealed inner envelope, but gives it to the penitent. On the inner envelope there will be some general instruction as to the executor of the rescript, such as: *"Discreto viro confessario ex approbatis ab Ordinario loci;"* then the confessor in this case, when giving the rescript to the penitent, will indicate to the penitent that he (the confessor) or any other approved confessor can open the envelope and execute the rescript at a time when the penitent makes his confession. Again, the inner envelope may contain the wording: *"Doctori in Theologia vel Iure Canonico;"* [3] and the confessor will inform the penitent of any priest who will be capable of executing the rescript.

When a confessor has executed a rescript of the Sacred Penitentiary, he must burn it or destroy it in some other way as soon as possible, that is, within three days,[4] under pain of *latae sententiae* excommunication.[5]

Article II. The Obligation of Obedience

A. Gravity of the Obligation

Since recourse implies that a censure has been contracted and absolved, and since a censure in turn implies that a grave sin has

[3] A rescript bearing this direction may be executed by confessors of the Society of Jesus with the permission of their superior and the consent of the penitent; *cf.* Arregui, *Summarium Theol. Mor.*, n. 617, 5, nota 1. Likewise, a doctorate in Sacred Scripture from the Pontifical Biblical Commission or the Pontifical Biblical Institute confers the same rights and produces the same canonical effects as a doctorate in theology; *cf.* Pius XI, const. *"Deus scientiarum Dominus,"* 24 Maii, 1931, Art. 10, § 3—*AAS,* XXIII (1931), 249.

[4] *Cf.* Bargilliat, *Praelectiones Juris Canonici* (37. ed., Parisiis: Baston, Berche et Pagis, 1923, 1924), I, n. 546, f; *cf.* also Marc-Gestermann-Raus, *Instit. Mor. Alph.*, n. 1552, 3, on the interpretation of *"quamprimum"* in ecclesiastical law.

[5] On the various practical notions regarding the rescript containing the mandates, *cf.* Ayrinhac-Lydon, *Penal Legislation,* n. 104, note (pp. 79, 80); Arregui, *Summarium Theol. Mor.*, n. 617, 5; Ferreres, *Instit. Can.*, II, n. 1009, f.

been committed, it is clear that the mandates will consist of instructions, a penance, and satisfaction which will bind the penitent under a grave obligation.[6] The mandates will vary according to the circumstances of the case, and its elements will be adapted and proportioned to the particular kind of crime committed and the specific censure contracted, as these will be known to the superior from their explicit mention in the letter of recourse. But this variance in the mandates will never affect the gravity of the obligation in such a way as to change it into a light obligation, and the mandates, though they may be more or less severe, will always constitute serious matter, and the penitent will be obliged to accept and fulfill them under pain of grave sin.

In general, the obligation to fulfill the mandates will follow the same rules as the obligation to fulfill a grave sacramental penance. The substance of the mandates must be fully carried out, and, if the manner of fulfilling it is prescribed, this also must be complied with under an obligation that will be ordinarily grave. It must be fulfilled by the penitent himself and not by any other, unless this is expressly permitted in the mandates, though the assistance or agency of others, it seems, may be used to some extent in certain elements, for example, the reparation of scandal and the restoration for harm or injury.

The confessor *per se* has no power to commute the mandates given by a superior, but if any commutation is needed, this should be requested of the superior. However, it seems that the exception allowed by moralists concerning the commutation of a sacramental satisfaction by an inferior may also be admitted here, namely, that if it is morally impossible for the penitent both to fulfill the mandates and to have recourse again to the superior for a commutation, the confessor can commute the mandates, acting on what might be called a presumed permission of the superior. But if the mandates comprise elements which bind throughout an extended period of time, as will usually happen with reference to the censure for *absolutio complicis,* it seems clear that the confessor could do no more than temporarily commute such elements or suspend the

[6] *Cf.* Cerato, *Censurae Vigentes,* p. 41.

obligation of observing them, that is, only until communication with the proper superior, either by the penitent personally or through the agency of the confessor, would cease to be morally impossible. Needless to say, a confessor would have to be most circumspect in commuting injunctions prescribed by a superior.

The obligation of obedience to the mandates ceases when they are properly fulfilled, as is obvious, also if the penitent is perpetually impeded both from observing the mandates and from obtaining a legitimate commutation.[7]

B. The Question of Reincidence

Although the obligation to obey the mandates undoubtedly binds under grave sin, there is a question concerning the mandates which has arisen since the promulgation of the Code, and which has aroused much discussion and diversity of opinion. The question is this: does the obligation of obedience to the mandates bind under pain of reincidence, that is, in such a way that, if after making recourse the penitent culpably fails to fulfill the mandates, he falls back into the same kind of censure as that from which he was absolved? The discussion here is not concerned, of course, with the case in which it is expressly stated in the mandates that the various elements must be fulfilled *sub poena reincidentiae,* but it considers the general case in which the obligation to fulfill the mandates arises from canon 2252.

Shortly before the Code this same doubt arose, and it was authentically settled by a response of the Holy Office to the effect that obedience to the mandates bound under pain of reincurrence of the censure.[8] However, with the promulgation of the Code, the doubt revived because of the wording of canon 2252, in which it is de-

[7] No specific treatment of this matter has been found in the works of canonists or moralists. For a discussion of the obligation to fulfill sacramental satisfaction, as considered by the moralists, *cf.* Aertnys-Damen, *Theol. Mor.*, II, nn. 323-326; Marc-Gestermann-Raus, *Instit. Mor. Alph.*, nn. 1721-1725; Vermeersch, *Theol. Mor.*, III, nn. 600, 601; Wouters, *Man. Theol. Mor.*, II, n. 356.

[8] S. C. S. Off., litt. 19 Augusti, 1891—*Fontes,* n. 1143; quoted above, Chapter II, note 120.

clared that those who are absolved in danger of death by a priest without any special faculty *"tenentur, postquam convaluerint, obligatione recurrendi, sub poena reincidentiae, ad illum qui . . . ; eorumque mandatis parendi."* The source of the new doubt is—does the phrase *"sub poena reincidentiae"* refer only to the words *"obligatione recurrendi,"* or must it also be applied to the words *"eorumque mandatis parendi"?*

Among the authors who consider this question, some simply maintain that obedience to the mandates binds under pain of reincidence, and they do not admit the opposite opinion; [9] others, indeed, hold the opinion affirming reincidence, but acknowledge that the negative opinion possesses probability, or at least gives rise to some doubt; [10] and others do not commit themselves, mentioning the af-

[9] *E. g.,* Blat, *Commentarium,* lib. V, pp. 111, 118; Pruemmer, *Manuale Iuris Canonici* (4. et 5. ed., Friburgi Brisgoviae: Herder, 1928), n. 569, 7; *Idem,* "Der kirchenrechtlich vorgeschriebene Rekurs bei der Absolution von Reservatfällen," *TPQ,* LXXVIII (1925), 763, 770; Eichmann, *Lehrbuch des Kirchenrechts auf Grund des Codex Iuris Canonici* (2. ed., Paderborn: Schöningh, 1926), p. 697; Wouters, *Man. Theol. Mor.,* II, n. 865, 2 e, 3 c (pp. 728, 729); Slater, *A Manual of Moral Theology* (6. ed., London: Burns Oates & Washbourne, 1928), II, 159, 160. Cappello, often cited for this opinion affirming reincidence, expresses it in *De Censuris* (ed. 1925 et 1933), n. 117, but seems to be alluding only to the case in which canon 2254, § 3, is applied in danger of death; in *De Poenitentia* (2. ed., 1929), n. 597, 7, he asserts that the penitent not fulfilling the mandates commits a sin, but, according to the better opinion, does not reincur the censure; when speaking of canon 2254, § 1, in *De Censuris* (ed. 1925 et 1933), n. 128, 17, he simply states the obligation of obedience to the mandates, without mention of reincidence. It is to be remarked that in this and the following notes on this question, references are made indiscriminately to authors who set forth their opinion under either canon 2252 or canon 2254, § 1, for the question of reincidence through failure to obey the mandates is here considered as being exactly the same in canon 2252 and canon 2254, § 1. *Cf.* below, Chapter VII, Article V, p. 217.

[10] *E. g.,* Creusen, *Epitome,* III, n. 452, 6; Cocchi, *Commentarium,* lib. V, pp. 122, 123; Kelly, *Jurisdiction of the Confessor,* pp. 98, 173, 174; Paban, "Absolutio a censuris in periculo mortis," *Bollettino del Clero Romano,* VIII (1927), 39, 40. The opinion denying reincidence for failure to obey the mandates has been incorrectly ascribed to Paban in a review in *Apollinaris,* I (1928), 200.

firmative opinion without comment, and granting the probability of the negative opinion.[11] On the other hand, some lean with uncertainty to the opinion denying reincidence; [12] while others maintain that the obligation of obedience to the mandates does not bind under pain of reincurrence of a censure, but that this penalty is attached only to the obligation of recourse.[13]

One of the main arguments in favor of the opinion affirming that the obligation to obey the mandates binds *sub poena reincidentiae* is that the very purpose of recourse is to secure the mandates. Since the obligation of recourse certainly binds under the penalty of reincurrence of a censure, the same sanction should be attached to the obligation of observing the purpose of recourse, namely, the acceptance and fulfillment of the mandates. However, the connection between recourse and the fulfillment of the mandates does not necessarily demand that the penalty attached to one must also be attached to the other. It may be that the legislator wished to stress the obligation of recourse to impress on the penitent the gravity of his crime in realizing that the case must be subjected to the

[11] *E. g.*, De Meester, *Compendium*, III, P. II, 182.

[12] *E. g.*, Chelodi, *Ius Poenale*, p. 42.

[13] *E. g.*, Arregui, *Summarium Theol. Mor.*, n. 617, 3; Vermeersch, *Theol. Mor.*, III, n. 476, 1; Cerato, *Censurae Vigentes*, p. 41; Salucci, *Diritto Penale*, I, 220; Coronata, *Instit. Iuris Can.*, IV, 177 (apparently by a printing mistake, Coronata refers to canon 2254 while treating this point in the section on danger of death and using the wording of canon 2252, expressing the same opinion on canon 2254, § 1, in another place, *viz.*, *op. cit.*, IV, 182); Reintjes, *De Absolutione Censurae*, pp. 23, 24; Motry, *Diocesan Faculties According to the Code of Canon Law*, The Catholic University of America, Canon Law Studies, n. 16 (Washington: The Catholic University of America, 1922), p. 122; Rainer, *Suspension of Clerics*, pp. 211, 212; Jone, "Die Absolutionsvollmachten in Todesgefahr," *TPQ*, LXXIX (1926), 237-239; Schwentner, "Die Excommunicatio Specialissimo Modo Reservata," *TPQ*, LXXVIII (1925), 288. *Cf.* also Raus and Roberti, as cited under canon 2254, § 1, in Chapter VII, note 272. *Cf.* also Cappello, *De Poenitentia*, n. 597, 7, as mentioned above, in the present chapter, note 9. Others who seem to hold this opinion, but do not express their view in an unequivocal manner, are: Genicot-Salsmans, *Instit. Theol. Mor.*, II, n. 574, 3; Sabetti-Barrett, *Compendium Theologiae Moralis* (32. ed., Neo Eboraci: Pustet, 1929), p. 1003; Davis, *Moral and Pastoral Theology* (New York: Sheed & Ward, 1935), III, pp. 450, 451, 453.

judgment of the competent superior and in receiving and perceiving the instructions, penance, and satisfaction comprising the mandates; and that he was content to leave the fulfillment of the mandates to be carried out according to the norms of moral theology, which, as will be seen presently, amply provide for the observance of the mandates without necessitating the reincurrence of the same kind of censure.

However this may be, if obedience to the mandates was intended to be included under the penalty of reincidence, the actual wording of canon 2252 has not placed this question beyond the sphere of doubt. Had there been no pre-Code legislation on this point, it would seem that the interpretation including the obligation of obedience to the mandates along with the obligation of recourse under the penalty of reincidence would be clearly extending the sense of canon 2252, bringing more under it than is expressly contained. For the phrase *"sub poena reincidentiae"* is inserted immediately after the words *"obligatione recurrendi"* and appears to be applied exclusively to the obligation of recourse; while, if the legislator wished to include both the recourse and the obedience to the mandates under the penalty, by the transfer of a single word the canon could have been clearly and simply worded: *". . . tenentur, postquam convaluerint, obligatione, sub poena reincidentiae, recurrendi . . . eorumque mandatis parendi."* But canon 2252 is not worded in this way, and that its actual wording on this point is not accidental is seen from the use of almost identical phrasing in canon 2254, § 1 [14] and in a decree of the Sacred Penitentiary.[15]

Some authors [16] invoke the pre-Code response of the Holy Office

[14] Canon 2254, § 1: " . . . iniuncto onere recurrendi, sub poena reincidentiae, . . . et standi eius mandatis."

[15] S. Poenit., decr. 16 Novembris, 1928: " . . . onus adhuc remaneat praedictis sacerdotibus ad S. Poenitentiariam recurrendi, sub poena excommunicationis . . . , et standi eius mandatis."—*AAS*, XX (1928), 398, 399; *cf.* above, Chapter V, note 67.

[16] *E. g.*, Blat, *Commentarium*, lib. V, pp. 112, 118; Cappello, *De Censuris*, n. 117; Creusen, *Epitome*, III, n. 452, 6. Vermeersch is not here mentioned with Creusen, for, as indicated above, he differs from Creusen on this point.

on the phrase *standi mandatis* as unassailable proof of the contention that the obligation of obedience to the mandates is still *sub poena reincidentiae*. But the overwhelming cogency attached to this response in connection with the interpretation of the present law is not quite patent. To clarify the issue, it will be well to repeat briefly what has already been discussed in this regard in the historical section. The constitution "*Apostolicae Sedis*," permitting the absolution from all censures in danger of death, imposed on the penitent after recovery the *obligatio standi mandatis Ecclesiae* when a censure reserved *speciali modo* had been absolved.[17] A question was submitted to the Holy Office as to whether the *obligatio standi mandatis Ecclesiae* bound *sub poena reincidentiae* and as to what the phrase *standi mandatis* meant. The response affirmed that the *obligatio standi mandatis* bound under pain of reincidence, and it declared that the obligation involved the burden of recourse and obedience to the mandates.[18] In other words, in the constitution "*Apostolicae Sedis*" there was no specific mention of the *obligatio recurrendi*, but only of the *obligatio standi mandatis*, and it was this latter single phrase which was declared to contain the two distinct elements, namely, the obligation of recourse and the obligation of obedience to the mandates, both elements binding under the penalty of the reincurrence of a censure. Consequently, there is not a perfect parity between the phrase *standi mandatis* of the pre-Code legislation and the similar phrase *mandatis parendi* of canon 2252 or the identical phrase *standi mandatis* of canon 2254, § 1. If, in these two canons, it were simply stated that there was an *obligatio standi mandatis*, without mention of the obligation of recourse, it would be properly interpreted in the light of the old

Concerning the uncertain position of Cappello on this general question, *cf.* above, in the present chapter, note 9.

[17] Pius IX, const. "*Apostolicae Sedis*," 12 Octobris, 1869, § 1, n. 12—*Fontes*, n. 552; quoted above, Chapter II, note 115. *Cf.* also the response of the Holy Office, June 17, 1891, restricting the obligation of recourse to cases in which absolution had been given from censures reserved *speciali modo*, as above, Chapter II, note 118.

[18] S. C. S. Off., litt. 19 Augusti, 1891—*Fontes*, n. 1143; quoted above, Chapter II, note 120.

law as containing the two elements of recourse and obedience to the mandates, both *sub poena reincidentiae.* But the phrases *standi mandatis* and *mandatis parendi* of the new law are explicitly distinguished from the obligation of recourse and no longer include it and, when the legislator made this distinction, according to the wording of canons 2252 and 2254, § 1 he apparently attached the penalty of reincidence to the obligation of recourse and not to the obligation of obedience to the mandates. Therefore, it is not admitted that the authentic interpretation of the phrase *standi mandatis* of the old law is impregnable proof for the opinion that the obligation of obedience to the mandates in the new law binds under penalty of reincurrence of a censure, since the legislator, in revising the manner of formulating the law, has seemingly not retained the old-law sanction for obedience to the mandates but has indicated the contrary—a thing that could have been easily and clearly avoided, if so desired.

In support of the opinion denying that obedience to the mandates binds *sub poena reincidentiae,* an argument is sometimes adduced from the fact that the phrase *eorumque mandatis parendi* is separated from the rest of canon 2252 by a semicolon, and this is taken as an indication that this phrase is entirely divorced from what precedes it. But this argument seems to have no value, for a semicolon was inserted for the sake of clarity between the prescription for recourse after absolution from *ab homine* censures and the prescription for recourse after absolution from the specified *a iure* censures, and if another semicolon were not added before the phrase *eorumque mandatis parendi,* this latter would then apparently pertain exclusively to the provision for *a iure* censures, which would be misleading. Therefore, the semicolon before *eorumque mandatis parendi,* instead of separating this phrase from what precedes it, appears to have been used intentionally to bind this phrase with the whole canon, and necessarily so, for by the omission of the final semicolon the obligation of obedience to the mandates would have been literally restricted to the prescription for censures *a iure.* In canon 2254, § 1, there is no explicit distinction between the recourse for *ab homine* censures and the recourse for *a iure* censures; no semicolon was needed to prevent confusion; no semicolon was then necessary before the words "*standi eius mandatis,*" and none was used; yet the *standi eius mandatis* of canon 2254, § 1, is absolutely parallel and identical with the *eorumque mandatis parendi* of canon 2252 with respect to the question whether or not it binds *sub poena reincidentiae.*

Similarly, little, if any, probatory value is to be found in the argument advanced by Chelodi [19] in support of the opinion denying reincidence. Quoting the responses of the Holy Office of August 19, 1891 [20] and January 13, 1892,[21] he draws the conclusion that only the recourse was prescribed *sub poena reincidentiae.* But in the first response the Holy Office clearly stated that obedience to the mandates was one of the elements of the *standi mandatis Ecclesiae,* binding *sub poena reincidentiae;* in the second, it was answering a particular question as to whether the obligation of recourse was *sub poena reincidentiae,* and it quoted only that part of the first response which applied to this question, namely, that the obligation of recourse was an element of *standi mandatis Ecclesiae* which bound under this penalty; but in the second response there is evidently no retraction of the assertion in the first response that obedience to the mandates was included under the penalty, for this point was not asked in the second question and was simply omitted in the response.

[19] *Ius Poenale,* p. 42.

[20] *Fontes,* n. 1143; quoted above, Chapter II, note 120.

[21] "6. Quoad absolutionem censurarum specialiter reservatarum in articulo mortis dubitatur: utrum infirmus si convalescit et onus non adimplet se praesentandi Superiori, in eamdem excommunicationem reincidat, an non.

"R. Ad 6. Detur decretum fer. IV, 19 Augusti, 1891 super dubiis quae sequuntur: '1. An obligatio standi mandatis Ecclesiae a Bulla *Apostolicae Sedis,* imposita sit sub poena reincidentiae, vel non?—2. An obligatio standi mandatis Ecclesiae in sensu Bullae *Apostolicae Sedis* idem sonet ac obligatio se sistendi coram S. Pontifice, vel an ab illa debeat distingui.—Resp. Ad 1. Affirmative ad primam partem; negative ad secundam.— Ad 2. Obligationem standi mandatis Ecclesiae importare onus sive per se sive per confessarium ad S. Pontificem recurrendi.—Sanctitas Sua resolutiones Eminentissimorum PP. adprobavit et confirmavit.' "—*Fontes,* n. 1147. Note that the question asked here concerns only recourse, and compare this response with the full text of the original decree, as in Chapter II, note 120.

However, the wording of canon 2252 on the obligation of obedience to the mandates, with its counterpart in canon 2254, § 1, seems to be sufficiently strong ground for denying that this obligation is *sub poena reincidentiae.* The same conclusion seems deducible from a comparison of these two sections with canon 2254, §§ 2, 3. In canon 2254, § 2, the recourse is supplied by the penitent's presenting himself before a privileged confessor for a new absolution, and *"mandata ab eodem accipiat."* There is nothing in that paragraph to indicate that the confessor must oblige the penitent to fulfill the mandates *sub poena reincidentiae;* indeed, it would seem strange that a specially authorized confessor, who, because of his special faculty, could absolve from the censure in ordinary circumstances without imposing mandates *sub poena reincidentiae,* would have to impose them in this manner simply because the penitent has already been absolved by another confessor with the obligation of recourse. Again, a marked contrast is immediately evident when a comparison is made between the uncertain wording of canons 2252 and 2254, § 1, regarding the mandates, and the clear and unmistakable wording of canon 2254, § 3, where it is beyond question that the mandates of the confessor bind *sub poena reincidentiae.* In this latter paragraph, since the recourse is dispensed with, the only element to which the penalty of reincidence can be attached is the mandates of the confessor. Moreover, if reincurrence of the same kind of censure followed failure to fulfill the mandates of the superior, this would seem to open the way to too much anxiety and scrupulosity on the part of the penitent, who has already escaped unquestionable reincidence by making recourse, and an ordinary confessor might well feel reluctant and incompetent to settle such doubts concerning the censure in these circumstances.

If it is not clear that the obligation of obedience to the mandates in the new law is not *sub poena reincidentiae,* there is obviously at least a doubt whether the penalty of the old law in this regard has been retained. How should this doubt be settled?

The supreme rule for interpreting penal law is: *"in poenis benignior est interpretatio facienda."* [22] But it may be objected

[22] Canon 2219, § 1. *Cf.* Chelodi, *Ius Poenale,* p. 25; Cappello, *De Censuris,* n. 46; De Meester, *Compendium,* III, P. II, 142; Salucci, *Diritto Penale,* I, 220.

that canon 2252, together with canon 882, does not constitute a penal law, and is not odious but favorable to the penitent, and therefore does not properly come under the rules for interpretation of penal law. But it is evident that that part of canon 2252 which prescribes recourse and obedience to the mandates, even though it occurs under the norms for absolution in Part II of Book V, is just as much a penal law as any canon in Part III of the same book.[23] A new delict is required, with all the necessary elements of a delict, including contumacy, and when this is verified, then a new censure of the same species as the one absolved is inflicted by the law.[24] Evidently, then, this meets all the requirements of a penal law. The question follows: in canon 2252 is there one delict or are there two delicts punishable by reincurrence of the same kind of censure; is the obligation of recourse alone, or is also the obligation of obedience to the mandates, subject to the penalty of reincidence? Without question, the obligation of recourse is *sub poena reincidentiae*. But what of the obligation of obedience to the mandates? This does not clearly come under the penalty, and since "*leges quae poenam statuunt . . . strictae subsunt interpretationi,*"[25] it should be considered as not affected by the penalty, and the *poena reincidentiae* should, in the absence of an authentic interpretation of the present law, be restricted to the obligation of recourse.[26]

If canon 6 is invoked, since there is question here of the existence of a penal law, not its n. 4 but its n. 5 is to be applied, and this is understood in the sense that any penalty of the old law which is not clearly retained in the Code is to be considered as abrogated.[27]

[23] The same is to be said of canon 2254.

[24] *Cf.* above, Chapter V, notes 110, 116, 117.

[25] Canon 19.

[26] A fundamental principle in all penal jurisprudence is to restrict penalties and to favor the culprit, as seen in the axioms: "*odia sunt restringenda*" and "*in dubio reo favendum est.*" *Cf.* Reg. 11, 15, 30, 44, R. J., in VI°. *Cf.* Salucci, *Diritto Penale,* I, 220; De Meester, *Compendium,* III, P. II, 142.

[27] Canon 6, n. 5: "Quod ad poenas attinet, quarum in Codice nulla fit mentio, spirituales sint vel temporales, medicinales vel ut vocant, vindicativae,

From all this discussion the conclusion follows that, unless the question is authentically solved to the contrary by the Holy See, it can be safely held that the obligation of obedience to the mandates does not bind under pain of reincurrence of the censure.

It may be objected that such a conclusion puts a premium on disobedience to the mandates, so that the penitent may flaunt them with impunity. But this is not true. Obedience to the mandates is certainly a grave obligation. If the penitent culpably fails or refuses to comply with the mandates, he commits a grave sin, from which he cannot be absolved until he does fulfill the mandates or seriously promises to do so.[28] Consequently, although the observance of the mandates is not obligatory under pain of reincurrence of the censure, it is well provided for by the norms of moral and pastoral theology, for the recusant penitent will not regain the state of grace except by ultimate compliance with the mandates.[29]

latae vel ferendae sententiae, eae tanquam abrogatae habeantur." *Cf.* Michiels, "De reservatione censurae latae sententiae praecepto peculiari adnexae," *ETL*, IV (1927), 619; Neuberger, *Canon 6*, p. 50; both quoted above, Chapter V, note 49.

[28] *Cf.* Aertnys-Damen, *Theol. Mor.*, II, n. 448, II: "Absolutio semper deneganda est hominibus certo indispositis. Certe indispositi sunt, qui . . . gravem obligationem implere detrectant." *Cf.* Marc-Gestermann-Raus, *Instit. Mor. Alph.*, n. 1813, 3, n. 1815: "Signa certae indispositionis praebent, . . . generatim, quicumque gravem obligationem cognitam implere renuunt. . . . Confessarius, quatenus est judex, absolutionem denegare debet incapacibus et certe indispositis."

[29] *Cf.* Schwentner, "Die Excommunicatio Specialissimo Modo Reservata," *TPQ*, LXXVIII (1925), 288: "Den Anordnungen der zuständigen Stelle hat der Pönitent Folge zu leisten (can. 2252), aber nicht bei Strafe der Reincidenz, diese bezieht sich sprachlich nur auf die *obligatio recurrendi;* mit dem unfolgsamen Pönitenten ist nach den Regeln der Pastoral zu verfahren."

SECTION II

THE ABSOLUTION FROM CENSURES IN THE MORE URGENT CASES

CHAPTER VII

THE USUAL METHOD—CANON 2254, § 1

Canon 2254, § 1. In casibus urgentioribus, si nempe censurae latae sententiae exterius servari nequeant sine periculo gravis scandali vel infamiae, aut si durum sit poenitenti in statu gravis peccati permanere per tempus necessarium ut Superior competens provideat, tunc quilibet confessarius in foro sacramentali ab eisdem, quoquo modo reservatis, absolvere potest, iniuncto onere recurrendi, sub poena reincidentiae, intra mensem saltem per epistolam et per confessarium, si id fieri possit sine gravi incommodo, reticito nomine, ad S. Poenitentiariam vel ad Episcopum aliumve Superiorem praeditum facultate et standi eius mandatis.

§ 2. Nihil impedit quominus poenitens, etiam post acceptam, ut supra, absolutionem, facto quoque recursu ad Superiorem, alium adeat confessarium facultate praeditum, ab eoque, repetita confessione saltem delicti cum censura, consequatur absolutionem; qua obtenta, mandata ab eodem accipiat, quin teneatur postea stare aliis mandatis ex parte Superioris supervenientibus.

§ 3. Quod si in casu aliquo extraordinario hic recursus sit moraliter impossibilis, tunc ipsemet confessarius, excepto casu quo agatur de absolutione censurae de qua in can. 2367, potest absolutionem concedere sine onere de quo supra, iniunctis tamen de iure iniungendis, et imposita congrua poenitentia et satisfactione pro censura, ita ut poenitens, nisi intra congruum tempus a confessario praefiniendum poenitentiam egerit ac satisfactionem dederit, recidat in censuram.

Article I. The More Urgent Cases

A. General Notions

It has been seen in the historical section of this work that, although the Church has always prescribed particular norms for the absolution from censures in ordinary cases, it has permitted deviations from these norms not only for absolution in danger of death, but also for absolution in other extraordinary circumstances. It has likewise been seen that the original provisions for absolution in extraordinary cases outside of danger of death, beginning in the twelfth century, gave way in the year 1886 to a new discipline which was gradually developed through responses of the Holy Office. This new discipline provided for absolution from reserved censures in what it termed the *"casus urgentiores,"* namely, danger of grave scandal or infamy, and the hardship of remaining in grave sin until a competent superior could be approached. It was this legislation on "the more urgent cases" which was substantially embodied in canon 2254 of the Code.

The number of the more urgent cases is variously regarded as two [1] or three,[2] depending on whether the danger of grave scandal or infamy is considered as constituting one or two distinct urgent cases. This slight divergency of opinion causes no difficulty, however, and there seems to be no objection to the consideration of the more urgent cases as either two or three. Lest there be any confusion, it is to be remarked here that throughout this work they are regarded as two distinct cases and are frequently referred to as the first or second *casus urgentior*, for this division seems to be favored by the wording of canon 2254, § 1. The important point is that the more urgent cases are only those mentioned in canon 2254, § 1.[3]

[1] Coronata, *Instit. Iuris Can.*, IV, 179; Cerato, *Censurae Vigentes*, pp. 43, 44; Salucci, *Diritto Penale*, I, 225; Cocchi, *Commentarium*, lib. V, p. 124.

[2] Cappello, *De Censuris*, n. 124, 2.

[3] Coronata (*Instit. Iuris Can.*, IV, 179) says: "Casus autem urgentiores a Codice definiuntur duo. Ex modo tamen loquendi Codicis haec definitio non videtur taxativa." If this is to be understood in the sense that there may be

For the use of the faculties of canon 2254, at least one of the more urgent cases must be verified, and this is for the validity of the absolution.[4] The same line of reasoning may be adduced with reference to this point as has been advanced above in connection with the circumstance of danger of death as necessary for the valid use of the faculties of canon 882.[5]

It is the office of the confessor in his prudence to judge whether or not a particular case is a *casus urgentior*. If he has at least a positive and probable reason for considering one of the more urgent cases to be present, even though he has some doubt in this regard, he can validly and licitly absolve, by virtue of canon 209 in conjunction with canon 2254.[6] Likewise, it is evident that what has been said relative to the judgment of danger of death may also be applied here, namely, that if the confessor prudently judges that a *casus urgentior* is verified in a particular case, the absolution is valid, even if subsequent events prove that that judgment was erroneous, as long as the penitent did not, in bad faith, falsely represent the case as a *casus urgentior*, for example, by asserting the

other general categories of more urgent cases besides those mentioned in canon 2254, it seems incorrect, for the use of the word *"nempe"* in canon 2254, § 1, clearly indicates that the enumeration is taxative, that is, all-inclusive.

[4] Cappello, *De Censuris*, n. 124, 1; Coronata, *loc. cit.*; De Meester, *Compendium*, III, P. II, 184. Coronata (*Ibid.*, nota 3) calls attention to the provision of canon 2247, § 3, for the validity of the absolution in a case which is not a *casus urgentior*, but in which the confessor is ignorant of the reservation.

[5] *Cf.* above, Chapter IV, Article I, p. 72.

[6] Canon 209 cannot be used without the application of the norms of canon 2254; otherwise, there would arise the anomaly that a penitent would escape the obligation of recourse when he is only doubtfully in a more urgent case, while another penitent would be bound by this obligation when a *casus urgentior* is certainly verified. If the censure itself or its reservation is doubtful, there is no need for the use of either canon 209 or canon 2254; when the censure is doubtful, it can be disregarded in the internal forum (*cf.* canons 2228; 2242, § 1; 2218, § 2), and if any absolution is given, it would only be an *absolutio ad cautelam* by any confessor according to canon 2253, n. 1; if the censure is certain but its reservation is doubtful, the reservation does not bind (canon 2245, § 4), and any confessor can absolve according to canon 2253, n. 1.

danger of scandal, while knowing that there certainly was no such danger.[7]

In passing, it is of practical value to call attention to an important point which will have its application elsewhere—that the use of canon 2254, unlike the analogous canon 2290 for *latae sententiae* vindictive penalties, is not restricted to occult cases of urgency.[8] Any restriction of this kind will arise only from the fact that the more urgent case is not verified in the particular circumstances, as will happen when a penitent, laboring under a public censure, does not find it hard to remain in sin; the other more urgent case of danger of grave scandal or infamy is *per se* inapplicable in such circumstances, and consequently the public censure could not be absolved by reason of canon 2254, since neither of the *casus urgentiores* would be verified. This matter will be treated in detail in the discussion on the absolution of public censures.[9]

B. *The Danger of Grave Scandal or Infamy*

The first *casus urgentior* mentioned in canon 2254 is as follows: *"si censurae latae sententiae exterius servari nequeant sine periculo gravis scandali vel infamiae."* Therefore, absolution can be granted by reason of canon 2254 if a *latae sententiae* censure cannot be observed without danger of grave scandal or infamy. This danger need not be certain or even very probable; but it is sufficient not only if there be probability of grave scandal or infamy, but even if there be probability of the mere *danger* of grave scandal or infamy.[10]

In general, "scandal" is defined as *"id omne quod proximo praebere potest ansam ruinae spiritualis, tum ipsa ruina spiritualis inde orta."* [11] It is divided into *scandalum activum* and *scandalum*

[7] *Cf.* above, as indicated in the present chapter, note 5.

[8] This is evident from the wording of canon 2254, § 1, especially when compared with canon 2290, § 1. *Cf.* also Coronata, *Instit. Iuris Can.*, IV, 252.

[9] *Cf.* below, in the present chapter, Article III, A, 3, p. 169. Note what is said in that place with regard to the public censure of suspension.

[10] *Cf.* Cappello, *De Censuris*, n. 124, 3; Rossi, "De sacerdotibus . . . ," *Perfice Munus*, XI (1936), 724.

[11] *Cf.* Marc-Gestermann-Raus, *Instit. Mor. Alph.*, n. 505.

passivum, the former being "*dictum vel factum minus rectum, praebens alteri occasionem ruinae spiritualis*,"[12] and the latter consisting in "*ipsa spiritualis proximi ruina, seu peccatum ad quod proximo occasio praebetur*." [13] Pertinent to canon 2254 is the notion that the "*factum minus rectum*" in *scandalum activum* may be an action which in itself is good or indifferent, but which has the appearance of evil in the eyes of others, for example, the omission of Mass on Sunday for a just cause unknown to others.[14] The examples ordinarily given with regard to the danger of scandal or infamy mentioned in canon 2254 are omission of the celebration of Mass by a priest or omission of the reception of Communion by a layman because of a *latae sententiae* censure, and these, although they may be indifferent in themselves, are capable of giving occasion to the spiritual harm of others in so far as they may lead to the presumption or conviction, spiritually detrimental to the onlooker, that the underlying reason for the omission is a crime. But canon 2254 seems to look primarily to those who suffer the spiritual harm, and not so much to those who occasion it. Consequently, it is concerned more with the *scandalum passivum*. This may be *scandalum datum*, if it arises from another's action which is evil or has the appearance of evil; or it may be *scandalum acceptum*, resulting from a good action of another. This latter scandal in turn is *scandalum pusillorum*, if it springs from weakness or ignorance, *scandalum pharisaicum*, if it arises from malice.[15]

Whenever, because of a *latae sententiae* censure, a person would be obliged to omit Communion, or a priest would have to refrain from saying Mass, or a party would be prevented from contracting marriage, or a priest would be barred from assisting at marriage, and the like, and it is foreseen that there is a probable danger that such will become an occasion for others, even through weakness or ignor-

[12] St. Thomas Aquinas, *Summa*, II. II, q. 43, a. 1.

[13] Marc-Gestermann-Raus, *loc. cit.*

[14] *Cf.* Marc-Gestermann-Raus, *loc. cit.*

[15] Authors differ on these divisions; the above are according to Marc-Gestermann-Raus, *Instit. Mor. Alph.*, n. 505; Aertnys-Damen, *Theol. Mor.*, I, nn. 376, 377.

ance, to commit a grave sin of any kind, such as detraction or rash judgment, then the censure can be absolved by reason of canon 2254. Likewise, this would apply if there were a probable danger of a grave diminution of virtue in others, or a serious lessening of esteem for religion or for the ministers of religion. Moreover, it seems that in this canon the term *"scandalum"* may be understood in a broader sense, as including not only what technically comes under the term, but also those things which are commonly considered as types of grave scandal, such as serious indignation or harmful rumors.[16] However, it would seem that the *scandalum pharisaicum*, arising purely from the malice of others, would not be sufficient in itself to allow the use of canon 2254; but such scandal may easily become a source of infamy to the person who omits an action because of a censure, and canon 2254 would then be applicable for this reason.

The *"infamia"* mentioned in canon 2254 seems, like the *"scandalum,"* to be qualified by the word *"gravis,"* [17] and consequently there would have to be at least a probable danger of serious infamy before this reason could be invoked for the use of canon 2254. In general, *infamia* may be defined as *"status laesae dignitatis ob diminutionem vel privationem existimationis,"* [18] or more clearly as *"amissio bonae existimationis apud probos et graves."* [19] Consequently, if there is a probable danger that one's good reputation among upright and serious-minded people will be lost or even notably diminished by the external observance of a *latae sententiae* censure,

[16] For these and other notions of *scandalum*, *cf.* Aertnys-Damen, *Theol. Mor.*, I, nn. 376-385; Marc-Gestermann-Raus, *Instit. Mor. Alph.*, nn. 505-515, 1550, 1; Vermeersch, *Theol. Mor.*, II, nn. 120-128; Wouters, *Man. Theol. Mor.*, I, nn. 546-553.

[17] *Cf.* Vermeersch, *Theol. Mor.*, III, n. 473, 1.

[18] *Cf.* Cocchi, *Commentarium*, lib. V, p. 192, adapting the definition of *existimatio* in Roman Law, as in D. (50. 13) 5. 1, namely, "existimatio est dignitatis inlaesae status, legibus ac moribus comprobatus, qui ex delicto nostro auctoritate legum aut minuitur aut consumitur." Note that, while Cocchi's adaptation is capable of expressing the notion of *infamia* in canon 2254, the converse of the Roman Law definition would strictly be *infamia iuris*, which is not meant in canon 2254.

[19] *Cf.* the notion of *infamia facti* as contained in canon 2293, § 3.

either because their suspicion of the crime would be converted into moral certitude,[20] or, it would seem, even because a strong suspicion would be aroused that the reason for the omission of the prohibited act is a crime, then the absolution from the censure can be granted according to canon 2254.

When canon 2254 speaks of the danger of scandal or infamy, it does not state, as it does with reference to the hardship of remaining in the state of grave sin, that there must be danger that the scandal or infamy will materialize before the confessor can apply for and obtain the proper faculties from a competent superior. But it seems that it must be understood in this sense, and be interpreted according to the old law, namely, that this *casus urgentior* is that in which absolution *cannot be deferred* without danger of grave scandal or infamy.[21] Therefore, this danger of scandal or infamy must be imminent to the extent that it will probably be verified before the confessor can obtain the proper faculties; if this is not the case, and the penitent will not be exposed to any danger of scandal or infamy before the confessor can secure the faculties for absolution from the superior, it would not be a *casus urgentior* and could not be invoked for the use of canon 2254.[22] However, this will seldom cause any difficulty, for ordinarily, when danger of scandal or infamy is used as the reason for absolving, it will be a case in which the penitent, immediately or shortly after his confession, must perform the act forbidden by the censure.[23]

It has been said [24] that, when the danger of scandal or infamy is the reason for granting absolution according to canon 2254, there

[20] Blat, *Commentarium,* lib. V, p. 115.

[21] *Cf.* S. C. S. Off., 23 Iunii, 1886—*Fontes,* n. 1102; quoted above, p. 56.

[22] Cocchi (*Commentarium,* lib. V, p. 124) seems to imply the opposite, namely, that the consideration of approaching the superior for faculties applies only to the case in which it is hard for the penitent to remain in grave sin. But if the danger of scandal or infamy is comparatively remote, so that the confessor can obtain the proper faculties and the penitent can return to him for absolution before the danger will actually arise, it is not seen how this can be regarded as a *casus urgentior.*

[23] *Cf.* Cappello, *De Censuris,* n. 124, 3.

[24] Salucci, *Diritto Penale,* I, 225, nota 1.

is question only of ***notorious latae sententiae*** censures, since, if they are occult, canon 2232 is applied to excuse from their observance.[25] But to say that the urgent case of danger of scandal or infamy is concerned only with notorious *latae sententiae* censures seems to be utterly incorrect. For, when a censure is notorious, there will be no danger of scandal or infamy in observing it in the external forum; rather the opposite will be the case, that there will be scandal from its non-observance.[26] Consequently, the danger of scandal or infamy can be taken as a cause for absolving according to canon 2254 only when the *latae sententiae* censure is occult,[27] at least in the place where the penitent must perform the act forbidden by the censure.

Regarding canon 2232, § 1, it must be noted that, except for a *latae sententiae* censure of suspension before a declaratory sentence, its application to censures will be rare in cases in which the penitent wishes to avoid infamy by proceeding to say Mass or receive Communion or perform any other act which requires the state of grace. For a censure presupposes a grave sin; [28] excommunication and personal interdict prevent the licit reception of the sacraments, and consequently must be absolved before the sin; [29] and actions such as the celebration of Mass or the reception of Communion cannot be licitly performed in the state of grave sin. Therefore, when a person is under an excommunication or a personal interdict, since he cannot be absolved from the sin until the censure is first removed, he will remain in the state of grave sin while he is under the censure, unless he regains the state of grace by an act of perfect contrition; but even in this supposition, no priest can say Mass

[25] Canon 2232, § 1: "Poena latae sententiae, sive medicinalis sive vindicativa, delinquentem, qui delicti sibi sit conscius, ipso facto in utroque foro tenet; ante sententiam tamen declaratoriam a poena observanda delinquens excusatur quoties eam servare sine infamia nequit, et in foro externo ab eo eiusdem poenae observantiam exigere nemo potest, nisi delictum sit notorium, firmo praescripto can. 2223, § 4."

[26] *Cf.* Cipollini, *De Censuris,* pp. 43, 44.

[27] *Cf.* Blat, *Commentarium,* lib. V, p. 115; Cipollini, *loc. cit.*

[28] Canons 2242, § 1; 2218, § 2.

[29] Canons 2260, § 1; 2275, n. 2; 2250, § 2.

and no one can receive Communion without first receiving sacramental absolution, except in those unusual circumstances in which, because of urgent necessity and the lack of a confessor, these are allowed after the guilty party makes an act of perfect contrition.[80]

Concerning the administration of the sacraments by priests under excommunication, suspension, or personal interdict, other canons provide for this,[81] and there is no need for the application of canon 2232. In general, however, for other actions forbidden by the three censures, canon 2232 can be used, but for licitness the state of grace must be regained according to the norms of law and of moral theology for actions which require the state of grace.

Although canon 2232 excuses from the observance of a *latae sententiae* censure before a declaratory sentence when there is danger of infamy, and although no irregularity would be contracted in such a case,[82] nevertheless this would not prevent the entire removal of the censure by absolution according to canon 2254 in danger of grave scandal or infamy.[83]

In general, then, it may be said that the *casus urgentior* of danger of grave scandal or infamy, when verified, can be invoked for the absolution, according to canon 2254, of any *latae sententiae* censure which is occult; but the censure *must* be occult, at least in the place in which the penitent wishes to exercise an act prohibited by the censure and in which the danger of scandal or infamy would arise from his failure to perform the act.[84]

C. *The Hardship of Remaining in Grave Sin*

The second *casus urgentior*, as given in canon 2254, is: "*si durum sit poenitenti in statu gravis peccati permanere per tempus*

[80] *Cf.* canons 807; 856. *Cf.* also Coronata, *Instit. Iuris Can.*, IV, 122; Marc-Gestermann-Raus, *Instit. Mor Alph.*, nn. 1550-1553.

[81] *Cf.* canons 2261; 2275, n. 2; 2284. However, that such a priest may act licitly, he must be in the state of grace, at least by an act of perfect contrition. *Cf.* Marc-Gestermann-Raus, *op. cit.*, nn. 1416, 1417, 1439.

[82] Coronata, *Instit. Iuris Can.*, IV, 122, nota 5; Rainer, *Suspension of Clerics*, p. 189.

[83] Blat, *Commentarium*, lib. V, p. 115.

[84] *Cf.* below, in the present chapter, Article III, A, 3, p. 171.

necessarium ut Superior competens provideat." In the pre-Code legislation it was necessary that the hardship of remaining in the state of grave sin be "*valde durum,*" [35] but, although the distinction may not be readily discernible in practice, in the present law it is required only that it be "*durum.*"

When is it hard for a penitent to remain in grave sin? No definite, objective norm can be given, for the hardship is to measured subjectively, dependent on the character and dispositions of each individual penitent. If, therefore, by the deferring of the absolution until the proper faculties could be obtained from a competent superior, the penitent would be saddened or displeased, or become anxious and lose his peace of soul because of the state of sin, or would show reluctance at the delay of absolution because of his lively desire to withdraw from the state of sin, then the hardship would be truly verified, and absolution could be given.[36] If the penitent does not possess these dispositions, it is agreed by all that the confessor can arouse them so as to be able to grant absolution,[37] and it would rather seem that the confessor not only *can* excite in the soul of the penitent a horor of sin, but that it is his *duty* to make this effort.[38] It is admitted by all that absolution can be given if it is hard for the penitent to remain in sin for even one day; [39] and it seems sufficient for the grant of absolution, if the penitent's peace of mind would require that he be not forced to remain in sin even for a single night.[40] If the faculty to absolve can

[35] *Cf.* S. C. S. Off., 16 Iunii, 1897—*Fontes,* n. 1187; quoted above, p. 59.

[36] *Cf.* Cappello, *De Censuris,* n. 124, 4; Cerato, *Censurae Vigentes,* p. 44; Salucci, *Diritto Penale,* I, 225; Cipollini, *De Censuris,* p. 44; De Meester, *Compendium,* III, P. II, 185; Blat, *Commentarium,* lib. V, p. 115; Rossi, "De sacerdotibus . . . ," *Perfice Munus,* XI (1936), 724.

[37] *E.g., cf.* Cappello, *loc. cit.;* De Meester, *loc. cit.;* Cipollini, *loc. cit.;* Coronata, *Instit. Iuris Can.,* IV, 179.

[38] *Cf.* Vermeersch-Creusen, *Epitome,* III, n. 454, 1, 2°.

[39] *Cf.* Cappello, *loc. cit.;* Coronata, *loc. cit.;* Vermeersch-Creusen, *loc. cit.;* Cerato, *loc. cit.;* Salucci, *loc. cit.;* De Meester, *loc. cit.;* Cavigioli, *De Censuris,* n. 58; Ayrinhac-Lydon, *Penal Legislation,* n. 102. *Cf.* also S. C. S. Off., 16 Iunii, 1897—*Fontes,* n. 1187; quoted above, as indicated in the present chapter, note 35.

[40] Coronata, *Instit. Iuris Can.,* IV, 179.

be obtained from the ordinary, or nuncio, or apostolic delegate on the same day on which the confession is made, the *casus urgentior* seems not to be verified; [41] yet in extraordinary circumstances the exception proposed by Cappello [42] appears admissible, that for certain persons who may possess special dispositions, such as clerics, priests, and religious, absolution may be granted even when faculties could be obtained in a few hours, whenever these persons would find it hard to remain in the state of grave sin for that amount of time. However, the suggestion offered by Rossi [43] may well be kept in mind, namely, that the confessor should not be scrupulous in inquiring about the number of hours or days during which the penitent can endure the state of grave sin without hardship, but if he finds from the dispositions of the penitent that he is reluctant to accept the deferring of absolution because of the necessity of remaining in sin, he can use canon 2254 and absolve.

However, the confessor must not by any means presume in every case that it will be hard for the penitent to remain in grave sin until the proper faculties can be obtained. Since the verification of the more urgent case, at least as prudently judged by the confessor, is for the validity of the absolution, the confessor must form a judgment according to the dispositions of the penitent, inquiring if necessary, and remembering that *"credendum est poenitenti."* [44] In practice, since the confessor can impress upon the penitent the seriousness of his condition and engender in him the dispositions whereby he will find it hard to remain in the state of grave sin, it may be stated, in the supposition that the confessor is successful in his efforts, that canon 2254 will almost always be available for the absolution of censures, at least for absolution with the obligation of recourse.[45]

[41] *Cf.* Vermeersch-Creusen, *Epitome,* III, n. 454, 1, 2°; De Meester, *Compendium,* III, P. II, 185, nota 3.

[42] *De Censuris,* n. 124, 4. *Cf.* also Rossi, "De sacerdotibus . . . ," *Perfice Munus,* XI (1936), 724.

[43] *Loc. cit.*

[44] *Cf.* Cipollini, *De Censuris,* p. 44; Coronata, *Instit. Iuris Can.,* IV, 179; Salucci, *Diritto Penale,* I, 225.

[45] *Cf.* Vermeersch, *Theol. Mor.,* III, n. 473, 2. However, note that, as

On this whole question of the hardship or remaining in grave sin, it is of practical value to note that canon 2254 can be used for absolution even if the penitent can withdraw from the state of sin by an act of perfect contrition, for this latter method is not the ordinary way of remitting sin and is not contemplated by the canon, which concerns the remaining in grave sin which has not been forgiven by sacramental absolution.[46]

With reference to the confessor's petition for faculties from a competent superior, it is important to advert to an analogous response of the Pontifical Commission on canons 1044 and 1045, § 3.[47] According to this declaration it is to be considered that the ordinary cannot be reached, if communication with him can be effected only by telephone or telegraph, but not by letter. Consequently, it is clear that, if a confessor cannot communicate with the proper superior by letter or by personal appearance before him within the time during which it is hard for the penitent to remain in grave sin, but can reach the superior only by telephone or telegraph, then the confessor can disregard such means of applying for faculties and can grant absolution by virtue of canon 2254, for the telephone and telegraph are not regarded as ordinary means of communication.

will be indicated immediately, the censure of suspension cannot be absolved simply by reason of the hardship of remaining in grave sin.

[46] *Cf.* Blat, *Commentarium,* lib. V, pp. 115, 116.

[47] "Utrum in casibus, de quibus in canonibus 1044 et 1045, § 3, censendum sit Ordinarium adiri non posse, cum nec per literas, nec per telegraphum nec per telephonum ad eum recurri potest; an etiam cum solum per literas impossibile est, licet per telegraphum vel telephonum id fieri possit.

"Resp. Negative ad 1am partem, affirmative ad 2am, seu ad effectum, de quo in cann. 1044 et 1045, § 3, censendum esse Ordinarium adiri non posse, si nonnisi per telegraphum vel telephonum ad eum recurri possit."— Pont. Comm., 12 Novembris, 1922, V—*AAS,* XIV (1922), 662, 663. It may be noted also that in 1891 the Holy Father prescribed that the Roman Congregations and Offices should not, as a general rule, admit requests for favors (*e. g.,* faculties and indults) which were made by means of the telegraph, and he announced through the Secretary of State that episcopal curias were to follow the same rule, since the same reasons applied equally to them; *cf.* litt. encyc. Secret. Stat., 10 Decembris, 1891—*Collectanea S. C. P. F.,* n. 1775.

Before this subject is brought to a close, it may be mentioned in general that the *casus urgentior* of the hardship of remaining in grave sin concerns the absolution of only those censures which prevent the licit reception of the sacraments, namely, excommunication and personal interdict, and does not include the censure of suspension, for in the case of suspension the state of grace can be regained by sacramental absolution while the suspension remains.[48]

Article II. The Grant of Absolution

A. The Confessor

According to canon 2254 *"quilibet confessarius"* can grant absolution from reserved *latae sententiae* censures in the more urgent cases. Therefore, any confessor can use canon 2254 for the benefit of those, but only those, for whom he possesses sacramental jurisdiction. Under the term "confessor" are included not only cardinals, ordinaries, and pastors, according to the extent of their jurisdiction,[49] but also the following: for the general faithful, secular and religious priests who are approved by the *Ordinarius loci* for the hearing of confessions; [50] for female religious, priests who possess the proper jurisdiction according to the norms of the law; [51] for exempt clerical religious, not only those who possess ordinary or delegated jurisdiction in the diocese, but also competent superiors of the institute according to the norms of the constitutions, and any member of the religious or secular clergy who has received delegated jurisdiction from these superiors; [52] and in general any priest to whom jurisdiction is supplied, in the particular circumstances and with reference to the particular penitent, by reason of common error or a positive doubt of law or of fact.[53] Canon 2254,

[48] Coronata, *Instit. Iuris Can.*, IV, 179; Raus, *Instit. Can.*, p. 698, nota 4; *Idem*, "Absolution von Zensuren l. s. ab homine," *TPQ*, LXXXIII (1930), 588; Rainer, *Suspension of Clerics*, p. 215. *Cf.* canons 2278, § 1; 2250, § 1.

[49] *Cf.* canons 239, § 1, nn. 1, 2; 873; 881.

[50] *Cf.* canons 874; 881, § 1.

[51] *Cf.* canons 876; 520-523.

[52] *Cf.* canons 874; 875, § 1; 518; 519.

[53] *Cf.* canon 209. *Cf.* Cappello, *De Censuris*, n. 126, 6.

therefore, does not confer jurisdiction, as does canon 882 in some cases, but it presupposes that the minister of absolution already possesses jurisdiction from some other source, and it extends the scope of this jurisdiction to embrace censures that it would not ordinarily comprise.

Since canon 2254 very directly concerns the good of souls, it is one of those canons which *"ex ipsa rei natura"* affect Orientals, and it can be used by confessors of any rite.[54]

Before he absolves, the confessor must, under pain of grave sin, impose on the penitent the obligation of recourse, unless it is a case in which the recourse will be morally impossible.[55] If the confessor would deliberately refrain from imposing the obligation of recourse in a case in which the obligation should be prescribed although he would commit a grave sin, the absolution would be valid, for the Code does not require this imposition of recourse under pain of invalidity of the absolution.[56] It is clear that in such a case the confessor would not contract the excommunication of canon 2338, § 1, or the suspension of canon 2366, for he would not be acting in contravention of these canons, since he possesses jurisdiction but uses it improperly.[57]

If the penitent unreasonably refuses to accept the obligation of recourse when it is morally possible, or does not intend to fulfill the mandates when they arrive, and rejects the alternative of going to a specially qualified confessor as provided for in canon 2254, § 2, the confessor cannot take it upon himself to dispense with the recourse and apply canon 2254, § 3, but must refuse absolution, for the penitent has not the requisite dispositions for absolution.[58]

[54] *Cf.* canon 1. *Cf.* Cappello, *De Censuris,* n. 132, 1; Rossi, "De sacerdotibus . . .," *Perfice Munus,* XI (1936), 724.

[55] *Cf.* Cappello, *De Censuris,* n. 127; Cocchi, *Commentarium,* lib. V, p. 125; Vermeersch-Creusen, *Epitome,* III, n. 454, 4, 1°; De Meester, *Compendium,* III, P. II, 186; Salucci, *Diritto Penale,* I, 232; Rossi, "De sacerdotibus . . .," *Perfice Munus,* XII (1937), 89.

[56] Coronata, *Instit. Iuris Can.,* IV, 180; Salucci, *loc. cit.;* Vermeersch-Creusen, *loc. cit.*

[57] *Cf.* Vermeersch-Creusen, *loc. cit.*

[58] *Cf.* Cerato, *Censurae Vigentes,* p. 44; Salucci, *Diritto Penale,* I, 227.

In canon 2254, § 1, as in the provision for absolution in danger of death in canons 882 and 2252, there is no mention of the phrase *"iniunctis de iure iniungendis,"* such as is found in canon 2254, § 3. However, the confessor must, as in every confession, impose a penance for the sin and enjoin those things commanded by the divine positive or natural law, such as the reparation of scandal, restitution of stolen goods, withdrawal from a Masonic or heretical sect, the dismissal of an accomplice in sin.[59] Since canon 2254, § 1, requires that recourse be made, the mandates which will come from the superior will provide for the penance for the censure and will indicate whatever is to be enjoined by ecclesiastical law.

B. The Penitent

The penitent contemplated in canon 2254 is any one of the faithful who has contracted a *latae sententiae* censure but cannot observe it in the external forum because of the danger of grave scandal or infamy, or who desires absolution from the censure because of the hardship of remaining in the state of grave sin during the time necessary for obtaining faculties from a competent superior.

The penitent may be of any rite whatsoever, whether Latin or Oriental, for canon 2254 very directly concerns the good of souls, and consequently Orientals should not be excluded from its benefits.[60] Apparently, also, an Oriental penitent can be validly and licitly absolved by a Latin confessor, and a Latin penitent by an Oriental confessor.[61] However, in the special provisions for Greek-Ruthenians in the United States, it is declared that Latin priests cannot absolve Greek-Ruthenian penitents from reserved sins and censures established by the Greek-Ruthenian ordinary, without his permission; nor can Greek-Ruthenian priests absolve from censures and reservations established by the Latin ordinary, without

[59] *Cf.* Cocchi, *Commentarium,* lib. V, p. 125.

[60] *Cf.* Cappello, *De Censuris,* n. 126, 8; Rossi, "De sacerdotibus . . . ," *Perfice Munus,* XI (1936), 725.

[61] *Cf.* canons 881, § 1; 905.

his permission.[62] But this restriction seems rather to refer to absolution in ordinary circumstances, and does not appear so stringent as to exclude the use of the faculties of canon 2254 for the more urgent cases.

Just as the penitent must have the proper dispositions before he can be absolved from his sins, so he must also have the requisite dispositions before he can be absolved from censures. These dispositions, when canon 2254, § 1, is to be applied, consist in the readiness to accept the obligation of recourse, to fulfill the things enjoined by the confessor, and to obey the instructions and injunctions which will be contained in the mandates of the superior. If the penitent unreasonably refuses to comply with any of these requisites, he cannot be absolved; if he intends to obviate the necessity of recourse by going to a specially qualified confessor, according to canon 2254, § 2, this is perfectly licit, and absolution can be granted; if the recourse is morally impossible, the confessor should apply the norm of canon 2254, § 3.[63]

When the penitent is one who has previously been absolved from a censure in danger of death or in a more urgent case, but has reincurred the same kind of censure through culpable failure to make the prescribed recourse, it is not sufficient for the confessor to urge him to make the omitted recourse; a new absolution must be given for the reincurred censure, and the recourse, if it is morally possible, must be again enjoined upon the penitent under pain of his falling back once more into the same kind of censure.

C. *Nature and Form of the Absolution*

Before the Code, the doubt arose as to whether the absolution granted in the more urgent cases was direct or indirect,[64] and a

[62] S. C. pro Eccl. Orient., decr., 1 Martii, 1929, Art. 31: " . . . Presbyteri vero latini absolvere non possunt fideles graeco-rutheni ritus a censuris et casibus reservatis ab Ordinario graeco-rutheno statutis, absque venia eiusdem. Vicissim idem dicatur de presbyteris graeco-ruthenis quoad censuras et reservationes statutas ab Ordinario latini ritus."—*AAS*, XXI (1929), 157, 158.

[63] *Cf.* Cerato, *Censurae Vigentes*, p. 44; Salucci, *Diritto Penale*, I, 227.

[64] For an explanation of this distinction, *cf.* above, p. 58; *cf.* also Cappello, *De Censuris*, n. 126, 9.

response of the Holy Office declared that the absolution was direct.[65]

Like the absolution granted in danger of death from reserved *ab homine* censures and censures reserved *specialissimo modo* to the Holy See, the absolution given from any reserved censure by reason of canon 2254, § 1, is an *absolutio ad reincidentiam.* Such an absolution, as has been mentioned in another place, is commonly considered to be a conditional absolution, based on a resolutive condition; so that the absolution produces its effect immediately, entirely removing the censure in the internal forum, but if the condition concerning the subsequent obligation of the penitent to make recourse is not fulfilled, a new censure of the same species is incurred.[66] However, this does not affect the confessor in his manner of absolving, for the condition implied in the *absolutio ad reincidentiam* arises from the law, not from the confessor, and *per se* the absolution is given absolutely by the confessor.[67]

If there is some doubt whether or not a particular case is a *casus urgentior,* but the confessor has a positive and probable reason for believing it to be such, he can absolve absolutely, for canon 209 will supply the necessary jurisdiction if the urgency of the case is not actually and objectively verified. When there is a doubt whether or not the penitent has incurred a censure, if it is a doubt of law, for example, whether or not a particular case is included under the terms of the law, then no absolution is necessary, for no penalty can be contracted for the violation of a doubtful law in those of its elements which are doubtful; if the doubt is a doubt of fact, an *absolutio ad cautelam* is given, which is a form of conditional absolution, by which the penitent is absolved from a doubtful censure in case it might have actually been incurred and absolution should be needed.[68] However, it is to be noted that

[65] S. C. S. Off., litt. 19 Augusti, 1891, ad 3—*Fontes,* n. 1143; quoted above, p. 58.

[66] *Cf.* what has been observed above regarding the nature of the absolution in danger of death, in Chapter IV, Article II, C, p. 83. *Cf.* canon 2248, § 3.

[67] *Cf.* Cerato, *Censurae Vigentes,* pp. 37, 38, 291, 292; Cappello, *De Censuris,* n. 95.

[68] *Cf.* canons 15; 19; 2219, § 1. *Cf.* Cappello, *De Censuris,* n. 94; Coronata, *Instit. Iuris Can.,* IV, 141.

an *absolutio ad cautelam* would be an application, not of canon 2254, but of canon 2253, n. 1, and consequently no obligation of recourse would be involved.

When the requisite dispositions of the penitent are doubtful, so that it is uncertain whether or not he has withdrawn from his contumacy, it seems that the confessor cannot absolve him conditionally from the censure, but must defer the absolution.[69] However, it a confessor has absolved absolutely when the penitent has only pretended to possess the dispositions required for the remission of his sins and censures, the absolution from the censure seems valid,[70] for the absolution from a censure can be valid even though the absolution from the sin is invalid, for example, in a sacrilegious confession.[71]

As will be seen presently, the absolution given by reason of canon 2254 is restricted to the sacramental forum. Accordingly, there is no need of any special form of absolution from the censure, for this is contained in that part of the customary form of sacramental absolution which begins with the words *"Dominus noster. . . "* It is also expressed in the short form of sacramental absolution, if by any chance there should be occasion to use this form, namely, *"Ego te absolvo ab omnibus censuris et peccatis, in nomine Patris, et Filii, ✠ et Spiritus Sancti.* Amen." The use

[69] *Cf.* Cappello, *op. cit.*, n. 89, 3, n. 94, 1; in this latter section Cappello limits to superiors the use of conditional absolution mentioned in canon 2239, § 1.

[70] *Cf.* Coronata, *Instit. Iuris Can.*, IV, 153. Cappello (*De Censuris*, n. 91, 2) maintains that if a confessor gives absolution to a penitent before his withdrawal from contumacy, the absolution is illicit and invalid, for the superior grants the faculty to absolve only under the express condition that contumacy has ceased, and Cappello cites canons 2241, § 1, 2242, §§ 1, 3, 2248 for this opinion. But, the illicitness being granted, the invalidity of the absolution from the censure does not seem clearly deducible from these canons, and one might rather say with Coronata (*loc. cit.*): "Si delinquens ficta poenitentiae signa dederit et ficte se reparaturum promiserit absolutio valere videtur, nisi forte absolvens conditionate absolvat, sub conditione nempe quod censuratus bene dispositus sit." *Cf.* canons 103, § 2; 104; 2238.

[71] *Cf.* D'Annibale, *Summula Theol. Mor.*, I, n. 336, nota 13; Coronata, *op. cit.*, IV, 143, 170, 171; Vermeersch, *Theol. Mor.*, III, n. 475.

of the form of sacramental absolution when absolution is granted from censures in the sacramental forum, as in canon 2254, is obligatory, binding at least *sub levi.*[72]

D. *The Forum of the Absolution*

The absolution granted by virtue of canon 2254 can be given by the confessor only "*in foro sacramentali,*" that is, only in connection with the act of sacramental confession, when the penitent confesses his sins and censures in the tribunal of Penance for the purpose of absolution.[73] Consequently, any use of canon 2254 outside the sacramental forum, even in the internal non-sacramental forum, is invalid.[74]

Therefore, absolution given by reason of canon 2254 does not remove the canonical effects of the censure in the external forum. But from this it cannot be deduced, as will be explained in another place, that this canon can be used only for occult censures, or that, when a penitent is so absolved, he must refrain from performing such actions in the external forum as will not cause scandal.[75]

Article III. The Object of the Absolution

A. *Latae Sententiae Censures*

The object of absolution granted according to canon 2254 consists of "*censurae latae sententiae,*" and when either of the more urgent cases is verified, any confessor "*ab eisdem, quoque modo reservatis, absolvere potest.*" Since *latae sententiae* censures may be of various kinds, and since authors have made restrictions re-

[72] *Cf.* canon 2250, § 3. *Cf.* Cappello, *De Censuris,* nn. 99, 100.

[73] *Cf.* Cappello, *De Censuris,* n. 126, 7; De Meester, *Compendium,* III, P. II, 185; Chelodi, *Ius Poenale,* p. 42, nota 6; Blat, *Commentarium,* lib. V, p. 116.

[74] *Cf.* Coronata, *Instit. Iuris Can.,* IV, 180.

[75] *Cf.* canon 2251. This matter relative to occult and public censures, indicated briefly here, will be treated at some length in the discussion of the absolution of public censures according to the norm of canon 2254; *cf.* below, in the present chapter, Article III, A, 3, p. 169.

garding the inclusion of certain of these censures under canon 2254 and have opened questions concerning the extension of this canon to other elements of penal law which are not *latae sententiae* censures, detailed consideration is here given to the different general types of *latae sententiae* censures, to the restrictions suggested by authors, and to the questions which have arisen concerning the inclusion of other elements of penal law which cannot be classified as *latae sententiae* censures.

1. *Latae Sententiae Censures A Iure.* In general, it may be said that all reserved *latae sententiae* censures which arise from either general or particular law are properly the object of the absolution which may be granted by reason of canon 2254. Whether or not this statement is to be restricted or extended will be seen in the course of the discussion in this article.

All *latae sententiae* censures which are reserved by general law to the Roman Pontiff,[76] to the Holy See in any manner, whether *specialissimo modo, speciali modo,* or *simpliciter,* or to the local or religious ordinary, can be absolved by reason of canon 2254; also *latae sententiae* censures which local or religious ordinaries have reserved to themselves by particular law.[77] If these censures are occult, there will be no difficulty, unless they have been brought before the judicial forum; [78] if they are public, certain considerations must be kept in mind, and this will call for a special treatment.[79]

If the *latae sententiae* censure, constituted by general or par-

[76] This matter of censures reserved personally to the pope is considered in detail below, in n. 6 under the present heading.

[77] *Cf.* Cappello, *De Censuris,* n. 126, 8; Coronata, *Instit. Iuris Can.,* IV, 179, 180; De Meester, *Compendium,* III, P. II, 185; Cerato, *Censurae Vigentes,* p. 43. Note that, according to canon 519, any confessor approved by the local ordinary for hearing confessions can absolve any religious from any censure reserved in his institute; in such a case, there would be no need to apply canon 2254. But canon 519 does not empower such confessors to absolve from censures reserved by common law to a religious ordinary.

[78] *Cf.* below, in n. 4 under the present heading.

[79] *Cf.* below, in n. 3 under the present heading.

ticular law, is a suspension, it can be absolved in the *casus urgentior* of danger of grave scandal or infamy, but not merely because of the hardship of remaining in the state of grave sin,[80] for suspension does not impede the licit reception of the sacraments, and absolution from the sins can be given for the recovery of the state of grace without the granting of absolution from the suspension.[81] This is a restriction which is not superadded to the wording of the canon, but arises from the nature of the canon, for in such circumstances the *casus urgentior* is not verified for the removal of the censure of suspension, and the provision of the canon is not to be applied.

The object of absolution considered here concerns *latae sententiae* censures reserved by common or particular law. Excommunication is always a censure; regarding suspension and interdict, in a doubt of law or in a doubt of fact which cannot be settled, they are presumed to be censures,[82] and therefore would be included under canon 2254, not only when they are clearly inflicted as censures, but also when there is doubt whether in a particular case they are censures or vindictive penalties. From the side of the *latae sententiae* element, it will usually be known whether or not a censure was inflicted as *latae* or *ferendae sententiae*. However, if there is a doubt whether a censure established in common or particular law is *latae* or *ferendae sententiae*, it is presumed to be *ferendae sententiae*.[83] In such a case, therefore, since the doubt presupposes that the censure has not been actually inflicted, as *ferendae sententiae*, by way of a judicial sentence or an extrajudicial decree (otherwise the penitent could hardly have such a doubt), then the censure can be regarded as a *ferendae sententiae* censure which has not yet been contracted, and there is no need

[80] *Cf.* Coronata, *Instit. Iuris Can.*, IV, 179; Vermeersch, *Theol. Mor.*, III, n. 473, 1; Raus, *Instit. Can.*, p. 698, nota 4; *Idem*, "Absolution von Zensuren l. s. ab homine," *TPQ*, LXXXIII (1930), 588; Rainer, *Suspension of Clerics*, p. 215.

[81] Compare canon 2278, § 1, with canons 2260, § 1 and 2275, n. 2; *cf.* canon 2250, § 1.

[82] Canon 2255, § 2.

[83] Canon 2217, § 2.

for the use of canon 2254; and if an *absolutio ad cautelam* is given, because of the consideration that the censure may have been *latae sententiae* and actually contracted, then, since the incurrence of the censure is doubtful,[84] its reservation is also doubtful and consequently non-existent,[85] and the confessor will apply, not canon 2254, but canon 2253, n. 1.

Not even the excommunication for *absolutio complicis in peccato turpi* has been excluded from canon 2254, § 1, and, since this is one of the most severely reserved censures, its inclusion serves to indicate the broad extent of the provisions for the more urgent cases. However, there is one censure which has been withdrawn entirely from canon 2254, namely, the *latae sententiae* excommunication incurred by a priest through contravention of canon 2388, § 1. This case, since its exclusion from canon 2254 is verified only under certain conditions, will call for special consideration.[86]

2. *Latae Sententiae Ab Homine Censures.* Since the promulgation of the Code a controversy has arisen as to whether or not *latae sententiae ab homine* censures can be absolved by reason of canon 2254. The question concerns *latae sententiae* censures which are established in particular precepts; for example, a bishop says to one of his priests: "You must not go to that place again, and if you do go, you are *ipso facto* suspended," and he may add, "and I reserve it to myself."

Despite the opinion of Michiels and Roberti, it seems sufficiently clear that there can be a censure which is at once both *latae sententiae* and *ab homine*.[87] Granting that there can be *latae sententiae ab homine* censures, are these included under canon 2254, or does this canon embrace only censures that are *latae sententiae a iure?*

[84] *Cf.* canons 2228; 2242, §§ 1, 2.

[85] *Cf.* canon 2245, § 4.

[86] It is discussed briefly in B of the present article, and in detail in Chapter X, Article IV.

[87] *Cf.* above, Chapter V, Article II, A, B, p. 91 ff.; the opinion of Michiels and Roberti is considered in detail, *ibid.*, A, 5.

Relative to the contention that *latae sententiae ab homine* censures cannot be absolved by reason of canon 2254, there are various indications which might lead one to that conclusion. In canon 2252, there is explicit provision for recourse to the one who inflicted the censure, if an *ab homine* censure was absolved, and to the Sacred Penitentiary, or to a bishop or some other ecclesiastic possessing the proper faculty, if absolution was granted from a censure reserved *specialissimo modo* to the Holy See. But in canon 2254 there is no mention of recourse to the one who inflicted the censure, but only to the Sacred Penitentiary, or to a bishop, or some other superior with the proper faculty, and since this is practically the same as the recourse prescribed in canon 2252 for censures reserved *specialissimo modo a iure,* it would seem to indicate that canon 2254 is intended only for *a iure* censures. Again, when canon 2253 offers norms for the ordinary absolution from censures, it inserts the saving clause regarding canon 2254 in its n. 3 on *a iure* censures, and this *"salvo praescripto can. 2254"* seems to be restricted to the *a iure* censures considered in canon 2253, n. 3, and not to apply to the *ab homine* censures in n. 2 of the same canon.

Concerning the authors who hold this negative opinion, namely, that which denies that *latae sententiae ab homine* censures can be absolved by reason of canon 2254, a few words of comment will be in order.

Cappello is considered as one of the most emphatic proponents of this view. However, it will be recalled that Cappello holds the rather unusual view that a *latae sententiae* censure is one which is attached to a law or a *general* precept in such a way that it is incurred *ipso facto.*[88] Consequently, it seems that Cappello does not recognize the existence of a *latae sententiae* censure attached to a particular precept,[89] which is the *latae sententiae ab homine* censure, and one searches in vain in his latest edition (1933) for the distinction of *latae sententiae* and *ferendae sententiae ab homine* censures. Therefore, although Cappello uses the argument from canon 2252 to conclude that *ab homine* censures are implicitly ex-

[88] *De Censuris* (ed. 1925 et 1933), n. 4, 3; *cf.* above, Chapter V, note 12.

[89] However, *cf.* above, Chapter V, note 13.

cluded from canon 2254, and this argument would apparently apply also to the *latae sententiae ab homine* censure, nevertheless, when he says that *ab homine* censures are *per se* excluded from canon 2254,[90] it seems that this must, in consistency with his opinion on *latae sententiae* censures, be referred only to *ab homine* censures which are *ferendae sententiae.*[91]

Blat [92] is also regarded as holding the negative opinion, but, after searching through a bewildering array of clauses, one is not quite certain as to the extent of Blat's exclusion of *latae sententiae ab homine* censures from canon 2254.

Cocchi [93] seems also to hold the negative opinion, but his wording is so ambiguous that he has been cited by Coronata [94] in favor of the opposite opinion.

Others simply assert that *ab homine* censures are excluded from canon 2254, and this must be properly interpreted as referring to all *ab homine* censures, whether *latae* or *ferendae sententiae.*[95]

On the other hand, canon 2254 states that all *latae sententiae* censures, no matter how reserved, may be absolved in the more urgent cases, and since it does not distinguish between *a iure* censures and *ab homine* censures, it seems that the distinction should not be made unless clearly demanded by the nature of the canon. Regarding the argument from the comparison of canons 2252 and 2254, § 1, it is useless to deny that the wording *"ad S. Poenitentiariam vel ad Episcopum aliumve Superiorem praeditum facultate"*

[90] *De Censuris* (ed. 1925), n. 132, 4; (ed. 1933), n. 133, 1.

[91] It is to be suspected that some authors who quote Cappello on this point, citing him in support of the exclusion of *latae sententiae ab homine* censures from canon 2254, have not related his opinion on *ab homine* censures in canon 2254 to his view on *latae sententiae* censures.

[92] *Commentarium,* lib. V, pp. 115, 116.

[93] *Commentarium,* lib. V, p. 124.

[94] *Instit. Iuris Can.,* IV, 179, nota 7.

[95] De Meester, *Compendium,* III, P. II, 185, nota 4; Wouters, *Man. Theol. Mor.,* II, n. 865, 2, b; Woywod, *A Practical Commentary on the Code of Canon Law* (3. ed., New York: Wagner, 1929), n. 2097; Aertnys-Damen, *Theol. Mor.,* II, n. 994 *bis;* Dargin, *Reserved Cases,* p. 86; Rossi, "De sacerdotibus . . . ," *Perfice Munus,* XII (1937), 16.

in canon 2254, § 1, seems at first sight to be referable only to the recourse for *a iure* censures, for it hardly appears likely that the Code would speak of recourse to a bishop or another superior possessing the proper faculty in the case of a censure which the bishop or superior has reserved to himself by a particular precept. In other words, the phrase *"praeditum facultate"* at first glance creates the impression that the recourse in question is prescribed after absolution has been given from some censure reserved to the Holy See, but for which a bishop or some other superior may have a *delegated faculty* to absolve and likewise to receive recourse.[96] But this notion of *"praeditum facultate"* as meaning "possessed of a delegated faculty" must not be urged too far; otherwise, there would appear to be no provision for recourse in the case of a censure reserved by law to a religious ordinary,[97] since he is not a bishop and, as he would have ordinary power to absolve in such a case,[98] he would not be a "superior endowed with a faculty" if "faculty" is taken in the sense of a delegated faculty; and again, the same would be true in the case of a censure which a major superior of an exempt clerical religious institute has reserved to himself, although it is admitted that such a censure can be absolved by reason of canon 2254.[99] Therefore, although the *"facultate praeditum"* in canon 2252 can mean only a delegated faculty, since there is question of a censure reserved *specialissimo modo,* for which only the Holy See would have ordinary power, nevertheless in canon 2254 the same phrase must be understood in a broader sense as referring to a bishop or superior who has the power to absolve, whether

[96] *Cf.* the analogous response on the words *"facultate praeditum"* in canon 2252, declaring that these words apply also to *"Episcopum"*—Pont. Comm., 12 Novembris, 1922, n. VIII—*AAS,* XIV (1922), 663; quoted above, Chapter V, note 77.

[97] *E.g., cf.* canon 2385.

[98] The provisions of canon 2237 and 2253, n. 3, by which ordinaries can absolve from censures reserved by common law to the ordinary, are considered as expressions of ordinary jurisdiction, not jurisdiction delegated by the law. *Cf.* Cappello, *De Censuris,* n. 122, e, n. 123, 6; Chelodi, *Ius Poenale,* p. 34; Sole, *De Delictis et Poenis,* n. 147, 3.

[99] *Cf.* Cappello, *op. cit.,* n. 126, 8.

that power be ordinary or delegated. If it is accepted in this sense, and recourse is to be made to the Sacred Penitentiary or to any bishop or other superior who has the power to absolve, then there seems to be no reason to exclude the *latae sententiae ab homine* censure from canon 2254 merely from the argument that there is no provision for the recourse. In a word, the prescription in canon 2254 for recourse is broader than the similar wording in canon 2252 for censures reserved *specialissimo modo a iure;* it must be broader, since recourse in canon 2254 is required after absolution from any reserved *latae sententiae* censure; and it is sufficiently broad to include *latae sententiae ab homine* censures without any absolute need of the specific wording *"ad illum qui censuram tulit"* for *ab homine* censures as in canon 2252.[100]

The wording of canon 2253, n. 3, seems to offer a real difficulty, though no mention of it has been found in any of the works of authors who exclude *latae sententiae ab homine* censures from canon 2254. The phrase *"salvo praescripto can. 2254"* in the above canon seems to refer only to its paragraph on censures reserved *a iure,* and not to its paragraph on *ab homine* censures. Unless that phrase can be extended to all matters in the canon to which it is applicable, namely, to both its paragraphs on reserved censures, which does not seem very probable, the solution of this difficulty is not readily seen. But it may be said that there seems to be no reason why there should not be an extraordinary absolution from *ab homine* censures as well as from censures reserved *a iure.* The *ab homine* censures have an extraordinary provision for absolution in danger of death, as is clear from canons 882 and 2252. Why should there not be an extraordinary provision for them in the more urgent cases? If they are *ferendae sententiae,* the *casus urgentiores,* as will be seen,[101] will rarely be verified; but if they are *latae sententiae,* there seems to be no less chance for the contingency of a more urgent case in their regard than for censures reserved by diocesan law, and these latter certainly come under canon 2254.

It must be remembered that there is so much obscurity in the

100 *Cf.* Collison, *Non Omnis Censura Ab Homine Est Reservata,* pp. 58-61.

101 *Cf.* below, in C of the present article.

Code in its provisions for *latae sententiae ab homine* censures, that such canons as 2254 and 2245 have given rise to the opinion of Michiels and Roberti that a *latae sententiae* censure attached to a particular precept is not *ab homine* but *tamquam a iure.*[102] The opinion of these authors has not been admitted in this work, for various reasons; yet, from the insistence upon the existence of *latae sententiae ab homine* censures, there remain the difficulties concerning their reservation and absolution.

To return to the question in this discussion: can *latae sententiae ab homine* censures be absolved by reason of canon 2254, or must they be excluded? The opinion affirming that they can be absolved has received rather wide support.[103] From this external authority and from the fact that the *latae sententiae ab homine* censure is not unquestionably excluded by the wording of canon 2254, it seems that the least that can be admitted is that there is a doubt of law, and, since "*favores convenit ampliari*" [104] and also since in a doubt of law the Church supplies jurisdiction,[105] it can safely be held that *latae sententiae ab homine* censures can be absolved by reason of canon 2254, unless the Holy See decides otherwise.

102 *Cf.* above, Chapter V, Article II, p. 101 ff.

103 *Cf.* Coronata, *Instit. Iuris Can.*, IV, 179; Cipollini, *De Censuris,* p. 44; Cerato, *Censurae Vigentes,* p. 28; Raus, *Instit. Can.*, p. 698; *Idem,* "Absolution von Zensuren l. s. ab homine," *TPQ,* LXXXIII (1930), 586, 587; Kelly, *Jurisdiction of the Confessor,* pp. 169, 170; Collison, *Non Omnis Censura Ab Homine Est Reservata,* pp. 58-61; Marc-Gestermann-Raus, *Instit. Mor. Alph.*, n. 1284, 3; Genicot-Salsmans, *Instit. Theol. Mor.*, II, n. 574, 2; Reintjes, *De Absolutione Censurae,* p. 32. To these, who are explicit on this point, may perhaps be added those who state in general that all *latae sententiae* censures, without exception, may be absolved, *e.g.*, Chelodi, *Ius Poenale,* p. 42; Salucci, *Diritto Poenale,* I, 225; Davis, *Moral and Pastoral Theology,* III, 452, 453. Besides, Roberti ("An censura latae sententiae per praeceptum constituta sit reservata," *Apollinaris,* VI [1933], p. 347) and Rainer (*Suspension of Clerics,* p. 215) maintain that the exact censure in question can be absolved, though they say it is not *ab homine* but *tamquam a iure,* and Rainer expressly says that no *ab homine* censure comes under canon 2254; so they agree with the above opinion *quoad rem, etsi non quoad nomen.*

104 Reg. 15, R. J. in VI°.

105 Canon 209.

Before the discussion on this question can be concluded, one more point calls for brief consideration. It has been stated in another place[106] that a *latae sententiae ab homine* censure which has not been expressly reserved in the particular precept can be regarded as not reserved. In such a case, since the censure is not reserved, there is no need for the application of canon 2254, which deals only with reserved censures, but the confessor will use canon 2253, n. 1, which does not entail any obligation of recourse. But the *latae sententiae ab homine* censure which, as has just been concluded above, may be considered as coming under canon 2254, is one which the superior has expressly reserved to himself in the particular precept; for example, "You must not go to that place, and if you do, you are *ipso facto* suspended, and I reserve the absolution to myself." If it is objected that in such a case there would be contempt of the superior's authority if an ordinary confessor would absolve by reason of canon 2254, the statement is here ventured that no more contempt is to be found in absolving from this censure than in absolving from one which the Code has expressly reserved to the Holy See; and if this is not admitted, it must be agreed that the necessity as found in the *casus urgentiores* removes even the semblance of contempt, and at any rate the matter will ordinarily be subjected to the judgment of the superior by means of the required recourse.[107]

3. *Public Censures.* When one compares the opening words of canon 2254 with those of canon 2290, he notices a significant difference, namely, that the provision for the remission of *latae sententiae* vindictive penalties in more urgent cases is expressly restricted to occult cases, while this restriction has been studiously omitted in the parallel canon on *latae sententiae* censures. Absolution according to canon 2254, then, may be given *"in casibus urgentioribus,"* and the text does not require that these more urgent cases be occult. In fact, Salucci has gone so far as to say that this canon applies only to notorious *latae sententiae* censures, since oc-

[106] *Cf.* above, Chapter V, Article II, B, p. 105.

[107] *Cf.* Cipollini, *De Censuris*, p. 44.

cult censures are provided for in canon 2232.[108] This opinion of Salucci has already been considered, and it has been said that when this view is referred to the *casus urgentior* of danger of scandal or infamy, it is *per se* incorrect, for generally there will be question rather of giving than of avoiding scandal by the non-observance of a notorious censure in the external forum.[109]

The best general statement that can be given on this point of the absolution of public censures is that offered by De Meester, who says that public censures can be absolved by reason of canon 2254, provided that one of the more urgent cases is verified, and that the requirements of canon 2251 are observed concerning the effects of this absolution in the external forum.[110]

It is nowhere positively stated in the Code that public censures can be absolved in the internal forum, but this notion is clearly implied in canon 2251, which states that a person who is absolved from a censure in the internal forum may act as absolved also in the external forum, provided that there is no danger of scandal from such actions in the external forum.[111] If the censure were occult, there would be no danger of scandal from actions in the external forum, so this provision of canon 2251 must include public censures, and it is commonly accepted in this sense.[112] Conse-

108 *Diritto Penale,* I, 225, nota 1.

109 *Cf.* above, in the present chapter, Article I, B, p. 149.

110 *Compendium,* III, P. II, 185, nota 5.

111 Canon 2251: "Si absolutio censurae detur in foro externo, utrumque forum afficit; si in interno, absolutus, remoto scandalo, potest uti talem se habere etiam in actibus fori externi; sed, nisi concessio absolutionis probetur aut saltem legitime praesumatur in foro externo, censura potest a Superioribus fori externi, quibus reus parere debet, urgeri, donec absolutio in eodem foro habita fuerit."

112 *Cf.* Cappello, *De Censuris,* nn. 97, 98, 109; Coronata, *Instit. Iuris Can.,* IV, 173; Sole, *De Delictis et Poenis,* n. 185; Chelodi, *Ius Poenale,* p. 40; Salucci, *Diritto Penale,* I, 216; Cipollini, *De Censuris,* pp. 35, 36; De Meester, *Compendium,* III, P. II, 179; Roberti, "An censura l.s. . . . ," *Apollinaris,* VI (1933), 346. Note, moreover, that De Meester (*loc. cit.*) says: "Absolutio pro foro interno passim datur, nostris diebus, etiam quando censura est publica et rarius recurritur ad absolutionem pro foro externo, nisi cum haereticis. Si quis censura *publice* mulctatus fuerit per sententiam *declara-*

quently, there would likewise be no juridical objection to the absolution of public censures by reason of canon 2254 in the more urgent cases, as long as the cases are actually verified.

Public *latae sententiae* censures, then, can be absolved according to canon 2254 when, and only when, at least one of the *casus urgentiores* is verified. The more urgent case of danger of grave scandal or infamy will not be verified for the absolution of a public censure, for the simple reason that a person who is commonly known to be under a censure will not occasion scandal or suffer infamy by failing to perform an act prohibited by the censure; in fact, the very opposite may be the case, namely, that the person would rather cause scandal by performing such an action.[113] However, it must be remembered that, according to the practice of the Sacred Penitentiary, censures, like delicts, may be occult by reason of the persons who know of them, by reason of the place, and by reason of the time.[114] Therefore, a censure that is known to a few persons, though public if these persons will spread it abroad, will be occult if they are of such a character that they will not divulge their knowledge of the censure to others; a censure may be public in one place, and occult in another; it may have been public in a certain place at one time, but has become occult in the same place with the passing of time. This is to be borne in mind for the proper understanding of the statement that public censures cannot be absolved simply because of the danger of scandal or infamy. Consequently, if it should happen that there is actually danger of scandal or infamy if a person fails to perform an act prohibited by a censure, because the censure, although public elsewhere or at some other time, is now *de facto* occult in the place in which the person is morally forced to place the act, he can be absolved, whether

toriam vel *condemnatoriam*, absolutio *per se* in foro *externo* semper danda est et publicanda." The question whether or not *latae sententiae* censures which have been brought to the judicial forum, or which have been juridically declared, are to be excluded from canon 2254 will be treated immediately, in nn. 4 and 5 under the present heading.

[113] *Cf.* Cipollini, *De Censuris*, pp. 43, 44.

[114] *Cf.* Rossi, "De sacerdotibus . . . ," *Perfice Munus*, XI (1936), 532, nota 2; 534, nota 1. Rossi, an official of the Sacred Penitentiary, presumably is well qualified to speak on such matters.

the *latae sententiae* censure is *a iure* or *ab homine.* It is said: "*de facto* occult in the place in which the penitent is morally forced to place the forbidden act in order to avoid scandal or infamy," and not "*de facto* occult in the place in which the confession is made."[115] The reason for this is as follows: if the penitent makes his confession in his own parish, wishing to act against the censure in that place, the censure must be indeed be occult in that place, which is the place of confession, otherwise the confessor cannot absolve, for there will be no danger of scandal or infamy; but if the penitent makes his confession either in his own parish or in some other parish, but must act against the censure in some place in which the public censure is *de facto* occult, then the confessor can absolve by reason of the danger of scandal or infamy, regardless of the fact that the censure is public or occult in the place of the confession. In other words, the public or occult nature of the censure does not necessarily affect the place of confession, but it does affect the place in which the penitent intends to act; and if the place of confession and the place of action are the same, as will ordinarily, but not always, happen, then the censure must be occult, otherwise the danger of scandal or infamy will not be verified.

Regarding the second of the *casus urgentiores,* namely, the hardship of remaining in grave sin until the confessor can obtain faculties from a competent superior, it makes no difference whether the *latae sententiae* censure is public or occult. Accordingly, if this more urgent case is verified, a public censure can be absolved by any confessor according to the norm of canon 2254, in order that the penitent may regain the state of grace. But after the absolution the penitent must by all means observe canon 2251, and therefore he cannot perform any actions in the external forum which are liable to cause scandal. Consequently, if there would be scandal if such a penitent, publicly considered to be still under censure, would receive Communion, he would have to refrain,[116] but nothing would prevent him from going to some

[115] This latter expression is used by Cappello (*De Censuris,* n. 133, 2) in reference to public *ab homine* censures.

[116] *Cf.* Sole, *De Delictis et Poenis,* n. 185. *Cf.* also the private response on this matter by the S. C. C., 18 Novembris, 1922, as translated in Bouscaren, *Canon Law Digest,*. I, 408, 409.

other place, where he is not known, to receive Communion there. If it is commonly known that the person has gone to confession, or if it will be presumed by the people that he has been absolved, for example, because he is now faithfully attending to his religious duties in contrast to his former conduct, then there will be no danger of scandal, and the person can perform all acts in the external forum, unless the superior forbids him to act as one absolved until he can prove his reception of absolution in the internal forum or demonstrate the legitimacy of the presumption of his absolution.[117] If the person can do neither of these, the superior can forbid him to act as one absolved, until he obtains absolution in the external forum; but if the person can demonstrate by proof or by legitimate presumption that he was absolved in the internal forum, it seems that the superior can no longer require him to observe the censure in the external forum.[118] However, this would not prevent the superior from demanding that the person make public satisfaction for his public crime.

There is one public censure which apparently cannot be absolved by reason of canon 2254,[119] and that is the public censure of suspension. Since it is public, *per se* it cannot be absolved in view of danger of scandal or infamy, for this ordinarily would not be verified; since it is a suspension, there is no urgent necessity to absolve from it by reason of the hardship of remaining in grave sin, for the sin can be absolved without the absolution of the censure.[120]

[117] *Cf.* canon 2251. *Cf.* Cappello, *De Censuris,* n. 98; Coronata, *Instit. Iuris Can.,* IV, 173, 174; De Meester, *Compendium,* III, P. II, 179; Chelodi, *Ius Poenale,* p. 40; Vermeersch-Creusen, *Epitome,* III, n. 450, 3; Ayrinhac-Lydon, *Penal Legislation,* n. 92; Rossi, "De sacerdotibus . . . ," *Perfice Munus,* XI (1936), 533, nota 2.

[118] *Cf.* Coronata, *loc. cit.;* Cappello, *loc. cit.;* Ayrinhac-Lydon, *op. cit.,* n. 93; Cipollini, *De Censuris,* pp. 28, 35, 36. Other authors, *e. g.,* De Meester (*loc. cit.*), say that the superior *can* accept the proof of absolution in the internal forum as sufficient for the external forum; but the wording of canon 2251 seems entirely in favor of the view explicitly mentioned by Coronata, that the superior *must* accept such proof as sufficient.

[119] That is, besides the censure, whether public or occult, which has been expressly excluded from canon 2254 by the Sacred Penitentiary; *cf.* below, in B of the present article.

[120] *Cf.* above, in the present chapter, note 48.

The general statement, therefore, still stands, namely, that public *latae sententiae* censures can be absolved by reason of canon 2254, provided that at least one of the more urgent cases is verified, and provided that the requirements of canon 2251 are observed regarding the effects of this absolution with respect to acts in the external forum.

4. *Censures Brought to the Judicial Forum.* It may happen that a delict or a *latae sententiae* censure confessed by a penitent has been already brought to the judicial forum, either to the contentious forum for the declaration of some juridical fact, or to the criminal forum for the declaration of the censure in the external forum.[121] Although the matter is disputed, it seems that for the present purposes a case may be considered to be brought to the judicial forum when the party has been legitimately cited.[122] Can a person in such circumstances be absolved by reason of canon 2254?

It is commonly held that, when a case has been brought to the contentious forum, the person must be absolved in the external forum, and that absolution in the internal forum is of no avail.[123] However, this concerns the ordinary absolution from censures. Does it apply also to the extraordinary absolution from censures? Certainly it does not restrict the power of the confessor when absolving in danger of death. But does it limit the power of the confessor who wishes to absolve in the other extraordinary circumstances, namely, in the more urgent cases?

This question is usually not mentioned in treatments of the absolution in the *casus urgentiores,* but the general statement is ordinarily made that the confessor can absolve from all *latae sententiae*

[121] *Cf.* canon 1552, § 2.

[122] For an outline of the various opinions on this point, *cf.* Coronata, *Instit. Iuris Can.,* IV, 136, nota 4. Note that the case considered in the present discussion refers to a censure brought to the judicial forum, but not yet declared; for a discussion of the case in which the censure has been declared, *cf.* n. 5 under the present heading.

[123] *Cf.* Cappello, *De Censuris,* n. 119; Coronata, *op. cit.,* IV, 137; De Meester, *Compendium,* III, P. II, 183.

censures. Cappello,[124] however, asserts that, if the delict has been brought before a judge of the external forum, the confessor *per se* cannot absolve from the censure in the more urgent cases, but that he can absolve for the sacramental forum if the penitent, properly disposed, is in a place in which the delict is utterly unknown, or if otherwise the penitent would be forced to remain in the state of grave sin for a long time.

If the legislator wished to exclude from the scope of canon 2254 censures brought to the judicial forum, it seems that he would have made express mention of this, as he has done in canon 2237, § 1, regarding public censures of this kind. But he has not done this in canon 2254, and, since the moral necessity implied in the more urgent cases removes even the semblance of contempt for ecclesiastical authority,[125] and since the matter will ordinarily be subjected to the judgment of the superior by means of recourse, there seems to be no reason why canon 2254 cannot be applied, provided that at least one of the more urgent cases is verified. If the censure is occult, in the sense that it has not, and presumably will not easily be, divulged,[126] then it can be absolved for either of the two cases of urgent necessity. If it is public, *per se* it cannot be absolved by reason of the danger of scandal or infamy, for this will ordinarily not exist in such a case; but it can be absolved if the penitent finds it hard to remain in the state of grave sin until the proper faculties can be obtained from the competent superior. There seems to be no particular reason for Cappello's statement that the penitent can be absolved if otherwise he would have to remain in grave sin for a *long* time, but it rather appears that the urgent case of hardship of remaining in grave sin is to be interpreted and applied in this case in the same way as for other *latae sententiae* censures. If the censure is public, however, it must be remembered that the penitent, after absolution in the sacramental forum, can perform only those acts in the external forum which will not be an occasion of scandal to others.[127]

[124] *De Censuris,* n. 133, 3.

[125] *Cf.* Cipollini, *De Censuris,* p. 44, on a similar point.

[126] *Cf.* canon 2197, nn. 1, 4.

[127] Canon 2251.

5. *Censures After a Declaratory Sentence.* It is commonly stated that a declaratory sentence does not influence the reservation or non-reservation of a *latae sententiae* penalty, but that when a censure is publicly declared, either judicially by a sentence or extra-judicially by a decree or precept according to the norm of canon 2225, *per se* it must be absolved in the external forum, and ordinarily the fact of absolution is to be published that the faithful may know of it.[128]

It must be noted, first of all, that the declaration of an *a iure* penalty does not make it an *ab homine* penalty, for a condemnatory sentence is the only one which causes an *a iure* penalty to become *ab homine.*[129] Secondly, there is a distinction between the declaration and the denunciation of a censure. The declaratory sentence is a juridical pronouncement by a competent authority that a person has contracted a *latae sententiae* penalty; the denunciation is the act of making public the fact that a penalty, already declared, has been contracted, so that the incurrence of the penalty becomes a matter of common knowledge, and this may be done in various ways, for example, by the insertion of the sentence in the official periodical.[130] When the declaratory sentence is made known generally, therefore, it involves the denunciation. But it may happen that the sentence is not made public, but is placed in the secret archives. In such a case, although the censure may be notorious with notoriety of law according to the norm of canon 2197, n. 2,[131] it may at the same time be occult, in the sense that it has not been and will not easily be divulged.[132]

[128] *Cf.* Coronata, *Instit. Iuris Can.*, IV, 121; Cappello, *De Censuris*, nn. 74-76, 109, 110, 133; De Meester, *Compendium*, III, P. II, 179; Rossi, "De sacerdotibus . . . ," *Perfice Munus*, XI (1936), 534.

[129] Canon 2217, § 1, n. 3. *Cf.* Cappello, *op. cit.*, n. 76, 10; Coronata, *op. cit.*, IV, 76-78, 163; Cerato, *Censurae Vigentes*, p. 17.

[130] *Cf.* Cappello, *op. cit.*, nn. 74-76, 78, 79; Coronata, *op. cit.*, IV, 121; De Meester, *Compendium*, III, P. II, 58; Cerato, *op. cit.*, pp. 17, 18.

[131] That is, if the sentence has become a *res judicata*, or if the person has made a juridical confession of the delict. Concerning the *res judicata*, *cf.* canons 1902-1904; 1880.

[132] *Cf.* canon 2197, nn. 1, 4. *Cf.* Coronata, *Instit. Iuris Can.*, IV, 14-18.

Consequently, a *latae sententiae* censure after a declaratory sentence cannot be regarded as *ferendae sententiae,* and it may be either public or occult. The question now arises: can a *latae sententiae* censure after a declaratory sentence be absolved according to the norms of canon 2254, and, if so, under what circumstances?

This question is not considered by most of the authors, but Cappello [133] has offered a solution. He asserts that if a censure has been declared publicly and with the name of the guilty party, absolution *per se* cannot be given in the sacramental forum in the more urgent cases, unless the penitent is in a place where the delict is unknown, or unless he would otherwise have to remain for a long time in the state of grave sin. However, this solution does not appear entirely satisfactory. The proper solution seems rather to consist of a combination of a statement made by Roberti [134] and of the conclusion mentioned above concerning the absolution from public censures; namely, that canon 2254 is not limited by any distinction between censures that are declared or not declared, but that absolution can be given from declared *latae sententiae* censures as long as at least one of the *casus urgentiores* is verified, and provided that the requirements of canon 2251 are observed concerning the effects of this absolution with regard to acts in the external forum.

Specifically, if the declared censure is public, *per se* it cannot be absolved simply by reason of the danger of grave scandal or infamy, for this ordinarily will not be verified; but whether it is public or occult, it can be absolved if it is hard for the penitent to remain in the state of grave sin until the confessor can obtain the proper faculties from the superior—applying, therefore, the usual interpretation of this hardship, or rather applying the actual wording of canon 2254, and not admitting the seemingly arbitrary view that absolution can be given only if otherwise the penitent would have

[133] *De Censuris,* n. 133, 4.

[134] "Absolutio in casibus urgentioribus nullam patitur distinctionem, sive quoad reservationem, sive quoad mandata, inter censuras declaratas et non declaratas. Ex quo arguitur declarationem nullo modo limitare absolvendi potestatem, salva, uti patet, facultate, quibusvis Superioribus facta, poenas urgendi in foro externo, nisi absolutio probetur aut legitime praesumatur (c. 2251)."—"An censura l. s. . . . ," *Apollinaris,* VI (1933), 347, 348.

to remain in grave sin for a long time. However, since a declaratory sentence will hardly be pronounced except in the case of a crime that is extraordinary or that is joined with unusual contumacy, the confessor should be very prudent in judging whether the contumacy has ceased and whether such a penitent really finds it a hardship to remain in sin until the proper superior can be approached; if prudence dictates that such is the case, he can then absolve simply by reason of this hardship experienced by the penitent. But the penitent, after absolution, must observe the prescriptions of canon 2251, that is, he must avoid all those acts in the external forum, but only those, which will cause scandal to others, and, if the absolution cannot be proved or legitimately presumed, he must obey the superior if the latter forbids him to act as one absolved in the external forum.

6. *Censures Reserved Personally to the Roman Pontiff.* There are certain *latae sententiae* censures which are reserved in a manner that is even more stringent than the *specialissimo modo* reservation to the Holy See, and these are the *latae sententiae* censures reserved personally to the Supreme Pontiff. They are all excommunications and may be classified under three headings, namely: those attached to delicts in the election of the Roman Pontiff; those attached to violations of the secret of the Holy Office; and those attached to violations of secrecy in causes of beatification and canonization.[185]

There are various *latae sententiae* excommunications attached to delicts in the election of the Roman Pontiff,[186] and the same

[185] *Cf.* Cappello, *De Censuris,* nn. 66, 207.

[186] *Cf.* Pius X, const. *"Vacante Sede Apostolica,"* 25 Decembris, 1904, nn. 37, 50, 51, 52, 69, 79, 80, 81, 82, 88. This constitution is the first among the documents appended to the Code. *Cf.* also canons 160; 2330. The number of the excommunications is considered as seven, by Leech (*A Comparative Study of the Constitution "Apostolicae Sedis" and the "Codex Juris Canonici,"* p. 13); as eight, by Coronata (*Instit. Iuris Can.,* IV, 344-349); as nine, by Cappello (*De Censuris,* nn. 565-578), and Cipollini (*De Censuris,* pp. 237-254); and as ten, by Cerato (*Censurae Vigentes,* p. 188). The main source of the divergency on the number is the treatment of the prescriptions on secrecy in nn. 51, 52, and 69 of the constitution.

constitution which established them decreed that, except in danger of death, they could be absolved by no one, not even the Cardinal Major Penitentiary, but only by the Roman Pontiff.[137]

The second type of censure reserved personally to the Holy Father is the *latae sententiae* excommunication incurred for violation of the secret of the Holy Office. The obligation of the secret of the Holy Office binds all members of the Holy Office in all matters pertaining to their duties; [138] also all who perform any office in the Sacred Consistorial Congregation, in matters concerning the election, character, and conduct of bishops, administrators apostolic, and other ordinaries, or concerning the erection or union of dio-

[137] " . . . ita ut hanc legem violantes excommunicationem ipso facto incurrant, a qua, sicut ab alia quavis et contra quoslibet in hac Constitutione imposita et irrogata, seu infra imponenda et irroganda poena excommunicationis, a nullo, ne a Maiori quidem Poenitentiario, cuiuslibet facultatis vigore, praeterquam a Romano Pontifice, nisi in mortis articulo, absolvi possint."—Pius X, const. *"Vacante Sede Apostolica,"* n. 51.

[138] *Cf.* canon 243, § 2. *Cf.* Pius X, motu propr. "Romanis Pontificibus," 17 Decembris, 1903, n. 4: " . . . huius Congregationis [S. Officii] id proprium est, quod eius membra et officiales ad suum munus fideliter obeundum inviolatumque in omnibus et cum omnibus secretum servandum sub poena teneantur excommunicationis maioris latae sententiae, ipso facto et absque alia declaratione incurrendae, a qua nonnisi a Nobis atque a Nostris pro tempore Successoribus Romanis Pontificibus, privative etiam quoad S. Poenitentiariam ipsumque D. Cardinalem Poenitentiarium, praeterquam in articulo mortis, absolvi queant; . . ."—*Fontes*, n. 657. *Cf.* also Benedict XIV, const. *"Sollicita ac provida,"* 9 Iulii, 1753, § 12— *Fontes*, n. 426. Regarding the competence of the Holy Office, *cf.* canon 247. Before 1917 matters relating to indulgences were in the care of the Holy Office, but they were not included under the special secrecy of the Holy Office; *cf.* Ordo Servandus In Sacris Congregationibus, Tribunalibus, Officiis Romanae Curiae, 29 Iunii, 1908, 29 Septembris, 1908, Pars II, Cap. VII, Art. I, n. 11—*AAS*, I (1909), 80. In 1917, competence concerning the use and concession of indulgences was transferred to the Sacred Penitentiary; *cf.* Benedict XV, motu propr. *"Alloquentes proxime,"* 25 Martii, 1917, IV, V—*AAS*, IX (1917), 167. By the same *motu proprio* (nn. I-III—*Ibid.*), the Congregation of the Index was abolished, and its former competency regarding the prohibition of books was assigned to the Holy Office; but even before this change, this matter was included under the secret of the Holy Office—*cf.* Ordo Servandus In Sacris Congregationibus . . . ," Pars II, Cap. VII, Art. VII, n. 2—*AAS*, I (1909), 98.

ceses; [139] and besides, anyone who is requested, under the secret of the Holy Office, to give information regarding individuals considered for promotion to the episcopate.[140] For violation of the secret of the Holy Office, besides *ferendae sententiae* penalties, there is a *latae sententiae* excommunication from which, except in danger of death, no one but the Roman Pontiff, not even the Cardinal Major Penitentiary, can absolve, according to various documents regarding this secret of the Holy Office.[141]

The third censure reserved personally to the pope is the *latae sententiae* excommunication incurred for the violation of secrecy by anyone who takes part in processes of beatification and canonization as conducted by the Sacred Congregation of Rites.[142] This excommunication was likewise established in such a way that no one but the Roman Pontiff, excluding even the Cardinal Major Penitentiary, could absolve from it except in cases of danger of death.[143]

[139] For the formula of the oath taken in this Congregation, *cf.* Ordo Servandus In Sacris Congregationibus . . ., Pars II, Cap. VII, Art. II, n. 4—*AAS,* I (1909), 82, 83. It is called the "*Sancti Officii iusiurandum,*" and is, in part, as follows: "Ego N. N. sub poena excommunicationis latae sententiae ipso facto et absque alia declaratione incurrendae, a qua, praeterquam in articulo mortis, a nullo nisi a Summo Pontifice, ipso quidem Cardinali Poenitentiario excluso, absolvi possim, et sub aliis poenis etiam gravissimis arbitrio Summi Pontificis mihi in casu transgressionis infligendis, spondeo, voveo ac iuro, inviolabile secretum me servaturum in omnibus et singulis quae ad Episcoporum, Administratorum Apostolicorum aliorumque Ordinariorum electionem, vitam, mores agendique rationem delata sint; itemque in omnibus quae ad dioecesium erectionem seu earumdem unionem spectent, exceptis dumtaxat iis quae in fine et expeditione eorumdem negotiorum legitime publicari contingat: . . ."

[140] *Cf.* response of the S. C. Consist., 25 Aprilis, 1917—*AAS,* IX (1917), 232, 233.

[141] *Cf.* above, in the present chapter, notes 138, 139. *Cf.* also S. C. Consist., 25 Aprilis, 1917, ad IV: "Excommunicatione, a quo [qua?] nemo, nisi Ipse Romanus Pontifex, excluso etiam Emño Cardinali Maiori Poenitentiario, absolvere potest; aliisque poenis ferendae sententiae, quae contra violatores secreti S. Officii a iure statutae sunt."—*AAS,* IX (1917), 232.

[142] *Cf.* canon 2037, §§ 1-3. *Cf.* also Ordo Servandus In Sacris Congregationibus . . ., Pars II, Cap. VII, Art. VIII, n. 4—*AAS,* I (1909), 99; S. R. C., decr. 15 Octobris, 1678, § 1, n. 3, §§ 3, 4—*Fontes,* n. 5626.

[143] *Cf.* the formula of the oath, as given by S. R. C., decr. 15 Octobris,

Can these censures which are reserved personally to the pope be absolved by reason of canon 2254? This question is fraught with serious difficulties, which have led authors to adopt entirely divergent opinions. Since, among these censures reserved personally to the pope, the excommunications attached to delicts in the election of the Roman Pontiff are the only ones mentioned in the Code, it is usually in connection with the commentary on canon 2330 that this divergency of opinion is manifested. But the same solution, whatever it may be, will equally apply to the other excommunications reserved personally to the pope.

On the one hand, it is clearly stated that the censures for delicts in the election of the Roman Pontiff can be absolved only by the pope, and by no one else, even the Cardinal Major Penitentiary, except in cases of danger of death; and canon 2330 declares that, regarding these penalties, the constitution *"Vacante Sede Apostolica"* alone is to be followed. Again, there is some similarity between the wording of this constitution in its reservation of the absolution, and the wording of a decree of the Sacred Penitentiary reserving exclusively to itself, under certain conditions, the absolution of a priest who has attempted marriage. For a time it was held by some that this decree did not exclude canon 2254, but a declaration of the Sacred Penitentiary emphatically stated that the faculties of canon 2254 were of no avail for this case.[144]

On the other hand, canon 2254 provides for absolution in the more urgent cases from all *latae sententiae* censures *"quoquo modo reservatis,"* and it contains no restriction regarding censures reserved personally to the pope.[145] Besides, the jubilee faculties of 1925 and 1934 give some indication that these censures can be absolved

1678, §§ 3, 4. It is, in part, as follows: " . . . iuro . . . servare secretum . . ., sub poena periurii, et excommunicationis latae sententiae, a qua nonnisi a Summo Pontifice (excluso etiam maiori Poenitentiario) praeterquam in mortis articulo absolvi possim."

[144] S. Poenit., decr., 18 Aprilis, 1936—*AAS*, XXVIII (1936), 242, 243; declar. 4 Maii, 1937—*AAS*, XXIX (1937), 283, 284. This matter is treated in detail in Chapter X, Article IV.

[145] For an example of an explicit, though partial, restriction of this kind, *cf.* canon 239, § 1, n. 1.

by reason of canon 2254. By these faculties all confessors were empowered to absolve from all sins and censures reserved by law to the Roman Pontiff or to the ordinary, and also from *ab homine* censures; but the restriction was made that, in absolving from censures reserved personally to the pope or *specialissimo modo* to the Holy See, the confessor could act only according to the norm of canon 2254.[146] True, this is not conclusive that censures reserved personally to the pope are included under the normal scope of canon 2254, for it may be that the faculties for these censures were contained only in the special concessions for the jubilees. But it is certain that the power to absolve from censures reserved *specialissimo modo* to the Holy See does proceed from canon 2254, without the need of jubilee faculties; [147] and the indication seems to be that the Holy Father, in granting these most ample faculties, intended to allow the absolution from censures reserved personally to himself or *specialissimo modo* to the Holy See only *ad normam iuris communis,* that is, outside of danger of death, only in the more urgent cases, and with the obligation of recourse when morally possible.[148]

It may be that canon 2330, occurring in the Code under Part III on the penalties for various delicts, refers only to the substance of the penalties and the manner in which they are incurred in matters concerning papal election,[149] and not to their absolution; otherwise, one would expect to find in canon 2254 some phrase such as "*salvo praescripto can. 2330.*"

The similarity between the wording of the various documents regarding absolution from the censures reserved personally to the pope and the wording of the above-mentioned decree of the Sacred Penitentiary with its exclusive reservation, cannot be urged too strongly, for, besides the fact that this decree is clearly a derogation from canon 2254, the case in point in the decree is vastly dif-

[146] Pius XI, const. "*Servatoris Iesu Christi,*" 25 Decembris, 1925, pars de facultatibus, III, IV—*AAS,* XVII (1925), 615, 616; const. "*Quod superiore anno,*" 2 Aprilis, 1934, VIII, n. 3, IX, n. 1—*AAS,* XXVI (1934), 144, 145.

[147] *Cf.* S. Poenit., 21 Aprilis, 1921—*AAS,* XIII (1921), 239.

[148] "When morally possible"—that is, excluding the censure of canon 2367, for which recourse must always be made.

[149] This seems to be indicated by Sole, *De Delictis et Poenis,* n. 353.

ferent from the censures reserved to the pope, since it is uncertain whether or not the guilty priest will be willing and able to meet the requirements implied in his amendment after attempting marriage, and his absolution is to be granted by the Sacred Penitentiary with a special form of procedure and under certain precautions and conditions prescribed by the Holy Father. On this point, it seems significant that Rossi, who correctly interpreted the aforesaid decree of the Sacred Penitentiary as excluding canon 2254,[150] indicates that canon 2254 can be used for censures reserved personally to the pope, when he speaks of the manner of making recourse for such censures after absolution in the more urgent cases.[151]

Among the authors there are those who explicitly deny the applicability of canon 2254 to the censures of the constitution "*Vacante Sede Apostolica,*" [152] and those who merely repeat the words of the constitution, without reference to canon 2254, but apparently excluding the absolution in the more urgent cases.[153] On the other side, there are those who explicitly affirm that these censures can be absolved by reason of canon 2254 in the more urgent cases.[154]

If canon 2254 applies to the censures for delicts in papal elections, it also applies to the other *latae sententiae* excommunications reserved personally to the pope, namely, those concerning the secret of the Holy Office and the secrecy in causes of beatification and canonization. This is clear from the identical manner in which all these censures are reserved, and it is recognized by those who assert

[150] "S. Poenit. Apos., Decretum 18 Aprilis, 1936—Annotationes," *Apollinaris,* IX (1936), 587, 588. *Cf.* also the subsequent comment on Rossi's interpretation, in *Apollinaris,* X (1937), 175.

[151] "De sacerdotibus . . . ," *Perfice Munus,* XII (1937), 90.

[152] *E. g.,* Cerato, *Censurae Vigentes,* p. 188; Woywod, *Practical Commentary,* n. 2183, note 60; Pistocchi, *I Canoni Penali del Codice Ecclesiastico* (Torino, Roma: Marietti, 1925), p. 76.

[153] *E. g.,* De Meester, *Compendium,* III, P. II, 244; Cavigioli, *De Censuris,* n. 80; Salucci, *Diritto Penale,* II, 84. However, *cf.* Salucci, *op. cit.,* I, 226.

[154] *E. g.,* Cappello, *De Censuris,* n. 565, 2; Chelodi, *Ius Poenale,* p. 85, nota 1; Cipollini, *De Censuris,* pp. 237, 238; Cocchi, *Commentarium,* lib. V, p. 260; Vermeersch-Creusen, *Epitome,* III, n. 530.

in general that canon 2254 applies to censures reserved personally to the pope.[155]

To come to a conclusion on this point, now that the matter has been discussed, it seems that the opinion affirming that canon 2254 can be used in the more urgent cases for absolution from censures reserved personally to the pope is sufficiently strong, and that it can safely be followed in practice unless the contrary should be decided by the Holy See.

B. The Excluded Latae Sententiae Censure

It is necessary to mention here, in connection with the absolution from *latae sententiae* censures in the more urgent cases, that there is one such censure which cannot be absolved by reason of canon 2254. It is not the excommunication for absolution of one's accomplice *in peccato turpi,* for this certainly comes under canon 2254, § 1, but the only restriction is that it cannot be absolved without the obligation of recourse, as mentioned in canon 2254, § 3.

Briefly, for the subject is to be treated in detail elsewhere,[156] the *latae sententiae* censure which has been withdrawn from the faculties of canon 2254 is the excommunication, reserved *simpliciter,* incurred by a priest who has attempted marriage, and who, for very grave reasons, is compelled to remain under the same roof as his accomplice. If he promises that he will, and there are sufficient indications that he can, observe perfect chastity under these circumstances in the future, the Sacred Penitentiary will consider the case in a special form of procedure and, if the nature of the case warrants it, will grant absolution under certain precautions and conditions prescribed by the Supreme Pontiff.

[155] *Cf.* Cappello, *op. cit.*, n. 126, 8; *cf.* also Rossi, "De sacerdotibus . . . ," *Perfice Munus,* XII (1937), 90. However, Coronata (*Instit. Iuris Can.*, IV, 344), when speaking of the censures of the constitution *"Vacante Sede Apostolica,"* though not committing himself, says: "Non censetur tamen prohibita absolutio ad normam can. 2254"; but when treating of the secret of the Holy Office and the secrecy in causes of beatification and canonization (*op. cit.*, IV, 162), he makes no reference to canon 2254, but simply says: "Pro absolutione semper recurrendum est ad Sacram Poenitentiariam." The reason for this distinction is not evident.

[156] *Cf.* below, Chapter X, Article IV.

Consequently, in such a case, when a priest has attempted marriage and must continue to live in the same house with his accomplice, the confessor can do nothing by reason of canon 2254, but must submit the case to the Sacred Penitentiary, which will not absolve unless the reasons for continued dwelling with the woman are justifiable, and unless there is evidence that the guilty priest can and will observe perfect chastity in the future.[157]

C. *The Question of Ferendae Sententiae Censures*

Before this question can be properly discussed, it must be noted that this section is devoted exclusively to *ferendae sententiae* censures, and its caption is not "the question of *ab homine* censures." Now, all *ferendae sententiae* censures, after their infliction, are *ab homine*, whether they proceed from law or from a particular precept.[158] But not all *ab homine* censures are *ferendae sententiae*, for there can be *latae sententiae ab homine* censures, and these latter have already received special consideration.[159] Therefore, to avoid confusion, it is important to observe that the present discussion is concerned only with *ferendae sententiae* censures.

An opinion has been advanced that, in the more urgent case of hardship of remaining in grave sin, the confessor can absolve by reason of canon 2254 from any excommunication or personal interdict, regardless of whether it is *latae sententiae* or *ferendae sententiae, a iure* or *ab homine.*[160] Likewise, general statements have appeared to the effect that *ab homine* censures (apparently, therefore, both *latae sententiae* and *ferendae sententiae*) can be absolved in the more urgent cases, and that canon 2254 can be used for all censures without exception.[161] Again, it has been said that, although *ab homine* censures *per se* do not come under canon 2254, neverthe-

[157] S. Poenit., decr. 18 Aprilis, 1936—*AAS*, XXVIII (1936), 242, 243; declar. 4 Maii, 1937—*AAS*, XXIX (1937), 283, 284; both quoted below, Chapter X, Article IV.

[158] Canon 2217, § 1, n. 3.

[159] *Cf.* above, in the present article, A, 2.

[160] Kelly, *Jurisdiction of the Confessor*, p. 170.

[161] Cerato, *Censurae Vigentes*, pp. 28, 43; Pruemmer, *Man. Theol. Mor.*, III, 356. However, *cf.* Pruemmer, *Man. Iuris Can.*, n. 569, 7.

less the confessor can absolve from these censures, even after a condemnatory sentence, if they are utterly unknown in the place where the penitent is, or if recourse for faculties is impossible or extremely difficult and the penitent would otherwise have to remain for a long time in the state of grave sin.[162]

On the other hand, it has been said that censures which have been inflicted by a sentence—apparently, therefore, signifying *ferendae sententiae* censures, or at least including them—cannot be absolved by reason of canon 2254, since they are public, at least in law, and the reputation of the guilty party is no longer intact.[163]

What is to be thought of these varying opinions? To say that *ferendae sententiae* censures can be absolved in both or either of the more urgent cases seems to have absolutely no basis in the wording of canon 2254, and it is *per se* incorrect. It is true that this canon, because of the manner in which it is formulated, might momentarily lead one to conclude that *ferendae sententiae* censures can be absolved in the *casus urgentior* of hardship of remaining in grave sin, for the words *"censurae latae sententiae"* are enclosed in the clause which expresses the other *casus urgentior.* But in canon 2254 the general declaration is made that, in the more urgent cases, the confessor *"ab eisdem, quoquo modo reservatis, absolvere potest."* To what does the *"ab eisdem"* refer? Unless one could in some way interpret it as including the *"status gravis peccati,"* which would not produce a sensible rendering in the context [164] and would be at variance with the clear meaning of the original provision incorporated in canon 2254,[165] it is evident that the *"ab eisdem, quoquo*

[162] Cappello, *De Censuris,* n. 133, 5. It has been remarked before that Cappello, because of his opinion on *latae sententiae* censures as attached only to laws or general precepts, must be speaking of *ferendae sententiae* censures when he uses the term *"ab homine"; cf.* above, Chapter V, note 12.

[163] *Cf.* Cocchi, *Commentarium,* lib. V, p. 124.

[164] Besides, if this interpretation were proper, there would be no dispute about the inclusion of reserved sins under canon 2254, and those who hold the affirmative view on this point would not have to draw on analogy as the source of their opinion. This question is treated below, in E of the present article.

[165] *Cf.* S. C. S. Off., 16 Iunii, 1897—*Fontes,* n. 1187; quoted above, p. 59.

modo reservatis" can refer only to the "*censurae latae sententiae.*" [166]

Per se, then, canon 2254 concerns only *latae sententiae* censures. Properly so, for in inflicting *ferendae sententiae* censures, the superior or judge will provide that all danger of scandal or infamy will be obviated—otherwise he will not impose the penalty—and it is not easily presumed that a delinquent, who because of his persevering contumacy has been personally subjected to a *ferendae sententiae* censure, will suddenly find it so hard to remain in the state of grave sin that he cannot wait for the confessor to obtain the proper faculties from the superior.[167] Again, canon 2232 does not provide for the non-observance of a *ferendae sententiae* censure because of the danger of infamy, for it is presupposed that no such danger will arise from the observance of *ferendae sententiae* censures. Consequently, the case will rarely, if ever, occur in which the *casus urgentiores* will be verified for *ferendae sententiae* censures.

Suppose, however, that such a case does arise in which, for example, the superior has not guarded against the danger of scandal or infamy, or, despite all presumptions to the contrary, it is actually hard for the penitent to remain in grave sin until the proper superior can be approached for the faculty to absolve. As has been mentioned, Cappello [168] asserts that an *ab homine* censure inflicted by a sentence can be absolved in the more urgent cases if the censure or the sentence is unknown in the place in which the penitent is staying, or if the application for faculties to absolve would be impossible or extremely difficult, so that the penitent would be forced to remain in grave sin for a long time. With Coronata [169] one wonders at the arguments underlying this opinion. Yet one agrees with Coronata in not rejecting the conclusion, but rather accepting it.

[166] *Cf.* Blat, *Commentarium,* lib. V, p. 116; Coronata, *Instit. Iuris Can.,* IV, 179, 180; De Meester, *Compendium,* III, P. II, 184, nota 7; Cocchi, *Commentarium,* lib. V, p. 124.

[167] *Cf.* canon 2223. *Cf.* Collison, *Non Omnis Censura Ab Homine Est Reservata,* p. 60.

[168] *De Censuris,* n. 133, 5.

[169] *Instit. Iuris Can.,* IV, 179, nota 7.

However, it seems that a broader solution than Cappello's may properly be proposed. It has been, and still is, maintained here that *ferendae sententiae* censures are not included under the wording of canon 2254, and that *per se* this canon cannot be applied to them, not only because of the omission of reference to them in the text, but also because the *casus urgentiores* will hardly be verified in their regard. Law contemplates ordinary contingencies; at times it may provide for the extraordinary, or even for the exceptional, as in canon 2254; but it ignores the accidental. If a more urgent case occurs in connection with *ferendae sententiae* censures, this will be *per accidens*. But granting the possibility of such a supposition, one inquires if there is any norm for the extraordinary absolution of *ferendae sententiae* censures. For danger of death there is; for urgent cases there is not. Yet, neither is there any positive exclusion of extraordinary absolution from these censures in the more urgent cases—simply an absence of provision, apparently as being unnecessary. But, in the supposition that such an absolution should become necessary in the sense of the more urgent cases, what is to be done? There seems to be no reason why, from analogy, canon 20 should not be invoked for the application of canon 2254 to *ferendae sententiae* censures. In employing the analogy, one must avoid any arbitrary limitations or extensions of canon 2254. Accordingly, though this will rarely be the case, if there is danger of scandal or infamy from the observance of any *ferendae sententiae* censure which is *de facto* occult, it can be absolved; and if, by chance, it should be hard for the delinquent to remain in grave sin until the proper superior can be approached for faculties, any *ferendae sententiae* excommunication or personal interdict can be absolved. Obviously, the same obligations must be observed as for *latae sententiae* censures, namely, the obligation of recourse to the competent superior according to the norm of canon 2254, if it is morally possible, and the obligation of obedience to the mandates of the superior, with the observance, besides, of the prescription of canon 2251 regarding the effects of this sacramental absolution in the external forum.

The conclusion, then, in brief is: *per se, ferendae sententiae* censures do not come under 2254; *per accidens,* and by analogy, this canon can be applied if, in some unusual case, one of the more urgent cases should be verified in connection with a *ferendae sententiae* censure.

D. The Question of Vindictive Penalties

Concerning vindictive penalties, it may be briefly and summarily said that canon 2254 does not at all apply to them, for they are completely provided for in canon 2290.[170] It is worthy of note that in canon 2290 the suspension or dispensation of the *latae sententiae* vindictive penalties can be granted only for occult cases in which the guilty person would otherwise be exposed to the risk of giving scandal or suffering infamy. This is only to be expected, for vindictive penalties do not prevent the reception of the sacraments, and consequently the *casus urgentior* of hardship of remaining in sin, as in canon 2254, would be futile in canon 2290; and since the only more urgent case with regard to *latae sententiae* vindictive penalties is the danger of scandal or infamy, the application of canon 2290 is restricted to occult cases, for otherwise the danger would not be verified. Therefore, although canon 2254 is analogous in form to canon 2290 and supplies a norm for canon 2290, § 2, for cases in which recourse is morally impossible, nevertheless it has an entirely different object from canon 2290 and has nothing to do with vindictive penalties.

E. The Question of Reserved Sins

A fair amount of support has been given to the opinion that, by analogy, canon 2254 can be used for the absolution of reserved sins. The reasons usually alleged are that, since the confessor can

[170] Canon 2290. "§ 1. In casibus occultis urgentioribus, si ex observatione poenae vindicativae latae sententiae, reus seipsum proderet cum infamia et scandalo, quilibet confessarius potest in foro sacramentali obligationem servandae poenae suspendere, iniuncto onere recurrendi saltem intra mensem per epistolam et per confessarium, si id fieri possit sine gravi incommodo, reticito nomine, ad S. Poenitentiariam vel ad Episcopum facultate praeditum et standi eius mandatis.

"§ 2. Et si in aliquo casu extraordinario hic recursus sit impossibilis, tunc ipsemet confessarius potest dispensationem concedere ad normam can. 2254, § 3."

absolve according to canon 2254 from *reservata cum censura,* which is greater, he can also absolve *a fortiori* from *reservata sine censura,* which is less; also that the original decree of the Holy Office of June 23, 1886, on the more urgent cases and a subsequent response of the Sacred Penitentiary concerned both reserved cases and reserved censures.[171]

However, with Coronata [172] it must be said that the force of the analogy is not very compelling. For in canon 2254 there is question of an *absolutio ad reincidentiam,* by reason of which the penitent falls back into the same kind of censure if he does not fulfill the obligations prescribed *sub poena reincidentiae.* But such an absolution could not be given with regard to reserved sins, for here there is no question of falling back into the same kind of censure, since there was no previous censure, or even into the same kind of sin.

The argument from the wording of the decree of the Holy Office of June 23, 1886, is without weight, for, although reference was made to reserved cases in the question, the response confined itself solely to the momentous provision for reserved censures.[173]

Similarly, very little can be drawn, with regard to reserved sins, from the proposed decree of the Sacred Penitentiary of November 7, 1888. This declared that the old discipline for reserved censures was not to be retained for reserved sins, but it did not apply the new discipline for censures to reserved sins.[174]

[171] *Cf.* Cappello, *De Censuris,* n. 125; Cipollini, *De Censuris,* pp. 44, 45; Ferreres, *Instit. Can.,* II, n. 1009, d; Arregui, *Summarium Theol. Mor.,* n. 614, 2. Farrugia (*De Casuum Conscientiae Reservatione iuxta Codicem Iuris Canonici,* 2. ed., Augustae Taurinorum: Marietti, 1922, pp. 61, 62, 65) held that, in the more urgent cases, the reservation of sins reserved to the ordinary ceased by virtue of canon 900, and absolution could be given without the obligation of recourse; but in the same cases, sins reserved to the pope could be absolved only with the obligation of recourse according to the norm of canon 2254. However, on this question of the cessation of reservation by reason of canon 900, the distinction between sins reserved to the ordinary and sins reserved to the pope no longer obtains, because of a response of the Pontifical Commission in 1925, as will be noted presently.

[172] *Instit. Iuris Can.,* IV, 180.

[173] *Cf. Fontes,* n. 1102; quoted above, p. 56.

[174] *Cf. Collectanea S. C. P. F.,* n. 1695, ad 1.

If any argument were to be drawn for the assimilation of reserved sins and reserved censures under the altered discipline of 1886, it seems it should be found in the response of the Holy Office of June 17, 1891.[175] In this it was said that the penalty of reincurrence of the same kind of censure affected not only censures and cases reserved *speciali modo* to the Roman Pontiff, but also those reserved *simplici modo*. But even here, despite the wording *"a censuris et casibus,"* the response apparently refers only to reserved censures, for the question concerns the reincurrence of the same kind of *censure*, which does not apply to reserved sins.

There appears, therefore, to be very little, if any, basis for applying canon 2254 to the absolution of reserved sins.[176] The provisions for reserved sins and for reserved censures should rather be kept apart, for the norms of canon 900 for the cessation of reservation with regard to sins, and consequently for their absolution, certainly do not apply to the reservation and absolution of censures,[177] and conversely it would seem that the norms for reserved censures should not be applied to reserved sins.

Moreover, there is apparently no need for the use of canon 2254 for reserved sins, since they are amply provided for in canon 900.[178] The latter canon enumerates various circumstances in which any and all reservations of sins cease, and this includes the sins reserved to

[175] *Fontes*, n. 1137; quoted above, p. 57.

[176] *Cf.* Vermeersch, *Theol. Mor.*, III, n. 476, 3; Dargin, *Reserved Cases*, p. 86; Kelly, *Jurisdiction of the Confessor*, pp. 170, 171.

[177] "1. Utrum *quaevis reservatio*, de qua can. 900, sit tantum ratione peccati an etiam ratione censurae.

"R. Ad 1. Affirmative ad primam partem, negative ad secundam."—Pont. Comm., 10 Novembris, 1925, VII—*AAS*, XVII (1925), 583.

[178] *Cf.* Dargin, *Reserved Cases*, p. 86. He says: "This canon [2254] refers only to absolution from reserved censures; it does not refer to absolution from sins reserved *ratione sui*. This is clear from the word *"Censurae"* in the canon itself and from the fact that the Code has already provided for the cessation of reservation of sins in urgent cases, in canon 900, No. 2. Consequently, it is not correct to extend canon 2254 to reserved sins as some authors do."

the pope.[179] Among these circumstances is that in which, in the prudent judgment of the confessor, the faculty to absolve cannot be asked of the legitimate superior without grave inconvenience to the penitent.[180] Cappello, a strong proponent of the application of canon 2254 to reserved sins,[181] says that this *grave incommodum* mentioned in canon 900 need only be truly probable and is present especially in the following cases: if there would be particular difficulty in returning to the confessor; if it would be very hard (*valde durum*) for the penitent to remain in the state of grave sin for three days, two days, or one day, or even because of special circumstances, for a few hours; if it is morally impossible to defer the absolution until faculties can be obtained orally or by letter from the ordinary or the vicar forane, because of the necessity of saying Mass or receiving Communion, which cannot be omitted without the danger of scandal or infamy; likewise, if it is to be feared that the penitent, because of the deferred absolution, would lose his present good dispositions, and would go away undisposed and not return.[182] Evidently, then, the meaning of the *grave incommodum* effecting the cessation of the reservation of sins is practically the same, according to Cappello, as the meaning of the *casus urgentiores* in canon 2254; for the danger of scandal or infamy is interpreted in the same manner, and the hardship of remaining in grave sin is understood as extending over the same period of time, but in canon 2254 it need only be *durum,* while with reference to canon 900 Cappello says it must be *valde durum.* The only difference, therefore, between the *casus*

[179] "2. Utrum canon 900 agat de reservatione casuum ab Ordinariis tantum an etiam a Sancta Sede statuta.

"R. Ad 2. Negative ad primam partem, affirmative ad secundam."—Pont. Comm., 10 Novembris, 1925, VII—*AAS,* XVII (1925), 583. The doubt evidently arose from the fact that the declaration of the Holy Office of July 13, 1916, n. 7, from which this canon was drawn almost word for word, considered only sins reserved by ordinaries; *cf. Fontes,* n. 1302.

[180] Canon 900. "Quaevis reservatio omni vi caret:

"2. Quoties . . ., prudenti confessarii iudicio, absolvendi facultas a legitimo Superiore peti nequeat sine gravi poenitentis incommodo."

[181] *De Censuris,* n. 125.

[182] *De Poenitentia,* n. 554. Vermeersch-Creusen (*Epitome,* II, n. 179) speak in the same sense.

urgentiores of canon 2254 and the *grave incommodum* of canon 900 is found in the distinction, according to Cappello, between *durum* in the former and *valde durum* in the latter, regarding the hardship of remaining in grave sin. But this distinction is rather tenuous, and quite elusive in practice, and it has not been made by other writers on this point.[183]

Consequently, it seems that one may conclude with Rossi [184] that, although canon 2254 is not applicable to reserved sins, the same cases of urgent necessity will be sufficient for the cessation of the reservation according to canon 900,[185] and the confessor can absolve from them by reason of the provision of canon 900 and without imposing the obligation of recourse.

However, it must be noted that in the case of the two sins reserved *ratione sui* to the Holy See the obligation of recourse will be involved because of other provisions. Regarding the reserved sin committed by a confessor who absolves obstinate adherents of *L'Action Française,* recourse must always be made, even if the

[183] *E. g.,* Dargin (*Reserved Cases,* p. 34) says: "Reservation also ceases as often as the confessor prudently judges that he cannot ask for faculties without grave inconvenience to the penitent; examples of such grave inconvenience would be, if the penitent would suffer loss of reputation, if it would be very difficult for the penitent to return to confession, if he could not omit celebrating Mass or receiving Communion without causing scandal, if the penitent would feel it a grave hardship to remain in the state of mortal sin during the time necessary to obtain the faculty to absolve." *Cf.* also Farrugia, *De Casuum Conscientiae Reservatione,* pp. 61, 62. When it has been said above that the *casus urgentiores* of canon 2254 are practically the same as the *grave incommodum* of canon 900, this is meant in the sense that the same circumstances which permit the use of canon 2254 for the absolution of reserved censures actually effect the cessation of the reservation of sins; but it is not denied that the *grave incommodum* of canon 900 can be interpreted in a broader sense than the *casus urgentiores* of canon 2254.

[184] "De sacerdotibus . . .," *Perfice Munus,* XII (1937), 15, 16. *Cf.* also De Meester, *Compendium,* III, P. II, 185, nota 6; Genicot-Salsmans, *Instit. Theol. Mor.,* II, n. 400; Dargin, *Reserved Cases,* pp. 86, 89.

[185] *Cf.* Cappello, *De Poenitentia* (ed. 1929), n. 554; n. 560, 2; n. 597; n. 604, 1, 5°; from this, it is hard to understand why Cappello, in *De Censuris* (ed. 1925 et 1933), n. 125, speaks of the application, by analogy, of canon 2254 for reserved sins for cases in which the reservation does not cease by virtue of canon 900. *Cf.* also Wouters, *Man. Theol. Mor.,* II, n. 385, 2, b.

reservation ceases according to canon 900 or in any other way.[186] Likewise, it will be practically the same if the confessor absolves from the one sin reserved *ratione sui* by the Code to the Holy See, namely, that of false accusation of solicitation, as mentioned in canon 894. This crime is generally considered to be the same as that which is reserved *speciali modo* to the Holy See *ratione censurae,* as enacted in canon 2363, and even if the reservation of the sin would cease according to canon 900 in a more urgent case, the absolution from the censure would entail the obligation of recourse as in canon 2254.[187]

F. The Question of Irregularities

In more urgent cases there is an extraordinary provision for the dispensation from irregularities, but it is not canon 2254. Canon 990 states that, in occult more urgent cases in which the ordinary cannot be approached and there is danger of grave harm or infamy, any confessor can dispense from all irregularities arising from delicts, except those incurred through voluntary homicide or abortion and those brought to the judicial forum, but only for the purpose that the penitent can licitly exercise orders already received.[188]

[186] ". . . Huius reservationis ea vis est ut in illis quoque casibus, in quibus iuxta canonicas dispositiones quaevis reservatio cessat, onus adhuc remaneat praedictis sacerdotibus ad S. Poenitentiariam recurrendi, sub poena excommunicationis specialiter Sanctae Sedi reservatae, intra mensem a die obtentae sacramentalis absolutionis, vel postquam convaluerint si aegroti, et standi eius mandatis."—S. Poenit., decr. 16 Novembris, 1928—*AAS,* XX (1928), 398. *Cf.* also Pius XI, const. *"Quod superiore anno,"* 2 Aprilis, 1934, IX, n. 1—*AAS,* XXVI (1934), 145.

[187] This question is treated in some detail in Chapter X, Article II. If the delinquent should escape the censure through ignorance, it seems that the confessor would have to follow the norms of canon 2363 before absolving from the sin; *cf.* Pius XI, litt. apos. *"Carissime in Christo,"* 15 Augusti, 1928, Indultum quoad confessionem . . ., n. 1—*AAS,* XXI (1929), 17.

[188] Canon 990. "§ 1. Licet Ordinariis vel per se vel per alium suos subditos dispensare ab irregularitatibus omnibus ex delicto occulto provenientibus, ea excepta de qua in can. 985, n. 4 aliave deducta ad forum iudiciale.

"§ 2. Eadem facultas competit cuilibet confessario in casibus occultis urgentioribus in quibus Ordinarius adiri nequeat et periculum immineat gravis

Since irregularities do not prevent the reception of the Sacrament of Penance and the recovery of the state of grace, there can be no *casus urgentior* of hardship of remaining in grave sin, as in canon 2254, and the other more urgent case of danger of scandal or infamy is amply provided for in canon 990.

Canon 2254, therefore, has nothing to do with irregularities, either directly or by analogy, but the confessor who, absolving from a reserved censure according to the norm of canon 2254, finds that there is also an irregularity arising from the violation of that censure,[189] will do well to remember the provision of canon 990.

Article IV. The Recourse

A. Recourse—By Whom

When a confessor absolves a penitent from a reserved censure according to the norm of canon 2254, he is bound under pain of grave sin to enjoin upon the penitent, when it is morally possible, the obligation of recourse.[190] This obligation of recourse directly and immediately affects the penitent, and it is clearly a grave obligation, for if it is deliberately and culpably neglected, it entails the reincurrence of the same kind of censure.[191]

The penitent may fulfill the obligation of recourse in various ways, but *per se* he must fulfill it in one of these ways. He may write or go personally to the competent superior for the mandates, but in many cases this will be morally or physically impossible; he may supply for recourse by receiving a new absolution from a specially qualified confessor, according to the norm of canon 2254, § 2; but he must make the recourse *"saltem per epistolam et per*

damni vel infamiae, sed ad hoc dumtaxat ut poenitens ordines iam susceptos exercere licite valeat."

Canon 985. "Sunt irregulares ex delicto:

"4. Qui voluntarium homicidium perpetrarunt aut foëtus humani abortum procuraverunt, effectu secuto, omnesque cooperantes."

[189] *Cf.* canon 985, n. 7.

[190] Concerning the nature of recourse, *cf.* above, Chapter V, Article I, p. 90.

[191] *Cf.* Cappello, *De Censuris*, nn. 127, 129; Rossi, "De sacerdotibus . . .," *Perfice Munus*, XII (1937), 89.

confessarium" if he cannot make it in some other way.[192] However, to preclude any misunderstanding, it must be said immediately that the penitent is never obliged to go to a specially qualified confessor; he may do so if he wishes, but he is not bound to satisfy the obligation of recourse by obtaining a new absolution in this manner; and the recourse may be considered as morally impossible and sufficient for the application of canon 2254, § 3, even if it would be easy for the penitent to approach a confessor who possesses a special faculty.[193]

The minimum required, then, is that the penitent make the recourse through the confessor by means of a letter; if this is impossible, the penitent himself must, if he can, write or go personally to the proper superior for the mandates.[194]

It may happen that the confessor cannot write for the penitent, for example, because he will not see the penitent again. In such a case, it is sometimes said that it is sufficient for the confessor to demand that the penitent himself write to the proper superior, either through some other confessor or personally, asking, in this latter case, for the rescript *in forma gratiosa*.[195] But, although a penitent *may* go to another confessor and ask him to undertake the recourse,[196] it is by no means clear that he *must* do so. Again, it cannot be said here what may be the ability of penitents in other

[192] *Cf.* Cappello, *op. cit.*, n. 129; Cocchi, *Commentarium*, lib. V, p. 124; Coronata, *Instit. Iuris Can.*, IV, 181, 182. With Coronata (*loc. cit.*), there seems to be no objection to the confessor's making the recourse personally, by a visit to the proper superior, provided, of course, that the name of the penitent is withheld, as it would be in a letter, and that the seal of confession is safeguarded in every other way; contrary to Salucci (*Diritto Penale*, I, 227), who asserts that the professor can make the recourse only by letter.

[193] *Cf.* Coronata, *op. cit.*, IV, 182, 183; Vermeersch-Creusen, *Epitome*, III, n. 454, 4, 2°; Vermeersch, *Theol. Mor.*, III, n. 473, 4.

[194] *Cf.* Cappello, *De Censuris*, n. 129; Cipollini, *De Censuris*, p. 46; De Meester, *Compendium*, III, P. II, 186.

[195] *Cf.* De Meester, *loc. cit.*, basing his statement on various responses of the Sacred Penitentiary, especially that of November 7, 1888, ad 5, as in *Collectanea S. C. P. F.*, n. 1695. *Cf.* also Blat, *Commentarium*, lib. V, p. 117.

[196] *Cf.* Cerato, *Censurae Vigentes*, p. 41; Genicot-Salsmans, *Instit. Theol. Mor.*, II, n. 574, 3, b; Jone, "Die Absolutionsvollmachten in Todesgefahr," *TPQ*, LXXIX (1926), 20.

lands to write for mandates, expressing the case with sufficient thoroughness and clarity and asking for rescripts *in forma commissoria* or *in forma gratiosa;* but it is agreed with Kelly [197] that, at least in this country, it will be rare that the penitent, unless he is a priest,[198] will be able to write or go personally to the competent superior without serious inconvenience.[199] Therefore, when the penitent is personally incapable of making recourse (which will generally be the case), if the confessor is prevented by some grave reason from writing for the penitent, or if the penitent will not be able to return to the confessor without serious inconvenience, this will be the place to apply canon 2254, § 3, and to absolve without the obligation of recourse.[200]

Suppose, however, that the confessor can write for the penitent, and that the penitent can return to the confessor to receive the mandates of the superior. Is the confessor obliged to undertake the recourse? It is generally said that the confessor would be obliged *ex caritate,* though it is not certain whether the obligation would be light or grave.[201] However, it seems that a distinction is in order. If the penitent can make the recourse in some other way, but would prefer to be spared embarrassment, difficulty, or hardship (that is, not a serious inconvenience, for this would excuse from the recourse), then the confessor should, in charity, undertake the recourse, but it is not evident that he would be bound *sub gravi*

[197] *Jurisdiction of the Confessor,* pp. 172, 173.

[198] Or perhaps a major cleric, or also a religious regarding censures reserved to his own major superior.

[199] *Cf.* Arregui (*Summarium Theol. Mor.,* n. 617, 5) for the following general statement on recourse to the Sacred Penitentiary: "Raro poenitens recurrere poterit et volet: unde confessarius ipse ad S. Paenitentiariam scribat."

[200] *Cf.* Aertnys-Damen, *Theol. Mor.,* II, n. 994 *bis,* III; Kelly, *Jurisdiction of the Confessor,* pp. 172, 173. A priest's ability to make recourse personally, as mentioned, precludes the possibility of absolving from the censure for *absolutio complicis in peccato turpi* without the obligation of recourse, as specified in canon 2254, § 3. This matter in general is considered in the treatment of "moral impossibility" in canon 2254, § 3, as below, Chapter IX, Article I.

[201] *Cf.* Cappello, *De Censuris,* nn. 128, 129; Vermeersch-Creusen, *Epitome,* III, n. 454, 3, 1°; Aertnys-Damen, *op. cit.,* II, n. 994 *bis,* I; Rossi, "De sacerdotibus . . . ," *Perfice Munus,* XII (1937), 89.

to do so. But if the recourse can be made in no other way than by a letter written by the confessor, and he is not excused by any just cause, it would seem that the confessor would be bound *sub gravi* and *ex munere confessarii* rather than *ex caritate.* For the confessor is not free to dispense with the obligation of recourse and to apply canon 2254, § 3, according to his own convenience, but there must be a serious cause of moral impossibility before he is allowed to do so. The penitent clearly has a grave obligation to make the recourse, and, if he can make it in no other way, he *must* make it *saltem per epistolam et per confessarium.* Consequently, it seems that, when the recourse can be made in no other way than through the confessor, there is a corresponding grave obligation on the part of the confessor to undertake the recourse, and not merely from charity, but from his office as confessor.

A question has arisen as to whether the penitent is bound by the obligation of recourse if the confessor has failed to impose it upon him. Coronata [202] offers a defense of the negative view, saying that the obligation of recourse does not arise from the law, for the law does not command the recourse, but rather commands the confessor to absolve with a resolutive condition depending on the fulfillment of recourse; that if the condition is not attached, it does not exist; also that, when the law wishes to oblige the penitent to make the recourse without being informed of it, it clearly expresses this, as in canon 2252.

However, the opposite view, supported by Cappello,[203] seems without doubt to be the only true interpretation. The difference between canons 2252 and 2254 on this point is that in the former the legislator has left it to the prudence of the confessor to inform the penitent of recourse, while in the latter, since the same grave reasons do not exist for the omission of this information, the confessor is explicitly bound to impose on the penitent the obligation of recourse. The distinction, then, concerns only the confessor's obligation to impose the recourse, not the penitent's obligation to

[202] *Instit. Iuris Can.*, IV, 180, nota 7.

[203] *De Censuris*, n. 127. *Cf.* also De Meester, *Compendium*, III, P. II, 186; Rossi, "De sacerdotibus . . . ," *Perfice Munus*, XII (1937), 89, nota 4.

fulfill it. Besides, as has been mentioned before,[204] the resolutive condition, which is commonly understood as being implied in an *absolutio ad reincidentiam,* and which is based on the fulfillment of recourse, does not affect the manner in which the confessor imparts absolution. For this condition is not added by the confessor to the form of absolution, but it arises from the law, so that, while the confessor *per se* absolves absolutely, the reincurrence of a censure is effected by reason of the law if the penitent culpably fails to fulfill the obligation of recourse within the prescribed time when he becomes aware of it.

Therefore, it seems clear that, when the penitent is already aware of the obligation of recourse, he is bound by it whether or not the confessor explicitly imposed it upon him; likewise, that the penitent is bound by the obligation of recourse when he becomes aware of it, even though the confessor failed to inform him of it. If the penitent cannot write or go personally to the competent superior, but can return to the confessor to whom he made the former confession, he would be bound to do so, so that the recourse can be made through that confessor, unless the penitent prefers to take advantage of the provision of canon 2254, § 2. But if the penitent himself cannot write or personally go to the competent superior and cannot return to the former confessor, or if the latter refuses to make the recourse when requested, then, although the penitent can make recourse through another confessor, it is not clear that he is bound to do this; [205] and in such a case, he can be regarded as affected by a serious inconvenience, which will excuse him from the recourse, if it is evident that he will never

[204] *Cf.* above, in the present chapter, Article II, C, p. 158.

[205] There is no certainty that a penitent must go to another confessor, repeat his confession, and ask the new confessor to undertake the recourse, when the recourse cannot be made through the first confessor to whom the penitent originally made his confession. If the penitent would go to another confessor to ask him to make the recourse, it seems that there would be no question of a *poena reincidentiae* for subsequent failure of the penitent to return to this confessor for the mandates, since the penitent has followed a course of action which, though very commendable, is not clearly obligatory.

again see the first confessor, or will see him only after a very long time.[206]

Another question has arisen, namely, that which concerns the penitent's obligation of recourse, if the confessor has promised to undertake it but has actually failed to do so. Cappello[207] states that in such a case the penitent *can* make the recourse, if he wishes, but does not seem to be bound by any strict obligation, and therefore would not reincur the same kind of censure for failure to make the recourse. He adds that, if the confessor who has undertaken the recourse should die or depart from the place, not to return, it is doubtful whether the penitent is still bound to make recourse. But the reasoning behind these statements is not quite clear. The obligation of recourse immediately and directly affects the penitent, who must fulfill it in some way. One of the ways in which the penitent can fulfill this obligation is by a letter written by the confessor; and if this is the only way in which recourse can be made, which will generally be the case unless the penitent is a priest, then the penitent is bound to perform it in this way, and it seems that the confessor has a corresponding obligation to assume the burden. But the confessor acts only as the *agent* of the penitent, and it does not appear that the confessor can accept the obligation of recourse in such a way that the penitent is entirely relieved of it; otherwise, there would apparently be no obligation of the penitent to return to the confessor to receive the mandates from the superior. It must be understood, of course, that there is no question of reincurrence of a censure by the penitent while the confessor is supposed to be performing the recourse, for the penitent has acted according to the law, and there is certainly no sin and no contumacy in the interim. It is here maintained, then, that, however the recourse is performed, the obligation always pertains to the penitent as the principal, and, if the service of the confessor is requisitioned, his action is only the action of an agent. Consequently, it seems that in theory the only proper conclusion is that

[206] *Cf.* below, in the present article, F, p. 215; *cf.* also above, Chapter V, Article V, C, p. 122.

[207] *De Censuris*, n. 128, 17. *Cf.* also Coronata, *Instit. Iuris Can.*, IV, 182.

advanced by Rossi,[208] namely, that when the confessor has assumed the burden of recourse but has actually failed to perform it, whatever may have been the reason, the penitent is bound *sub poena reincidentiae* to make the recourse within a month from the time at which he discovers that the confessor has abandoned the recourse. For *per se* the penitent is bound by the obligation of recourse until it is fulfilled. But in practice, the same answer may be given here as has been offered for the preceding question. If the penitent cannot return to the original confessor, or if the latter refuses to accept the burden of writing for the mandates, then the penitent can, if he wishes, go to another confessor and ask him to accept the burden of recourse, or can go to a specially qualified confessor, as is indicated in canon 2254, § 2. But, unless the penitent is personally capable of recourse but prefers not to perform it personally, he is not bound to accept either of the two methods just mentioned, and would not be subject to the penalty of reincidence; and when he cannot without serious inconvenience personally write or go to the proper superior for the mandates, then, if this serious inconvenience may be regarded as lasting indefinitely, he can be considered as excused from the obligation of recourse.[209]

B. Recourse—To Whom

The recourse prescribed by canon 2254, § 1, is to be made *"ad S. Poenitentiariam vel ad Episcopum aliumve Superiorem praeditum facultate."* Whether the recourse is to be made to one or the other of these will depend on the nature of the censure which was absolved in the more urgent case.

If the censure absolved by reason of canon 2254, § 1, was a *latae sententiae ab homine* censure which the superior expressly reserved to himself, the recourse is made to that superior who inflicted it, or to his own competent superior, successor, or delegate, provided that the last-named is a canonical superior.[210] The same is to be said if, in some extraordinary case, a *ferendae sententiae* censure has been absolved according to canon 2254, § 1, by reason

[208] "De sacerdotibus . . . ," *Perfice Munus,* XII (1937), 89, nota 6.

[209] *Cf.* the references as indicated above, in the present chapter, note 206.

[210] *Cf.* canon 2245, § 2, with canon 2254, § 1.

of analogy, but in this case it is to be noted that, if the censure was inflicted by a judge who is not a canonical superior, he has no power to receive the recourse or to give the mandates.[211]

If the absolved censure was one reserved by common or particular law to the local or religious ordinary, the recourse is to be made respectively to one of those competent superiors who in law are considered as local or religious ordinaries.[212]

If the absolved censure was reserved *simpliciter* to the Holy See, and the case was occult, recourse can be made to the local ordinary; and if the penitent is a member of an exempt clerical religious institute, recourse can be made also to the competent major superior of the penitent, and this major superior will usually be the penitent's provincial or general.[213] For other censures reserved to the Holy See, recourse *per se* is to be made to the Sacred Penitentiary. However, it may be that the local ordinary or the apostolic delegate has a faculty to absolve and consequently is competent to receive recourse and give the mandates. So it may be best in most cases, unless it is clear that the local ordinary or the apostolic delegate would not have the proper faculty, and provided that there is no danger to the seal of confession, to make the recourse through one of these authorities.[214] The title used in such a case is *Reverendissime Domine,* instead of *Eminentissime Princeps,* for the latter is employed when the letter is sent directly to the Cardinal Major Penitentiary. If the local ordinary or the apostolic delegate is incapable of accepting the recourse, he will send the letter in proper form to the Sacred Penitentiary.

It is to be noted that the bishop is not competent to receive recourse simply by reason of his office, in cases of censures reserved to the Holy See, for it is clear from an analogous response on canon 2252 that the words "*praeditum facultate*" in canon 2254, § 1,

[211] *Cf.* canon 2236, § 3, with canon 2254, § 1. The competent superior in such a case would be the one in whose authority the judge acted, or also the Sacred Penitentiary, since the matter here treated concerns the internal forum.

[212] *Cf.* canons 198; 488, n. 8.

[213] *Cf.* canons 2237, § 2; 198; 488, n. 8.

[214] *Cf.* Kelly, *Jurisdiction of the Confessor*, pp. 174, 175.

qualify "*Episcopum*" as well as "*aliumve Superiorem.*"[215] Therefore, although the purpose of recourse is not to receive absolution or faculties for absolution, the bishop or superior must possess the power to absolve from the censure concerned before he can receive the recourse as a competent superior and give the mandates.

When the penitent was absolved by reason of canon 2254, § 1, from a censure reserved personally to the Roman Pontiff, the recourse can be made directly to the Holy Father, but it can also be made to the Sacred Penitentiary, and the Cardinal Major Penitentiary will take care of the case, either giving the mandates himself, if he should happen to have a faculty for a certain number of cases, or referring the matter to the Supreme Pontiff in a private audience.[216]

If a Greek-Ruthenian penitent, living in the United States, was absolved from a censure reserved to his ordinary, the recourse is made to that ordinary; namely, to the Greek-Ruthenian ordinary residing at Philadelphia, Pennsylvania, if the penitent is a Galician; to the Greek-Ruthenian ordinary whose chancery is situated at Homestead, Pennsylvania, if the penitent has come from, or is descended from a family which has come from Russian Podocarpathia, Hungary, or Jugo-Slavia.[217]

If an Oriental penitent of any rite has contracted one of the censures reserved *specialissimo modo* to the Holy See,[218] and has been absolved in virtue of canon 2254, § 1, recourse is to be made to the Sacred Penitentiary, which is competent in the internal forum in matters pertaining to Orientals.[219]

[215] Pont. Comm., 12 Novembris, 1922—*AAS,* XIV (1922), 663; quoted above, Chapter V, note 77.

[216] *Cf.* Cappello, *De Censuris,* n. 128, 16; Rossi, "De sacerdotibus . . . ," *Perfice Munus,* XII (1937), 90.

[217] *Cf.* S. C. pro Eccl. Orient., 1 Martii, 1929, prooemium et Art. 31—*AAS,* XXI (1929), 152, 157, 158. For the addresses of these two ordinaries, *cf. The Official Catholic Directory* (New York: Kenedy, 1937), pp. 593, 596.

[218] That Orientals are bound by the laws concerning these four censures, *cf.* S. C. S. Off., decr. 21 Iulii, 1934—*AAS,* XXVI (1934), 550.

[219] S. C. pro Eccl. Orient., 26 Iulii, 1930—*AAS,* XXII (1930), 394; quoted above, Chapter V, note 71. *Cf.* also the decree of the Holy Office as in the preceding note of the present chapter.

In the case in which a censure has been reincurred because of culpable failure to perform the required recourse after absolution either in a more urgent case or in danger of death, and absolution has been granted from the reincurred censure according to canon 2254, § 1, the recourse is exactly the same as for a censure which has been incurred for the first time, has not been complicated by reincidence, and has been absolved by reason of canon 2254, § 1. For the reincurred censure is the same in species as the original censure, whether *ab homine,* reserved to the ordinary or to the Holy See in any manner, or reserved personally to the pope.

Similar to the discipline existing immediately before the Code,[220] in no case can recourse, properly so-called, be made to a confessor who merely enjoys the faculty to absolve from the respective censure in the sacramental forum.[221] For the recourse must be made to the Sacred Penitentiary or to a bishop or other *superior* enjoying the faculty. The ordinary confessor who possesses a special faculty is not a superior, and the only part he can play is that in which the penitent personally comes to him in the tribunal of Penance to seek a new absolution according to canon 2254, § 2, and thus relieve himself of the burden of recourse that would otherwise have to be made to a competent superior.

C. *Recourse—For What Censures*

It may be said very simply and briefly that recourse is prescribed whenever any censure has been absolved by reason of canon 2254, § 1.[222] This implies two factors, namely, that the censure is a

[220] *Cf.* S. C. S. Off., 19 Decembris, 1900, ad 3—*Fontes,* n. 1249; quoted above, p. 61.

[221] *Cf.* Cappello, *De Censuris,* n. 128, 14. On this point there is much ambiguity in the works of authors (*e. g.,* Creusen, *Epitome,* III, n. 454, 3, 2°; Cocchi, *Commentarium,* lib. V, p. 124) who indiscriminately apply the term *recursus* to the application to a competent superior for his mandates and to the approach of a specially qualified confessor, as in canon 2254, § 2, for a new absolution. These notions are distinct and should not be confused. *Cf.* below, Chapter VIII, Article I, B, p. 221.

[222] It is not to be objected that the excommunication for *absolutio complicis* involves recourse even if it has been absolved according to canon 2254, § 3, for this censure cannot be absolved by reason of canon 2254, § 3, without

reserved censure, and that the confessor, in absolving, possesses no special faculty for the reserved censure he absolves, but uses the faculties of canon 2254, § 1. If the censure is not reserved, canon 2253, n. 1, is to be applied rather than canon 2254. If the censure is reserved, but the confessor has the faculty to absolve from it through some source other than canon 2254, then there is no need to use this canon, but again the confessor follows the norms for ordinary absolution as in canon 2253, nn. 2, 3; for example, when a confessor who enjoys the faculties of regulars absolves from a censure reserved by common law to the bishop,[223] or when a confessor, by reason of delegated diocesan faculties (in those dioceses in which the faculties are actually delegated by the bishop, and according to the extent in which they are delegated), absolves from a censure reserved by common law to the bishop or from an occult censure reserved *simpliciter* to the Holy See.[224]

The conclusion, therefore, is as follows: the recourse obliges when, and only when, some reserved censure, whatsoever be the manner in which it is reserved, has been absolved by reason of the faculties of canon 2254, § 1.

D. Recourse—When

According to canon 2254, § 1, the confessor can absolve, "*iniuncto onere recurrendi, sub poena reincidentiae, intra mensem* . . ." The penitent, then, is given a month within which he can comply with the obligation of recourse.

Canonists are not entirely at one in their consideration of the manner in which this month is to be computed. Coronata [225] asserts that the month is computed from the moment the absolution is given,[226] or from the day on which the obligation of recourse

the obligation of recourse, but only according to canon 2254, § 1, or theoretically but not practically, according to canon 2254, § 2. The above general statement, therefore, stands.

[223] *Cf.* Vermeersch-Creusen, *Epitome,* I, n. 727, 5; Aertnys-Damen, *Theol. Mor.,* II, n. 1067.

[224] *Cf.* canons 2237; 199.

[225] *Instit. Iuris Can.,* IV, 180, 181.

[226] *Cf.* canon 34, § 2. The same view seems to be held by Cocchi, *Com-*

becomes known to the penitent. Others [227] say that the month is calculated from the day of absolution or from the day on which the penitent becomes aware of the obligation of recourse. Cipollini [228] reckons the month according to canon 32, § 2, with canon 34, § 3, nn. 1, 4. Vermeersch-Creusen,[229] Roberti,[230] and Blat,[231] explicitly indicate that the day of the absolution is not included in the computation of the month, Roberti saying that the calculation is based on canon 34, § 3, nn. 1, 3, and Blat referring to canon 34, § 3, nn. 3, 4.

What, then, is the correct manner of computing this month allowed to the penitent for recourse?

The first supposition will be the case in which the penitent has been informed by the confessor of the obligation of recourse, or in which he knows of this obligation from some other source at the time of his absolution. The *tempus a quo* does not depend on the free choice of the penitent, and consequently the month would not be computed from moment to moment, as in canon 34, § 2; but the *tempus a quo* is explicitly assigned as the time of absolution, and therefore the computation must follow the norms of canon 34, § 3.

First, then, the month is to be taken as it is in the calendar and does not necessarily consist of thirty days.[232] Secondly, since it is hardly conceivable that the absolution will coincide with the beginning of the day, the day of absolution is not computed, and the month will be completed at the end of that day in the following month which numerically bears the same date as the day of absolution; for example, if the absolution was granted on January 6,

mentarium, lib. V, p. 124; Rossi, "De sacerdotibus . . .," *Perfice Munus*, XII (1937), 89.

227 *E. g.*, Cappello, *De Censuris*, n. 127; De Meester, *Compendium*, III, P. II, 186.

228 *De Censuris*, p. 45.

229 *Epitome*, III, n. 454, 3, 3°.

230 *De Delictis et Poenis*, I, Pars I, n. 318 (p. 364), as quoted by Raus, "Der Zusatz 'sub poena reincidentiae' . . .," *TPQ*, LXXXIX (1936), 126, 127.

231 *Commentarium*, lib. V, p. 117.

232 Canon 34, § 3, n. 1. *Cf.* also canon 32, § 2: ". . . nisi mensis et annus dicantur sumendi prout sunt in calendario."

the month allowed for recourse ends at midnight of February 6.[233] Thirdly, if the following month has not a day with numerically the same date as the day on which absolution was given, the month allotted for recourse will be completed at midnight of the last day of this following month; for example, if absolution was given on January 30, the month for recourse ends at midnight of February 28, or, in leap year, February 29.[234]

However, these various features of the computation should not create any confusion, for the confessor need only call to mind the date on which he is absolving, and then tell the penitent that the recourse must be made, under pain of reincurrence of the same kind of censure, before the end of the day in the next month which bears the same number; for instance, if he absolves on January 16, the recourse is to be made before midnight of February 16. Besides, the recourse in most cases will be made through the confessor, who will very likely not defer it till the last moment; if he should neglect it for over a month, he will *per se* be guilty of sin, but there will be no question of reincidence, either for the confessor, since he cannot reincur a censure which he never contracted, or for the penitent, for he is not at fault.

The month allowed for recourse is *tempus utile,* and consequently the time during which the penitent is unaware of the obligation of recourse or is unable to fulfill it is not computed.[235] Therefore, since the time is *tempus utile,* the obligation of recourse does not cease after a month of continuous time, when serious inconvenience has prevented the making of recourse during part or all of that time, but it perseveres during a month of days which offer opportunity for recourse. Apparently it is with reference to the computation of the month as continuous time that the statement is made that the time limit of one month is *ad urgendam obliga-*

[233] Canon 34, § 3, nn. 2, 3.

[234] Canon 34, § 3, n. 4.

[235] *Cf.* canon 35. *Cf.* Coronata, *Instit. Iuris Can.*, IV, 181; Cocchi, *Commentarium*, lib. V, p. 124; De Meester, *Compendium*, III, P. II, 186; Blat, *Commentarium*, lib. V, p. 117; Kelly, *Jurisdiction of the Confessor*, p. 173; Rainer, *Suspension of Clercis*, pp. 216, 217.

tionem rather than *ad finiendam obligationem.*[236] For the phrase *ad urgendam obligationem* is hardly to be applied to the time limit of one month in canon 2254, § 1, when it is calculated as *tempus utile*. The reason is that, when a month of *tempus utile* has passed, the penitent has failed to fulfill the obligation of recourse during a period which offered opportunity for recourse, and he immediately becomes subject to the penalty of reincidence. Thereupon, his obligation is not to make recourse for the censure previously absolved, but to seek a new absolution from the new censure.

It has been said [237] that, when the penitent has been impeded from making the recourse during the month, he must make it immediately upon the cessation of the impediment. This does not seem to be true. Since the supposition is that the penitent was prevented from making recourse, the continuous time of one month was not *tempus utile,* none of the time available for recourse has passed, and the penitent has a whole month of *tempus utile* after the cessation of the impediment for the fulfillment of his obligation. Again, it may happen that the penitent is impeded, for example, by sickness, from making recourse during part of the month indicated by the confessor for recourse, but has opportunity to make the recourse on other days. When the penitent is making the recourse personally, since he has a month of days on which there is opportunity for the fulfillment of his obligation, for every day on which he is entirely prevented from making recourse the original month is to be prolonged by an additional day. Each of such additional days must be available for recourse before being included in the period of *tempus utile,* and each is to be a full day of twenty-four hours from midnight to midnight.[238]

The foregoing matter on the first consideration, namely, the case in which the penitent knows of the obligation of recourse at

[236] *Cf.* Vermeersch-Creusen, *Epitome,* III, n. 454, 3, 3°; Cocchi, *loc. cit.*; De Meester, *loc. cit.*; Rossi, "De sacerdotibus . . . ," *Perfice Munus,* XII (1937), 89. Concerning the eventual cessation of an imposed obligation of recourse when its fulfillment continues to be impossible because of a grave inconvenience, *cf.* below, in the present article, F, p. 215.

[237] *Cf.* Rossi, *Ibid.,* nota 5.

[238] *Cf.* canon 32, § 1.

the time of his absolution, is also to be applied with due adaptation to the second consideration, namely, the case in which the penitent has been ignorant of the obligation of recourse. Theoretically, the obligation begins at the time of his absolution, but, since the month allowed is *tempus utile,* it is not actually computed until he becomes aware of the obligation.[239] When he does learn of this obligation, the month is to be computed in the same manner as has been indicated regarding the usual case in which the confessor informs the penitent of the obligation at the time of his absolution, except that the *tempus a quo* in this second instance is the time at which the penitent learned of the obligation of recourse.

Before this point can be concluded, it must be noted that it is sufficient that the recourse be *begun* within a month, and it is not necessary that the mandates of the superior be received by the penitent within the month, or even that the letter of recourse should have reached the superior within this time.[240]

E. Recourse—In What Manner

The point under discussion here concerns the manner of making recourse when this is done by letter, and the purpose is to indicate what must be expressed in this petition to the superior for his mandates.

In general, the recourse by letter is to be made in such a way that the case with all its necessary circumstances is exactly and properly stated, a fictitious name being used to designate the penitent.[241] The letter, then, is to contain the following elements: the title of the superior, *e. g., Eminentissime Princeps;* a fictitious name for the penitent; the nature of the censure or censures absolved, and the crime or crimes, with their number and any necessary circumstances, such as the fact that the crime is public, if such is

[239] Concerning the possibility of the cessation of the obligation of recourse because of ignorance, *cf.* below, in the present article, F, p. 215.

[240] *Cf.* above, Chapter V, note 92, on similar matter concerning the recourse after absolution in danger of death; *cf.* also Roberti, *De Delictis et Poenis,* I, Pars I, n. 318 (p. 364), as quoted by Raus, "Der Zusatz 'sub poena reincidentiae' . . .," *TPQ,* LXXXIX (1936), 126, 127.

[241] Cappello, *De Censuris,* n. 128, 13.

the case; mention that the penitent, properly disposed, was absolved in a more urgent case according to the norm of canon 2254, § 1; expression of the fact that the penitent is prepared to accept and fulfill the mandates of the superior; indication of any unusual circumstances which would hinder the penitent from performing in their entirety the mandates ordinarily prescribed for the case in question; the date; the real name and address of the confessor to whom the mandates are to be sent. These factors will be sufficiently expressed if the letter is worded according to the formulae to be found in Appendix I of this work, with proper adaptations as demanded by the nature and particular circumstances of the individual case.

Special information must be added to the above in cases in which recourse is made to the Sacred Penitentiary regarding the censure for ***absolutio complicis in peccato turpi.*** The quality of the delinquent priest must be indicated, *e. g.*, whether he is a pastor or an assistant. Mention must likewise be made of the number of accomplices he has absolved since his last confession, or the number of times he has absolved the same accomplice.[242] The letter of recourse may also include reference to the manner in which the censure was contracted, whether by absolving the accomplice, or by pretending to absolve, or by absolving after inducing the accomplice not to confess the sin of complicity which had not yet been remitted.[243] Again, it will be proper to suggest, if the case warrants it, that the guilty priest will not be able to withdraw from his office as pastor, because of serious reasons, for a certain period of time.[244] According to these divergent factors the mandates of

[242] *Cf.* Vermeersch, *Theol. Mor.*, III, n. 502.

[243] *Cf.* canon 2367. Included also under canon 2367, § 2, is the case in which a confessor has persuaded a person, either within or outside of sacramental confession, that impure actions to be committed by them are not sinful or at least not gravely sinful, and then has absolved or pretended to absolve the person when the latter mentioned only other sins in confession; *cf.* S. C. S. Off., decr. 16 Novembris, 1934—*AAS*, XXVI (1934), 634. Regarding the reference to the various types of this crime in the letter of recourse, *cf.* Arregui, *Summarium Theol. Mor.*, n. 617 (p. 408), nota 1.

[244] *Cf.* Cappello, *De Censuris*, n. 580.

the Sacred Penitentiary will very probably vary to a considerable degree.

The matter will offer little difficulty in any case in which the confessor can write the letter of recourse and the penitent can return to him to accept the mandates of the superior. If the confessor cannot write within a month, or the penitent cannot return to him when the mandates will reasonably be expected, and the recourse cannot be made in any other way, the confessor should absolve according to canon 2254, § 3. But such an absolution, without the obligation of recourse, cannot be granted for the censure contracted for *absolutio complicis.*[245] Consequently, in this case the recourse must be made in some way, and there are various ways in which the obligation can be fulfilled.

First, the priest who has contracted the censure of canon 2367 and has been absolved according to canon 2254, § 1, may go to some other confessor to whom he can return for the mandates, explain the case to him, and ask him to undertake the recourse.[246]

Secondly, the priest may write the letter of recourse himself, using a fictitious name, expressing the wording of the formula in the first person instead of the third, and asking that the mandates be sent to some confessor, whose real name and address he mentions in the letter.[247] He then notifies the confessor, either in or outside of confession, that the mandates are to be expected, and he subsequently goes to the confessor to receive the mandates when they arrive from the Sacred Penitentiary.

Thirdly, the priest may, if he wishes, write personally to the Sacred Penitentiary, expressing the formula in the first person, signing his own name and address, and asking that the mandates be sent to him *in forma gratiosa,* so that there will be no need of an executor of the rescript.[248]

[245] Canon 2254, § 3. *Cf.* the discussion of this matter in Chapter IX, Article V, A, p. 255.

[246] *Cf.* above, in the present chapter, note 196.

[247] *Cf.* Arregui, *Summarium Theol. Mor.*, n. 617 (p. 408), nota 1, formula 2; Salucci, *Diritto Penale,* I, 231, nota 1, formula 2; Bargilliat, *Praelectiones Juris Canonici,* I, n. 545, c.

[248] *Cf.* De Meester, *Compendium,* III, P. II, 186.

Fourthly, when the guilty priest is being absolved by a confessor to whom he cannot return, he can act in the following manner. The penitent gives this confessor the name and address of another confessor to whom the penitent will be able to go to receive the mandates. The first confessor writes the letter of recourse in the usual way, but asks that the mandates be sent to that confessor whom the penitent-priest has indicated. In the meantime, the penitent goes to the second confessor and advises him (in the confessional, if the penitent wishes to conceal his identity), that the mandates will come from the Sacred Penitentiary, and that he will return to this second confessor to accept the mandates.[249]

Fifthly, Cappello [250] asserts that, when the confessor will not see the priest-delinquent again, the ordinary method of handling the recourse is the following. The confessor asks the priest his name and address. Then the confessor writes to the Sacred Penitentiary, explaining the case in the usual manner, but asking permission to transmit the mandates to the penitent by mail. Then, when the confessor receives the mandates, he sends them to the penitent, using the name and address he has previously learned from him. However, if the guilty priest does not wish to give his name and address to the confessor—and he can never be obliged to do so [251]—he may choose one of the other methods of making recourse, but the recourse must be made in some way.

A letter of recourse to a local or religious ordinary, or to any competent superior below the Holy See, will usually be written in the vernacular, or possibly in Latin; that to the Sacred Penitentiary may be written in any language, but Latin is preferable.[252]

Since it is "sacred and inviolable" that absolutely nothing done by the officials of the Sacred Penitentiary should be other than gratuitous,[253] there is no need of sending any fee with the letter of

[249] *Cf.* Cappello, *De Censuris,* n. 582, for a formula which implies this manner of proceeding.

[250] *Op. cit.*, n. 131, 3, n. 580.

[251] *Cf.* Genicot-Salsmans, *Instit. Theol. Mor.*, II, n. 574, 3, c.

[252] *Cf.* Cappello, *De Censuris,* n. 128, 16; Coronata, *Instit. Iuris Can.*, IV, 182; Pruemmer, *Man. Theol. Mor.*, III, 304.

[253] Pius XI, const. *"Quae divinitus Nobis,"* 25 Martii, 1935, n. 10—*AAS,* XXVII (1935), 111, 112.

recourse to the Sacred Penitentiary. However, the sending of a small sum to cover the cost of return postage is not prohibited.

The letter is to be sealed securely and is to be sent directly to the proper superior, or, if the nature of the case requires, directly to the Sacred Penitentiary.[254] Although the name of the penitent is fictitious, under no circumstances is a confessor to send the details of a case to a procurator or agent, so that the latter may prepare the case better for presentation to the Sacred Penitentiary. If the services of an agent are employed, any letter of recourse sent to him to be presented to the proper superior or Sacred Penitentiary must be enclosed in a separate envelope, which he is strictly forbidden to open, for, although there is hardly any possibility of his knowing the identity of the penitent concerned, he is not to be acquainted with matters of conscience or with anything pertaining to sacramental confession.[255]

F. Recourse—The Excusing Cause

The recourse prescribed by canon 2254, § 1, is to be performed *"si id fieri possit sine gravi incommodo."* The serious inconvenience mentioned in this paragraph of canon 2254 is sometimes considered as the correlative of the moral impossibility provided for in canon 2254, § 3, in such a way that the serious inconvenience is expressed as a saving clause referring to § 3, and the moral impossibility is simply an explanation of the serious inconvenience in § 1.[256] But the provision of canon 2254, § 3, is sufficient in itself to derogate from the obligation of recourse in canon 2254, § 1, without any need of a saving clause in the latter paragraph. The better interpretation, therefore, seems to be that suggested by Cipollini,[257] that the

[254] This is not to be understood as precluding the possibility of making recourse to the Sacred Penitentiary through the bishop or the apostolic delegate.

[255] *Cf.* S. Poenit. monitum (without date)—*AAS*, XXVII (1935), 62; Schaaf, "The Seal of Confession: New Precautions," *Ecclesiastical Review*, XCII (1935), 540, 541. *Cf.* also S. C. S. Off., instr. 9 Iunii, 1915—not in *AAS*, but translated in Bouscaren, *Canon Law Digest*, I, 413, 414.

[256] *Cf.* Coronata, *Instit. Iuris Can.*, IV, 182.

[257] *De Censuris*, p. 48. Cappello (*De Censuris*, n. 128, 11) seems to indicate the same notion but is not so clear as Cipollini

moral impossibility of § 3 refers to the case in which the confessor foresees at the time of the confession that the recourse will be morally impossible and consequently absolves without the obligation of recourse; while the serious inconvenience in § 1 concerns the case in which the confessor, not foreseeing any difficulty of recourse, imposes the obligation when he absolves, but a serious inconvenience subsequently arises to prevent the recourse.

In general, it may be said that the *grave incommodum* need not be certain, but is sufficient if it is truly probable; that it can be spiritual or temporal, moral or physical, affecting oneself or involving another; and that ordinarily it will consist in a danger of scandal or infamy because of the fact that the penitent's crime is liable to become known to unauthorized persons through revelation of the contents in the letter of recourse or in the mandates of the superior.[258] Before the time of the present Code it was declared that the general danger that the letters might be opened by civil authorities was not sufficient to excuse from the obligation of making recourse, since the true name of the penitent was not to be mentioned in the letter.[259] But if there should actually be danger in a particular case that the letter would be opened by someone other than the proper authority, and that the identity of the penitent would become known, with the consequent danger of scandal or infamy or of violation of the seal of confession, then such danger would clearly be a sufficient cause at least to defer the recourse.[260]

The grave inconvenience may be of various kinds. For instance, the confessor has sent the letter of recourse, but the penitent cannot now return to him to receive the mandates of the superior because of ill health, or because of an unexpected change of residence to a

[258] *Cf.* Cappello, *De Censuris*, n. 128, 11.

[259] "6. Utrum tuta conscientia doceatur et in praxim deducatur, ut quidam volunt, propter hodiernum periculum ne aperiantur epistolae a potestate civili, non requiri ut epistola ad Summum Pontificem dirigatur in casibus urgentioribus, vel quando adiri nequit Papa.

"R. Ad 6. Negative, cum in precibus nomina et cognomina sint supprimenda."—S. Poenit., 7 Novembris, 1888—*Collectanea S. C. P. F.*, n. 1695.

[260] *Cf.* Coronata, *Instit. Iuris Can.*, IV, 184; Cappello, *De Censuris*, n. 128, 11; De Meester, *Compendium*, III, P. II, 188; Cocchi, *Commentarium*, lib. V, p. 126.

place at a great distance from the confessor, and the penitent cannot write or go personally to the superior. But it would be as futile as it is impossible to attempt an enumeration of the ways in which a *grave incommodum* might arise. A prudent judgment will dictate whether or not the circumstances in a particular case constitute a serious inconvenience preventing recourse.

The serious inconvenience will be tantamount to moral impossibility of making recourse and, since it is here considered in the case in which it arises after the obligation of recourse has been imposed, it is evident that it will at least suspend that obligation. When the grave inconvenience ceases, the recourse must be undertaken within the proper time and according to any required manner that is possible,[261] for *per se* the obligation of recourse remains until it is fulfilled.

Can the obligation of recourse eventually cease because of the persistence of a grave inconvenience? And another question regarding the cessation of the obligation of recourse may here be asked, namely,—can a long-continued ignorance of this obligation ultimately bring about its cessation?

These two questions have been treated together in some detail in reference to the recourse after absolution in danger of death.[262] It will suffice here, then, to restate the conclusions deduced in that discussion, namely: if a serious inconvenience preventing recourse, or if ignorance of the obligation of making recourse, lasts for a *very long time,* or if the serious inconvenience is foreseen as destined to last for a *very long time,* then the obligation can be considered as not binding; and a very long time, according to an analogy drawn from the old law, can be regarded as that which extends over at least five years, over an indefinite period of time (provided that it is not clearly less than five years), or over one's lifetime.

G. *Recourse—The Sanction*

The obligation of recourse binds the penitent "*sub poena reinci-*

[261] This is to be understood according to what has been said above regarding the computation of time for the recourse and the ways in which recourse is to be performed; *cf.* above, in the present article. D, p. 205; A, p. 195.

[262] *Cf.* above, Chapter V, Article V, C, D, p. 121 ff.

dentiae," so that if he culpably fails to make the prescribed recourse within the required time, he reincurs the same kind of censure as that from which he was absolved. Therefore, whatever may have been the nature of the original censure absolved by reason of canon 2254, § 1, whether it was *ab homine* or *a iure,* whether reserved to the ordinary, or to the Holy See in any manner, or personally to the pope, the reincurred censure is specifically the same. Except for the following two points of variation—namely, that reincidence according to canon 2254 applies to all reserved censures, while that of canon 2252 concerns only reserved *ab homine* censures and censures reserved *specialissimo modo* to the Holy See, and that the obligation of recourse *per se* begins after absolution in the more urgent cases, but only after recovery from danger of death—what has been said of reincidence with reference to canon 2252 will also apply to the sanction determined in canon 2254. Therefore, these two easily recognizable factors being excluded,[263] the same is to be said here as has been discussed in connection with reincidence for failure to make recourse after recovery from danger of death, and it is considered sufficient here to indicate the conclusions and to refer back to the previous discussion.[264]

The conclusions, in general, are as follows. Since there is question of the reincurrence of a *new* censure, specifically the same but numerically distinct from the former censure, all the requisites for the incurrence of a censure must be verified; so the penitent must know of the penalty and must not be affected by any cause that would preclude grave sin or that would otherwise excuse him from contracting the censure, such as ignorance, inadvertence, or forgetfulness.[265] This being presupposed, the penitent who does not, within a month of time which daily offers opportunity (*tempus utile*), write or go personally to the proper superior for his mandates, or entrust to the confessor the writing of the letter of re-

[263] Obviously there is excluded also the consideration of reincidence in the case in which the confessor has applied canon 2254, § 3, when absolving in danger of death; this will be treated in detail under canon 2254, § 3.

[264] *Cf.* Chapter V, Article VI, p. 124.

[265] *Cf.* above, Chapter V, notes 110, 116, 117; *cf.* also Cipollini, *De Censuris*, p. 47; Blat, *Commentarium*, lib. V, pp. 116, 117.

course, relapses into the same kind of censure as that from which he was absolved. Likewise, when the letter of recourse has been written by the confessor (and the recourse need only be *begun* within the month allowed by canon 2254, § 1), if the penitent does not return to him to accept the mandates of the superior within the time reasonably determined by the confessor, he reincurs the same kind of censure, provided that the confessor did not demand that the penitent return to him in less time than a month of *tempus utile* after absolution as allowed by the law.[266]

Article V. The Mandates

The nature of the *mandata,* the gravity of the obligation to obey them, and the question of reincidence in cases in which they are not fulfilled, have all been treated at considerable length when this matter was discussed in relation to canon 2252.[267] It has been stated in that place that the question of reincidence for failure to obey the mandates is regarded in this work as being exactly the same both in canon 2252 and in canon 2254, § 1,[268] and the nature of these mandates and the obligation to obey them are likewise the same. Lest repetition become endless, only the main conclusions will be restated here, while the development of the arguments will be found in the previous discussion on the mandates under canon 2252.

First, the obligation of obedience to the mandates binds without doubt under pain of grave sin.[269]

Secondly, there is the question of reincidence, when this penalty is not expressly stated in the mandates of the superior or provided

[266] *Cf.* above, Chapter V, notes 112, 113.

[267] *Cf.* above, Chapter VI, p. 129 ff.

[268] All authors who have been consulted on this point are consistent in their view, either affirmative or negative, concerning reincidence in canons 2252 and 2254, § 1, with the exception of Salucci, who, when treating canon 2252 (*Diritto Penale,* I, 220), argues at length that the censure is not reincurred through failure to obey the mandates, but in discussing canon 2254, § 1 (*op. cit.,* I, 226), simply asserts that both the recourse and the obedience to the mandates are *sub poena reincidentiae.*

[269] *Cf.* above, Chapter VI, Article II, A, p. 130.

for by particular norms,[270] but when the obligation of obedience and the question of the penalty depend on the wording of canon 2254, § 1. Despite the opinion of those who claim that obedience to the mandates binds *sub poena reincidentiae*,[271] the view that the obligation does not bind under this penalty has sufficient grounds to be held safely in practice,[272] and the obligation to obey the mandates will be sufficiently provided for by the norms of moral theology regarding the subsequent absolution of the penitent who refuses to fulfill a grave obligation.[273]

[270] *Cf.* S. Poenit., monita, 31 Iulii, 1924, V, concerning the obligation of penitents to obey, *sub poena reincidentiae,* the orders of the ordinary when they have been absolved from public censures by reason of jubilee faculties—*AAS,* XVI (1924), 338, 339.

[271] *Cf.* above, Chapter VI, notes 9, 10.

[272] *Cf.* above, Chapter VI, notes 12, 13; also Chapter VI, Article II, B, in its entirety; *cf.* also Coronata, *Instit. Iuris Can.,* IV, 182, nota 4; Chelodi, *Ius Poenale,* p. 43; Raus, "Der Zusatz 'sub poena reincidentiae' beim kirchenrechtlichen Rekurs gemäss can. 2254, § 1," *TPQ,* LXXXIX (1936), 125; Roberti, *De Delictis et Poenis,* I, Pars I, nn. 318, 323, as quoted by Raus, *loc. cit.*

[273] *Cf.* above, Chapter VI, notes 28, 29.

CHAPTER VIII

THE ALTERNATIVE METHOD—CANON 2254, § 2

Canon 2254, § 2. Nihil impedit quominus poenitens, etiam post acceptam, ut supra, absolutionem, facto quoque recursu ad Superiorem, alium adeat confessarium facultate praeditum, ab eoque, repetita confessione saltem delicti cum censura, consequatur absolutionem; qua obtenta, mandata ab eodem accipiat, quin teneatur postea stare aliis mandatis ex parte Superioris supervenientibus.

ARTICLE I. THE CIRCUMSTANCES

A. *"Etiam post acceptam absolutionem"*

WHEN a penitent has been absolved from a reserved censure by reason of canon 2254, § 1, with the obligation of recourse, he may still go to some confessor who has a special faculty for that censure, receive absolution after confessing again at least the crime and censure, and thus free himself from the obligation of recourse, or, if recourse has already been made, from the obligation of obeying the mandates that will subsequently come from the superior. Before the legislation of the Code there was a controversy on this question, but it has been definitely settled in canon 2254, § 2.[1]

Since canon 2254, § 2, from its very wording—*"nihil impedit quominus . . . "*—is a privilege and a benefit to the penitent, it is to be understood in the sense that, although the penitent may avail himself of it if he wishes, he is never obliged to accept it.[2]

The opinion has been advanced that, since canon 2254, § 2, says *"etiam post acceptam, ut supra, absolutionem,"* the provision of this paragraph cannot be used *ante acceptam absolutionem,* for the

[1] *Cf.* Cappello, *De Censuris,* n. 130, 6.

[2] *Cf.* Coronata, *Instit. Iuris Can.,* IV, 182, 183; Vermeersch-Creusen, *Epitome,* III, n. 454, 4, 2°; Vermeersch, *Theol. Mor.,* III, n. 473, 4.

hypothesis is that the penitent is to go to some specially authorized confessor different from the first confessor.[3] But, unless something is here being overlooked in the discussion of this point, there is no difficulty whatsoever.[4] If the penitent goes to a specially authorized confessor without having previously been absolved according to canon 2254, § 1, the provision of canon 2254, § 2, is unnecessary, for the confessor simply uses his special faculty[5] according to the norm of canon 2253, without imposing any obligation of recourse. But if the penitent goes to a specially authorized confessor after having been absolved by virtue of canon 2254, § 1, then the provision of canon 2254, § 2, is very necessary to preclude the notion that, since absolution has already been granted with the obligation of recourse, the faculty of the specially authorized confessor is no longer of any avail. The above-mentioned opinion must not be accepted in the sense that a specially authorized confessor cannot use his faculty until the penitent has been absolved from a reserved censure in a more urgent case according to the norm of canon 2254, § 1; this would indeed be unintelligible. The conclusion, therefore, is that a specially authorized confessor can use his special faculty whether the penitent has or has not been already absolved according to canon 2254, § 1.[6] But if the confessor employs his special faculty in a case in which absolution has not previously been granted according to canon 2254, § 1, he is following the norm, not of canon 2254, § 2, but of canon 2253, n. 2 or n. 3.

[3] *Cf.* De Meester, *Compendium,* III, P. II, 187, nota 4.

[4] It may be that De Meester's interpretation of canon 2254, § 2, as a form of recourse has led him to this conclusion. As noted under the following heading, this acceptance of canon 2254, § 2, is not admitted in this work.

[5] This term "special faculty" is not used in this discussion in the restricted sense attached to it in canon 2253, n. 3, as being that particular faculty which empowers its possessor to absolve in ordinary cases from censures reserved *speciali modo* to the Holy See; but it is used in the general sense as being some faculty which a confessor enjoys for a reserved censure outside of danger of death and the more urgent cases. Such a confessor is referred to in the present discussion and throughout the work as a "specially authorized confessor" or a "specially qualified confessor," as distinguished from a "simple confessor."

[6] *Cf.* Cappello, *De Censuris,* n. 130, 1; Coronata, *Instit. Iuris Can.,* IV, 183.

It will ordinarily be the case that the specially authorized confessor of canon 2254, § 2, will be different from the confessor who absolved the penitent according to canon 2254, § 1. However, the distinction between confessors as implied by the canon rests rather on the differentiation between confessors who are specially authorized and confessors who enjoy no special faculty, and it is not necessarily based upon the specification of separate individuals. Consequently, if it should happen that the same confessor, who has absolved the penitent with the obligation of recourse, should subsequently obtain a special faculty for the absolved censure, and if the penitent should return to him before the recourse is begun or before the mandates of the superior are received, there appears to be no reason why the confessor cannot use this special faculty according to the norm of canon 2254, § 2, even though in identity he is not an *alius confessarius.*

B. "Facto quoque recursu"

The penitent's presentation of himself to a privileged confessor as contemplated in canon 2254, § 2, is rather widely accepted as a form of recourse, with more than a few authors using the terms *"recursus"* and *"recurrere"* to express it.[7] It cannot be denied that these terms are broad enough to express what is meant in canon 2254, § 2; the only objection is that they seem too broad and much wider in meaning than the terms *"recurrendi"* and *"recursus"* in canon 2254, §§ 1, 3, and consequently are apt to create confusion. For "recourse," in its use in canon 2254, §§ 1, 3, is to be understood in a strict, technical sense as an application for mandates after absolution has been received; but if *"recurrere"* is used to express the provision of canon 2254, § 2, it has the broader and more general meaning of "to go" to a specially authorized confessor. Not the term *"recurrat,"* but *"adeat,"* has been used in canon 2254, § 2, and it is respectfully suggested that the notions be kept apart, as they have been in the canon.[8]

[7] *Cf.* Coronata, *Instit. Iuris Can.*, IV, 183; De Meester, *Compendium,* III, P. II, 187; Creusen, *Epitome,* III, n. 454, 3, 2°; Cocchi, *Commentarium,* lib. V, p. 124; Cappello, *De Censuris,* n. 130, 1, 2 (however, *cf. op. cit.*, n. 128, 14).

[8] Cerato (*Censurae Vigentes,* p. 44), has used the words *"adire"* and

The penitent's appearance before a specially authorized confessor, although it is somewhat similar to recourse and indeed supplies for recourse, is not strictly a recourse as the term is used in canon 2254, §§ 1, 3.[9] The proper concept seems to be that, *instead* of making recourse, a penitent who has been absolved with the obligation of recourse can go to a specially authorized confessor and, after repeating the confession of the sin for which he incurred the censure, receive a new absolution; or if the penitent has already made recourse to the competent superior, he can go to a confessor possessing a special faculty, receive a new absolution, accept the mandates of the confessor, and release himself from the mandates which will come from the superior. In the old law, it was explicitly denied that *recourse* could be made to a confessor with a subdelegated faculty,[10] and this old law has been retained in the Code, for, as is evident from canon 2254, § 1, *recourse* can be made only to the Sacred Penitentiary or to the bishop or other *superior* with the proper faculty. Yet this does not prevent the penitent from going to a confessor with the proper faculty to receive a new absolution from him.

Canon 2254, § 2, then, is a provision, not for recourse, but for a new absolution. Is this a new development, originated by the Code? In the footnotes which he added to the Code, Gasparri has cited only one source for canon 2254, § 2, and that is the abovementioned response of the Holy Office, which denied that recourse could be made to a confessor with a subdelegated faculty.[11] But the provision that the specially authorized confessor *can absolve* bears a striking resemblance to a letter of the Holy Office [12] regarding recourse after absolution in danger of death, and which Gasparri has cited for canon 2254, § 1. Recalling that recourse in these

"adeundi," and in thus adhering to the wording of canon 2254, § 2, has avoided confusion. *Cf.* also Kelly, *Jurisdiction of the Confessor,* p. 175.

[9] *Cf.* Sole, *De Delictis et Poenis,* n. 195; Ayrinhac-Lydon, *Penal Legislation,* n. 105; Vermeersch, *Theol. Mor.,* III, n. 473, 3, n. 474; Kelly, *loc. cit.*

[10] S. C. S. Off., 19 Decembris, 1900, ad 3—*Fontes,* n. 1249; quoted above, p. 61.

[11] *Cf.* the preceding note.

[12] 19 Augusti, 1891, ad 2—*Fontes,* n. 1143; quoted above, Chapter II, note 120.

circumstances obliged at that time for censures reserved *speciali modo* to the Holy See, one sees a very obvious similarity between canon 2254, § 2, and that response of the Holy Office, which is, in part: "Obligationem standi mandatis Ecclesiae importare onus sive per se sive per confessarium, recurrendi ad S. Pontificem, eiusque mandatis obediendi, *vel novam absolutionem petendi ab habente facultatem absolvendi* a censuris S. Pontifici speciali modo reservatis." The reason why this provision was not included in canon 2252 seems clear. The legislator, determining in the Code the *specialissimo modo* reservation as a new form of reservation embracing only four censures, attached the obligation of recourse after absolution in danger of death only to these four censures, and to *ab homine* censures, and implicitly to the three censures reserved to the pope personally. Apparently he considered that it would be futile to retain the notion of a new absolution in these cases, since it will hardly happen that there will be a confessor with such faculties. Anyone who enjoys these faculties will usually be a superior, but even if he is not, canon 2252, unlike canon 2254, allows that *recourse* be made to him without the need of a new absolution.[18] But it may easily happen that a confessor has a faculty for some censure for which recourse is prescribed in canon 2254, § 1, since this obligation affects all reserved censures after absolution in the more urgent cases; and it seems quite clear that canon 2254, § 2, is an adaptation of the above-quoted provision which arose in connection with recourse after absolution in danger of death.

If canon 2254, § 2, is not a provision for recourse, how is one to explain the nature of this new absolution, since the crime and censure have already been remitted by the absolution given according to canon 2254, § 1? The concept is here submitted that canon 2254, § 2, is a kind of *restitutio in integrum,* a restoration of the *status quo ante,* a sort of fiction of law by which the case of the penitent, in so far as the canonical effects of the censure are concerned, is considered as being presented for the first time, so that

[18] Canon 2252: ". . . tenentur . . . obligatione recurrendi . . . ad S. Poenitentiariam vel ad Episcopum aliumve facultate praeditum . . ." Canon 2254, § 1: ". . . iniuncto onere recurrendi . . . ad S. Poenitentiariam vel ad Episcopum aliumve Superiorem praeditum facultate . . ."

the specially authorized confessor can use his special faculty as if no previous action had been taken in the case. The confessor could use his special faculty for the censure in ordinary cases, outside the *casus urgentiores,* without imposing the obligation of recourse, and the law has granted the favor to the penitent that, even though his case has already been handled according to the norm of canon 2254, § 1, and the guilt of the sin and censure removed, the confessor is not to be prohibited the use of his faculty, and the penitent is not to be denied the advantage of that faculty, unless the case has been definitely closed by the reception of the mandates from the superior.[14]

It may be objected that the foregoing discussion is a demonstration of needless hair-splitting and that, whether or not canon 2254, § 2, provides for a form of recourse, the actual result is the same. But its value will appear from the light it sheds upon the following dispute.

The opinion of Sole,[15] namely, that a penitent absolved according to canon 2254, § 1, cannot make recourse to a specially authorized confessor, but must make it to the Sacred Penitentiary, the bishop or some other superior with the proper faculty, has been cated by Creusen [16] in the sense that recourse to a competent superior must always be made even if absolution has been granted according to the norm of canon 2254, § 2. But Creusen has drawn a conclusion that is not contained in Sole's words and has rejected a view that he wrongly ascribes to Sole. Similarly, Salucci [17] has attributed the same opinion to Sole and has rejected the latter's appeal to the old law for the view that recourse cannot be made to a confessor who possesses a special faculty. Salucci himself maintains that canon 2254, § 1, gives the general rule for recourse, but that canon 2254, § 2, is an exception to the rule that recourse must be made to a competent superior. The source of the discrepancy, as readily appears from the above discussion, lies in the manner of interpreting canon 2254, § 2. Creusen and Salucci consider it a

[14] *Cf.* below, in the present chapter, Article II, D, p. 229.

[15] *De Delictis et Poenis,* n. 195.

[16] *Epitome,* III, n. 454, 3, 2°.

[17] *Diritto Penale,* I, 228, nota 1.

form of recourse; Sole does not. And Sole seems to be correct, for, although canon *2254*, § *2*, supplies for and eliminates the obligation of recourse, in itself it is not strictly a recourse.[18] Consequently, Sole is not to be understood in the sense that recourse must be made to a competent superior even after absolution has been given according to canon *2254*, § *2*.

Whether or not one construes canon *2254*, § *2*, as a form of recourse, the conclusion remains as follows: if a penitent, absolved according to canon *2254*, § 1, with the obligation of recourse, avails himself of the provision of § *2* of this canon before making the recourse, he is no longer bound to make recourse; [19] if he has already made recourse to the superior and then goes to a specially authorized confessor for absolution, he is no longer bound to observe the mandates which will come from the superior, but it is sufficient that he observe those imposed by the confessor.

However, De Meester [20] and Blat [21] maintain that, although the penitent can go to a specially authorized confessor if recourse has been made to a superior, he cannot do so if the recourse has been made to the Sacred Penitentiary, since canon *2254*, § *2*, says *"facto quoque recursu ad Superiorem."* But the Sacred Penitentiary is also a competent superior for the internal forum, and it is clear that the *"Superiorem"* in canon 2254, § 2, is used in the general sense in which it is employed in the wording *"Superior competens"* of canon 2254, § 1, where it manifestly embraces also the Sacred Penitentiary; so that even if recourse has already been made to the Sacred Penitentiary, the penitent can go to a specially authorized confessor and receive a new absolution without being obliged to observe the mandates which will subsequently come from the Sacred Penitentiary.[22]

[18] This is also indicated in the discussion as to whether the words *"hic recursus"* in canon 2254, § 3, refer only to canon 2254, § 1, or also to canon 2254, § 2; *cf.* below, Chapter IX, Article I, p. 235.

[19] *Cf.* Cappello, *De Censuris*, n. 130, 1, 2; Coronata, *Instit. Iuris Can.*, IV, 183; De Meester, *Compendium*, III, P. II, 187; Vermeersch-Creusen, *Epitome*, III, n. 454, 3, 2°; Salucci, *Diritto Penale*, I, 228, nota 1, n. 4.

[20] *Loc. cit.*

[21] *Commentarium*, lib. V, p. 119.

[22] *Cf.* Coronata, *Instit. Iuris Can.*, IV, 183, nota 2.

It is of high practical importance that the phrase "*facto quoque recursu ad Superiorem*" was inserted in canon 2254, § 2; otherwise an inferior, such as a specially authorized confessor, might very well consider that the case was no longer a *res integra*, but that the mandates of the superior were absolutely to be awaited and obeyed.[23]

Canon 2254, § 2, can be used as long as the penitent has not actually received the mandates of the superior; once he has received these, the case is definitely closed, and he can no longer go to a specially authorized confessor for this case.[24]

Article II. The Absolution

A. The Confessor

For the use of canon 2254, § 2, the confessor must be one who is "*facultate praeditus*," that is, one who has a faculty for ordinary cases to absolve from the censure confessed by the penitent. His power to absolve, therefore, must proceed from some other source than from the faculties of canon 882 for danger of death or the faculties of canon 2254, §§ 1, 3, for the more urgent cases. For canon 2254, § 2, is neither a grant nor an extension of faculties, but presupposes that the minister of absolution is a specially authorized confessor in the sense that he enjoys a special faculty.

A religious who enjoys the privileges of regulars is a specially authorized confessor regarding censures reserved by common law to the bishop.[25] Likewise, an ordinary is a specially qualified confessor for his subjects regarding censures he has reserved to himself and censures reserved to him by the common law, unless the latter are public and have been brought to the contentious forum of some other ordinary;[26] also for occult censures reserved *simpliciter* to the Holy See;[27] and for all censures from which he has the power to

[23] *Cf.* Vermeersch-Creusen, *Epitome*, III, n. 454, 3, 2°.

[24] Coronata, *op. cit.*, IV, 183.

[25] *Cf.* Vermeersch-Creusen, *Epitome*, I, n. 727, 5; Aertnys-Damen, *Theol. Mor.*, II, n. 1067.

[26] *Cf.* canons 198; 488, n. 8; 2253, nn. 2, 3; 2237, § 1. *Cf.* Coronata, *Instit. Iuris Can.*, IV, 137; Cappello, *De Censuris*, nn. 122, 123.

[27] *Cf.* canon 2237, § 2.

absolve by reason of quinquennial faculties (if he is a local ordinary) or particular indults. Similarly, all confessors to whom these faculties have been delegated or subdelegated by the ordinary, according to the extent in which the faculties have been given, are competent to act as provided for by canon 2254, § 2; [28] and any confessor approved by the local ordinary has the power to absolve in ordinary cases from censures reserved in a religious institute.[29]

An apostolic delegate can absolve as in canon 2254, § 2, according to the extent of the faculties delegated to him.[30] Cardinals can do the same with reference to all censures except those reserved *specialissimo modo* to the Holy See and those attached to the revelation of the secret of the Holy Office.[31]

All of these have faculties to absolve outside of danger of death and the more urgent cases, and, as far as their jurisdiction extends, they can use the norm of canon 2254, § 2, to grant a new absolution in the sacramental forum to a penitent who has already been absolved with the obligation of recourse according to canon 2254, § 1.

B. *The Object of the Absolution*

There is no censure which by its very nature is excluded from the scope of canon 2254, § 2, with one exception. This exception concerns the case in which a priest has contracted the excommunication of canon 2388, § 1, for having attempted marriage, and is forced by very grave reasons to continue dwelling with his accomplice, even though he intends to practice perfect chastity in the future. This censure, under the foregoing conditions, although in theory it is still reserved *simpliciter* to the Holy See, has been explicitly withdrawn from the provisions of canon 2254 and has been reserved exclusively to the Sacred Penitentiary. It not only cannot be absolved by virtue of canon 2254, §§ 1, 3, but it cannot be absolved even by one who has faculties to absolve in ordinary cases

[28] *Cf.* canons 2253, nn. 2, 3; 2245, § 2; 199.

[29] Canon 519. It must be noted that canon 519 confers no power on such confessors to absolve from censures reserved *by common law* to religious superiors.

[30] *Cf.* canon 267, § 2.

[31] *Cf.* canon 239, § 1, n. 1.

from censures reserved *simpliciter* to the Holy See. Consequently, this censure in these particular circumstances cannot be absolved according to canon 2253, n. 3, by one who possesses the faculty to absolve from censures reserved *simpliciter* to the Holy See, but only by the Sacred Penitentiary; and it cannot be absolved by reason of canon 2254 whether together with or apart from the obligation of recourse. Since no one, except only the Sacred Penitentiary, is a *confessarius facultate praeditus* for this case, it is evident that canon 2254, § 2, is not applicable to it. Moreover, the supposition of canon 2254, § 2, that the penitent has already been absolved according to canon 2254, § 1, with the obligation of recourse, will not be verified, for canon 2254, § 1, cannot be used for this particular case.[82]

In theory, every censure which can be absolved by reason of canon 2254, § 1, falls also under the provision of canon 2254, § 2. Not even the censure for *absolutio complicis* is excluded.[83] But whatever may be the theoretical side, in practice the application of canon 2254, § 2, will be decidedly limited. For it will rarely, if ever, happen that a confessor will enjoy the faculty to absolve in ordinary cases from censures reserved *specialissimo modo* to the Holy See, and unless he is an apostolic delegate or an ordinary with special delegation, he will hardly have such a faculty for censures reserved *speciali modo* to the Holy See. Therefore, the extent of the object of absolution according to canon 2254, § 2, is not directly restricted because of the nature of the censure concerned, but the limitation will arise in many cases from the lack of a confessor possessing the proper faculty.

C. *The Matter of Confession*

Canon 2254, § 2, presupposes that the penitent has already been absolved from his crime and censure according to the norm of canon 2254, § 1, with the obligation of recourse. The crime cannot revive, for it has been completely remitted, and the only way in

[82] A detailed discussion of this case will be found in Chapter X, Article IV. *Cf.* also above, Chapter VII, Article III, B, p. 184.

[83] Kelly, *Jurisdiction of the Confessor*, p. 175.

which the penitent could again become guilty of such a crime would be to commit another sin of the same kind. The censure was absolved with an *absolutio ad reincidentiam,* namely, in such a way that the penitent would incur another censure of the same species if he culpably failed to perform the prescribed recourse within the proper time. When the penitent wishes to release himself from the obligation of recourse, or from the necessity of observing the superior's mandates when recourse has already been made, and for this purpose goes to a specially authorized confessor, he must repeat the confession *"saltem delicti cum censura."* Both the delict and the censure must, therefore, be mentioned in this new confession. *At least* these must be mentioned, for, since there is question of sacramental confession, all necessary matter for confession must also be confessed. Consequently, not only the delict with the censure must be confessed, even though the censure has already been remitted and the delict is now only sufficient matter and not necessary matter; but also any mortal sin which has been committed since the last worthy confession, and in general every mortal sin which has not yet been directly submitted to the power of the keys, must likewise be confessed, for if they are deliberately concealed, the confession will be sacrilegious.[34]

D. The Grant of Absolution

To understand the nature of canon 2254, § 2, and the manner in which it produces its effects is not an easy task. Coronata,[35] considering the provision of canon 2254, §. 2, as a form of recourse, claims that the obligation of confessing at least the delict and censure in order to obtain the benefits of this paragraph arises from the positive precept of the Church, which requires this new confession in order to break down further the contumacy of the delinquent. But this notion does not impress one as being very cogent, for contumacy is supposed to have ceased when absolution is given from a censure,[36] and there is no question of further breaking down

[34] *Cf.* Cipollini, *De Censuris,* pp. 47, 48.

[35] *Instit. Iuris Can.,* IV, 183.

[36] *Cf.* canons 2248, §§ 1, 2; 2250, § 1; 2242, § 3.

contumacy which no longer exists. Besides, as has been discussed above,[87] the provision of canon 2254, § 2, viewed in the light of the old law, is not properly and strictly a form of recourse as this term is used in canon 2254, §§ 1, 3, for recourse in these latter paragraphs is not at all concerned with absolution, but only with mandates.

To repeat and amplify what has already been indicated regarding the nature of canon 2254, § 2, it seems that this provision has evolved from such considerations as the following. The penitent has gone to a confessor without any special faculty and has been absolved from a reserved censure by reason of canon 2254, § 1, with the obligation of recourse and of obedience to the mandates of the superior. Before he makes the recourse, or before he receives the mandates, he discovers he could have gone to another confessor who has a special faculty for the censure and who in ordinary circumstances, outside of the *casus urgentiores,* could have absolved him without the obligation of recourse and consequently without question of the reincurrence of the censure, but only with the imposition of mandates. This penitent, who has already shown good will by having the censure remitted according to canon 2254, § 1, should not be in a less favorable position than another penitent who has not done this, but has submitted the case for the first time to a specially authorized confessor. Thereupon, the Church makes the positive declaration that, even though the delict and censure have already been absolved, the penitent may once again confess them, this time to a specially authorized confessor, and this confessor can use his special faculty in the same way as if no previous absolution had been granted, and with the same canonical effect as would be produced if this specially authorized confessor used his faculty in ordinary circumstances, namely, that there is no subsequent obligation of recourse, and that it is sufficient to obey the mandates imposed by this confessor. In brief, the penitent is not to be deprived of the advantage of the specially authorized confessor's faculty, even if he has already been absolved according to the norm of canon 2254, § 1.

[87] *Cf.* the present chapter, Article I, B, p. 221.

The foregoing consideration may be illustrated by the following example. A person who has contracted a censure reserved by the common law to the local ordinary goes to a confessor and is absolved by reason of canon 2254, § 1, with the obligation of recourse *sub poena reincidentiae.* Before making the recourse, or, if recourse has been made, before receiving the mandates of the superior, he learns that a religious confessor with the privileges of regulars could have absolved him from this censure without the obligation of recourse. He goes to this confessor and presents the case to him, confessing the delict and censure. The confessor knows that he could have absolved the penitent without any difficulty and without any obligation of recourse if the censure were being confessed for the first time, for that is the benefit of his faculty. Then he recalls the provision of canon 2254, § 2, that, even if the penitent has already been absolved according to canon 2254, § 1, and even if recourse has already been made, the case is not considered as closed until the penitent receives the mandates of the superior, and the Church allows him to use his faculty and grant the penitent a new absolution, imposing proportionate mandates, but freeing the penitent from the obligation of recourse, or, if recourse has been made, releasing the penitent from the obligation of observing the mandates which will subsequently come from the superior.

Consequently, the repeated confession of at least the delict and the censure seems to be prescribed not only that the specially authorized confessor, from his knowledge of the case, may give proportionate mandates, but especially that he may be able to use his special faculty to absolve.

The absolution granted according to canon 2254, § 2, like that in canon 2254, §§ 1, 3, can be given only in the sacramental forum, for there is question only of going to another *confessor* possessed of the proper faculty.[38] It has been said,[39] however, that if the new confessor has jurisdiction in the external forum, the absolution can be given outside the Sacrament of Penance. This statement is true, in the supposition that the confessor is also qualified to grant abso-

[38] *Cf.* Blat, *Commentarium,* lib. V, p. 119.

[39] *Cf.* Salucci, *Diritto Penale,* I, 229.

lution to the individual penitent from the particular censure in the external forum. But such an absolution would not be an application of canon 2254, § 2. It does not even pertain *per se* to the recourse as in canon 2254, § 1, for this recourse concerns the petition for mandates, and not the request for absolution in the external forum. It would rather pertain to canon 2251, regarding the absolution in the external forum of a penitent who has already been absolved in the internal forum. The absolution provided for in canon 2254, § 2, therefore, is granted only within the Sacrament of Penance.

Per se the absolution is given absolutely and according to the customary form used for sacramental absolution.[40]

If the confession is sacrilegious or null on the part of the penitent, nevertheless the canonical effect of canon 2254, § 2, concerning the censure is produced, namely, the cessation of the obligation of recourse and of obedience to the mandates of the superior, provided that, with reference to the latter obligation, the penitent observes the mandates prescribed by the confessor.[41]

In canon 2254, § 2, there is no explicit prescription, as there is in canon 2254, § 3, that the confessor is to absolve, *iniunctis de iure iniungendis*. The same phrase is also omitted in canon 2254, § 1, apparently because the matters to be enjoined according to the law will be provided for in the mandates of the superior. When the mandates of the superior are replaced by those of the specially authorized confessor, it seems clear that the latter should enjoin not only those things which the divine-natural and divine-positive laws demand, but also, as the confessor of canon 2254, § 3, must do, those required by ecclesiastical law, as the superior would do if he were giving the mandates.[42]

Article III. The Mandates

Besides enjoining the things required by divine-natural, divine-positive, and ecclesiastical law, the specially authorized confessor

[40] *Cf.* canon 2250, § 3.

[41] *Cf.* Cipollini, *De Censuris*, pp. 47, 48.

[42] The elements included under the phrase *"iniunctis de iure iniungendis"* are considered below, Chapter IX, Article II, p. 241.

of canon 2254, § 2, must also give mandates for the penitent to observe. These, in general, will consist of the penance and satisfaction for the censure according to the manner in which these will be explained under the discussion of the penance and satisfaction in canon 2254, § 3.[43] However, it is important to note here that, although the penance and satisfaction as given by the confessor of canon 2254, § 3, unquestionably bind *sub poena reincidentiae,* there is no indication that the mandates imposed in accordance with the norm of canon 2254, § 2, bind in the same way. This seems logical, for the superior would not be bound to give the mandates in such a way that they oblige under pain of reincurrence of the censure, and the same seems true of the specially authorized confessor, who shares the special faculty of the superior, and who could absolve in ordinary cases from the censure concerned without imposing mandates *sub poena reincidentiae.* Moreover, unless his faculty has been delegated to him under this condition that he impose mandates *sub poena reincidentiae,* it appears that the specially authorized confessor not only is not bound to absolve with an *absolutio ad reincidentiam,* but that he cannot do so, since a confessor can absolve in this manner only in the cases expressed in the law,[44] and in canon 2254, § 2, there is no mention of reincidence. However, the mandates of the specially authorized confessor, since they are imposed for a censure, must be grave, and they will certainly bind the penitent under pain of grave sin. But there is no necessity for this confessor to impose a special penance for the sin as distinct from the penance for the censure, for it can be presumed that the penance for the sin has already been prescribed by the confessor who absolved according to canon 2254, § 1. Consequently, the mandates of the specially authorized confessor will be concerned only with the censure.

It has been said[45] that, when a penitent is absolved by a specially authorized confessor according to the norm of canon 2254, § 2, he is bound to fulfill the mandates of the confessor and cannot observe the mandates that will come from the superior when re-

[43] *Cf.* below, Chapter IX, Article III, p. 246.

[44] *Cf.* Cappello, *De Censuris,* n. 94, 1, n. 95, 7.

[45] *Cf.* Chelodi, *Ius Poenale,* p. 43.

course has been made. There seems to be reason for this view, in the fact that the case appears to be closed by the penitent's acceptance of the confessor's mandates.[46] However, canon 2254, § 2, says that the penitent, after the new absolution, is to accept the mandates of the confessor, "*quin teneatur postea stare aliis mandatis ex parte Superioris supervenientibus.*" Although he is freed from the obligation of observing the subsequent mandates of the superior, this wording of the canon favors the more common opinion that the penitent can, if he wishes, await the mandates of the superior and fulfill them instead of the mandates of the specially authorized confessor.[47]

[46] *Cf.* Woywod, *Practical Commentary,* n. 2096.

[47] *Cf.* Cappello, *De Censuris,* n. 130, 5; Coronata, *Instit. Iuris Can.,* IV, 183; De Meester, *Compendium,* III, P. II, 188; Salucci, *Diritto Penale,* I, 228, nota 1, n. 2; Rossi, "De sacerdotibus . . . ," *Perfice Munus,* XII (1937), 228.

CHAPTER IX

THE EXCEPTIONAL METHOD—CANON 2254, § 3

Canon 2254. § 3. Quod si in casu aliquo extraordinario hic recursus sit moraliter impossibilis, tunc ipsemet confessarius, excepto casu quo agatur de absolutione censurae de qua in can. 2367, potest absolutionem concedere sine onere de quo supra, iniunctis tamen de iure iniungendis, et imposita congrua poenitentia et satisfactione pro censura, ita ut poenitens, nisi intra congruum tempus a confessario praefiniendum poenitentiam egerit ac satisfactionem dederit, recidat in censuram.

Article I. The Circumstances

When the recourse as prescribed in canon 2254, § 1, is morally impossible, the confessor can absolve without the obligation of recourse, except for the case of *absolutio complicis in peccato turpi*, and in place of the recourse he enjoins the things required by law and he also imposes a fitting penance and satisfaction which must be fulfilled under pain of reincurrence of the censure.[1]

The fact that canon 2254, § 3, provides for the absolution without the obligation of recourse when *"hic recursus"* is morally impossible, has led to some confusion. The source of the difficulty is that some authors have interpreted canon 2254, § 2, as a form of recourse, and consequently they are at loss to understand whether the *"hic recursus"* of canon 2254, § 3, refers to the recourse as in canon 2254, § 1, or to what they consider as recourse in canon 2254, § 2, or to both.[2] But the provision of canon 2254, §2 for

[1] Throughout this discussion of canon 2254, § 3, even if the censure for *absolutio complicis* is not expressly mentioned as excluded, it is to be understood as excluded, together with the specific case under canon 2388, § 1, as will be mentioned concerning these in the present chapter, Article V.

[2] *E. g., cf.* Creusen, *Epitome*, III, n. 454, 3, 2°.

a new absolution is not properly a recourse, and the only thing that need be considered in the discussion of the moral impossibility of "*hic recursus*" is the recourse of canon 2254, § 1. This is evident not only from the development of the pre-Code legislation on the more urgent cases,[3] but also from a comparison of canon 2254 with the parallel canon 2290 on the extraordinary remission of *latae sententiae* vindictive penalties, in which canon there is no provision corresponding to canon 2254, § 2, but its "*hic recursus*" of § 2 clearly and exclusively refers to the recourse in its § 1. Moreover, if canon 2254, § 2, were a form of recourse, the "*hic recursus*" of § 3 would logically refer solely to § 2, which no one admits. Consequently, in the treatment of the moral impossibility of recourse, as in canon 2254, § 3, the provision of canon 2254, § 2 can be entirely disregarded, as not being a recourse and as being outside the purview of canon 2254, § 3. There is no intention of denying, however, that a confessor could absolve a penitent according to canon 2254, § 1, with the obligation of recourse, when the penitent promises to supply for a morally possible recourse by going within a month to a specially authorized confessor according to the norm of canon 2254, § 2.[4] But even if it were easy for the penitent to go to a specially authorized confessor for a new absolution, this would not be reason for refusing absolution as in canon 2254, § 3, without the obligation of recourse, and for granting it only as in canon 2254, § 1; for canon 2254, § 2, is granted as a privilege to the penitent, which he may use if he wishes, but which is never to be construed to his disadvantage.[5]

Since canon 2254, § 3 refers back to the recourse in canon 2254, § 1, there is a question which calls for consideration before the nature of the moral impossibility is explained. It has been mentioned that, concerning the recourse *intra mensem* as in canon 2254, § 1, the month is commonly accepted as *tempus utile* and as being *ad urgendam obligationem* rather than *ad finiendam obligationem*.[6]

[3] *Cf.* above, Chapter III, Article III.

[4] *Cf.* Coronata, *Instit. Iuris Can.*, IV, 181, nota 5; Cerato, *Censurae Vigentes*, p. 44.

[5] *Cf.* Vermeersch, *Theol. Mor.*, III, n. 473, 4.

[6] *Cf.* above, Chapter VII, Article IV, D, p. 207.

Consequently, when the obligation of recourse has been actually imposed, the penitent is still bound to fulfill it even if he has been unable to perform the recourse within a month of actual time from his absolution. However, when the confessor, before absolving, foresees that the penitent will not be able to discharge the obligation of recourse within a month, it appears that he must form his judgment on the calculation of the month as *tempus continuum*;[7] otherwise the provision of canon 2254, § 3 would be practically useless, for in the computation of *tempus utile* the time is not considered to begin until the person is able to act, and there would be a contradiction in a norm for moral impossibility which is based on a calculation that presumes that the person is able to act. Therefore, except with reference to the censure for *absolutio complicis*, the confessor can absolve without imposing the obligation of recourse when he foresees that the recourse will be morally impossible within one calendar month from the date on which he is absolving.

Moral impossibility of recourse is interpreted in harmony with the responses of the Holy Office which supplied the basis of canon 2254, § 3, together with the addition of any serious inconvenience as also being a form of moral impossibility impeding recourse.

First of all, recourse is morally impossible if neither the penitent nor the confessor can make the recourse even by letter to the Sacred Penitentiary or to the proper superior, and it is hard for the penitent to go to another confessor.[8] The hardship of going to another confessor has been interpreted by various authors in the sense that, if it is hard for the penitent to go to a specially authorized confessor as mentioned in canon 2254, § 2, then, in the supposition that neither confessor nor penitent can make recourse at least by letter, the confessor can absolve as in canon 2254, § 3; [9] but if the penitent would not find it hard to go to a specially authorized

[7] *Cf.* canon 35. *Cf.* Coronata, *Instit. Iuris Can.*, IV, 181.

[8] *Cf.* S. C. S. Off., 9 Novembris, 1898—*Fontes*, n. 1207; quoted above, p. 60. This response, referring only to recourse to the Sacred Penitentiary, must, of course, be interpreted at the present according to the adaptation of the old law concerning recourse, as in canon 2254, § 1.

[9] *Cf.* Cappello, *De Censuris*, n. 131, 2; Coronata, *Instit. Iuris Can.*, IV, 184; Rossi, "De sacerdotibus . . .," *Perfice Munus*, XII (1937), 90.

confessor, the first confessor apparently should absolve according to canon 2254, § 1, and oblige the penitent to satisfy for the recourse by going to the confessor enjoying a special faculty. However, as has been mentioned in connection with canon 2254, § 2, there is no circumstance in which a penitent is obliged to use the privilege of eliminating recourse by going to a specially authorized confessor in order to obtain a new absolution, and canon 2254, § 2 is never to be construed to the disadvantage of the penitent. In canon 2254, § 3, it is stated that absolution can be given without the obligation of recourse if "*hic recursus*" is morally impossible. But "*hic recursus*" evidently is the recourse *intra mensem saltem per epistolam et per confessarium* mentioned in canon 2254, § 1. When the phrase "*per medium confessarii*" is found in the pre-Code decrees of the Holy Office on absolution from reserved censures in the more urgent cases, it invariably refers to that individual confessor whom the penitent approached for absolution in the more urgent case. Likewise, the words "*per confessarium*" in canon 2254, § 1, seem to refer to that particular confessor. The only other confessor mentioned in canon 2254 is the specially authorized confessor of canon 2254, § 2, to whom the penitent *may* go, if he wishes, to receive a new absolution and thus supply for recourse which has already been imposed. There is nothing about the penitent's obligation to make recourse through some other confessor than the one by whom he is absolved, whether or not it would be easy for the penitent to go to another confessor and ask him to undertake the recourse. The entire matter apparently pertains solely to the penitent and to the confessor from whom the penitent receives absolution from a censure in a more urgent case. Furthermore, it appears that it will almost always be hard for a penitent to go to another confessor and repeat to him the confession of the sin and censure,[10] in order that this new confessor may undertake the recourse. It is in harmony with this interpretation that the view is being held, as remarked by Cocchi,[11] that the moral impossibility of recourse is verified if neither the penitent nor the confessor to whom he made his confession can perform

[10] *Cf.* Vermeersch, *Theol. Mor.*, III, n. 473, 2 (p. 396), for this statement in a different application.

[11] *Commentarium*, lib. V, p. 126, nota 1.

the recourse at least by letter.[12] It seems that this opinion regarding moral impossibility of recourse may be held, not only because almost every penitent will feel reluctance in being asked to go to another confessor and repeat the confession, but mainly because in the present law on the more urgent cases there is no clear obligation for the penitent to make the recourse through any other confessor than the one by whom he is absolved from a reserved censure by virtue of canon 2254, § 1.

Moral impossibility of recourse may arise in a second way, namely, if, even though the confessor can write the letter of recourse, the penitent cannot return to him and is unable to make the recourse himself, and finds it hard to go to another confessor.[13] Concerning the hardship of going to another confessor, the same may be said here as has just been mentioned. Again, it will nearly always happen that the penitent will not be able, without serious inconvenience, to go personally to the superior for the mandates; and even though he may know how to write, he will practically always, unless he is a priest, be *"scribendi impar"* in this regard, that is, unequal to the task of writing a competent and accurate letter of recourse.[14] Therefore, if the confessor foresees that the penitent will not be able to return to him to receive the superior's mandates and is unable to make the recourse by personal appearance or by letter, he can absolve him according to canon 2254, § 3 without the obligation of recourse. It seems that this would obtain also in a case in which it is only probable that the confessor will see the penitent again, or will see him only after a long time. [15]

The third manner in which recourse is morally impossible consists in the situation in which there is any serious inconvenience preventing recourse. The broad meaning and extent of the serious in-

[12] *Cf.* Salucci, *Diritto Penale,* I, 227; Aertnys-Damen, *Theol. Mor.,* II, n. 994, *bis,* III; Kelly, *Jurisdiction of the Confessor,* p. 173; Vermeersch-Creusen, *Epitome,* III, n. 454, 4, 2°.

[13] *Cf.* S. C. S. Off., 5 Septembris, 1900—*Fontes,* n. 1247; quoted above, p. 60.

[14] *Cf.* Kelly, *Jurisdiction of the Confessor,* p. 173; Arregui, *Summarium Theol. Mor.,* n. 614, 3, n. 617, 5. The phrase *"scribendi impar"* is used in the response of the Holy Office cited in the preceding note.

[15] Cappello, *De Censuris,* n. 131, 2.

convenience has already been considered in the discussion of the *grave incommodum* mentioned in canon 2254, § 1.[16] The same explanation of serious inconvenience applies here, but it may be repeated that, in connection with canon 2254, § 1, the *grave incommodum* is not foreseen by the confessor, but arises subsequently to the absolution and suspends or excuses from the imposed obligation of recourse; while in canon 2254, § 3, the serious inconvenience is foreseen by the confessor as destined to endure for at least a month, and he absolves without imposing the obligation of recourse.

The moral impossibility of recourse may easily be verified when people go to confession during missions or other spiritual exercises, for it will usually happen that they will not be able, at least for some uncertain period of time, to revisit the priest who conducted the exercises and receive from him the mandates of the superior.[17] This supposes, of course, that the people have made their confession to the missionary, and not to some priest stationed in the parish. The same conclusion in respect of moral impossibility is ordinarily true when a layman confesses to a priest who is assisting at a parish over a week end or for a very short time, and who will probably not return to that parish or may return only at some uncertain and indefinite time in the distant future.[18] However, if such a priest comes from some other parish in the same city or from a short distance, so that there would be no serious inconvenience for the penitent to go to him to receive the mandates of the superior, the recourse would not be morally impossible.

These, then, are the ways in which recourse is morally impossible, and in such circumstances the confessor can absolve without imposing the obligation of recourse, except for the case of *absolutio complicis* and the specific case under canon 2388, § 1; instead of the recourse he enjoins the things required by law and he also prescribes a penance and satisfaction which must be fulfilled under pain of reincurrence of the censure.

16 *Cf.* above, Chapter VII, Article IV, F, p. 213. *Cf.* Cappello, *op. cit.*, n. 128, 11, n. 131, 2; Coronata, *Instit. Iuris Can.*, IV, 184.

17 *Cf.* Coronata, *loc. cit.;* Cocchi, *Commentarium*, lib. V, p. 126.

18 *Cf.* Cappello, *De Censuris*, n. 131, 2, for the general notion underlying this application.

Article II. The Things to be Enjoined

Before the confessor absolves he must enjoin upon the penitent the things required by law. It is commonly held that the phrase "*iniunctis de iure iniungendis*" involves three things, namely: satisfaction to an injured party for damage inflicted; reparation of scandal; and, besides a sacramental satisfaction, a salutary penance.[19] This interpretation has received such wide support that it is not without misgivings and hesitancy that the opinion is here advanced that, whatever may be the merit of such an interpretation with reference to the phrase "*iniunctis de iure iniungendis*" as found in rescripts from the Sacred Penitentiary, this commonly accepted view is at fault in accepting that phrase in this sense in canon 2254, § 3.

In canon 2254, § 3, there are three things which the confessor must do, namely: 1. he must enjoin the things required by law; 2. he must impose a penance for the censure; 3. he must impose a satisfaction for the censure. The penitent's observance of the things enjoined according to the requirements of law is not *sub poena reincidentiae;* but on the other hand, "*poenitens, nisi intra congruum tempus a confessario praefiniendum poenitentiam egerit ac satisfactionem dederit, recidat in censuram.*"

To attack the root of the difficulty immediately, what is the satisfaction which the confessor must impose under pain of reincidence? Cerato [20] understands the satisfaction as synonymous with the penance. But Cipollini [21] very properly asks why the canon has not only expressly mentioned both the penance and the satisfaction for the censure, but has also distinguished between the performance of the penance and the giving of the satisfaction. Then he concludes that the satisfaction does not refer to the reparation of scan-

[19] *Cf.* Cappello, *op. cit.*, n. 101, n. 131, 4; Coronata, *Instit. Iuris Can.*, IV, 184; De Meester, *Compendium*, III, P. II, 176; Cipollini, *De Censuris*, p. 49; Sole, *De Delictis et Poenis*, n. 198; Salucci, *Diritto Penale*, I, 229; Cerato, *Censurae Vigentes* pp. 36, 263-265; Blat, *Commentarium*, lib. V, p. 120; Kelly, *Jurisdiction of the Confessor*, p. 176; Ayrinhac-Lydon, *Penal Legislation*, n. 106, b.

[20] *Censurae Vigentes*, p. 265.

[21] *De Censuris*, pp. 49, 50.

dal or harm because this is already included in the *iniunctis de iure iniungendis,* but that the satisfaction consists in some work by which the absolved penitent may show his submission and obedience to the Church, and that consequently the confessor could simply impose the obligation of living a good life as the satisfaction. But would it be advisable for the confessor to impose such an obligation under pain of reincurrence of a censure, as the satisfaction must be imposed? If he did, would the penitent reincur the same kind of censure after committing another mortal sin of any kind? Or when would he seriously fail against this obligation of leading a good life to such an extent that the *satisfactio sub poena reincidentiae* is not given within the time specified by the confessor?

It is generally said, as has been mentioned, that the things to be enjoined according to law are: 1. the satisfaction to an injured party; 2. the reparation of scandal; 3. besides the sacramental satisfaction, a salutary penance. Now, first of all, it is absolutely clear that the penance to be imposed by the confessor for the censure, according to canon 2254, § 3, is distinct from the *iniunctis de iure iniungendis* and must be performed *sub poena reincidentiae.* Therefore, the common opinion, although it may be true in other instances, is unquestionably incorrect when, in reference to canon 2254, § 3, it includes the "salutary penance" for the censure under the *iniunctis de iure iniungendis.* Secondly, concerning the term "satisfaction" as found in the above opinion, if the "sacramental satisfaction" refers to the penance for the sin as distinct from the penance for the censure, as is to be presumed, it seems correct to include it under the *iniunctis de iure iniungendis,* for apparently there should be a distinct penance for the sin and for the censure, but the sacramental penance can be immediately eliminated as a possible explanation of the *satisfactio pro censura;* if the "satisfaction to an injured party" is intended as the *satisfactio pro censura,* then it should not be included in the phrase "*iniunctis de iure iniungendis*" in the treatment of canon 2254, § 3; for the things to be enjoined and the satisfaction are distinguished in this place and have a different binding force, the first to be observed *sub gravi* or *sub levi* according to the particular character of the various things enjoined, and the second to be observed *sub poena reincidentiae.*

In canon 2254, § 3, is the phrase *"imposita congrua . . . satisfactione pro censura"* meaningless, or, if not, what does it mean? From the wording of the canon, it seems evident that the *satisfactio pro censura* is distinct not only from the *iniunctis de iure iniungendis* but also from the *poenitentia pro censura*. In what, then, does it consist?

The true interpretation, it seems, should be based on wording similar to that of canon 2254, § 3 in canon 2242 regarding contumacy. In this canon it is said that a person is contumacious who does not desist from the crime or who refuses to do penance with the due reparation of harm and scandal; that, on the other hand, contumancy is considered to have ceased when the delinquent has truly repented of his crime and has given fitting satisfaction for harm and scandal, or has at least seriously promised to do so.[22] The two elements for the cessation of contumacy, then, are: 1. penance; 2. satisfaction for harm and scandal. To transfer the wording of canon 2242, § 3 and adapt it in negative form to the formulation of canon 2254, § 3, it seems that it could be paraphrased as follows: "Contumaciam non desiisse dicendum est, nisi reus poenitentiam egerit et simul ipse congruam satisfactionem pro damnis et scandalo dederit aut saltem serio promiserit." Perhaps this would supply an answer to Cipollini's question as to why canon 2254, § 3, contains an explicit distinction between the penance and the satisfaction, and why it has emphasized this distinction in the wording *"poenitentiam egerit ac satisfactionem dederit."* Apparently, according to canon 2254, § 3, the legislator considers that the penitent who has been absolved without the obligation of recourse, but who has subsequently failed gravely to manifest his protested repentance by means of the performance of the prescribed penance, or who has seriously failed to give the required satisfaction, is still contuma-

[22] Canon 2242. "§ 2. . . . contumax est qui . . . a delicto non desistit vel patrati delicti poenitentiam cum debita damnorum et scandali reparatione agere detrectat . . ."

"§ 3. Contumaciam desiisse dicendum est, cum reum vere delicti commissi poenituerit et simul ipse congruam satisfactionem pro damnis et scandalo dederit aut saltem serio promiserit; iudicare autem utrum poenitentia vera sit, satisfactio congrua aut eiusdem promissio seria, necne, illius est, a quo censurae absolutio petitur."

cious; and he punishes the contumacy evidenced in the omission of penance or satisfaction by the reincurrence of the censure.

Consequently, it is here respectfully maintained that the *satisfactio pro censura* in canon 2254, § 3 consists of the reparation of harm and scandal, and that the common opinion, including the reparation of harm and scandal under the *iniunctis de iure iniungendis*, is faulty when it is applied to canon 2254, § 3.[23]

To restate in briefest form the conclusion deduced from this discussion and to obviate all confusion—the common opinion on the *iniunctis de iure iniungendis* claims that this phrase embraces three things: the satisfaction to an injured party; the reparation of scandal; lastly, besides a sacramental satisfaction, a salutary penance. But it is here maintained that in canon 2254, § 3 the salutary penance is not one of the things to be enjoined according to the law, but that it is the *poenitentia pro censura*, expressly mentioned in this canon; also, that the satisfaction to an injured party and the reparation of scandal are not among the things to be enjoined according to the law, but rather constitute the *satisfactio pro censura*.[24]

What, then, is to be included under the phrase "*iniunctis de iure iniungendis*"? It would be impossible to attempt an enumeration of the things to be enjoined according to the law, for these will

[23] It is not denied that an objection may be raised against this view because of such wording as is found mentioned by Pius XI, const. "*Servatoris Iesu Christi*," 25 Decembris, 1925, pars de facultatibus, III: ". . . caveat autem confessarius ne quemquam publica censura irretitum in foro conscientiae Deo reconciliet, nisi is paratus sit intra sex menses Ecclesiae satisfacere et scandalum damnumque reparare."—*AAS*, XVII (1925), 616. In this there is evidently a distinction between the satisfaction and the reparation of harm and scandal; but in this instance, it is not clear what the "*Ecclesiae satisfacere*" would mean unless it refers to the penance to be imposed for the censure, and in canon 2254, § 3, the penance is explicitly distinguished from the satisfaction for the censure.

[24] It is interesting to note that De Smet (*De Absolutione Complicis et Sollicitatione*, 2. ed., Brugis: Beyaert, 1921, n. 132), when speaking of the crime of false accusation of solicitation, includes under the *iniunctis de iure iniungendis* the retractation of the denunciation and the reparation of harm, and then he immediately refers to them as the *satisfactio* to be performed *sub poena reincidentiae* within the time specified by the confessor.

vary with the particular case. However, a few examples may be given.

If a person has incurred the censure for attempting marriage before a non-Catholic minister, he must be required to have the marraige convalidated or to leave his accomplice. This is demanded by natural law.

When someone has contracted a public censure, before he is absolved he should be required to avoid any acts in the external forum that would cause scandal to those who are unaware of his absolution. This arises from the natural law and is confirmed by canon 2251.[25]

Before a penitent is absolved from the excommunication contracted for joining a Masonic sect, he should be required to abjure the sect before the confessor; to denounce all ecclesiastics and religious known to him as members of the sect;[26] and to promise to relinquish all books, manuscripts, and emblems which pertain to the sect, so that they may be sent to the Holy Office, or, if grave reasons prevent this, at least to destroy them.[27]

When a person has contracted a censure for reading forbidden books, the confessor before absolving must demand that the person give the books to the ordinary or to the confessor or to someone with the faculty to keep forbidden books, or at least that he promise to destroy them.[28]

It is obligations such as these that the confessor must enjoin upon the penitent before absolving him, and it seems that it is such

[25] *Cf.* also S. C. C., 18 Novembris, 1922— not in *AAS*, but translated in Bouscaren, *Canon Law Digest*, I, 408, 409.

[26] *Cf.* canon 2336, § 2.

[27] *Cf.* these norms as given for the use of jubilee faculties, by Pius XI, const. *"Quod superiore anno,"* 2 Aprilis, 1934, IX, 4—*AAS*, XXVI (1934), 145. *Cf.* also the norms to be followed by bishops in the use of quinquennial faculties granted by the Sacred Penitentiary, as in Formula IV of the faculties of 1934, section VI, n. 5—translation in Bouscaren, *Canon Law Digest*, II, 15.

[28] *Cf.* this norm as given for the use of jubilee faculties, as in S. Poenit., monita, 3 Aprilis, 1934, XI—*AAS*, XXVI (1934), 151. *Cf.* also the prescriptions of the Sacred Penitentiary concerning the use of the quinquennial faculties it grants to bishops, in the faculties of 1934, Formula IV, section VI, n. 2—translation in Bouscaren, *op. cit.*, II, 14, 15.

that are to be included under the phrase *"iniunctis de iure iniungendis."*

Article III. The Penance and Satisfaction

A. Nature of the Penance and Satisfaction

Besides a sacramental penance for the crime, the confessor must impose a distinct penance for the censure.[29] It seems that for the crime, the confessor should impose the same kind of grave penance that he would prescribe if there were no censure attached to the sin, although it may perhaps be mitigated to some extent because of the imposition of another penance for the censure. However, it is not the penance for the crime, but the penance for the censure, which is proposed as the subject of this discussion.

The penance for the censure must be a grave penance, as is evident from the penalty attached to its culpable omission, namely, the reincurrence of a censure.[30] Since there is no authentic declaration of the Sacred Penitentiary on this question, there is a notable discrepancy among the authors in their consideration of the various degrees of grave penances. The principal penances are enumerated in canon 2313, § 1, and consist of determined prayers, pilgrimages and other works of piety, fasts, alms, and spiritual exercises for a brief time in a religious house.

Since there are two factors in the gravity of a penance, namely, the seriousness of the work prescribed, and the length of time over which it is extended, it is practically impossible to give any definite norm which will apply in all cases; for example, it would be far less serious to be obliged to say a rosary every day for a week than to fast or make a pilgrimage every day for a week. Even for an objective norm, much must depend on the prudent judgment of the confessor. However, some such norms have been given by authors and may be mentioned here.

[29] *Cf.* Coronata, *Instit. Iuris Can.*, IV, 184; Cappello, *De Censuris*, n. 101, n. 132, 4; Cerato, *Censurae Vigentes*, pp. 265, 296, 297; Kelly, *Jurisdiction of the Confessor*, p. 176; De Meester, *Compendium*, III, P. II, 176; contrary to Cipollini, *De Censuris*, pp. 49, 50.

[30] Blat, *Commentarium*, lib. V, p. 121.

It is generally agreed that a grave penance is one which corresponds to a good work prescribed *sub gravi* by the Church, or which, because of its notable quantity or quality, would be obligatory *sub gravi* if it were prescribed by the Church.[31]

Coronata [32] says that such a penance is to be enjoined for censures of less importance. He considers as a *poenitentia gravis et longa* one which is to be repeated each day for a month, or once a week for three months. As a *poenitentia gravis et diuturna,* to be prescribed for the most serious censures, he regards one which is to be performed each day for three months; each week for six months; or every month for one or two years.

Cappello [33] considers that the *poenitentia longa* and the *poenitentia diuturna* are synonymous, and says that such a penance would be one that is to be performed each week for a month; each day for a week; or many times during an entire day. He regards as a *poenitentia gravis et valde diuturna* one to be performed each month for half a year; each week for two months; or every day for two or three weeks.

Cerato [34] gives the following norms: a grave penance would extend over six months and would consist of the recitation of the rosary three times a week, or of fasting once a week, or of confession each month; a *poenitentia longa* is one performed at least once a week for a year; a *poenitentia diuturna,* one which is prolonged for three years.

Vermeersch [35] insists on the relative character of the penance, but also gives as an example of a penance that is objectively *gravis et diuturna* the daily recitation of the rosary for three months, or the weekly approach to the sacraments for six months, or the monthly approach for a year.

From the wide divergency of opinion manifested by these four authors, the impossibility of indicating any particular objective

[31] *Cf.* Cappello, *De Censuris,* n. 101; Coronata, *Instit. Iuris Can.,* IV, 184.

[32] *Loc. cit.*

[33] *Loc. cit.*

[34] *Censurae Vigentes,* pp. 260-263, 296.

[35] *Theol. Mor.,* III, n. 613.

norm seems quite obvious. It must be left to the judgment of the confessor to determine what penance, in its combined elements of the seriousness and difficulty of the good work and of the length of time for which it is to be prolonged, is proportionate to the particular censure. Above all, he is to consider the character and ability of the penitent, recall that he is the minister not only of divine justice but of divine mercy, and provide for both the divine honor and the salvation of souls.[86]

Concerning the satisfaction for the censure, it has been demonstrated in the preceding article that the only interpretation which gives any meaning to the *satisfactio pro censura* of canon 2254, § 3 is that which is deduced in harmony with canon 2242, and that the satisfaction consists of the reparation of harm and scandal. There is hardly any author who gives an explicit interpretation of the *satisfactio pro censura*. However, Blat,[87] asserting that the reparation of harm and scandal is included under the *iniunctis de iure iniungendis,* says that the satisfaction for the censure comprises, for example, the protestation found in the form of absolution in the Roman Ritual, or the reparation of honor or reputation. But it is hard to believe that such a protestation is the satisfaction to be given *sub poena reincidentiae* within the time determined by the confessor. And the reparation of honor or reputation seems simply to be part of the obligation to repair harm and scandal. It may be said here that, if there is any plausible explanation of the meaning of the *satisfactio pro censura* besides the one here adduced, namely, that it consists of the reparation of harm

[86] *Cf.* canons 887; 888, § 1. *Cf.* an analogous response of the S. Poenit., 8 Aprilis, 1890: ". . . Potestne iniungi poenitentia per tres tantum menses, verum pluribus per hebdomadam vicibus adimplenda, quando praescripta est *gravis et diuturna,* ac per unum solum mensem cum statuta fuit *gravis poenitentia salutaris* . . . ?

"R. In praefinienda poenitentiae qualitate, gravitate, duratione, etc., quae dispensantis aut delegati arbitrio iuri conformi remittuntur, neque severitatis, neque humanitatis fines esse excedendos, rationemque habendam conditionis aetatis, infirmitatis, officii, sexus, etc., eorum quibus poena irrogari iniungitur." —*Collectanea S. C. P. F.,* n. 1725.

[87] *Commentarium,* lib. V, pp. 120, 121. *Cf.* also Cocchi, *Commentarium,* lib. V, p. 127.

and scandal, it has not been found in the writings of any author consulted in the preparation of the present work.

According to this interpretation it will be necessary to require the satisfaction only when scandal has actually been given and has not been repaired, and when harm has been inflicted and its reparation has not been made or condoned or rejected.[38] Consequently, there would be no necessity for satisfaction, as distinct from the penance for the censure, for example, in the case of a person who has incurred an occult censure for reading a forbidden book.

When harm has been inflicted and has not yet been repaired, the confessor must require that the penitent make restoration for it in the best possible way. For example, if a person has contracted the excommunication for the usurpation of ecclesiastical goods, he should be required to restore them according to his ability; if a person has unjustly inflicted physical harm on a cleric by striking him, before he is absolved from the censure he should be placed under the obligation of repaying any expenses, as far as he is able, that arose from his action.

When scandal has been given, the divine law demands that it be repaired, and the reparation should be made in the way which the confessor judges is best.[39] For instance, if a person has publicly incurred the censure for contracting a marriage before a non-Catholic minister, and the scandal has not yet been repaired in any way, the confessor should not only enjoin the convalidation of the marriage or the separation of the parties, but should require that this be done in some manner by which the scandal will be effectively eliminated.

The time within which the penance is to be performed and the satisfaction given is to be determined specifically by the confessor.

[38] *Cf.* Coronata, *Instit. Iuris Can.*, IV, 184; Cerato, *Censurae Vigentes*, pp. 36, 37. Both of these authors are speaking of the satisfaction to an injured party or the reparation of scandal as included under the things to be enjoined; but the same conclusion applies also to the above interpretation.

[39] *Cf.* S. Poenit., 10 Decembris, 1860, ad 27: "Reparationem scandali esse necessariam de iure divino, eamque faciendam esse meliori modo quo potest prudenti iudicio Ordinarii seu Confessarii."—*ASS*, I (1865-1866), 566.

With regard to the satisfaction, the time prescribed for the reparation of harm and scandal should ordinarily not exceed six months.[40]

If a confessor would deliberately refrain from imposing the penance and satisfaction, the absolution would be clearly illicit, but it seems that it would not be invalid, for the obligation of imposing these and also of enjoining the things required by the law seems to be rather a prescription than a *conditio sine qua non.*[41]

B. The Sanction

When the confessor imposes the penance and satisfaction upon the penitent, he must specify the time within which they are to be performed, and he must inform the penitent that, if they are not fulfilled within the prescribed time, the same kind of censure will be reincurred.[42] If the time has not been determined, there can be no question of reincidence, as is evident from the wording of canon 2254, § 3, and from the fact that it would never be certain when the censure would be reincurred if there were no terminus within which the obligation must be fulfilled. In such a case, Coronata [43] asserts that the time could be determined by another confessor; but this seems rather dubious, and it appears that in these circumstances the penitent would be bound *sub gravi* to perform the penance and give the satisfaction, but not *sub poena reincidentiae.* However, if the confessor has specified the time, but has failed to inform the penitent of the penalty of reincidence, it seems that this could be declared by a subsequent confessor, for this penalty arises from the law.

It is not necesary that the same time be determined for both the penance and the satisfaction, since these are distant factors, but a definite time must be specified for each, whether it is the

[40] *Cf.* this norm as given for the use of jubilee faculties by Pius XI, const. *"Servatoris Iesu Christi,"* 25 Decembris, 1925, pars de facultatibus, III—*AAS,* XVII (1925), 616; quoted above, in the present chapter, note 23.

[41] *Cf.* Salucci, *Diritto Penale,* I, 233, 234, quoting Wernz, *Ius Decretalium,* VI, 184 (n. 176), nota 177. *Cf.* also Cerato, *Censurae Vigentes,* p. 37, with reference to absolution in the non-sacramental forum without the imposition of satisfaction; he considers it illicit but valid.

[42] *Cf.* Coronata, *Instit. Iuris Can.,* IV, 185; Salucci, *op. cit.,* I, 229.

[43] *Loc. cit.*

same or different, for the penitent reincurs the same kind of censure unless he has both performed the penance and given the satisfaction within the prescribed time.

Since there is question of reincidence, the penance and satisfaction should be imposed in such a way as to leave the least possible chance for doubt. A definite penance should be prescribed for a specified time. Regarding the satisfaction, generalities should not be prescribed, or there will always be uncertainty and anxiety about the reincurrence of the censure. The satisfaction should be as specific as the case allows. For example, in the restoration for damage or harm inflicted, the ability of the penitent to repair it should be considered, and then a definite prescription should be made, so that, if the penitent seriously fails to observe it within the determined time, he reincurs the censure. For the reparation of scandal, such things as leading a good life can hardly be imposed *sub poena reincidentiae;* but particular obligations should be prescribed according to the nature of the case, such as the retractation of heretical statements before those to whom they were originally made; the actual departure from an accomplice or the convalidation of a scandalous marriage in such a way that the scandal will be removed; the going to confession within stated intervals for a certain length of time, when this will suffice to nullify the scandal; and, in general, those specific things should be required which will provide that the scandal in the particular case will be repaired in the manner that seems best in the prudent judgment of the confessor.[44]

For the reincurrence of a censure the same factors are necessary as for the incurrence of a censure, for it is a new censure of the same species which is incurred, and before it can be contracted, there must be a new delict, external, grave, consummated, and joined with contumacy.[45]

[44] *Cf.* S. Poenit., 10 Decembris, 1860, ad 27—*ASS,* I (1865-1866), 566.

[45] *Cf.* canons 2228; 2242, § 1. *Cf.* Cappello, *De Censuris,* n. 95, 3, 6, 8, n. 131, 6; Cocchi, *Commentarium,* lib. V, pp. 115, 116, 126; Coronata, *Instit. Iuris Can.,* IV, 140, 141; Chelodi, *Ius Poenale,* p. 43; Blat, *Commentarium,* lib. V, p. 121; Cerato, *Censurae Vigentes,* p. 38; Sole, *De Delictis et Poenis,* n. 152, 3; Rossi, De sacerdotibus . . . ," *Perfice Munus,* XII (1937), 228.

In canon 2254, § 3 there are apparently two delicts, namely, the culpable omission of the penance, and the culpable omission of the satisfaction, either of which is sufficient to involve the reincurrence of the censure.[46] Likewise, the culpable neglect or rejection of either of these elements involves contumacy.[47]

If either or both the penance and satisfaction were entirely omitted without any excusing cause within the time prescribed by the confessor, it is clear that the delict or delicts are perfect and consummated, and the same kind of censure is reincurred.[48] But Coronata[49] has raised the question as to whether the reincidence takes place if the penance or satisfaction was partially, but not completely, fulfilled. He responds that, if at least half of the penance and satisfaction was fulfilled, it seems that the censure would not be reincurred, although the obligation of completing the penance and satisfaction would remain. There appears to be good reason for this opinion, for the penance, although it may consist of various grave elements, for example, reciting the rosary each day for a month, should be imposed as a unit, for it is to be a penance, not penances; and the same applies to the satisfaction. To take the example just given, it would impress one as being rather harsh to say that a penitent would reincur a censure for culpably omitting one rosary among the thirty prescribed. Consequently, it seems justifiable to say that, if the greater part of both the penance and the satisfaction has been fulfilled, there would be at least uncertainty whether or not the double delict is perfect and consummated, and the reincurrence of the censure would not take place, though the penitent would still be bound to complete the penance and satisfaction.[50]

[46] *Cf.* Coronata, *Instit. Iuris Can.*, IV, 185; Blat, *Commentarium*, lib. V, p. 121; Salucci, *Diritto Penale*, I, 229.

[47] *Cf.* canon 2242, §§ 2, 3.

[48] *Cf.* Coronata, *Instit. Iuris Can.*, IV, 185.

[49] *Loc. cit.* Coronata seems to be the only author who has considered this matter in detail.

[50] Coronata, *loc. cit.; cf.* also Blat, *Commentarium*, lib. V, p. 121; however the latter is not entirely clear in his statement on giving the satisfaction *"saltem in parte ipsius gravi."*

Article IV. The Absolution

Very little need be said here concerning the absolution granted according to canon 2254, § 3, for in its various elements it is practically the same as the absolution given by reason of canon 2254, § 1, which has already been treated at length. The minister of absolution is the same; the forum of the absolution is the same, namely, the sacramental forum; the nature and form of the absolution are likewise the same, but the penalty of reincidence, implied in the *absolutio ad reincidentiam* granted according to canon 2254, § 3, is based on the fulfillment of the penance and satisfaction imposed by the confessor, while that in canon 2254, § 1 depends on the fulfillment of the obligation of recourse.

Concerning the object of the absolution given according to canon 2254, § 3, *per se* it is exactly the same as that in canon 2254, § 1, with the same excluded case and an additional exception, as will be discussed in the following article. However, the inapplicability of canon 2254, § 3 will arise in some instances, not from the nature of the censure, but from the character of the person who confesses it. For, especially in some of the more serious censures, such as those reserved personally to the pope, it will occasionally happen that the censures have been incurred by persons for whom recourse will not be morally impossible, namely, priests or others who will be able to make recourse at least by writing the letter personally. Consequently, with the exception of the two censures about to be treated, the limitation of the application of canon 2254, § 3 will arise, not from any definite exclusion of censures from its scope, but from the fact that the condition for its use, namely, moral impossibility of recourse, will not be verified in some cases.

Before the two excluded cases are considered, a question may be raised here regarding absolution. If a person, unable to make recourse, personally, would deliberately choose a confessor to whom he cannot return and would receive absolution without the obligation of recourse, while he could as easily have gone to another confessor who would have granted absolution with the obligation of recourse, would the absolution be illicit, invalid, or both? Suppose the case of a person who goes to his parish church to confess a reserved censure in a more urgent case; he discovers that the pastor is hearing confessions, and also that a visiting priest, who will not return, is in another confessional; knowing that, if he confesses to the pastor, he will have to make recourse through the pastor and obey the mandates of the superior, he goes to the visiting priest, confesses the censure, receives absolution, and accepts the penance and satisfaction imposed by the confessor. In brief, he has forced the use of canon 2254, § 3 to escape recourse, when he could have been absolved according to canon 2254, § 1. What is to be said of his absolution?

The law evidently supposes that canon 2254, § 3 is to be employed only when the norm of canon 2254, § 1 is morally impossible, and the usual method of absolution in the more urgent cases is to be followed, where possible, rather than the exceptional method. Canon 2254, § 1 *must* be used when, in the actual circumstances of a case being confessed, the recourse is morally possible, for the confessor is not free to dispense with the obligation of recourse and replace it with the imposition of a penance and satisfaction; and if the confessor deliberately acted in this way, the absolution, though valid, would be illicit on his part. In the case supposed above, the recourse was not morally impossible before the confession, for it could have been satisfied if the confession had been made to the pastor. But when the censure is confessed to the visiting priest, there is apparently no obligation for him to send the penitent to the pastor to repeat the confession in order to be absolved according to canon 2254, § 1; and, *de facto,* in these circumstances the recourse is morally impossible, since the penitent cannot make the recourse personally and cannot return to the visiting priest for the mandates of the superior. Consequently, in the presumption that the *casus urgentior* is verified, namely, that there is danger of scandal or infamy, or hardship for the penitent to remain in grave sin, the absolution is valid. It is also licit on the part of confessor and penitent, if the conditions of canon 2254, § 3 concerning injunctions, penance, and satisfaction are observed, for canon 2254, § 3 is a complete provision for absolution in the more urgent cases, just as is canon 2254, § 1. But the action of the penitent before the confession, in forcing the use of canon 2254, § 3 in place of canon

2254, § 1, is a circumvention of the law, for the spirit of the law contemplates the application and acceptance of the usual method in the more urgent cases, rather than the exceptional method. However, such a circumvention could not be set down with any certainty as seriously sinful. The case, indeed, will be more theoretical than practical, for it will rarely happen that anyone except a person well versed in the law would think of acting in this way, and such a person will ordinarily be capable of making recourse personally by letter, and consequently should be absolved according to canon 2254, § 1, with the obligation of recourse.

Article V. The Excluded Cases

A. The Censure in Canon 2367

If recourse is morally impossible, absolution can be granted according to canon 2254, § 3, without the obligation of recourse, *"excepto casu quo agatur de absolutione censurae de qua in can. 2367."* The excommunication incurred for absolution of one's accomplice *in peccato turpi*, therefore, is explicitly excluded from the provision of canon 2254, § 3.

It is asserted by some authors [51] that the reason for the exclusion of this censure is because it is presumed that a priest can make the recourse personally, and consequently the recourse is not morally impossible simply because it cannot be made through the confessor. This is one reason, but another seems to be that the Sacred Penitentiary desires to take action in this case and not leave it to the judgment of a confessor, so that, to use the terms employed by certain authors, the restriction is not only *"in odium sacerdotis,"* but also *"in odium criminis."* [52] For this crime, besides possessing a special gravity, involves future dangers to souls, and the Sacred Penitentiary wishes to provide particular precautions that the same harm may not occur again. This crime is one of the two abuses

[51] *E. g.*, Coronata, *Instit. Iuris Can.*, IV, 185; Sole, *De Delictis et Poenis*, n. 197; Lega, *De Delictis et Poenis* (2. ed., Romae, 1910), n. 146 (p. 205).

[52] *Cf.* Salucci, *Diritto Penale*, I, 231; De Meester, *Compendium*, III, P. II, 188, nota 5. *Cf.* also Cappello, *De Censuris*, n. 131, 3; Cipollini, *De Censuris*, pp. 48, 49.

of the sacrament of Penance which Pope Benedict XIV treated in his constitution *"Sacramentum Poenitentiae"*;[53] the other is the crime of *sollicitatio ad turpia.* Very probably this latter crime would also be excluded from canon 2254, § 3, if it were not provided for in another way.[54] For, although there is no *latae sententiae* censure for *sollicitatio,*[55] the penitent who has been solicited must denounce the confessor within a month after being informed of this obligation, and the obligation of denunciation binds under pain of a *latae sententiae* excommunication which cannot be absolved until the person has at least promised seriously to fulfill it.[56] In this way the case will be brought to the attention of the Holy Office, and suitable measures will be taken to prevent any recurrence of the crime. But this method is not used for the censure contracted because of *absolutio complicis,* and the only way in which this censure would escape the notice of the Holy See would be by an absolution given according to canon 2254, § 3. Consequently, this seems to be the principal reason why it has been excluded from this part of canon 2254; if the only reason for the restriction were the ability of priests to make recourse personally, a general limitation regarding censures contracted by priests would have been more logical.[57]

The exclusion of the censure of canon 2367 from canon 2254, § 3, is worded so plainly and definitely that some authors maintain that the recourse must always be made, without exception.[58] When the confessor cannot make the recourse, and he foresees that the delinquent priest, because of some impediment, will not be able to make it personally within a month, but will be able to make it later,

[53] 1 Iunii, 1741—document V appended to the Code.

[54] Curiously enough it was this crime, instead of *absolutio complicis,* which, apparently by mistake, was excluded in canon 2254, § 3, in the original edition of the Code; *cf. AAS,* IX (1917), Pars II, 426. *Cf.* also Vermeersch, *Theol. Mor.,* III, n. 474.

[55] *Cf.* canon 2368, § 1.

[56] Canons 904; 2368, § 2.

[57] *Cf.* Salucci, *Diritto Penale,* I, 231.

[58] *E. g.,* Vermeersch-Creusen, *Epitome,* III, n. 454, 4, 2; Cavigioli, *De Censuris,* n. 58; Raus, *Instit. Can.,* p. 699; Blat, *Commentarium,* lib. V, p. 120; Kelly, *Jurisdiction of the Confessor,* p. 175. *Cf.* also Ayrinhac-Lydon, *Penal Legislation,* n. 106, a.

some say that the confessor *must* prorogue the time for recourse, specifying a definite time within which it must be made *sub poena reincidentiae*; [59] others say that the confessor *can* prorogue the time for recourse.[60] Lega, writing before the Code on the exclusion of the censure for *absolutio complicis* from the norms for absolution without recourse in the more urgent cases, maintained that, if the delinquent priest were prevented from writing (for example, because of sickness), there would be no reason to except him from the absolution without recourse; [61] and this opinion has received considerable support since the promulgation of the Code, several authors adding that not only sickness, as mentioned by Lega, but any other serious cause or grave inconvenience preventing recourse, such as the danger of infamy from the opening of the letter, would suffice for the granting of the absolution without the obligation of recourse.[62]

What is to be deduced from this variety of opinions, some maintaining the absolute exclusion of the censure for *absolutio complicis* from canon 2254, § 3, others asserting the possibility or the obligation of proroguing the time for recourse, and others admitting that absolution without recourse can be granted in any circumstances of grave inconvenience?

Regarding the notion of the prorogation of the time for recourse, several points call for consideration. In the assumption

[59] *Cf.* Cappello, *De Censuris,* n. 131, 5; Chelodi, *Ius Poenale,* p. 43.

[60] *Cf.* Coronata, *Instit. Iuris Can.,* IV, 185; De Meester, *Compendium,* III, P. II, 188; Salucci, *Diritto Penale,* I, 230.

[61] "In rescripto diei 7 Iunii, 1899, fit exceptio de sacerdote qui absolvit complicem in peccato turpi; et hoc ita intelligi debet, nempe sacerdotem, non comprehendi in indulta exemptione a danda epistola ad S. Sedem; quia sacerdos non est illiteratus; sed si casus fingatur, eum morbo impediri quominus scribat, ratio non adest cur excludatur ab indulto generali."—*De Delictis et Poenis,* n. 146 (p. 205). For the response of the Holy Office of June 7, 1899, *cf. Fontes,* n. 1224; explained above, p. 60.

[62] *Cf.* Cappello, *De Censuris,* n. 131, 3; Coronata, *Instit. Iuris Can.,* IV, 185; De Meester, *Compendium,* III, P. II, 188; Cerato, *Censurae Vigentes,* pp. 44, 45; Sole, *De Delictis et Poenis,* n. 197; Pruemmer, *Man. Theol. Mor.,* III, 304; Rossi, "De sacerdotibus . . .," *Perfice Munus,* XII (1937), 229. The opinion of Lega is also indicated without comment by Cocchi, *Commentarium,* lib. V, p. 127; Chelodi, *Ius Poenale,* p. 43, nota 4; it seems to be rejected by Salucci, *Diritto Penale,* I, 231.

that the month allowed for recourse in canon 2254, § 1, is *tempus utile* (and it seems clear that it must be understood in this sense), any prorogation of this period would be simply an increase of the number of days on which the penitent would have opportunity for recourse. But there is no basis for the contention that the confessor can add to the month of *tempus utile,* and that he can eliminate the penalty of reincidence for a penitent who has with grave culpability failed to make the recourse within a month of days which offered opportunity for recourse. On the other hand, it would be an injustice to threaten a priest, guilty of the crime of *absolutio complicis,* with the penalty of reincidence for failure to make the recourse within, for instance, four or six months of continuous time, when the opportunity for recourse and consequently the computation of the *tempus utile* will begin only at a later date. For the penitent's obligation to make recourse, when he has been absolved according to canon 2254, § 1, becomes effective only when he is able to make the recourse.

Besides, the opinion which maintains that the confessor *can* prorogue the time for recourse is open to the further objection that the confessor is seemingly *free* to extend a period of continuous time for recourse; the apparent alternative, in case the confessor does not choose to extend the time, is that he will absolve without the obligation of recourse. But the law supposes no such freedom of choice on the part of the confessor, and the opinion which affirms such freedom seems gratuitous and arbitrary in permitting so much power of decision to the confessor.

As has been mentioned, it seems that the presumption that priests can make recourse personally by letter is not the only reason for the exclusion of the censure of canon 2367 from canon 2254, § 3, but that the more important reason is that the Sacred Penitentiary wishes to handle such cases itself by its mandates, so as to provide suitable safeguards against future repetition of this abuse of the Sacrament of Penance. Canon 2254, § 3, states that, when the recourse that is to be prescribed in accordance with canon 2254, § 1, is morally impossible, any *latae sententiae* censure can be absolved without the penitent's being obliged to make the recourse, except the one censure mentioned in canon 2367. It does not demand that recourse be made after absolution from this censure even if the recourse is morally impossible. This would be contradictory, for recourse very obviously cannot be made as long as it is morally impossible. But there is no contradiction in canon 2254, § 3. It has been said, in the discussion on moral impossibility of recourse, that canon 2254, § 3, can be applied when it is foreseen that the recourse cannot be made within a month, and that this month must be regarded as a month of continuous time if the confessor will be in any way able to form a judgment of the moral impossibility, since *tempus utile* presupposes ability to act. In harmony with this, it seems clear that the prescription of canon 2254, § 3, consists in the requirement that recourse be made after absolution from the censure for *absolutio complicis* even if the recourse will be morally impossible for a month of continuous time. In other words, canon 2254, § 3, simply is not to be applied to this case. Consequently, the opinion which maintains that a priest, guilty of the crime of *absolutio complicis,* can be absolved without the obligation of recourse if sickness or any serious inconvenience renders it morally impossible for him to make the recourse within a month, seems to be in direct opposition to the explicit wording of the law. Only canon 2254, § 1, is to be applied for the absolution of the censure of canon 2367, so that recourse must be made at whatsoever time it becomes morally possible, and must be made *sub poena reincidentiae* within one month of *tempus utile,* that is, within one month of days which offer opportunity for recourse. It may be that in some cases the *tempus utile* will never begin, for the reason that there will never be opportunity to make the recourse. In such cases the obligation to make recourse will remain suspended and will never become effective. In other cases the opportunity to make recourse may arise only after the obligation of recourse has been suspended for a considerable time, but if the recourse is not then performed within a month of days which offer opportunity for recourse, the penalty of reincidence is incurred.

In the continued assumption that the confessor cannot make the recourse, or that the delinquent priest cannot return to him for the mandates, the following opinion is here advanced concerning the obligation of recourse which binds a priest absolved in a more urgent case from the censure for *absolutio complicis.* If the priest who has contracted the censure of canon 2367 can make the recourse personally—and this must be presumed in a priest—he must do so. However, if he prefers not to write the letter of recourse himself, though able to do so, he can choose some other method of making recourse,[63] but he must fulfill the obligation of recourse in some way. The period of time within which the recourse must be made is one month of *tempus utile,* that is, a month of days which offer opportunity for recourse; and ordinarily for a priest who enjoys good health this month of *tempus utile* will coincide with a month of continuous time. If the recourse is culpably omitted within a month of *tempus utile,* the priest again incurs a censure reserved *specialissimo modo* to the Holy See. In a word, the censure inflicted for the crime of *absolutio complicis* is entirely outside the provision of canon 2254, § 3, and in a more urgent case it can be absolved only according to the norm of canon 2254, § 1.

It may be remarked that, when the Sacred Penitentiary grants the faculty to absolve from the censure for *absolutio complicis,* it usually requires that the delinquent priest abstain from ever again hearing the confession of his former accomplice; [64] besides, it ordinarily enjoins that, if the priest has presumed to absolve three or more accomplices or the same accomplice three or more times since his last confession,[65] he must refrain from the office of hearing confessions as soon as possible, within a time to be determined by the confessor, which time cannot be protracted beyond three months if

[63] *Cf.* above, Chapter VII, Article IV, E, p. 211.

[64] *Cf.* also Pius XI, const. *"Servatoris Iesu Christi,"* 25 Decembris, 1925, pars de facultatibus, III—*AAS,* XVII (1925), 615.

[65] "Since his last confession"—this interpretation is based on a response of the S. Poenit., 5 Martii, 1925—*cf. Ecclesiastical Review,* LXXV (1926), 67, 68; also translation in Bouscaren, *Canon Law Digest,* I, 859. Formerly, the interpretation contemplated the commission of the crime of *absolutio complicis* three times during the course of one's entire priestly life, and was based on a response of the S. Poenit., 5 Iunii, 1901, ad 1—*ASS,* XXXIV (1901, 1902), 186, 187; also in *Ecclesiastical Review,* XXV (1901), 250, 251. The latter interpretation is still held by Coronata, *Instit. Iuris Can.,* IV, 528.

the delinquent is an ordinary confessor, nor beyond six months if he is a pastor.[66]

B. The Specific Case Under Canon 2388, § 1

This matter is to be treated in considerable detail in the following chapter,[67] so a brief mention of the case will be sufficient under the present heading. When a priest has attempted marriage, and, although he promises to observe perfect chastity in the future, is obliged by very serious reasons to continue dwelling with his accomplice, he can be absolved only by the Sacred Penitentiary, unless he is in danger of death. This case has been explicitly withdrawn from the faculties of canon 2254, § 1, and *a fortiori* it cannot be absolved by reason of canon 2254, § 3.

Consequently, there are two cases, and only two, which are positively excluded from the norm for absolution without recourse in the more urgent cases: the excommunication reserved *specialissimo modo* to the Holy See for *absolutio complicis,* as enacted in canon 2367; and, in the specific circumstances indicated above, the excommunication reserved *simpliciter* to the Holy See for marriage attempted by a priest, for this censure can never be absolved in the more urgent cases, even with the obligation of recourse, but only in danger of death.

[66] *Cf.* Cappello, *De Censuris,* n. 179, 2; Pistocchi, *Canoni Penali,* pp 227, 228; Coronata, *loc. cit.*

[67] Chapter X, Article IV.

CHAPTER X

SPECIAL CASES IN RELATION TO CANON 2254

ARTICLE I. HERESY, SCHISM, AND APOSTASY FROM THE FAITH

Canon 2314, § 1. Omnes a christiana fide apostatae et omnes et singuli haeretici aut schismatici:

1. Incurrunt ipso facto excommunicationem;

2. . . .

3. . . .

§ 2. Absolutio ab excommunicatione de qua in § 1, in foro conscientiae impertienda, est speciali modo Sedi Apostolicae reservata. Si tamen delictum apostasiae, haeresis vel schismatis ad forum externum Ordinarii loci quovis modo deductum fuerit, etiam per voluntariam confessionem, idem Ordinarius, non vero Vicarius Generalis sine mandato speciali, resipiscentem, praevia abiuratione iuridice peracta aliisque servatis de iure servandis, sua auctoritate ordinaria in foro exteriore absolvere potest; ita vero absolutus, potest deinde a peccato absolvi a quolibet confessario in foro conscientiae. Abiuratio vero habetur iuridice peracta cum fit coram ipso Ordinario loci vel eius delegato et saltem duobus testibus.

It is not intended to discuss here the case of heretics or schismatics who wish to convert to the Catholic Church; for them there is need of investigation concerning their baptism, a juridical abjuration of their errors, and absolution in the external forum.[1] The

[1] For a treatment of these matters, *cf.* MacKenzie, *The Delict of Heresy in Its Commission, Penalization, Absolution,* The Catholic University of America, Canon Law Studies, n. 77 (Washington: The Catholic University of America, 1932), pp. 113-116; Cappello, *De Censuris,* n. 215; Coronata, *Instit. Iuris Can.,* IV, 291-296; Cocchi, *Commentarium,* lib. V, p. 228; Vermeersch-Creusen, *Epitome,* III, n. 513, III, 2°; Ayrinhac-Lydon, *Penal Legislation,* n. 203; Woywod, *Practical Commentary,* nn. 2155-2158. *Cf.* especially S. C. S. Off., 20 Iulii, 1859—*Fontes,* n. 953; also S. C. S. Off., litt. 8 Martii, 1882—*Fontes,* n. 1073. Concerning the reception of schismatical Russians into the Church, *cf.* Pont. Comm. pro Russia, monit. 12 Ianuarii, 1929—*AAS,* XXI (1929), 94; instr. 26 Augusti, 1929—*Ibid.,* 608-610.

present consideration contemplates the case of those persons who have been baptized and reared in the Catholic Faith, but have contracted the excommunication of canon 2314 by subsequently falling into heresy, schism, or apostasy from the Faith.[2]

If the censure is occult, there is no difficulty to prevent the application of canon 2254, with or without the obligation of recourse according to the circumstances, in either of the more urgent cases, namely, in danger of grave scandal or infamy, or in the hardship of remaining in grave sin until the faculty can be obtained.[3] The confessor receives the penitent's private abjuration of heresy or schism and gives the proper injunctions, such as the removal of the occasion of relapse or the destruction of heretical or schismatical books; if recourse is to be made, it is directed to the Sacred Penitentiary or to the bishop or another superior if these latter have a faculty for excommunications reserved *speciali modo* to the Holy See.

Even if the delict was public, canon 2254 may be applicable, not in the *casus urgentior* of danger of scandal or infamy, for *per se* this will not be verified in such a case, but in the more urgent case of hardship of remaining in grave sin until the confessor can procure faculties. However, in this case, the penitent is bound to observe the prescription of canon 2251 in avoiding any acts in the external forum which would create scandal; and he can be forced to refrain from acting in the external forum as one absolved, if his sacramental absolution cannot be proved or legitimately presumed.[4]

[2] For the notion of heresy, apostasy, and schism, *cf.* canon 1325, § 2: "Post receptum baptismum si quis, nomen retinens christianum, pertinaciter aliquam ex veritatibus fide divina et catholica credendis denegat aut de ea dubitat, haereticus; si a fide christiana totaliter recedit, apostata; si denique subesse renuit Summo Pontifici aut cum membris Ecclesiae ei subiectis communicare recusat, schismaticus est." For an explanation of these notions, *cf.* Cappello, *op. cit.*, nn. 208-213; Coronata, *op. cit.*, IV, 278-287; Ayrinhac-Lydon, *op. cit.*, nn. 191-200; Sole, *De Delictis et Poenis*, nn. 313-316; Cerato, *Censurae Vigentes*, pp. 142-144.

[3] *Cf.* MacKenzie, *The Delict of Heresy*, pp. 111-113; Cocchi, *Commentarium*, lib. V, p. 227; Vermeersch-Creusen, *Epitome*, III, n. 513, III, 1°; Ayrinhac-Lydon, *op. cit.*, n. 203.

[4] *Cf.* MacKenzie, *loc. cit.* *Cf.* the general discussion of the absolution of public censures, above, Chapter VII, Article III, A, 3, p. 169. *Cf.* also the norm

The difficulty arises when the delict of heresy, schism, or apostasy has been brought in any way to the external forum of the ordinary. Can canon 2254 be employed to grant absolution in the internal forum in such circumstances? According to canon 2314, § 2, the ordinary can grant absolution in the external forum when the case has been brought to that forum. Does this exclude all possibility of absolution in the internal forum according to the norm of canon 2254? It seems not, for in canon 2314, § 2, it is said that the ordinary *can* grant absolution in the external forum; it is not said that he *must* grant it in the external forum, to the exclusion of any previous absolution in the internal forum in a more urgent case. Consequently, it appears that *per se* there is no exclusion of sacramental absolution according to canon 2254, as long as one of the *casus urgentiores* is verified. However, the sacramental absolution will usually be of little avail in these circumstances, as regards its effects in the external forum, for, even if it is granted, the penitent will ordinarily have to obtain an absolution in the external forum before he can enjoy the benefits of reinstatement in the communion of the faithful.[5]

given for the use of the jubilee faculties of 1934—Pius XI, const. *"Quod superiore anno,"* 2 Aprilis, 1934, IX, 3: "Haereticos vel schismaticos, qui fuerint publice dogmatizantes, ne absolvant, nisi ii, abiuratis saltem coram ipso confessario haeresi vel schismate, scandalum, ut par est, iam reparaverint, aut promiserint sese, ut par est, efficaciter reparaturos."—*AAS*, XXVI (1934), 145. A similar norm was given for the use of the jubilee faculties of 1925; *cf.* Pius XI, const. *"Servatoris Iesu Christi,"* 25 Decembris, 1925, pars de facultatibus, V—*AAS*, XVII (1925), 616.

[5] *Cf.* MacKenzie, *The Delict of Heresy*, pp. 111, 113: "If the delict of heresy had been notorious, either in fact or by *judicial process*, there is less possibility of applying this canon [2254]. Such penitents are, *ex hypothesi*, already disgraced and cannot plead that they fall within the provisions of the first clause of the canon. It is possible, but rather improbable, that obdurate heretics of this type will be so moved with compunction and religious fervor, that they will find it hard to delay their reconciliation with the Church for even a few days. However, if this possibility were actualized in a given case, the canon might be applied, especially if the delinquent takes immediate steps to notify the general public of his repentance. . . . If the penitent has been sentenced in the external forum, mere sacramental absolution will not suffice to free him from the prohibitions which the sentence brought upon him in regard to his external religious life. . . . It will be nec-

The conclusion, therefore, is that, although there is no absolute prohibition against the use of canon 2254 in a more urgent case when a censure for heresy, apostasy, or schism has been brought to the external forum of the ordinary, and although this absolution granted according to canon 2254 will restore the penitent to the state of grace, nevertheless the absolution from the censure in the sacramental forum will be generally useless to remove the inhibitions of action involved in the censure. Moreover, for such cases brought to the external forum, in many dioceses the confessor will have or will with little difficulty be able to obtain the delegated faculty to receive the juridical adjuration of the delinquent and to absolve him in the external forum, *"servatis de iure servandis,"* especially regarding the reparation of scandal. This absolution also produces its effect in the internal forum,[6] and subsequently any confessor can absolve from the sin of heresy, apostasy, or schism without any necessity of recourse.[7]

Article II. False Accusation of Solicitation

Canon 2363. Si quis per seipsum vel per alios confessarium de sollicitationis crimine apud Superiores falso denuntiaverit, ipso facto incurrit in excommunicationem speciali modo Sedi Apostolicae reservatam, a qua nequit ullo in casu absolvi, nisi falsam denuntiationem formaliter retractaverit, et damna, si qua inde secuta sint, pro viribus reparaverit, imposita insuper gravi ac diuturna poenitentia, firmo praescripto can. 894.

Canon 894. Unicum peccatum ratione sui reservatum Sanctae Sedi est falsa delatio, qua sacerdos innocens accusatur de crimine sollicitationis apud iudices ecclesiasticos.[8]

There is little doubt that the most perplexing problem in the

essary to secure absolution in the external forum." *Cf.* also the discussion of the absolution of censures brought to the judicial forum or declared by a judicial sentence, above, Chapter VII, Article III, A, 4, 5, p. 174 ff.

[6] Canon 2251.

[7] Canons 2314, § 2; 2246, § 3.

[8] *Cf.* Benedict XIV, const. *"Sacramentum Poenitentiae,"* 1 Iunii, 1741, § 3—document V appended to the Code.

study of absolution in the more urgent cases is that which arises from the relation of canon 2254 to canon 2363. On the one hand, it is asserted in canon 2363 that absolution cannot be given in any case, unless a formal retractation of the false charge has been made and the harm repaired; on the other hand, in canon 2254 a most general power is granted for absolution in the more urgent cases, and these may be verified before the accusation has been formally retracted and the harm actually repaired. Difficulties arise from the interpretation of the "formal retractation," from the question whether canon 2363 restricts absolution only in cases of ordinary absolution or also in the extraordinary cases, and from the consideration as to whether a serious promise of retractation and reparation is sufficient to meet the requirements of the canon. In response to these difficulties, almost every conceivable shade of opinion has appeared, resulting in a conglomeration of views which produce nothing but bewilderment.

Chelodi [9] and Augustine [10] maintain that neither in danger of death nor in the more urgent cases can absolution be given unless the formal retractation has been made and the damage repaired, Augustine admitting that if the judicial retractation is impossible because of the physical or mental condition of the penitent, the confessor can receive the retractation and then report to the authorities, provided, of course, that the seal of confession is safeguarded.

Coronata [11] and Cappello [12] claim that the formal retractation is none other than that which is made in juridical form before the competent superior, namely, the local ordinary or the Holy Office or the special delegate of either. Since it will not happen in one case in a thousand that a person in a more urgent case is making his confession to the local ordinary or his delegate or to the delegate of the Holy Office, canon 2254 is useless according to this opinion.[13]

[9] *Ius Poenale,* p. 118.

[10] *Commentary,* VIII, 425.

[11] *Instit. Iuris Can.,* IV, 505, 506.

[12] *De Censuris,* n. 290.

[13] Cappello (*op. cit.,* n. 291) says that the *falso denuntians* can be absolved according to canon 2254, § 1, with the obligation of recourse; but he seems

Others admit that, in the more urgent cases, it is sufficient if the penitent gives the confessor a written and signed retractation, or retracts the false accusation beforehand in the presence of two witnesses, for both methods are formal in the sense that they can be used for the removal of the effect of the judicial denunciation; but these authors contend that a promise to make the retractation is not sufficient, though it will suffice regarding the reparation of harm.[14]

Still another opinion acknowledges that the two methods of retractation just mentioned are sufficient in the *casus urgentior* of danger of scandal or infamy, and if neither can be performed, a serious promise to fulfill the obligation of retracting the false accusation will suffice; but in the more urgent case of hardship of remaining in grave sin until the proper faculties can be procured, canon 2363 is to be strictly observed.[15]

Finally, De Smet alone has been found to admit that canon 2254, § 3 can be used if the recourse is morally impossible,[16] and that, if the retractation cannot be made at least by a signed letter given to the confessor or by admission of the false accusation before two witnesses, a promise of retractation and of reparation of harm

to be speaking only of the reserved sin of canon 894, according to his opinion on the analogous absolution of reserved sins by reason of canon 2254.

[14] *Cf.* Vermeersch-Creusen, *Epitome,* III, n. 565, 2; Sole, *De Delictis et Poenis,* n. 416, 5; Cocchi, *Commentarium,* lib. V, p. 328; Ayrinhac-Lydon, *Penal Legislation,* n. 325, c; Cipollini, *De Censuris,* pp. 129-131; De Meester, *Compendium,* III, P. II, 268, nota 5; Salucci, *Diritto Penale,* II, 274; Genicot-Salsmans, *Instit. Theol. Mor.,* II, n. 400. Woywod ("False Accusation of Solicitation," *Homiletic and Pastoral Review,* XXXVIII [1938], 720) says it is not advisable to absolve a penitent after a mere promise of retractation.

[15] *Cf.* Cerato, *De Delicto Sollicitationis* (Patavii: typis Seminarii, 1922), pp. 115, 116; *Idem, Censurae Vigentes,* p. 171; Wouters *Man. Theol. Mor.,* II, n. 895, XIII, nota 1 (pp. 767, 768). Pistocchi (*Canoni Penali,* p. 216) quotes this opinion of Cerato and seems to accept it.

[16] *De Absolutione Complicis et Sollicitatione* (2. ed., Brugis: Beyaert, 1921), n. 130. Cocchi (*Commentarium,* lib. V, p. 328) expressly states that the obligation of recourse is one of the conditions for absolution in the more urgent cases; *cf.* also De Meester, *Compendium,* III, P. II, 268, nota 5.

will suffice not only in danger of death,[17] but also in either of the two more urgent cases.[18]

What is to be drawn from this variety of conflicting opinions on the relation between canons 2254 and 2363? Utter uncertainty is the first and deepest impression. What course, then, is to be followed?

Despite the fact that the opinion of De Smet is solitary amid a variety of views which contradict one or the other of its elements, it is here accepted, and the following statement is made: in either of the more urgent cases, as well as in danger of death, if a formal retractation is impossible, either before the competent superior or by way of a signed letter given to the confessor or an attestation to the truth before two witnesses, a serious promise to retract the false accusation and to repair the harm will suffice for the grant of absolution either with or without the obligation of recourse, that is, according to canon 2254, § 1, or canon 2254, § 3.

How is such a conclusion deduced? First of all, a word may be said regarding the statement in reference to danger of death. If a person is actually at the point of death, can hardly speak, much

[17] "Retractatio illa stricte loquendo esset facienda coram Superiore coram quo denuntiatio est delata; sed, si id obtineri non possit, sufficit ut poenitens quacumque scripta declaratione subsignata, vel et orali declaratione coram duobus testibus, denuntiationem formaliter retractet, cum promissione debitam ulterius instituendi retractationem, si convaluerit; imo si aliter omnino fieri nequeat, non auderemus dicere quod non sufficiat sola seria, cui plene confidi queat, promissio de debita retractatione postea peragenda."—*Op. cit.*, n. 128.

[18] "Et quidem poenitens, non tantum non est absolvendus antequam poenitentiam acceptaverit ac denuntiationem retractaverit et damna pro posse reparaverit, *aut saltem illa praestanda spoponderit;* sed et pro executione praefiniendum est a confessario tempus congruum, non excedendum, idque sub poena reincidentiae in eamdam censuram, si poenitens, intra illius temporis terminos, non 'poenitentiam egerit ac satisfactionem dederit.' "—*Op. cit.*, n. 132. The *"illa praestanda spoponderit"* evidently does not refer only to the *"damna,"* for it would be without sense to say that the penitent must at least "promise to give harm"; the *"illa"* clearly refers to both the retractation and the reparation. The above citation is in reference to the application of canon 2254, § 3; regarding the statement that De Smet does not distinguish between the two *casus urgentiores*, but admits that absolution can be given from the censure of canon 2363 if either of them is verified, *cf. op. cit.*, n. 129.

less write, and the confessor is the only one present, must the confessor refuse to absolve because he cannot obtain a formal retractation? Evidently not, as long as the penitent has the proper dispositions and is willing or can be presumed to be willing to retract the false accusation in case of recovery. In such a case, the confessor should, if he can, obtain the penitent's permission to use his knowledge outside of confession and to do what he can to repair the harm in place of the penitent.[19] If the penitent is unable to give even this, it is unfortunate for the accused priest, just as it would be if the penitent died without making confession, but it seems clear that the properly disposed penitent should be absolved. Here, then, is one case in which absolution can be given without a previous formal retractation, contrary to the wording of canon 2363, according to which the penitent *"nequit ullo in casu absolvi"* until he has actually made a formal retractation and repaired the harm. This, of course, is an extreme case—a case of physical impossibility—but it should serve to illustrate the point. If the danger of death arises from any intrinsic or extrinsic cause, and the penitent is in sufficient possession of his faculties, then the retractation should be obtained either in writing or before two witnesses, and if this is impossible, the promise of making the retractation and reparation of scandal as soon as possible must be demanded before giving absolution; otherwise, the penitent is not properly disposed.

To come to the point which this article professedly proposes to consider—the conclusion has been stated that the censure of canon 2363 can be absolved with or without the obligation of recourse in either of the more urgent cases if, when the person is unable to give a signed retractation to the confessor or retract the false accusation before two witnesses, he at least makes a serious promise to make the retractation and repair the harm. To indicate the reasons for this opinion will involve a brief discussion of the views which have been indicated above.

First, it is not at all clear that the formal retractation mentioned in canon 2363 consists solely of a judicial statement made before the local ordinary or the Holy Office or the delegate of either;

[19] *Cf.* Cipollini, *De Censuris*, p. 130.

if it were certain, the opinion asserting that the signed retractation given to the confessor or the testimony before witnesses is sufficient, could not have received such wide acceptance.

Secondly, there are those who, though not distinguishing between the more urgent cases, admit that a promise is sufficient for the reparation of harm, but deny that a promise is sufficient for the retractation. But canon 2363 does not lend any support to the distinction between a promise of retractation and a promise of reparation; it simply says that absolution cannot be given unless the formal retractation has been made and the harm repaired; and consequently, the sufficiency of a promise should be maintained for neither or for both.

Thirdly, there are those who distinguish between the more urgent cases, saying that a promise of retractation is sufficient in the case of danger of scandal or infamy, but not in the case of hardship of remaining in grave sin until the proper faculties can be procured. But these two cases have been made parallel in canon 2254; their scope of application does not depend on the gravity of the censure, but upon their verification in a particular case—for example, the first *casus urgentior* will *per se* not be verified in the case of a public censure, but the second can be verified in this instance; consequently, the distinction that a promise of retractation is sufficient in one of the more urgent cases but not in the other, seems arbitrary.

Finally, there is the view which permits the absolution with the obligation of recourse, according to canon 2254, § 1, but not without this obligation, as in canon 2254, § 3. But the law has not made this distinction; what it has done is to permit the absolution of the censure for *absolutio complicis* according to canon 2254, § 1, while forbidding the absolution according to canon 2254, § 3; but it makes no such distinction regarding the censure of canon 2363.

On the one hand, canon 2363 is strict in its requirements; on the other hand, canon 2254 is almost limitless in its application. Should canon 2254, with canon 882, be restricted to meet the literal requirements of canon 2263; or should canon 2363 be interpreted to allow the range of application of canons 2254 and 882? If formal juridical retractation and actual reparation must be made before absolution, the emergency provisions for extraordinary cases are practically nullified for this particular censure. If these requirements are regarded as literally meant for ordinary cases, in which a confessor has the faculty to absolve, but must not use it until the requisites are fulfilled—and if, for extraordinary cases, a promise is considered as sufficient, as it is for other censures [20] —then both the ordinary and the extraordinary provisions for absolution are preserved intact. This, of course, involves the same objection that has been made to the other opinions, namely, a distinction where the law does not distinguish—a distinction between ordinary and extraordinary absolution, not in the sense that retractation and reparation are to be made in the one and disregarded in the other, but in the sense that these requirements are *actually* to be made before the one and at least *promised* before the other. But it must be noted that the conditions for the use of canon 2254 amply provide against any evasion of the requirements of canon 2363. If a person is absolved according to canon 2254, § 1 after promising to make retractation and reparation, he must make recourse to the competent superior and must receive the mandates either directly from the Sacred Penitentiary or by returning to the confessor; otherwise, he reincurs the same kind of censure, and the whole case is the same as if he had never been absolved. If the person is absolved according to canon 2254, § 3, before the absolution the confessor must not only assign a proportionate penance (which would be *gravis et diuturna* for this case, according to canon 2363), but he must also impose a satisfaction, which, as has been demonstrated,[21] consists in the reparation of harm and scandal, and if the penitent in this case does not fulfill the satisfaction by retracting the false accusation and repairing the harm within the time specified by the confessor, he reincurs the same kind of censure.[22]

[20] *Cf.* canon 2242, § 3.

[21] *Cf.* above, Chapter IX, Articles II and III, p. 241 ff.

[22] Note that De Smet (*De Absolutione Complicis et Sollicitatione*, n. 132), although asserting that the retractation and the reparation of harm come under the *iniunctis de iure iniungendis* of canon 2254, § 3, nevertheless states that, if a promised retractation and reparation are not performed within the time determined by the confessor, the penitent reincurs the censure; *cf.* above, in the present chapter, note 18.

Has the Church, at any time since the promulgation of the Code, admitted that in special circumstances a promise to retract the accusation and to repair the harm is sufficient for absolution? It has. In the jubilee faculties of 1925, it was stated that confessors could absolve penitents guilty of false denunciation of solicitation, if the penitents had formally retracted the accusation, or if they showed that they were seriously prepared to retract it as soon as possible and to repair any harm that had arisen from the calumny.[23] Here, then, was a situation in which, not to mention danger of death, there was no danger of scandal or infamy, and no special hardship of remaining in sin other than that which would arise from the penitent's being prevented from gaining the jubilee indulgences; yet any ordinary confessor was given the faculty to absolve, without the obligation of recourse, from the reserved sin of canon 894 and the reserved censure of canon 2363 as long as the penitent at least showed readiness to make the retractation and repair the harm as soon as possible. This, indeed, is no direct proof that a promise of retractation and reparation is sufficient for the use of the faculties of canon 2254, but it at least serves as an indication that this opinion is not radically incompatible with the practice of the Church.

Concerning the reserved sin of canon 894, which is generally considered as being the same crime which is punished additionally with the reserved censure of canon 2363,[24] it has been said in another

[23] Pius XI, const. *"Servatoris Iesu Christi,"* 25 Decembris, 1925, pars de facultatibus, VII: "Qui falsam sollicitationis denuntiationem admiserit, is ne absolvatur, nisi aut eam formaliter retractaverit, aut saltem ad eam quamprimum retractandam atque ad sarcienda calumniae damna serio paratum se praebeat."—*AAS,* XVII (1925), 616. No mention of this faculty was made in the jubilee faculties of 1934, and the Sacred Penitentiary simply applied the wording of canon 2363 to the reserved sin of canon 894; *cf.* S. Poenit., monita, 3 Aprilis, 1934, VII—*AAS,* XXVI (1934), 151.

[24] *Cf.* Cappello, *De Censuris,* n. 287; Coronata, *Instit. Iuris Can.,* IV, 507; Cocchi, *Commentarium,* lib. V, pp. 324-326; Vermeersch-Creusen, *Epitome,* III, n. 565, 1; De Meester, *Compendium,* III, P. II, 268, 269; Woywod, "False Accusation of Solicitation," *Homiletic and Pastoral Review,* XXXVIII (1938), 719. The opposite opinion, maintaining that canons 894 and 2363 contemplate different crimes, is held by Cerato, *De Delicto Sollicitationis,* pp. 113, 114; Motry, *Diocesan Faculties,* pp. 108-113.

place [25] that, in the same urgent circumstances in which canon 2254 can be used for the absolution of a reserved censure, the reservation of the sin ceases by virtue of canon 900.[26] Consequently, if the censure of canon 2363 can be absolved according to canon 2254, the reservation of the sin will not cause any difficulty.[27]

If the confessor absolves according to canon 2254, § 3, besides enjoining the things demanded by law, and requiring the satisfaction consisting in the reparation of scandal and harm, he must impose a "*poenitentia gravis et diuturna,*" according to canon 2363, for this crime. The matter of penances has been considered elsewhere [28] and needs no repetition here.

Before this discussion is brought to a close, it may be advisable to emphasize the previously stated conclusion that the promise of retractation and reparation is here considered as sufficient for the use of the faculties of canon 2254 *only when the retractation cannot be actually obtained in any form.* It will be comparatively rare that a retractation cannot be obtained in some form, especially in the *casus urgentior* of hardship of remaining in grave sin, but if this contingency should arise, it is here contended that a serious promise of retractation and reparation is sufficient for the grant of absolution, not only in a case of danger of death, but also in either of the more urgent cases.

[25] *Cf.* above, Chapter VII, Article III, E, p. 189 ff.

[26] In danger of death, the reservation ceases by reason of canon 882.

[27] In answer to the objection that such an opinion destroys all effectiveness of the reservation of sins to the pope, it may be observed that there are only two sins reserved *ratione sui* to the pope, or rather to the Holy See; that of canon 894 is also reserved *ratione censurae,* and if it is absolved according to canon 2254, recourse must be made to the Sacred Penitentiary, or, if recourse is morally impossible, the confessor must impose mandates similar to those of the Holy See and obligatory *sub poena reincidentiae;* the other sin reserved *ratione sui,* namely, that incurred by a confessor who deliberately absolves obstinate adherents of *L'Action Française,* always entails the obligation of recourse, even if the reservation ceases according to the norm of canon 900. *Cf.* above, Chapter VII, note 186.

[28] *Cf.* above, Chapter IX, Article III, p. 246 ff.

Article III. Apostasy and Flight From Religious Institutes

Canon 2385. Firmo praescripto can. 646, religiosus, apostata a religione, ipso iure incurrit in excommunicationem, proprio Superiori maiori vel, si religio sit laicalis aut non exempta, Ordinario loci in quo commoratur, reservatam, ab actibus legitimis ecclesiasticis est exclusus, privilegiis omnibus suae religionis privatus; et si redierit, perpetuo caret voce activa et passiva, ac praeterea aliis poenis pro gravitate culpae a Superioribus puniri debet ad normam constitutionum.

Canon 2386. Religiosus fugitivus ipso facto incurrit in privationem officii, si quod in religione habeat, et in suspensionem proprio Superiori maiori reservatam, si sit in sacris; cum autem redierit, puniatur secundum constitutiones, et si constitutiones nihil de hoc caveant, Superior maior pro gravitate culpae poenas infligat.

It is sometimes said [29] that, since apostasy from a religious institute [30] is usually public, and since the competent superior can be reached without difficulty, canon 2254 is not to be used for absolution from the excommunication of canon 2385,[31] but the penitent is to be sent to his religious superior to confer with him concerning return to the institute or secularization. However, it may happen that, although the crime is known to members of the institute, it

[29] *Cf.* Cocchi, *Commentarium,* lib. V, p. 368; Genicot-Salsmans, *Instit. Theol. Mor.,* II, n. 608.

[30] Canon 644. "§ 1. Apostata a religione dicitur professus a votis perpetuis sive sollemnibus sive simplicibus qui e domo religiosa illegitime egreditur cum animo non redeundi, vel qui, etsi legitime egressus, non redit eo animo ut religiosae obedientiae sese subtrahat.

"§ 2. Malitiosus animus, de quo in § 1, iure praesumitur, si religiosus intra mensem nec reversus fuerit nec Superiori animum redeundi manifestaverit."

[31] There seems to be no sufficient ground for the opinion excluding female religious from this censure. *Cf.* Cappello, *De Censuris,* n. 389, 2; Coronata, *Instit. Iuris Can.,* IV, 629; Cocchi, *loc. cit.;* Ayrinhac-Lydon, *Penal Legislation,* n. 357; Cavigioli, *De Censuris,* n. 164; Smith, *The Penal Law for Religious,* The Catholic University of America, Canon Law Studies, n. 98 (Washington: The Catholic University of America, 1935), pp. 95, 96. Contrary to Cerato, *Censurae Vigentes,* p. 102; Cipollini, *De Censuris,* p. 179; Pistocchi, *Canoni Penali,* pp. 309, 310.

has not been divulged to outsiders and is not liable to be divulged, and the delinquent religious finds that, in the place in which he is staying, there would be danger of grave scandal or infamy if he would omit the celebration of Mass or the reception of Communion. Likewise, there may be hardship of remaining in the state of grave sin until the ordinary can be approached, just as there may be in the case of any other censure reserved to the ordinary. If either of these two circumstances should be verified in a particular case, there seems to be no reason why the provision of canon 2254 should not be applied, provided that the penitent has the proper dispositions. Among the proper dispositions he must have is the readiness to rectify his status, either personally or through a representative, by arranging for his return to the institute or for a dispensation from his religious vows.

It will be rare that canon 2254, § 3, will be applicable in such a case, for even if the recourse cannot be made through the confessor, the religious himself can hardly be regarded as incapable of making personal recourse to the superior, if not by going to him, then at least by a personal letter. If he prefers not to write the letter personally, he may make the recourse in some other way,[32] but it will be very seldom that he can be excused from the obligation of recourse on the grounds of its moral impossibility.

When the confessor makes the recourse for the penitent, he directs it to the major superior, if the penitent is a member of an exempt clerical religious institute; [33] to the local ordinary of the place in which the penitent is staying, in the case of any other religious.

However, it must be noted that there will hardly be any case in which it will be sufficient to make recourse for the internal forum, since the status of the apostate religious will practically always have to be rectified in the external forum, either by reinstatement in the institute or by dispensation from his vows. Consequently, if the con-

[32] *Cf.* above, Chapter VII, Article IV, E, p. 211.

[33] With reference to confessors approved by the local ordinary for the hearing of confessions, it must be recalled that canon 519 grants no power to such confessors to absolve from censures reserved *by common law* to religious superiors.

fessor has any part in assisting the delinquent to rectify the situation, it will not be in his capacity as confessor, but simply as an intermediary in the external forum; and it will not be enough to give a fictitious name for the religious in the letter to the superior, but the true name must be given, either as known outside of confession or from confessional knowledge used with the permission of the penitent.

Since the apostate religious is *per se* bound to return without delay to his institute,[34] the recourse will ordinarily be provided for by his communication with his superior at his return; if it is morally impossible for him to return, and he is willing to obey the mandates of the superior, there seems to be no reason to deny him absolution in the internal forum in a *casus urgentior,* and it will be incumbent upon him to satisfy the obligation of recourse either by personally presenting himself to the superior or writing to him, or by using an intermediary for the external forum.

Canon 2385 preserves intact the provision of canon 646, and if the apostasy from the religious institute is complicated by the fact that the religious has taken flight with a person of the opposite sex, he is *ipso facto* dismissed from the institute,[35] and, although *per se* he is still bound by his vows,[36] he cannot be readmitted to the religious institute.[37] Consequently, in such a case an apostate religious absolved by reason of canon 2254 would have to seek a dispensation from his vows.

[34] Canon 645, § 1.

[35] Canon 646, § 1, n. 2. If the religious has attempted marriage, he contracts the excommunication of canon 2388, § 2; moreover, if he is in sacred orders and has attempted marriage, he also incurs the excommunication of canon 2388, § 1.

[36] Canon 669, § 1.

[37] "I. An declaratio facti, de qua in canone 646, § 2, requiratur ad hoc ut Religiosus ipso facto habendus sit tanquam legitime dimissus.

"II. An praescriptum canonis 672, § 1, extendatur etiam ad Religiosos ipso facto dimissos ad normam canonis 646.

"R. Ad I. Negative.

"Ad II. Negative."—Pont. Comm., 30 Iulii, 1934, III—*AAS,* XXVI (1934), 494. *Cf.* canon 672, § 1. *Cf.* Smith, *Penal Law for Religious,* p. 107.

Regarding fugitives from religious institutes,[38] the only *latae sententiae* censure which could call for the use of canon 2254 is the censure of suspension incurred by a fugitive in sacred orders.[39] If there is hardship of remaining in grave sin until the faculties can be obtained, this in itself is no reason for the use of canon 2254, for the sin can be absolved while the suspension remains.[40] However, if there should be danger of scandal or infamy from the observance of the suspension in a particular case, even though the delinquent can be absolved from the sin and can then invoke canon 2232, § 1, to disregard the censure as long as the danger of scandal or infamy lasts, nevertheless there seems to be sufficient reason to apply canon 2254 and to grant absolution from the censure in these circumstances.[41] For canon 2232, § 1, appears to be an added provision for the contingency in which absolution cannot be obtained; but when the confessor can grant absolution and entirely remove the censure, it would seem that he should follow this course and release the penitent from the censure, rather than constrain the penitent to remain under the censure and to disregard it in the danger of infamy. Ordinarily, canon 2254, § 3, will be inapplicable in the case considered here, and absolution will be granted only with the obligation of recourse, since recourse should not be morally impossible for a cleric in major orders. Regarding recourse, it must be noted with reference to the present case that, although the censure may be unknown to those persons among whom the delinquent is forced to perform a prohibited act in order to avoid the danger of scandal or infamy, it may easily be known to the superiors of the delinquent, and the case will have to be handled in such a way that the recourse will acquaint the superiors with the rectified status of the individual religious. Such a form of recourse, informing the superiors of the name of the penitent and

[38] Canon 644. "§ 3. Fugitivus est qui, sine Superiorum licentia, domum religiosam deserit cum animo ad religionem redeundi."

[39] That this suspension is a censure, *cf.* Cappello, *De Censuris*, n. 539, 1; Coronata, *Instit. Iuris Can.*, IV, 631; Rainer, *Suspension of Clerics*, p. 235; Smith, *Penal Law for Religious*, p. 101.

[40] Canon 2250, § 1.

[41] *Cf.* Blat, *Commentarium*, lib. V, p. 115.

of his absolution in the sacramental forum, can obviously be made only from knowledge obtained outside of confession or from confessional knowledge used with the permission of the penitent, to preclude a violation of the seal of confession.

However, it may happen that the crime was entirely occult, is known only to the delinquent himself, and is in no danger of coming to the knowledge of others. If the religious does not wish to betray his crime by having it brought to the attention of his superior, it seems that, as has just been mentioned, he can be absolved by reason of canon 2254 in the *casus urgentior* of danger of scandal or infamy, with the obligation of recourse. Then, although the censure is reserved to the major superior, the recourse could be made to the Sacred Penitentiary, whose mandates would provide against revelation of the crime through any *ipso facto* privation of offices as determined by canon 2386, and would indicate the injunctions to be observed and the penance to be performed in accordance with the constitutions of the institute, or, in the absence of such specific constitutions, in proportion to the gravity of the crime. If, in such a case, there would be no danger of violation of the seal of confession in sending the letter of recourse to the superior, with a fictitious name to designate the penitent, the competent superior would unquestionably be the major superior [42] if the fugitive religious is a member of an exempt clerical institute; apparently the same is true if the institute is clerical but not exempt; [43] if the fugitive is a cleric in major orders in a lay institute [44] in which the major superior is not a cleric, it is generally said that the competent superior is the local ordinary,[45] but it may happen that such a superior in an exempt lay institute, such as the Hospitallers of St. John of God, actually possesses jurisdiction in the nonsacramental fora, despite the provision of canon 118 that only clerics

[42] *Cf.* canon 488, n. 8, with the possible restriction of canon 501, § 3.

[43] *Cf.* Coronata, *Instit. Iuris Can.*, IV, 631; Vermeersch-Creusen, *Epitome*, III, n. 590; Cocchi, *Commentarium*, lib. V, p. 369.

[44] *Cf.* canon 488, n. 4. A *religio laicalis* is one in which the majority of the members are not priests.

[45] *Cf.* Vermeersch-Creusen, *loc. cit.;* Cocchi, *loc. cit.;* Ayrinhac-Lydon, *Penal Legislation*, n. 360, 2.

can possess jurisdiction.[46] However, when a confessor is writing a letter of recourse from knowledge gained in the confessional, he should ordinarily write to the Sacred Penitentiary in such an unusual case as the one under discussion, for there may easily be at least a suspicion concerning the identity of the delinquent if recourse is made to the superior, and consequently this latter method of recourse may involve danger of violation of the seal of confession.

Article IV. Attempted Marriage by a Priest

Canon 2388, § 1. Clerici in sacris constituti vel regulares aut moniales post votum sollemne castitatis, itemque omnes cum aliqua ex praedictis personis matrimonium etiam civiliter tantum contrahere praesumentes, incurrunt in excommunicationem latae sententiae Sedi Apostolicae simpliciter reservatam; clerici praeterea, si moniti, tempore ab Ordinario pro adiunctorum diversitate praefinito, non resipuerint, degradentur, firmo praescripto can. 188, n. 5.

§ 2. Quod si sint professi votorum simplicium perpetuorum tam in Ordinibus quam in Congregationibus religiosis, omnes, ut supra, excommunicatio tenet latae sententiae Ordinario reservata.

Occasionally during the course of this work reference has been made to a censure which, although neither *ab homine* nor reserved *specialissimo modo* to the Holy See, entails the obligation of recourse if it is absolved in danger of death, and which is entirely excluded from the faculties of canon 2254. The case concerns any priest who has attempted marriage, and who, because of very grave reasons, is obliged to continue dwelling with his accomplice, although he intends to observe perfect chastity in the future.

The present discipline for this case originated in 1936, in the following decree of the Sacred Penitentiary.[47]

[46] For a discussion of this question, *cf.* Smith, *Penal Law for Religious*, pp. 101-103.

[47] *AAS*, XXVIII (1936), 242, 243.

SACRA PAENITENTIARIA APOSTOLICA

Absolutio Sacerdotum ab Excommunicatione, ob Attentatum Etiam Civile Tantum Matrimonium, et Actu Cum Muliere Caste Conviventium Eorumque Admissio ad Participationem Sacramentorum More Laicorum Sacrae Paenitentiariae Apostolicae Exclusive Reservatur.

DECRETUM

Lex sacri coelibatus inter Latinos adeo Sanctae Ecclesiae curae semper fuit atque est ut, si agatur de sacerdotibus, fere nunquam super ea retroactis temporibus dispensatum fuerit, nunquam prorsus, ne in mortis quidem periculo, in praesenti disciplina dispensetur.

Cum tamen, nequitia temporum, contingere aliquando soleat ut infelix aliquis sacerdos, suae vocationis oblitus in sacrilegum concubinatum lapsus, ob matrimonium etiam civiliter tantum attentatum aliasque gravissimas rationes, a cohabitatione sub eodem tecto cum suae desertionis complice, etsi forte tandem ad cor reversus, cessare impediatur, ideoque ad suae eiusdemque suae complicis conscientiae consulendum, data fide de absoluta perfectaque in posterum continentia perpetuo servanda, ad participationem sacramentorum more laicorum petat admitti, Sancta eadem Ecclesia, pro sua erga devios etiam filios materna sollicitudine, ei, quantum in se est, si et quando peculiaria id suadeant rerum adiuncta, subvenire non renuit. Quod quidem cum conscientiam praesertim respiciat, Sacrae Paenitentiariae Apostolicae *exclusive* reservari congruum visum est.

Re igitur collata per infrascriptum Cardinalem Maiorem Paenitentiarium cum Ssmo D. N. Pio divina providentia Pp. XI, eadem Sanctitas Sua, in audientia diei 14 mensis Martii vertentis anni, eidem Cardinali Maiori Paenitentiario impertita, suprema Sua auctoritate decernere ac statuere dignata est ut, firma excommunicatione, de qua in canone 2388, § 1, absolutio ab ea in casu supra exposito et consequens supplicantis admissio ad sacramenta more laicorum suscipienda, ab ipsa tantum Sacra Paenitentiaria Apostolica, servata speciali procedendi forma et sub peculiaribus quibusdam cautelis et conditionibus ab eadem Sanctitate Sua patefactis ac praescriptis, concedi possint; et si forte concedantur ab aliquo sacerdote in periculo mortis, maneat obligatio ad ipsam Sacram Paenitentiariam recurrendi, ut praescribitur canone 2252 pro censuris a iure Sanctae Sedi specialissimo modo reservatis.

Hoc autem Decretum Sibi relatum in alia audientia diei 28 eiusdem mensis idem Ssm̃us Dominus Noster in omnibus adprobare et confirmare dignatus est, mandans ut, quo solet modo, publici iuris fiat.

Contrariis quibuscumque etiam speciali mentione dignis non obstantibus.

Datum Romae, ex Aedibus Sacrae Paenitentiariae Apostolicae, die 18 Aprilis 1936.

L. Card. Lauri, *Paenitentiarius Maior.*

L. ✠ S. S. Luzio, *Regens.*

In the decree, although it was explicitly mentioned that the censure under the specific circumstances was reserved solely to the Sacred Penitentiary, there was no express exclusion of canon 2254, and, while some commentators clearly or implicitly indicated that canon 2254 was no longer applicable to this case,[48] there were others who maintained that canon 2254, § 1, could still be used.[49]

With little delay the Sacred Penitentiary, in the following declaration of 1937,[50] emphasized very clearly that, according to the meaning and wording of its previous decree, the censure was so reserved to itself that no one, by reason either of canon 2254, § 1, or of any other faculty, could grant absolution from it except in danger of death.

[48] *Cf.* Rossi, "S. Poenit. Apos., Decretum 18 Aprilis, 1936—Annotationes," *Apollinaris,* IX (1936), 587, 588; Fliesser, "Absolutio et ad participationem sacramentorum admissio sacerdotum in attentato matrimonio abhinc caste viventium," *TPQ,* LXXXIX (1936), 822; Verhamme, "Decretum 18 Aprilis, 1936—Notae," *Collationes Brugenses,* XXXVI (1936), 336, 337.

[49] *Cf.* Beijersbergen, "Decretum 18 Aprilis, 1936—Annotationes," *Periodica,* XXV (1936), 202; Bergh, "Absolution de prêtres mariés civilement," *NRT,* LXIII (1936), 914, 915.

[50] *AAS,* XXIX (1937), 283, 284.

SACRA PAENITENTIARIA APOSTOLICA
DECLARATIO

Super Decreto Quod Incipit "Lex Sacri Coelibatus" Diei 18 Aprilis 1936

Evulgato per Commentarium Officiale Apostolicae Sedis (vol. XXVIII, pag. 242) Decreto, quod incipit "Lex sacri coelibatus" diei 18 aprilis 1936, quo absolutio ab excommunicatione de qua in can. 2388, § 1, quando agatur de sacerdote qui, matrimonio civiliter attentato, ad cor dein reversus, ad participationem sacramentorum more laicorum petat admitti, data quidem fide de absoluta perfectaque in posterum continentia perpetuo servanda, quamvis tamen ob gravissimas rationes cessare non valeat a cohabitatione sub eodem tecto cum suae disertionis complice, Sacrae Paenitentiariae Apostolicae, excepto casu periculi mortis, reservatur, non defuerunt nec desunt Canonistae et Moralistae qui docuerint ac doceant casum hunc nihil differre a casu aliarum censurarum, quae in casibus urgentioribus remitti possunt sub quibusdam conditionibus et clausulis a quocumque confessario vi can. 2254.

Haec interpretatio, a praefati Decreti nedum sensu sed et littera prorsus absona, nullo modo defendi potest, eo praesertim quia expresse edicitur absolutionem de qua agitur "*ab ipsa tantum Sacra Paenitentiaria Apostolica,* servata speciali procedendi forma et sub peculiaribus quibusdam cautelis et conditionibus ab eadem Sanctitate Sua patefactis ac praescriptis," concedi posse.

Nihilominus, ad omnem, si quae adhuc forte superesset, dubitationem penitus auferendam, Ssmus Dominus Noster, in audientia infrascripto Card. Paenitentiario Maiori die 10 aprilis anni currentis impertita ad rem opportune interrogatus, suprema Sua auctoritate declarandum et, quo solet modo, publici iuris faciendum mandavit, hanc esse mentem Legislatoris, scilicet: Absolutionem a censura, de qua supra, ita esse Sacrae Paenitentiariae reservatam ut nemo unquam, excepto casu periculi mortis, ab ea absolvere possit, non obstante qualibet facultate, sive per can. 2254, § 1, sive per privilegium, sive denique per aliud quodcumque ius ceteroquin concessa.

Datum Romae, e Sacra Paenitentiaria, die 4 maii 1937.

L. Card. Lauri, *Paenitentiarius Maior.*

L. ✠ S. S. Luzio, *Regens.*

It was now indubitably manifest that the case mentioned in these documents could not be absolved according to the norm of canon 2254. However, this case is very specific, and is not at all coextensive with the legislation of canon 2388, § 1. Consequently, it is necessary to define the elements which constitute this censure reserved exclusively to the Sacred Penitentiary, and to indicate what censures, contracted through violations of canon 2388, § 1, can still be absolved by reason of canon 2254.

That a censure incurred by reason of canon 2388, § 1, be reserved solely to the Sacred Penitentiary, to the exclusion of canon 2254, the following three elements must be verified:

1. the party seeking absolution must be a priest;
2. he must have attempted marriage;
3. he must intend to continue living in the same house with his accomplice.

All three of these elements must be present in the case; if any one of them is lacking, the case can be settled according to the general norms for absolution.[51]

In the first place, therefore, if the person seeking absolution has contracted the excommunication of canon 2388, § 1, but is *not a priest*, the absolution is not exclusively reserved to the Sacred Penitentiary, and canon 2254 is applicable. Consequently, whether the person who has attempted marriage is a deacon or subdeacon or a religious in solemn vows, or is the accomplice who attempted marriage either with a priest or with any of the others just mentioned, the absolution is not exclusively reserved to the Sacred Penitentiary, but can be granted according to the general norms of Canon Law and moral theology.

Secondly, if the party is a priest but *did not attempt marriage*, even though he is living in concubinage with the woman, there is no

[51] Rossi, "S. Poenit. Apos., Decretum 18 Aprilis, 1936—Annotationes," *Apollinaris*, IX (1936), 587, 588; for a general confirmation of Rossi's opinion after the appearance of the declaration, *cf.* "S. Poenit. Apos., Declaratio 4 Maii, 1937—Annotationes," *Apollinaris*, X (1937), 175. *Cf.* also Rossi's reiteration of this opinion in *Perfice Munus* after the publication of the declaration, as cited in the following note.

reservation to the Sacred Penitentiary, for there is no censure, since the penalty is inflicted for attempted marriage.

Thirdly, if the party is a priest and has attempted marriage, but is *no longer living with his accomplice,* whether because she has died or because they have separated, the censure is not exclusively reserved to the Sacred Penitentiary.[52]

To restate the case, the only circumstances in which a censure contracted by reason of canon 2388, § 1, is exclusively reserved to the Sacred Penitentiary are those in which a *priest has attempted marriage and intends to continue dwelling under the same roof with his accomplice.* Whether or not the priest intends to observe perfect chastity in the future does not affect the reservation; it does affect the absolution, for if he does not intend to observe perfect chastity, he certainly will not be absolved by the Sacred Penitentiary, for he will not be dispensed from celibacy,[53] and he will unquestionably be lacking in the proper dispositions if he has no intention of avoiding sin; if he does intend to observe perfect chastity, he will be absolved by the Sacred Penitentiary if circumstances warrant the absolution.

It is hardly necessary to say that, although in many circumstances a censure contracted by reason of canon 2388, § 1, will not be exclusively reserved to the Sacred Penitentiary, it will gener-

[52] On these points, *cf.* Rossi, "S. Poenit. Apos., Decretum 18 Aprilis, 1936—Annotationes," *Apollinaris,* IX (1936), 587, 588; *Idem,* "De sacerdotibus qui matrimonium etiam civile tantum contrahere praesumpserint quoad absolutionem a censura de qua in can. 2388, § 1," *Perfice Munus,* XII (1937), 404. *Cf.* also Bergh, "Absolution de prêtres mariés civilement," *NRT,* LXIII (1936), 914, 915, compared with his article of the same title in *NRT,* LXIV (1937), 774; Lopez, "De reconciliatione sacerdotis, qui matrimonium attentare praesumpsit," *Periodica,* XXVI (1937), 505, 506; Beijersbergen, "Decretum 18 Aprilis, 1936—Annotationes," *Periodica,* XXV (1936), 202, 203; Verhamme, "Decretum 18 Aprilis, 1936—Notae," *Collationes Brugenses,* XXXVI (1936), 337.

[53] That is, unless it should be the extraordinary case in which he could prove that his ordination to the priesthood was invalid, or that his ordination did not entail the obligations of the clerical state because he was forced into it through grave fear, and never subsequently ratified it at least by the exercise of orders; *cf.* canon 214.

ally be no easy matter to handle such a case. When canon 2254 is employed for the grant of absolution—and it is applicable in any case except that specified in the two documents of the Sacred Penitentiary as excluded from this canon—its requirements must be fulfilled, and the general norms of moral theology must be observed.

Regarding such censures (with the exclusion, therefore, of the case reserved to the Sacred Penitentiary, since this is outside the application of canon 2254 and beyond the power of any confessor except for the case of danger of death), the following points may be noted. The penitent must be willing to remove the occasion of sin and also to repair any scandal which has arisen from his crime; otherwise, he will not have the proper dispositions for absolution. If he is a cleric or a religious, canon 2254, § 3, will usually be inapplicable, for it will not be common that recourse, at least by a personal letter, will be morally impossible. If he is a cleric in major orders, he must be ready to rectify his status through recourse, by a reduction to the lay state granted by the Holy See; [54] and if he is a deacon or a subdeacon, he may be able to obtain a dispensation from celibacy,[55] so that the marriage may be convalidated or, if possible, sanated. If the penitent who had attempted marriage is a religious in solemn vows, he has contracted the excommunication of canon 2388, § 1,[56] and he must rectify his status; by attempting marriage, he has been *ipso facto* dismissed from his institute,[57] but although he cannot be received back into the institute,[58] *per se* he

[54] *Cf.* canon 211, § 1. If the penitent is a cleric in minor orders, he does not incur the excommunication of canon 2388, § 1, and if he has contracted a valid marriage, according to canon 132, § 2, he is *ipso facto* reduced to the lay state.

[55] *Cf.* Rossi, "De sacerdotibus . . . ," *Perfice Munus,* XII (1937), 404, nota 1; Beijersbergen, "Decretum 18 Aprilis, 1936—Annotations," *Periodica,* XXV (1936), 203.

[56] If he is at the same time a cleric in major orders, he incurs a double excommunication by reason of canon 2388, § 1; if he is a religious in simple perpetual vows, he incurs the excommunication of canon 2388, § 2.

[57] Canon 646, § 1, n. 3.

[58] Pont. Comm., 30 Iulii, 1934, III, ad 2—*AAS,* XXVI (1934), 494; quoted above, in the present chapter, note 37.

is still bound by his vows,[59] and before he is absolved from the censure, he must be willing to apply for a dispensation from the vows.

Various other situations may also arise, for many circumstances may enter such cases from the combination of major orders with solemn or simple vows, or of solemn vows with major or minor orders. Regarding simple vows, further considerations may be involved by reason of their nature as perpetual or temporary, or as ceasing or not ceasing because of the crime. Each of these circumstances will call for a different solution, and each must be provided for when absolution is given according to canon 2254.

It is to be remarked that any censure contracted by reason of canon 2388, § 1, is still reserved only *simpliciter* to the Holy See; even the specific case for which absolution is reserved exclusively to the Sacred Penitentiary is still reserved *simpliciter* to the Holy See, but for all practical purposes its reservation is more strict than any *specialissimo modo* reservation.[60] If some case other than that excluded from canon 2254 arises, and it is occult, whether materially or formally occult,[61] recourse can be made to the ordinary [62] after absolution has been granted according to canon 2254, § 1, unless the nature of the case demands that the question of status be rectified by the Holy See, for example, in the case of a deacon or subdeacon who has incurred the censure of canon 2388, § 1. If the censure is public, absolution can be given for the internal sacramental forum according to canon 2254, and the absolved penitent can perform any action in the external forum that will not cause scandal,[63] for example, receiving Communion in some other parish where he is not known; but usually recourse will have to be made

[59] Canon 669, § 1. If the constitutions of his institute provide for the *ipso facto* dispensation from his vows when he is dismissed, *e.g.*, by reason of canon 646, he should report his status to the major superior.

[60] *Cf.* Rossi, "De sacerdotibus . . . ," *Perfice Munus*, XII (1937), 405; Fliesser, "Decretum 18 Aprilis, 1936—Notae," *TPQ*, LXXXIX (1936), 882; Beijersbergen, "Decretum 18 Aprilis, 1936—Annotationes," *Periodica*, XXV (1936), 201, 202.

[61] *Cf.* canon 2197, n. 4.

[62] *Cf.* canons 2254, § 1; 2237, § 2.

[63] *Cf.* canon 2251.

to the Sacred Penitentiary, preferably through the bishop or apostolic delegate, and the penitent will be obliged to observe the mandates. Canon 2254, § 3, will ordinarily be applicable, to excuse from the obligation of recourse, only in the case of a layman or laywoman who has contracted the censure of canon 2388 and is unable to make recourse through the confessor; and in this case, the confessor must enjoin the things demanded by law, and also impose a proportionate penance and a fitting satisfaction to be fulfilled *sub poena reincidentiae* within the determined time.

It has been mentioned above that, if a priest who has attempted marriage is no longer living with his accomplice, the absolution is not reserved exclusively to the Sacred Penitentiary. Consequently, canon 2254, § 1, could be used for absolution in the sacramental forum. Suppose, however, that such a priest wishes to be reinstated in the priesthood and to return to the exercise of the ministry. Like any major cleric who has attempted marriage, he has not only incurred the censure of canon 2388, § 1, but he has also contracted an irregularity.[64] According to the present practice, absolution from the censure in the external forum and dispensation from the irregularity are reserved to the Holy Office. Therefore, the priest who wishes to be absolved in the external forum and be dispensed from the irregularity, so that he may return to the exercise of his orders, should present his case to the Holy Office through his ordinary. If the ordinary informs the Holy Office that the priest is truly penitent, the Holy Office will grant absolution from the censure in the external forum and the permission to receive the sacraments *more laicorum*, the irregularity, however, remaining intact. If it is clear, after a long time of trial, that the priest has persevered in his good conduct, the Holy Office, after again consulting the ordinary, may dispense from the irregularity, but only for the celebration of Mass under special precautions. In general, the requirements of the Holy Office in such a case are: that a sincere repentance has been proved by long experiment; that there has been a real separation from, and absolute desertion of the accomplice; and that, if a civil marriage has been attempted, a civil divorce or separation be

[64] Canon 985, n. 3.

first obtained. These are the norms that are followed in such cases, but, especially if any children have been born of the union, little can be hoped regarding the return of the priest to the exercise of his orders, and ordinarily the only solution will be a reduction to the lay state.[65]

Finally, to return to the specific case which the Sacred Penitentiary has reserved exclusively to itself, some practical observations may be made before this discussion is concluded. First of all, for the sake of clarity, the case may be briefly restated. It is the case of a priest who has attempted marriage, and who, because of very grave reasons, must continue to dwell under the same roof as his accomplice, although he intends to practice perfect chastity in the future. It is needless to repeat that canon 2254 is inapplicable to this case. However, it will be helpful for the confessor who is confronted with such a case to know how it is handled.

If the case is occult, it is handled entirely between the Sacred Penitentiary and the confessor. If it is public, the Sacred Penitentiary requires, with the permission of the penitent as a preclusion of any violation of the seal of confession, the opinion of the ordinary on the case. The confessor presents the details of the case to the Sacred Penitentiary, explaining the reasons which prevent the separation of the priest from his accomplice. Before it will act, the Sacred Penitentiary will weigh the seriousness of the reasons, and will demand certitude of the future observance of chastity and efficacious removal of scandal. The ability and willingness of the priest to lead a life of chastity in the future must be proved by the fact that he has actually practiced continence for a sufficient length of time to give moral certitude that he will continue to observe perfect and absolute chastity for the remainder of his life. There must be a removal of scandal. If the case is occult, no danger of scandal will be present. If it is public, namely, if the delinquent's priesthood and cohabitation with the woman are known, the scandal will be best removed by a departure of the parties to some other place where they are not known. If this cannot be done, those who know of the crime should be disposed to look upon the

[65] *Cf.* Lopez, "De reconciliatione sacerdotis, qui matrimonium attentare praesumpsit," *Periodica,* XXVI (1937), 504, 505.

grant of absolution, not as a reason for further scandal, but as a cause for gratitude to God for the conversion of a sinner. This is why the opinion of the ordinary is required in a public case, for he can best judge of the character of his flock and decide whether and how the scandal can be eliminated. Again, if there is danger of scandal from the priest's approach to the sacraments or from his continued dwelling with the woman, the Sacred Penitentiary provides against it by demanding in its rescript that the priest obviate this scandal by explaining to the persons concerned the nature and conditions of the favor he has received. In general, the scandal that is considered must be true scandal, not merely *scandalum pusillorum* or *scandalum pharisaicum*.

When the Sacred Penitentiary grants absolution, it does so in a rescript in *forma commissoria necessaria*, requiring, therefore, the intervention of an executor. The faculty to absolve will be exercised in the sacramental forum, but the Sacred Penitentiary will ordinarily provide in its rescript that this absolution in the internal forum and the permission to continue living with the woman in the manner of brother and sister can be proved in the external forum. In this case the rescript will contain the prescription that it be executed with the correct names of the parties, and be preserved either at the Sacred Penitentiary itself or in secret archives of the episcopal curia.[66] The whole matter of absolution, consequently, will follow the norm of canon 2251 regarding its effects in the external forum, and when provision is made that the absolution can be proved in this forum, the superior can no longer insist upon the observance of the censure in the external forum until absolution has been obtained in that forum. No conflict should arise, however, for if the case is public, the superior of the external forum has already been consulted before absolution has been granted; if it is occult, there will be no danger of scandal, and the case will not be brought to the attention of the superior. The only case which might cause difficulty, therefore, would be one which was formerly occult but has become public; but usually this contingency will be adequately met by the provision of the Sacred Penitentiary in its

[66] This is similar to the norm of canon 1047.

rescript, that the absolution in the internal forum will be capable of proof before the superior of the external forum.[67]

To conclude, this case, as specified in its particular details in the two documents of the Sacred Penitentiary, is the one and only censure which is absolutely and entirely excluded from canon 2254. Every other censure can be absolved by virtue of this canon, provided that at least one of the more urgent cases is verified, and that there is a willingness to assume the obligations prescribed by the canon. May canon 2254, with its correlative canons 882 and 2252 for absolution in danger of death, fulfill the ardent desires of a solicitous Mother, and contribute much to the good of souls!

[67] On this entire matter of absolution by the Sacred Penitentiary in this case, *cf.* Rossi, "De sacerdotibus qui matrimonium etiam civile tantum contrahere praesumpserint quoad absolutionem a censura de qua in can. 2388, § 1," *Perfice Munus,* XII (1937), 463, 464, 590-593; Lopez, "De reconciliatione sacerdotis, qui matrimonium attentare praesumpsit," *Periodica,* XXVI (1937), 502-504.

CONCLUSION

As a result of this dissertation, it is believed:

1. that a clearer, more thorough, and more consecutive outline has been given of the historical development of the extraordinary absolution from censures in its twofold aspect of absolution in danger of death and in other extraordinary cases from the time of its origin up to the promulgation of the Code, than has yet appeared; and especially that the place of public penance in the evolving discipline on absolution from censures has been more lucidly indicated than in any recent work.

2. that the granting of absolution in danger of death, under the present law, by any validly ordained priest, whatever be his status, has been established as *per se* licit, contrary to the view of several authors, with the possibility of illicitness arising only *per accidens*.

3. that the view maintaining the non-reservation of *latae sententiae* censures which are attached to particular precepts without express reservation has received some confirmation, despite the insistence that such censures are *ab homine;* and that the seldom mentioned opinion asserting the non-obligation of recourse after absolution from such censures in danger of death, has been demonstrated as a logical deduction from this previous conclusion.

4. that the various censures *a iure* and the reserved sin which entail recourse after recovery when absolution has been given in danger of death have been treated in a clearer and more unified manner than in other works.

5. that the time-element with reference to recourse after absolution in danger of death and in the more urgent cases has been more thoroughly explained than has hitherto been done.

6. that the view denying the reincurrence of a censure for failure to obey the mandates of the superior, as mentioned in canons 2252 and 2254, has received considerable support.

7. that the varying applicability of the two more urgent cases mentioned in canon 2254 has been explained more thoroughly than in other works, with the result that questions such as the one regarding the absolution from public censures find a clearer solution.

8. that the opinion affirming that *latae sententiae ab homine* censures can be absolved by reason of canon 2254 has received confirmation.

9. that the question regarding the possibility of absolution from *ferendae sententiae* censures according to the norm of canon 2254 has been treated more clearly than in other works.

10. that the question regarding the absolution from reserved sins by reason of canon 2254 has been given more thorough consideration than is to be found in any other single work.

11. that more definite norms have been given concerning the possibility of the cessation of the obligation of recourse through serious inconvenience or ignorance, than are to be found elsewhere.

12. that the nature of the absolution given according to canon 2254, § 2, has received more careful consideration than heretofore.

13. that the circumstances constituting moral impossibility of recourse have been presented in a more comprehensive manner than in other treatments on this subject.

14. that the exception from absolution without recourse, namely, the censure of canon 2367, has been given more careful study in the light of a comparison of the opinions of various authors on the matter with the proper interpretation of canon 2254, § 3.

15. that the different elements referring to the mandates, as mentioned in canon 2252 and in the three paragraphs of canon 2254, have been treated more thoroughly than in other works.

16. that the common opinion, stating that the things to be enjoined according to law, as required by canon 2254, § 3, consist in satisfaction to an injured party, reparation of scandal, and a salutary penance, has been demonstrated to be erroneous; and that the *satisfactio pro censura,* explicitly demanded by canon 2254, § 3, has been shown to consist in the reparation of harm and scandal.

17. that the involved question regarding the absolution in more urgent cases from the reserved sin and reserved censure incurred because of false accusation of solicitation has received more careful attention and more comprehensive treatment than is to be found elsewhere.

18. that the censure inflicted for attempted marriage by a priest, excluded from canon 2254 by the Sacred Penitentiary within little more than the last two years, and hitherto treated only in scattered articles in periodicals, has received a more practical and more easily intelligible consideration than would otherwise be available to the ordinary confessor.

19. that, in general, the entire matter concerning the absolution from censures in danger of death and in the more urgent cases according to the present law—matter that is so practical and valuable for the confessor—has been discussed more thoroughly in this than in any other volume or combination of volumes, as is only to be expected of a specialized study of such proportions.

APPENDIX I

FORMULAE FOR RECOURSE

A. General form for recourse after absolution in danger of death.

Beatissime Pater (Pope):
Eminentissime Princeps (Cardinal):
Reverendissime Domine (Archbishop or Bishop):

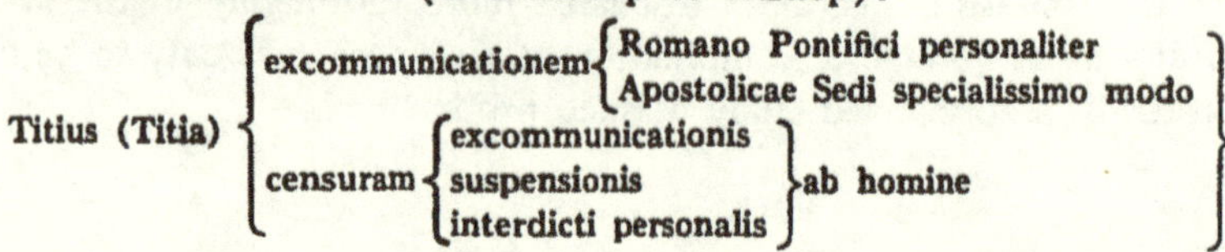

Titius (Titia) { excommunicationem { Romano Pontifici personaliter / Apostolicae Sedi specialissimo modo } / censuram { excommunicationis / suspensionis / interdicti personalis } ab homine }

reservatam contraxit propter . . . (*indicate the crime*). Rite dispositus (disposita) et versans in periculo mortis, absolutus (absoluta) fuit ab infrascripto confessario ad normam can. 882, 2252. Per has litteras obligationi recurrendi satisfacit, promittens omnia mandata se accepturum (accepturam) ac fideliter exsecuturum (exsecuturam).

Et Deus, etc.

(date) (true name and address of confessor)

(N. B. In these various formulae, the wording "Et Deus, etc." is set down without any further addition.)

B. General form for recourse after absolution in a more urgent case.

Beatissime Pater:
Eminentissime Princeps:
Reverendissime Domine:

Titius (Titia) contraxit censuram { excommunicationis / suspensionis / interdicti personalis }

{ Romano Pontifici personaliter / Sedi Apostolicae { specialissimo modo / speciali modo / simpliciter } / Ordinario } reservatam propter . . . (*indicate the crime*).

Rite dispositus (disposita) et versans in casu urgentiori, absolutus (absoluta) fuit ab infrascripto confessario ad normam can. 2254, § 1. Per has litteras obligationi recurrendi satisfacit, promittens omnia mandata se accepturum (accepturam) ac fideliter exsecuturum (exsecuturam).

Et Deus, etc.

(date) (true name and address of confessor)

C. Forms for recourse to the Sacred Penitentiary.

Address:

All' Eminentissimo Cardinale Penitenziere Maggiore
Palazzo del S. Officio
Roma, Italia.

(Recourse to the Sacred Penitentiary may be made through the local ordinary or the apostolic delegate.)

1. *Recourse through a confessor who will see the penitent again.*

Eminentissime Princeps:

Titius, vicarius cooperator, semel (bis, ter) absolvit complicem in peccato turpi, ideoque contraxit excommunicationem (duas, tres excommunicationes) specialissimo modo Sedi Apostolicae reservatam (reservatas). Rite dispositus et versans in casu urgentiori, absolutus fuit ab infrascripto confessario ad normam canonis 2254, § 1. Obligationi recurrendi nunc satisfacit, asseverans ad omnia mandata S. Poenitentiariae exsequenda se esse paratum. Animadvertendum existimo, Titium, propter peculiaria adjuncta, {non posse intra tres menses / nullo modo posse} officium confessiones audiendi dimittere (*if this is true, and as the case may be*).

Et Deus, etc.

(date) (true name and address of confessor)

2. *Recourse through a confessor who will not see the penitent again, but knows his name and address and intends to send the rescript to him through the mail.*

Eminentissime Princeps:

Titius, parochus, tres complices in peccato turpi ab ultima confessione absolvit, ideoque excommunicationem specialissimo modo Sedi Apostolicae reservatam ter contraxit. Poenitentia ductus, et versans in casu urgentiori, ad me, infrascriptum confessarium, venit, cui absolutionem ad normam canonis 2254, § 1, concedi. Ad S. Poenitentiariam per has litteras recurrit, promittens omnia quae-

cumque mandata se accepturum ac fideliter exsecuturum. Animadvertendum existimo, Titium, propter peculiaria adjuncta,
{ non posse intra sex menses
  nullo modo posse } dimittere officium paroeciale quo
fungitur (*if such is the case*). Cum Titius ad me reverti nequit, rogo ut mihi tribuatur facultas transmittendi per publicos tabelliones aliove modo rescriptum hujus S. Tribunalis.

Et Deus, etc.

(date) (true name and address of confessor)

3. *Form for recourse when the penitent writes the letter, asking that the rescript be sent to some confessor.*

Eminentissime Princeps:

Ego, Titius, complicem in peccato turpi semel absolvi, et idcirco excommunicationem Sedi Apostolicae specialissimo modo reservatam contraxi. Ad poenitentiam reversus, absolutus fui in casu urgentiori ad normam canonis 2254, § 1. Humillime per has litteras recurrens, promitto quibusvis mandatis me fideliter oboediturum. Faveat Eminentia Vestra rescriptum remittere ad infrascriptum confessarium, quem ad id accipiendum ac implendum adibo.

Et Deus, etc.

(date) Dignetur E. V. rescriptum dirigere ad:
(name and address of confessor)

4. *Form for recourse when the penitent writes the letter, asking that the rescript be sent directly to him.*

Eminentissime Princeps:

Ego complicem in peccato turpi semel absolvi, et idcirco excommunicationem Sedi Apostolicae specialissimo modo reservatam contraxi. Ad poenitentiam reversus, absolutus fui in casu urgentiori ad normam can. 2254, § 1. Humillime per has litteras recurrens, promitto quibusvis mandatis me fideliter oboediturum. Faveat Eminentia Vestra rescriptum in forma gratiosa remittere ad me infrascriptum.

Et Deus, etc.

(date) (true name and address of penitent)

D. Form for recourse to the Apostolic Delegate.

Address:
Most Reverend Amleto Cicognani
1811 Biltmore Street
Washington, D. C.

Your Excellency:

Titius incurred the excommunication, reserved in a special way to the Holy See, for reading a forbidden book. Since he was properly disposed and had already destroyed the book, when asking for absolution in a more urgent case, he was absolved by me according to the norm of canon 2254, § 1. He now fulfills the obligation of recourse, promising to perform the penance and observe the instructions which Your Excellency will impose.

Respectfully,

(date) (Confessor—name and address)

E. Form for recourse to the local ordinary.

Address:
Most Reverend ....
(chancery address—as in *The Official Catholic Directory*)

Your Excellency:

Titia contracted the excommunication, reserved to the ordinary, for the crime of abortion. Being properly disposed and asking for absolution in a more urgent case, she was absolved by me according to the norm of canon 2254, § 1. She now fulfills the obligation of recourse, promising to perform the penance and observe the instructions which Your Excellency will impose.

Respectfully,

(date) (Confessor—name and address)

APPENDIX II

FACULTIES OF THE APOSTOLIC DELEGATE AND BISHOPS OF THE UNITED STATES REGARDING CENSURES AND IRREGULARITIES

A. Faculties of the Apostolic Delegate

1. To absolve, both in the forum of conscience and in the external forum, after enjoining the things required by law according to the nature of the case, from all censures reserved by law in either a simple or special manner to the Holy See.

2. To dispense those already ordained, for the celebration of Mass and also for the acquisition and retention of ecclesiastical benefices, from all irregularities whatsoever, arising either *ex delicto* or *ex defectu,* as long as no scandal and no detriment to sacred functions is caused thereby, except the irregularities mentioned in canon 985, n. 4, and provided that, in cases of the crime of heresy or schism, an abjuration is first made to the one who grants absolution.

(These faculties are the ones mentioned in Caput I, nn. 4, 5, of the list of faculties granted to Nuntios, Internuntios, and Apostolic Delegates since the Code; Latin version in Vermeersch-Creusen, *Epitome Iuris Canonici,* I, Appendix I; an English translation in Bouscaren, *Canon Law Digest,* I, 175-187).

B. Faculties of the Bishops of the United States

1. To absolve all penitents (except heretics whose purpose is to spread heresy among the faithful) from all censures and ecclesiastical penalties incurred because of heresy either in the absence or in the presence of others, after the penitent has denounced according to law those whom he may know to be teaching the heretical doctrine and any ecclesiastical and religious persons who may have been his accomplices in this matter; or, if for just reasons this denunciation cannot be made before the absolution, after the penitent has seriously promised to make the denunciation as soon as he can and in the best manner possible, and, in every case, only after he has secretly abjured the heresy before the one absolving; and with the imposition of a grave salutary penance according to the seriousness of the excesses committed, together with the frequentation of the sacraments, and the obligation of retracting the heresy before the persons in whose presence it was manifested and of repairing scandal.

2. To absolve from censures and ecclesiastical penalties those who have defended or have knowingly, without proper permission, read or retained books of apostates, heretics, or schismatics which defend apostasy, heresy, or schism, or those books which have been prohibited by name through apostolic letters; after enjoining a suitable salutary penance and obliging the penitent, in as far as it may be possible, to destroy the books or to turn them over to the ordinary or confessor before absolution is granted.

3. To absolve from censures those who have directly or indirectly impeded the exercise of ecclesiastical jurisdiction of either the internal or the external forum, and have had recourse for this purpose to any civil authority.

4. To absolve from the censures and ecclesiastical penalties established with reference to duelling, but only in cases which have not been brought to the external forum; after imposing a grave salutary penance and enjoining the other things required by law.

5. To absolve from censures and ecclesiastical penalties those who have joined a Masonic sect or any similar association which conspires against the Church or legitimate civil authority; on condition that the penitents entirely withdraw from the respective sect or association and abjure it; that, according to canon 2336, § 2, they denounce all ecclesiastical and religious persons whom they may know to be members; and that they turn over to the one granting absolution all books, manuscripts, and insignia which pertain to the society and which they still possess, so that these may be cautiously sent as soon as possible to the Holy Office, or at least destroyed, if just and grave causes require this; with the imposition of a grave salutary penance according to the seriousness of the offense, together with the frequentation of the sacraments and the obligation of repairing scandal.

6. To absolve from censures and ecclesiastical penalties those who, without proper permission, have entered the enclosure of religious of either sex in solemn vows, and also those who brought them in or who permitted them to enter; provided that this was not done for any gravely criminal purpose of any kind, even though the purpose was not effected nor the matter brought to the external forum; with the imposition of a suitable salutary penance according to the seriousness of the offense.

7. To dispense from the irregularity arising from voluntary homicide or abortion, mentioned in canon 985, n. 4, but solely that the penitent may be able to exercise orders which he has already received; after imposing upon him the obligation, first, of having recourse to the Sacred Penitentiary within a month, at least by a letter written by the penitent himself or by another, the true name of

the penitent being withheld, explaining all the circumstances of the case, and especially indicating how many times the crime was committed, and, secondly, of obeying the mandates of the Sacred Penitentiary.

(These faculties are contained in nn. 1-6, 9, among the faculties granted by the Sacred Penitentiary in Section 6 of Formula IV of the quinquennial faculties which the bishops of the United States possess in their present form through 1939; a translation of this entire set of faculties is found in Bouscaren, *Canon Law Digest,* II, 5-18.)

APPENDIX III

LIST OF RESERVED *LATAE SENTENTIAE* CENSURES

I. Excommunications

A. Reserved Personally to the Roman Pontiff

They are incurred by:

1. Those who commit delicts in the election of the Roman Pontiff—canon 2330.

2. Those who violate the secret of the Holy Office.

3. Those who violate secrecy in causes of canonization and beatification.

B. Reserved in a Most Special Manner to the Holy See

They are incurred by:

1. Those who throw away the Consecrated Species, or carry them off or keep them for an evil purpose—canon 2320.

2. Those who lay violent hands on the person of the Roman Pontiff—canon 2343, § 1, n. 1.

3. Confessors who absolve or pretend to absolve an accomplice *in peccato turpi*, or who absolve after inducing the accomplice not to confess the sin of complicity—canon 2367.

4. Confessors who dare to violate directly the seal of confession—canon 2369, § 1.

C. Reserved in a Special Manner to the Holy See

They are incurred by:

1. Those guilty of the crime of apostasy, heresy, or schism—canon 2314.

2. Those suspected of heresy who do not amend within six months after being warned—canon 2315.

3. Those who publish books of apostates, heretics, or schismatics, defending apostasy, heresy, or schism; also those who defend or deliberately read or retain, without the proper permission, such books or other books forbidden by name by apostolic letter—canon 2318.

4. Those without priestly orders who pretend to celebrate Mass or hear sacramental confession—canon 2322, n. 1.

5. Those who appeal to an ecumenical council against the Roman Pontiff—canon 2332.

6. Those who have recourse to civil authority to impede letters or acts of the Holy See or its legates; those who directly or indirectly forbid the promulgation or execution of the same; and those who injure or terrorize others because of such letters or acts—canon 2333.

7. Those who issue laws, precepts, or decrees against the liberty or rights of the Church; and those who have recourse to civil authority and thereby directly or indirectly impede the exercise of ecclesiastical jurisdiction—canon 2334.

8. Those who dare to bring civil suit against cardinals, legates of the Holy See, major officials of the Roman Curia in matters pertaining to their office, or their own ordinary—canon 2341.

9. Those who lay violent hands on the person of a cardinal, legate of the Holy See, patriarch, archbishop, or bishop—canon 2343, §§ 2, 3.

10. Those who usurp or retain goods or rights of the Roman See—canon 2345.

11. Those who forge or falsify documents of the Holy See or knowingly make use of such documents—canon 2360, § 1.

12. Those who falsely accuse a confessor to superiors of the crime of solicitation—canon 2363.

D. Reserved in a Simple Manner to the Holy See

They are incurred by:

1. Those who traffic in indulgences—canon 2327.

2. Those who join Masonic or similar societies—canon 2335.

3. Those who, without the proper faculty, dare to absolve from an excommunication reserved in a most special or special manner to the Holy See—canon 2338, § 1.

4. Those who aid or abet an *excommunicatus vitandus* in the crime for which he was excommunicated; and clerics who knowingly admit and communicate with such an excommunicate in divine services—canon 2338, § 2.

5. Those who dare to bring civil suit against any bishop other than their ordinary, or against an abbot or prelate *nullius,* or against the highest superior of a religious institute of pontifical right —canon 2341.

6. Those who violate the papal enclosure of nuns; and those who admit such persons within the enclosure—canon 2342, n. 1.

7. Women who violate the enclosure of religious men in solemn vows; and those who admit women within the enclosure—canon 2342, n. 2.

8. Nuns who illicitly leave their papal enclosure—canon 2342, n. 3.

9. Those who dare to usurp ecclesiastical goods and turn them to their own use, or to prevent their fruits from coming to those to whom they rightfully belong—canon 2346.

10. Those who take any part in a duel; those who deliberately witness it; and those who culpably permit or fail to prohibit it—canon 2351, § 1.

11. Clerics in sacred orders and religious in solemn vows who dare to attempt marriage; also their accomplices—canon 2388, § 1.

12. Those who commit simony in connection with any ecclesiastical office, benefice, or dignity—canon 2392, n. 1.

13. Those who carry off, destroy, hide, or substantially change any document pertaining to the episcopal curia—canon 2405.

E. Reserved to the Ordinary

They are incurred by:

1. Catholics who attempt marriage before a non-Catholic minister—canon 2319, § 1, n. 1.

2. Catholics who enter marriage with an agreement to educate any or all of their children outside the Catholic Church—canon 2319, § 1, n. 2.

3. Catholics who knowingly dare to offer their children to a non-Catholic minister for baptism—canon 2319, § 1, n. 3.

4. Catholic parents, or those taking the place of the parents, who deliberately have their children brought up or instructed in a non-Catholic religion—canon 2319, § 1, n. 4.

5. Those who make false relics, or knowingly sell or distribute them or expose them for public veneration—canon 2326.

6. Those who lay violent hands on the person of a cleric or a religious of either sex—canon 2343, § 4.

7. Those who effectively procure abortion—canon 2350, § 1.

8. Religious guilty of the crime of apostasy from their institute—canon 2385.

9. Religious in simple perpetual vows who dare to attempt or contract marriage; also their accomplices—canon 2388, § 2.

II. Interdicts

A. An interdict, reserved in a special manner to the Holy See, is incurred by moral persons who appeal to an ecumenical council against the Roman Pontiff—canon 2332.

B. An interdict *ab ingressu ecclesiae*, reserved to the ordinary, is incurred by those who freely grant ecclesiastical burial to infidels, or to notorious apostates from the faith, heretics, schismatics, members of Masonic or similar societies, or to excommunicated or interdicted persons after a judicial sentence—canons 2339; 1240, § 1.

III. Suspensions

A. Reserved to the Holy See

1. A general suspension is incurred by any cleric who, through simony, has knowingly conferred or received ecclesiastical orders or has deliberately administered or received other sacraments—canon 2371.

2. A suspension *a divinis* is incurred by anyone who dares to receive ecclesiastical orders from one who is excommunicated, suspended, or interdicted after a declaratory or condemnatory sentence, or from a notorious apostate, heretic, or schismatic—canon 2372.

3. A general suspension is incurred by a cleric in sacred orders who, as a religious in perpetual vows, was dismissed from his religious institute for some crime less serious than those mentioned in canon 670—canon 671, n. 1.

4. A suspension *a divinis* is incurred by priests who leave Europe for America or the Philippine Islands with deliberate disregard of the prescriptions determined in a decree of the Sacred Consistorial Congregation of December 30, 1918—*AAS,* XI (1919), 39-43; *cf.* also Cocchi, *Commentarium,* lib. V, p. 220.

B. Reserved to the Ordinary

1. A suspension *ab officio* is incurred by any cleric who, without the permission of the ordinary of the place, brings civil suit against a cleric inferior to a bishop, or against any religious inferior to the highest superior of an institute of pontifical right—canon 2341.

2. A general suspension, reserved to the major superior, is incurred by a cleric in sacred orders who is a fugitive from his religious institute—canon 2386.

BIBLIOGRAPHY

Sources

Acta Apostolicae Sedis, Commentarium Officiale, Romae, 1909-

Acta Sanctae Sedis, 41 vols., Romae, 1865-1908.

Augustinus, Antonius, *Antiquae Decretalium Collectiones Commentariis et Emendationibus Illustratae,* Parisiis, 1621.

Bouscaren, T. Lincoln, *The Canon Law Digest,* 2 vols., Milwaukee: Bruce, 1934-1937.

Bullarum Diplomatum et Privilegiorum Sanctorum Romanorum Pontificum Taurinensis Editio, 25 vols., Augustae Taurinorum, 1857-1872.

Canones et Decreta Sacrosancti Oecumenici Concilii Tridentini, Romae: ex typographia polyglotta S. C. de Propaganda Fide, 1882.

Codex Iuris Canonici Pii X Pontificis Maximi iussu digestus Benedicti Papae XV auctoritate promulgatus, Romae: Typis Polyglottis Vaticanis, 1917.

Codicis Iuris Canonici Fontes cura Emi. Petri Card. Gasparri editi, 7 vols., Romae (later Civitate Vaticana): Typis Polyglottis Vaticanis, 1923-1935. (Vol. VII ed. *cura et studio Emi Iustiniani Card. Serédi.*)

Collectanea S. Congregationis de Propaganda Fide, 2 vols., Romae: Typographia Polyglotta S. C. de Propaganda Fide, 1907.

Corpus Iuris Canonici, ed. Lipsiensis 2., Aemilius Ludouicus Richter—Aemilius Friedberg, ed. anastatice repetita, 2 vols., Lipsiae: Tauchnitz, 1928.

Decretales D. Gregorii Papae IX, una cum Glossis Restitutae, Romae, 1582.

Denzinger, Henr., et Bannwart, Clem., *Enchiridion Symbolorum, Definitionum et Declarationum de Rebus Fidei et Morum,* 16. et 17. ed., Friburgi Brisgoviae: Herder, 1928.

Friedberg, Aemilius, *Quinque Compilationes Antiquae,* Lipsiae, 1882.

Jaffé, Philippus, *Regesta Pontificum Romanorum ab condita Ecclesia ad annum post Christum natum MCXCVIII,* 2 vols. in 1, Lipsiae, 1881.

Liber Sextus Decretalium, una cum Clementinis et Extravagantibus Earumque Glossis Restitutis, Romae, 1582.

Mansi, Joannes, *Sacrorum Conciliorum Nova et Amplissima Collectio,* 53 vols., Parisiis, 1901-1927.

Migne, Jacques Paul, *Patrologiae Cursus Completus, Series Graeca,* 161 vols., Parisiis, 1856-1866.

——— *Patrologiae Cursus Completus, Series Latina,* 221 vols., Parisiis, 1844-1864.

Reference Works

Aertnys, Josephus, et Damen, Cornelius, *Theologia Moralis secundum Doctrinam S. Alfonsi de Ligorio,* 11. ed., 2 vols., Taurinorum Augustae: Marietti, 1928.

Alphonsus Liguori, St., *Theologia Moralis*, ed. L. Gaudé, 4 vols., Romae, 1905-1912.

Alterius, Marius, *Disputationes de Censuris Ecclesiasticis*, 2 vols., Romae, 1616.

Arregui, Antonius, *Summarium Theologiae Moralis*, 10. ed., Bilbao: El Mensajero del Corazón de Jesús, 1927.

Ayrinhac, H. A., and Lydon, P. J., *Penal Legislation in the New Code of Canon Law*, revised edition, New York: Benziger, 1936.

[Bachofen], Charles Augustine, *A Commentary on the New Code of Canon Law*, 8 vols.; Vol. IV: *On the Sacraments (Except Matrimony) and Sacramentals*, 3. ed., St. Louis, Mo.: Herder, 1925; Vol. VIII: *Penal Code*, 2. ed., St. Louis, Mo.: Herder, 1924.

Barbosa, Augustinus, *Collectanea Doctorum tam Veterum quam Recentiorum in Jus Pontificium Universum*, 6 vols. in 3, Lugduni, 1716.

Bargilliat, Michael, *Praelectiones Juris Canonici*, 37. ed., 2 vols., Parisiis: Baston, Berche et Pagis, 1923-1924.

Batiffol, Pierre, *Etudes d'Histoire et de Théologie Positive*, 1re série, 4. ed., 2 vols., Paris, 1906; "Les Origines de la Pénitence," Vol. I, pp. 45-222.

Bernardus Papiensis, *Summa Decretalium*, ed. Ern. Laspeyres, Ratisbonae, 1860.

Blat, Albertus, *Commentarium Textus Codicis Iuris Canonici*, 6 vols., Romae, 1921-1927; Liber V, *De Delictis et Poenis*, Romae: Collegio "Angelico," 1924.

Böckhn, Placidus, *Commentarius in Jus Canonicum Universum*, 5 vols. in 3, Salisburgi, 1776.

Cappello, Felix M., *De Censuris iuxta Codicem Iuris Canonici*, Augustae Taurinorum: Marietti, 1919.

——— *Tractatus Canonico-Moralis de Censuris iuxta Codicem Iuris Canonici*, 2. ed., Taurinorum Augustae: Marietti, 1925; 3. ed., Taurinorum Augustae: Marietti, 1933. (The third edition is used throughout, except where explicit mention is made of the first or second edition.)

——— *Tractatus Canonico-Moralis de Sacramentis*; Vol. II, Pars I, *De Poenitentia*, 2. ed., Taurinorum Augustae: Marietti, 1929.

Cavigioli, Joannes, *De Censuris Latae Sententiae Quae in Codice Juris Canonici Continentur Commentariolum*, Torino: Libreria Editrice Internazionale, 1918.

Cerato, Prosdocimus, *Censurae Vigentes Ipso Facto a Codice Iuris Canonici Excerptae*, 2. ed., Patavii: Typis Seminarii, 1921.

——— *De Delicto Sollicitationis*, Patavii: Typis Seminarii, 1922.

Chelodi, Joannes, *Ius Poenale et Ordo Procedendi in Iudiciis Criminalibus iuxta Codicem Iuris Canonici*, Tridenti: Libr. Edit. Tridentum, 1925.

Cicognani, Amleto, *Canon Law*, authorized English version, by J. O'Hara and F. Brennan, Philadelphia: Dolphin Press, 1934.

Cipollini, Albertus, *De Censuris Latae Sententiae iuxta Codicem Iuris Canonici*, Taurini: Marietti, 1925.

Cocchi, Guidus, *Commentarium in Codicem Iuris Canonici,* 5 vols. in 8, Taurinorum Augustae, 1922-1930; Liber V, *De Delictis et Poenis,* 2. ed., Taurinorum Augustae: Marietti, 1928.

Collison, Paulus J., *Non Omnis Censura Ab Homine Est Reservata,* Dissertatio ad Gradum Doctoris in Facultate Iuris Canonici Consequendum Scripta apud Pontificium Institutum Angelicum, Romae, 1935; typis impressa Lovanii: Bibliotheca S. Alphonsi, 1936.

Conran, Edward J., *The Interdict,* The Catholic University of America, Canon Law Studies, n. 56, Washington: The Catholic University of America, 1930.

Coronata, Matthaeus Conte a, *Institutiones Iuris Canonici,* 5 vols., Taurini (Italia): Marietti, 1928-1936; Vol. IV, *De Delictis et Poenis,* 1935.

D'Annibale, Josephus, *Summula Theologiae Moralis,* 5. ed., 3 vols., Romae: Desclée, Lefebvre et Soc., 1908.

Daremberg, Ch., et Saglio, Edm., *Dictionnaire des Antiquités Grecques et Romaines,* 5 vols. in 9, Paris, 1873.

Dargin, Edward V., *Reserved Cases According to the Code of Canon Law,* The Catholic University of America, Canon Law Studies, n. 20, Washington: The Catholic University of America, 1924.

Davis, Henry, *Moral and Pastoral Theology,* Heythrop Theological Series, II, 4 vols., New York: Sheed & Ward, 1935.

De Meester, Alphonsus, *Juris Canonici et Juris Canonico-Civilis Compendium,* nova ed., 3 vols. in 4, Brugis: Desclée, De Brouwer et Sii, 1921-1928.

De Smet, Aloysius, *De Absolutione Complicis et Sollicitatione,* 2. ed., Brugis: Beyaert, 1921.

Eichmann, Eduard, *Lehrbuch des Kirchenrechts auf Grund des Codex Iuris Canonici,* 2. ed., Paderborn: Schöningh, 1926.

Enciclopedia Italiana, Milan: Treccani, 1929-

Farrugia, Nicolaus, *De Casuum Conscientiae Reservatione,* 2. ed., Augustae Taurinorum: Marietti, 1922.

Ferraris, F. Lucius, *Prompta Bibliotheca, Canonica, Juridica, Moralis, Theologica, nec non Ascetica, Polemica, Rubricistica, Historica,* ed. Migne, 8 vols., Parisiis, 1860-1863.

Ferreres, Joannes, *Institutiones Canonicae,* 2. ed., 2 vols., Barcinone: Subirana, 1920.

Fournier, Paul, *Les Officialités au Moyen Age,* Paris, 1880.

Frank, Fr., *Die Bussdisciplin der Kirche von den Apostelzeiten bis zum siebenten Jahrhundert,* Mainz, 1867.

Galtier, Paulus, *De Paenitentia,* Parisiis: Beauchesne, 1923.

Genicot, Eduardus, et Salsmans, I., *Institutiones Theologiae Moralis,* 11. ed., 2 vols., Bruxellis: Dewit, 1927.

Giraldi, Ubaldus, *Expositio Juris Pontificii juxta Recentiorem Ecclesiae Disciplinam,* 3 vols. in 2, Romae, 1769.

Gonzalez Tellez, Emmanuel, *Commentaria Perpetua in Singulos Textus Quinque Librorum Decretalium Gregorii IX*, 5 vols. in 4, Lugduni, 1715.

Grandclaude, Eugenius, *Jus Canonicum juxta Ordinem Decretalium*, 3 vols., Parisiis, 1883.

Hefele, Carolus, et Leclercq, Henricus, *Histoire des Conciles*, 9 vols. in 18, Paris, 1907-1921.

Hinschius, Paul, *System des katholischen Kirchenrechts*, 6 vols., Berlin, 1869-1897.

Hollweck, Joseph, *Die kirchlichen Strafgesetze*, Mainz, 1899.

Hostiensis, Cardinalis (Henricus de Segusio), *Commentaria in Quinque Decretalium Libros*, 5 vols. in 3, Venetiis, 1581.

——— *Summa Aurea*, Venetiis, 1570.

Huguenin, Ludovicus, *Constitutionis "Apostolicae Sedis" Brevis Explanatio*, Parisiis, 1877.

Hyland, Francis E., *Excommunication, Its Nature, Historical Development and Effects*, The Catholic University of America, Canon Law Studies, n. 49, Washington: The Catholic University of America, 1928.

Joannes Andreae, *In Sex Decretalium Libros Novella Commentaria*, 6 vols. in 5, Venetiis, 1581.

Kelly, James P., *The Jurisdiction of the Confessor According to the Code of Canon Law*, New York: Benziger, 1929.

King, James I., *The Administration of the Sacraments to Dying Non-Catholics*, The Catholic University of America, Canon Law Studies, n. 23, Washington: The Catholic University of America, 1924.

Kober, F., *Der Kirchenbann nach den Grundsätzen des canonischen Rechts*, Tübingen, 1863.

Konings, Antonius, *Theologia Moralis*, 5. ed., 2 vols., Neo Eboraci, 1882.

Konings, Antonius, et Putzer, Joseph, *Commentarium in Facultates Apostolicas*, 4. ed., Neo Eboraci, 1897.

Lea, Henry C., *A History of Auricular Confession and Indulgences in the Latin Church*, 3 vols., Philadelphia, 1896.

Leech, George L., *A Comparative Study of the Constitution "Apostolicae Sedis" and the "Codex Juris Canonici,"* The Catholic University of America, Canon Law Studies, n. 15, Washington: The Catholic University of America, 1922.

Lega, Michael, *Praelectiones in Textum Iuris Canonici—De Delictis et Poenis*, 2. ed., Romae, 1910.

Lehmkuhl, Augustinus, *Theologia Moralis*, 10. ed., 2 vols., Friburgi Brisgoviae, 1902.

Leurenius, Petrus, *Forum Ecclesiasticum, in quo Jus Canonicum Universum Explanatur*, 5 vols. in 3, Venetiis, 1729.

MacKenzie, Eric F., *The Delict of Heresy in Its Commission, Penalization, Absolution*, The Catholic University of America, Canon Law Studies, n. 77, Washington: The Catholic University of America, 1932.

Makée, P.-Ch., *Institutiones Juris Ecclesiastici tum Publici tum Privati,* 2 vols., Romae, Parisiis, Friburgi, 1897.

Marc, Cl., Gestermann, F. X., et Raus, J. B., *Institutiones Morales Alphonsianae,* 19. ed., 2 vols., Lugduni: Vitte, 1933.

Morinus, Joannes, *Commentarius Historicus de Disciplina in Administratione Sacramenti Poenitentiae Tredecim Primis Seculis in Ecclesia Occidentali, et huc usque in Orientali Observata,* Parisiis, 1651.

Motry, Hubert Louis, *Diocesan Faculties According to the Code of Canon Law,* The Catholic University of America, Canon Law Studies, n. 16, Washington: The Catholic University of America, 1922.

Neuberger, Nicolas J., *Canon 6, or the Relation of the Codex Juris Canonici to Preceding Legislation,* The Catholic University of America, Canon Law Studies, n. 44, Washington: The Catholic University of America, 1927.

Noldin, H., et Schmitt, A., *De Sacramentis,* 19. ed., Oeniponte: Rauch, 1929.

Noldin, H., et Schönegger, A., *De Censuris,* 20. et 21. ed., Oeniponte: Rauch, 1928.

Panormitanus, Abbas (Nicolaus de Tudeschis), *Commentaria in Quinque Libros Decretalium,* 5 vols. in 7, Venetiis, 1588.

Pennacchi, Josephus, *Commentaria in Constitutionem Apostolicae Sedis,* 2 vols., Romae, 1883.

Phillips, Georgius, et Vering, Fridericus, *Compendium Iuris Ecclesiastici,* 1. Latin version from 3. German ed., Ratisbonae, 1875.

Pichler, Vitus, *Jus Canonicum secundum Quinque Decretalium Titulos Explicatum,* Ravennae, 1741.

Pignataro, Felix, *De Disciplina Poenitentiali Priorum Ecclesiae Saeculorum Commentarius,* Romae, 1904.

Pirhing, Ernricus, *Jus Canonicum Nova Methodo Explicatum,* 5 vols. in 4, Dilingae, 1674-1678.

Pistocchi, Mario, *I Canoni Penali del Codice Ecclesiastico Esposti e Commentati,* Torino-Roma: Marietti, 1925.

Poschmann, Bernhard, *Die abendländische Kirchenbusse im frühen Mittelalter,* Breslauer Studien zur historischen Theologie, Band XVI, Breslau: Müller & Seiffert, 1930.

Probst, Ferdinand, *Kirchliche Disciplin in den drei ersten christlichen Jahrhunderten,* Tübingen, 1873.

Prümmer, Dominicus M., *Manuale Iuris Canonici,* 4. et 5. ed., Friburgi Brisgoviae: Herder, 1927.

——— *Manuale Theologiae Moralis secundum Principia S. Thomae Aquinatis,* 4. et 5. ed., 3 vols., Friburgi Brisgoviae: Herder, 1928.

Rainer, Eligius G., *Suspension of Clerics,* The Catholic University of America, Canon Law Studies, n. 111, Washington: The Catholic University of America, 1937.

Raus, Joannes B., *Institutiones Canonicae juxta Novum Codicem Juris,* 2. ed., Lugduni, Parisiis: Vitte, 1931.

Rauschen, Gerhard, *Eucharist and Penance in the First Six Centuries of the Church*, authorized translation from 2. German ed., St. Louis, Mo.: Herder, 1913.

Reiffenstuel, Anacletus, *Jus Canonicum Universum*, 5 vols. in 7, Parisiis, 1864-1870.

Reintjes, Gulielmus, *De Absolutione Censurae*, Dissertatio ad obtinendum gradum Doctoratus in Facultate Juris Canonici in Pontificio Collegio "Angelico" de Urbe Elaborata, 1925. [Not printed.]

Richter, Aemilius L., *Lehrbuch des katholischen und evangelischen Kirchenrechts*, 8. ed., 1 vol. in 2, Leipzig, 1886.

Sabetti, Aloysius, et Barrett, Timotheus, *Compendium Theologiae Moralis*, 32. ed., Neo Eboraci: Pustet, 1929.

Salucci, Raffaele, *Il Diritto Penale secondo il Codice di Diritto Canonico*, 2 vols., Subiaco: Tipografia dei Monasteri, 1926-1930.

Santi, Franciscus, *Praelectiones Juris Canonici*, 2 vols., Ratisbonae, Neo Eboraci, Cincinnati, 1886.

Schmalzgrueber, Franciscus, *Jus Ecclesiasticum Universum*, 5 vols. in 12, Romae, 1843-1845.

Schmitz, Herman J., *Die Bussbücher und die Bussdisciplin der Kirche*, Mainz, 1883.

Schulte, Johannes F. von, *Die Geschichte der Quellen und Literatur des Canonischen Rechts von Gratian bis auf die Gegenwart*, 3 vols., Stuttgart, 1875-1880.

Slater, Thomas, *A Manual of Moral Theology*, 6. ed., 2 vols., London: Burns, Oates & Washbourne, 1928.

Smith, Mariner T., *The Penal Law for Religious*, The Catholic University of America, Canon Law Studies, n. 98, Washington: The Catholic University of America, 1935.

Smith, S. B., *Elements of Ecclesiastical Law*, 6. ed., 3 vols., New York, 1887.

Sole, Iacobus, *De Delictis et Poenis—Praelectiones in Lib. V Codicis Iuris Canonici*, Romae: Pustet, 1920.

Suarez, Franciscus, *Opera Omnia*, ed. C. Berton, 26 vols., Parisiis, 1856-1866; Vol. XXIII, *De Censuris in Communi*.

Teetaert, Amédée, *La Confession aux Laiques dans l'Eglise Latine depuis le VIIIe jusqu'au XIVe Siècle*, Universitas Catholica Lovaniensis, Dissertationes ad gradum magistri in Facultate Theologica consequendum conscriptae, Series II, Tomus 17, Wetteren, Bruges, Paris: De Meester, Beyaert, Gabalda, 1926.

Thesaurus, Carolus, *De Poenis Ecclesiasticis Praxis Absoluta et Universalis*, nova Romana ed. U. Giraldi, Romae, 1831.

Thesaurus Linguae Latinae, Lipsiae, 1904-

Vacandard, E., *Etudes de Critique et d'Histoire Religieuse*, 2me série, 3. ed., Paris: Lecoffre, 1914; "Les Origines de la Confession Sacramentelle," pp. 51-125.

Vacant, E., Mangenot, E., et Amann, A., *Dictionnaire de Théologie Catholique*, Paris, 1903-

Van Espen, Zegerus B., *Scripta Omnia*, 4 vols., Lovanii, 1753.

——— *Tractatus Historico-Canonicus de Censuris Ecclesiasticis*, Lovanii, 1753; (included as separate unit in *Scripta Omnia*, Vol. IV).

Van Hove, A., *Prolegomena ad Codicem Iuris Canonici*, Commentarium Lovaniense in Codicem Iuris Canonici, Vol. I, Tom. I, Mechliniae et Romae: Dessain, 1928.

Vecchiotti, Septimius, *Institutiones Canonicae*, 16. ed., 3 vols., Augustae Taurinorum, 1875.

Vermeersch, Arthurus, *Theologiae Moralis Principia, Responsa, Consilia*, 2. ed., (except Vol. II—1. ed.), 4 vols., Brugis: Beyaert, 1926-1928.

Vermeersch, A., et Creusen, J., *Epitome Iuris Canonici*, 3. ed., 3 vols., Mechliniae et Romae: Dessain, 1927-1928.

Watkins, Oscar D., *A History of Penance*, 2 vols., London: Longmans, Green & Co., 1920.

Wernz, Franciscus X., *Ius Decretalium*, 6 vols., Romae et Prati, 1906-1913.

Wouters, Ludovicus, *Manuale Theologiae Moralis*, 2 vols., Brugis: Beyaert, 1932-1933.

Woywod, Stanislaus, *A Practical Commentary on the Code of Canon Law*, 3. ed., 2 vols., New York: Wagner, 1929.

Periodicals

Apollinaris, Romae, 1928—

Archiv für katholisches Kirchenrecht, Innsbruck, 1857-1861; Mainz, 1862—

Bollettino del Clero Romano, Roma, 1920—

Collationes Brugenses, Bruges, 1895—

Ecclesiastical Review, The [originally *The American Ecclesiastical Review*], Philadelphia, 1889—

Ephemerides Theologicae Lovanienses, Brugis, 1924—

Homiletic and Pastoral Review, The, New York, 1900—

Irish Ecclesiastical Record, The, Dublin, 1864—

Jus Pontificium, Romae, 1921—

Monitore Ecclesiastico, Il, Romae, 1876—

Nouvelle Revue Théologique, Tournai, 1869—

Perfice Munus, Torino, 1926—

Periodica de Re Canonica et Morali utili praesertim Religiosis et Missionariis, Bruges, 1905—

Theologisch-praktische Quartalschrift, Linz, 1832—

Articles

Beijersbergen, H., "Decretum 18 Aprilis, 1936—Annotationes," *Periodica*, XXV (1936), 199-203.

Bergh, E., "Absolution de prêtres mariés civilement," *Nouvelle Revue Théologique*, LXIII (1936), 914, 915; LXIV (1937), 774.

Cappello, Felix, "De absolutione a censuris 'ab homine' ac de metu relate ad censuras," *Nouvelle Revue Théologique*, XLVII (1920), 525-531.

[?] "Il Codice di Diritto Canonico—Riassunto e Dilucidazioni," *Il Monitore Ecclesiastico*, serie 4, vol. 4 (vol. 34—1922), 146-149.

Creusen, J., "De Reservatione Censurae Praecepto Latae," *Jus Pontificium*, IV (1924), 26-29.

——— "La réserve des censures 'ab homine,'" *Nouvelle Revue Théologique*, LV (1928), 436-444.

Fliesser, Josef, "Absolutio et ad participationem sacramentorum admissio sacerdotum in attentato matrimonio abhinc caste viventium," *Theologisch-praktische Quartalschrift*, LXXXIX (1936), 821-824.

Friedle, Theod., "Ueber die Absolutio a Censuris in articulo mortis," *Archiv für katholisches Kirchenrecht*, XXX (1873), 185-203.

Galtier, Fr., "De ignorantia et errore in censurarum specialissimo modo reservatarum absolutione," *Periodica*, XVII (1928), 55-68.

Jone, Heribert, "[Absolutio] In casibus urgentioribus," *Theologisch-praktische Quartalschrift*, LXXXIII (1930), 357-363.

——— "Die Absolutionsvollmachten in Todesgefahr," *Theologisch-praktische Quartalschrift*, LXXIX (1926), 12-21, 237-250.

Kelly, James P., "Faculties of Absolving and Dispensing in Danger of Death," *Ecclesiastical Review*, LXXXV (1931), 255-277.

[Kelly, James P.?], "Faculties of Confessor in Case of Danger of Death," *Ecclesiastical Review*, XCI (1934), 411-413.

Kinane, J., "The Reservation of Censures 'Latae Sententiae' Imposed by a Particular Precept," *Irish Ecclesiastical Record*, XL (1932), 528-534.

Lopez, Ulpianus, "De reconciliatione sacerdotis, qui matrimonium attentare praesumpsit," *Periodica*, XXVI (1937), 501-506.

Meurer, Christian, "Die rechtliche Natur der Pönitenzen der katholischen Kirche in historischer Entwicklung," *Archiv für katholisches Kirchenrecht*, XLIX (1883), 177-217.

Michiels, Gommarus, "De reservatione censurae latae sententiae praecepto peculiari adnexae," *Ephemerides Theologicae Lovanienses*, IV (1927), 180-194, 613-619.

Paban, Ceslaus M., "Absolutio a censuris in periculo mortis," *Bollettino del Clero Romano*, VIII (1927), 39, 40.

Prümmer, Dominicus M., "Der kirchenrechtlich vorgeschriebene Rekurs bei der Absolution von Reservatfällen," *Theologisch-praktische Quartalschrift*, LXXVIII (1925), 763-770.

Raus, Joannes B., "Absolution von Zensuren l. s. ab homine," *Theologisch-praktische Quartalschrift*, LXXXIII (1930), 585-588.

——— "Der Zusatz 'sub poena reincidentiae' beim kirchenrechtlichen Rekurs gemäss can. 2254, § 1," *Theologisch-praktische Quartalschrift*, LXXXIX (1936), 123-128.

Roberti, Franciscus, "De Absolutione in Periculo Mortis," *Apollinaris,* I (1928), 102, 103.

——— "An censura latae sententiae per praeceptum constituta sit reservata," *Apollinaris,* VI (1933), 341-348.

Rossi, Joseph, "De sacerdotibus qui matrimonium etiam civile tantum contrahere praesumpserint quoad absolutionem a censura de qua in can. 2388, § 1," *Perfice Munus,* XI (1936), 346-350, 400-403, 473-476, 530-534, 654-659, 719-725; XII (1937), 15-18, 86-91, 227-231, 335-339, 403-407, 461-464, 532-536, 590-593, 661-664. (This series of articles covers a much broader field than its title indicates, including among other things an extensive explanation of the extraordinary absolution from censures in general.)

——— "S. Poenitentiaria Apostolica, Decretum 18 Aprilis, 1936—Annotationes," *Apollinaris,* IX (1936), 587, 588.

[?], "S. Poenit. Apos., Declaratio 4 Maii, 1937—Annotationes," *Apollinaris,* X (1937), 175.

Schaaf, Valentine T., "The Seal of Confession: New Precautions," *Ecclesiastical Review,* XCII (1935), 540, 541.

Schwentner, B., "Die excommunicatio specialissimo modo reservata," *Theologisch-praktische Quartalschrift,* LXXVIII (1925), 283-291.

Verhamme, A., "Decretum 18 Aprilis, 1936—Notae," *Collationes Brugenses,* XXXVI (1936), 336, 337.

[Vermeersch, A.?], "Annotationes—De absolutione in periculo mortis," *Periodica,* XVII (1928), 41, 42.

Woywod, Stanislaus, "False Accusation of Solicitation," *Homiletic and Pastoral Review,* XXXVIII (1938), 718-722.

ABBREVIATIONS

AAS—*Acta Apostolicae Sedis.*
AKKR—*Archiv für katholisches Kirchenrecht.*
ASS—*Acta Sanctae Sedis.*
ETL—*Ephemerides Theologicae Lovanienses.*
Fontes—*Codicis Iuris Canonici Fontes.*
MPG—Migne, *Patrologia, Series Graeca.*
MPL—Migne, *Patrologia, Series Latina.*
NRT—*Nouvelle Revue Théologique.*
TPQ—*Theologisch-praktische Quartalschrift.*

Universitas Catholica Americae
WASHINGTON, D. C.
Facultas Juris Canonici
No. 113
1938

ALPHABETICAL INDEX

BIOGRAPHICAL NOTE

Francis Edwin Moriarty was born on April 9, 1909, at Boston, Massachusetts. After receiving his primary education in Our Lady of Perpetual Help School, he attended the Boston Latin School, from which he was graduated in June, 1926. He then went to the Redemptorist preparatory college at North East, Pennsylvania, and at the end of two years he entered the novitiate of the same Congregation at Ilchester, Maryland, where he was professed on August 2, 1929. Pursuing his seminary studies at Mount Saint Alphonsus, Esopus, New York, he was ordained to the priesthood by His Eminence, Patrick Cardinal Hayes, on June 17, 1934. After he had completed his final year of theology in 1935, he was sent to the Catholic University of America, from which he received the Baccalaureate in Canon Law in June, 1936, and the Licentiate in Canon Law in June, 1937.

CANON LAW STUDIES

1. Freriks, Rev. Celestine A., C.PP.S., J.C.D., Religious Congregations in Their External Relations, 121 pp., 1916.
2. Galliher, Rev. Daniel M., O.P., J.C.D., Canonical Elections, 117 pp., 1917.
3. Borkowski, Rev. Aurelius L., O.F.M., J.C.D., De Confraternitatibus Ecclesiasticis, 136 pp., 1918.
4. Castillo, Rev. Cayo, J.C.D., Disertacion Historico-Canonica sobre la Potestad del Cabildo en Sede Vacante o Impedida del Vicario Capitular, 99 pp., 1919 (1918).
5. Kubelbeck, Rev. William J., S.T.B., J.C.D., The Sacred Penitentiaria and Its Relation to Faculties of Ordinaries and Priests, 129 pp., 1918.
6. Petrovits, Rev. Joseph, J.C., S.T.D., J.C.D., The New Church Law on Matrimony, X-461 pp., 1919.
7. Hickey, Rev. John J., S.T.B., J.C.D., Irregularities and Simple Impediments in the New Code of Canon Law, 100 pp., 1920.
8. Klekotka, Rev. Peter J., S.T.B., J.C.D., Diocesan Consultors, 179 pp., 1920.
9. Wanenmacher, Rev. Francis, J.C.D., The Evidence in Ecclesiastical Procedure Affecting the Marriage Bond, 1920 (Printed 1935).
10. Golden, Rev. Henry Francis, J.C.D., Parochial Benefices in the New Code, IV-119 pp., 1921 (Printed 1925).
11. Koudelka, Rev. Charles J., J.C.D., Pastors, Their Rights and Duties According to the New Code of Canon Law, 211 pp., 1921.
12. Melo, Rev. Antonius, O.F.M., J.C.D., De Exemptione Regularium, X-188 pp., 1921.
13. Schaaf, Rev. Valentine Theodore, O.F.M., S.T.B., J.C.D., The Cloister, X-180 pp., 1921.
14. Burke, Rev. Thomas Joseph, S.T.D., J.C.D., Competence in Ecclesiastical Tribunals, IV-117 pp., 1922.
15. Leech, Rev. George Leo, J.C.D., A Comparative Study of the Constitution "Apostolicae Sedis" and the "Codex Juris Canonici," 179 pp., 1922.
16. Motry, Rev. Hubert Louis, S.T.D., J.C.D., Diocesan Faculties According to the Code of Canon Law, II-167, pp., 1922.
17. Murphy, Rev. George Lawrence, J.C.D., Delinquencies and Penalties in the Administration and the Reception of the Sacraments, IV-121 pp., 1923.
18. O'Reilly, Rev. John Anthony, S.T.B., J.C.D., Ecclesiastical Sepulture in the New Code of Canon Law, II-129 pp., 1923.
19. Michalicka, Rev. Wenceslas Cyrill, O.S.B., J.C.D., Judicial Procedure in Dismissal of Clerical Exempt Religious, 107 pp., 1923.
20. Dargin, Rev. Edward Vincent, S.T.B., J.C.D., Reserved Cases According to the Code of Canon Law, IV-103 pp., 1924.

21. Godfrey, Rev. John A., S.T.B., J.C.D., The Right of Patronage According to the Code of Canon Law, 153 pp., 1924.
22. Hagedorn, Rev. Francis Edward, J.C.D., General Legislation on Indulgences, II-154 pp., 1924.
23. King, Rev. James Ignatius, J.C.D., The Administration of the Sacraments to Dying Non-Catholics, V-141 pp., 1924.
24. Winslow, Rev. Francis Joseph, O.F.M., J.C.D., Vicars and Prefects Apostolic, IV-149 pp., 1924.
25. Correa, Rev. Jose Servelion, S.T.L., J.C.D., La Potestad Legislativa de la Iglesia Catolica, IV-127 pp., 1925.
26. Dugan, Rev. Henry Francis, A.M., J.C.D., The Judiciary Department of the Diocesan Curia, 87 pp., 1925.
27. Keller, Rev. Charles Frederick, S.T.B., J.C.D., Mass Stipends, 167 pp., 1925.
28. Paschang, Rev. John Linus, J.C.D., The Sacramentals According to the Code of Canon Law, 129 pp., 1925.
29. Pointek, Rev. Cyrillus, O.F.M., S.T.B., J.C.D., De Indulto Exclaustrationis necnon Saecularizationis, XIII-289 pp., 1925.
30. Kearney, Rev. Richard Joseph, S.T.B., J.C.D., Sponsors at Baptism According to the Code of Canon Law, IV-127 pp., 1925.
31. Bartlett, Rev. Chester Joseph, A.M., LL.B., J.C.D., The Tenure of Parochial Property in the United States of America, V-108 pp., 1926.
32. Kilker, Rev. Adrian Jerome, J.C.D., Extreme Unction, V-425 pp., 1926
33. McCormick, Rev. Robert Emmett, J.C.D., Confessors of Religious, VIII-266 pp., 1926.
34. Miller, Rev. Newton Thomas, J.C.D., Founded Masses According to the Code of Canon Law, VII-93 pp., 1926.
35. Roelker, Rev. Edward G., S.T.D., J.C.D., Principles of Privilege According to the Code of Canon Law, XI-166 pp., 1926.
36. Bakalarczyk, Rev. Richardus, M.I.C., J.U.D., De Novitiatu, VIII-208 pp., 1927.
37. Pizzuti, Rev. Lawrence, O.F.M., J.U.L., De Parochis Religiosis, 1927. (Not Printed.)
38. Bliley, Rev. Nicholas Martin, O.S.B., J.C.D., Altars According to the Code of Canon Law, XIX-132 pp., 1927.
39. Brown, Mr. Brendan Francis, A.B., LL.M., J.U.D., The Canonical Juristic Personality with Special Reference to its Status in the United States of America, V-212 pp., 1927.
40. Cavanaugh, Rev. William Thomas, C.P., J.U.D., The Reservation of the Blessed Sacrament, VIII-101 pp., 1927.
41. Doheny, Rev. William J., C.S.C., A.B., J.U.D., Church Property: Modes of Acquisition, X-118 pp., 1927.
42. Feldhaus, Rev. Aloysius H., C.PP.S., J.C.D., Oratories, IX-141 pp., 1927.
43. Kelly, Rev. James Patrick, A.B., J.C.D., The Jurisdiction of the Simple Confessor, X-2008 pp., 1927.

44. NEUBERGER, REV. NICHOLAS J., J.C.D., Canon 6 or the Relation of the Codex Juris Canonici to the Preceding Legislation, V-95 pp. 1927.
45. O'KEEFE, REV. GERALD MICHAEL, J.C.D., Matrimonial Dispensations, Powers of Bishops, Priests, and Confessors, VIII-232 pp., 1927.
46. QUIGLEY, REV. JOSEPH A. M., A.B., J.C.D., Condemned Societies, 139 pp., 1927.
47. ZAPLOTNIK, REV. JOHANNES LEO, J.C.D., De Vicariis Foraneis, X-142 pp., 1927.
48. DUSKIE, REV. JOHN ALOYSIUS, A.B., J.C.D., The Canonical Status of the Orientals in the United States, VIII-196 pp., 1928.
49. HYLAND, REV. FRANCIS EDWARD, J.C.D., Excommunication, Its Nature, Historical Development and Effects, VIII-181 pp., 1928.
50. REINMANN, REV. GERALD JOSEPH, O.M.C., J.C.D., The Third Order Secular of Saint Francis, 201 pp., 1928.
51. SCHENK, REV. FRANCIS J., J.C.D., The Matrimonial Impediments of Mixed Religion and Disparity of Cult, XVI-318 pp., 1929.
52. COADY, REV. JOHN JOSEPH, S.T.D., J.U.D., A.M., The Appointment of Pastors, VIII-150 pp., 1929.
53. KAY, REV. THOMAS HENRY, J.C.D., Competence in Matrimonial Procedure, VIII-164 pp., 1929.
54. TURNER, REV. SIDNEY JOSEPH, C.P., J.U.D., The Vow of Poverty, XLIX-217 pp., 1929.
55. KEARNEY, REV. RAYMOND A., A.B., S.T.D., J.C.D., The Principles of Delegation, VII-149 pp., 1929.
56. CONRAN, REV. EDWARD JAMES, A.B., J.C.D., The Interdict, V-163 pp., 1930.
57. O'NEIL, REV. WILLIAM H., J.C.D., Papal Rescripts of Favor, VII-218 pp., 1930.
58. BASTNAGEL, REV. CLEMENT VINCENT, J.U.D., The Appointment of Parochial Adjutants and Assistants, XV-257 pp., 1930.
59. FERRY, REV. WILLIAM A., A.B., J.C.D., Stole Fees, V-136 pp., 1930.
60. COSTELLO, REV. JOHN MICHAEL, A.B., J.C.D., Domicile and Quasi-Domicile, VII-201 pp., 1930.
61. KREMER, REV. MICHAEL NICHOLAS, A.B., S.T.B., J.C.D., Church Support In the United States, VI-136 pp., 1930.
62. ANGULO, REV. LUIS, C.M., J.C.D., Legislation de la Iglesia sobre la intencion en la application de la Santa Misa, VII-104 pp., 1931.
63. FREY, REV. WOLFGANG NORBERT, O.S.B., A.B., J.C.D., The Act of Religious Profession, VIII-174 pp., 1931.
64. ROBERTS, REV. JAMES BRENDAN, A.B., J.C.D., The Banns of Marriage, XIV-140 pp., 1931.
65. RYDER, REV. RAYMOND ALOYSIUS, A.B., J.C.D., Simony, IX-151 pp., 1931.
66. CAMPAGNA, REV. ANGELO, PH.D., J.U.D., Il Vicario Generale del Vescovo, VII-205 pp., 1931.

67. Cox, Rev. Joseph Godfrey, A.B., J.C.D., The Administration of Seminaries, VI-124 pp., 1931.
68. Gregory, Rev. Donald J., J.U.D., The Pauline Privilege, XV-165 pp., 1931.
69. Donohue, Rev. John F., J.C.D., The Impediment of Crime, VII-110 pp., 1931.
70. Dooley, Rev. Eugene A., O.M.I., J.C.D., Church Law on Sacred Relics IX-143 pp., 1931.
71. Orth, Rev. Clement Raymond, O.M.C., J.C.D., The Approbation of Religious Institutes, 171 pp., 1931.
72. Pernicone, Rev. Joseph M., A.B., J.C.D., The Ecclesiastical Prohibition of Books, XII-267 pp., 1932.
73. Clinton, Rev. Connell, A.B., J.C.D., The Paschal Precept, IX-108 pp., 1932.
74. Donnelly, Rev. Francis B., A.M., S.T.L., J.C.D., The Diocesan Synod, VIII-125 pp., 1932.
75. Torrente, Rev. Camilo, C.M.F., J.C.D., Las Processiones Sagradas, V-145 pp., 1932.
76. Murphy, Rev. Edwin, J., C.PP.S., J.C.D., Suspension Ex Informata Conscientia, XI-122 pp., 1932.
77 MacKenzie, Rev. Eric F., A.M., S.T.L., J.C.D., The Delict of Heresy in Its Commission, Penalization, Absolution, VII-124 pp., 1932.
78. Lyons, Rev. Avitus E., S.T.B., J.C.D., The Collegiate Tribunal of First Instance, XI-147 pp., 1932.
79. Connolly, Rev. Thomas A., J.C.D., Appeals, XI-195 pp., 1932.
80. Sangmeister, Rev. Joseph V., A.B., J.C.D., Force and Fear as Precluding Matrimonial Consent, V-211 pp., 1932.
81. Jaeger, Rev. Leo A., A.B., J.C.D., The Administration of Vacant and Quasi-Vacant Episcopal Sees in the United States, IX-229 pp., 1932.
82. Rimlinger, Rev. Herbert T., J.C.D., Error Invalidating Matrimonial Consent, VII-79 pp., 1932.
83. Barrett, Rev. John D. M., S.S., J.C.D., A Comparative Study of the Third Plenary Council of Baltimore and the Code, IX-221 pp., 1932.
84. Carberry, Rev. John J., Ph.D., S.T.D., J.C.D., The Juridical Form of Marriage, X-177 pp., 1934.
85. Dolan, Rev. John L., A.B., J.C.D., The Defensor Vinculi, XII-157 pp., 1934.
86. Hannan, Rev. Jerome D., A.M., S.T.D., LL.B., J.C.D., The Canon Law of Wills, IX-517 pp., 1934.
87. Lemieux, Rev. Delisle A., A.M., J.C.D., The Sentence in Ecclesiastical Procedure, IX-131 pp., 1934.
88. O'Rourke, Rev. James J., A.B., J.C.D., Parish Registers, VII-109 pp., 1934.
89. Timlin, Rev. Bartholomew, O.F.M., A.M., J.C.D., Conditional Matrimonial Consent, X-381 pp., 1934.

90. WAHL, REV. FRANCIS X., A.B., J.C.D., The Matrimonial Impediments of Consanguinity and Affinity, VI-125 pp., 1934.
91. WHITE, REV. ROBERT J., A.B., LL.B., S.T.B., J.C.D., Canonical Ante-Nuptial Promises and the Civil Law, VI-152 pp., 1934.
92. HERRERA, REV. ANTONIO PARRA, O.C.D., J.C.D., Legislacion Ecclesiastica sobrael Ayuno y la Abstinencia, XI-191 pp., 1935.
93. KENNEDY, REV. EDWIN J., J.C.D., The Special Matrimonial Process in Cases of Evident Nullity, X-165 pp., 1935.
94. MANNING, REV. JOHN J., A.B., J.C.D., Presumption of Law in Matrimonial Procedure, XI-111 pp., 1935.
95. MOEDER, REV. JOHN M., J.C.D., The Proper Bishop for Ordination and Dimissorial Letters, VII-135 pp., 1935.
96. O'MARA, REV. WILLIAM A., A.B., J.C.D., Canonical Causes for Matrimonial Dispensations, IX-155 pp., 1935.
97. REILLY, REV. PETER, J.C.D., Residence of Pastors, IX-81 pp., 1935.
98. SMITH, REV. MARINER T., O.P., S.T.Lr., J.C.D., The Penal Law for Religious, VII-169 pp., 1935.
99. WHALEN, REV. DONALD W., A.M., J.C.D., The Value of Testimonial Evidence in Matrimonial Procedure, XIII-297 pp., 1935.
100. CLEARY, REV. JOSEPH F., J.C.D., Canonical Limitations on the Alienation of Church Property, VIII-141 pp., 1936.
101. GLYNN, REV. JOHN C., J.C.D., The Promoter of Justice, XX-337 pp., 1936.
102. BRENNAN, REV. JAMES H., S.S., M.A., S.T.B., J.C.D., The Simple Convalidation of Marriage, VI-135 pp., 1937.
103. BRUNINI, REV. JOSEPH BERNARD, J.C.D., The Clerical Obligations of Canons 139 and 142, X-121 pp., 1937.
104. CONNOR, REV. MAURICE, A.B., J.C.D., The Administrative Removal of Pastors, VIII-159 pp., 1937.
105. GUILFOYLE, REV. MERLIN JOSEPH, J.C.D., Custom, XI-144 pp., 1937.
106. HUGHES, REV. JAMES AUSTIN, A.B., A.M., J.C.D., Witnesses in Criminal Trials of Clerics, IX-140 pp., 1937.
107. JANSEN, REV. RAYMOND J., A.B., S.T.L., J.C.D., Canonical Provisions for Catechetical Instruction, VII-153 pp., 1937.
108. KEALY, REV. JOHN JAMES, A.B., J.C.D., The Introductory Libellus in Church Court Procedure, XI-121 pp., 1937.
109. McMANUS, REV. JAMES EDWARD, C.SS.R., J.C.D., The Administration of Temporal Goods in Religious Institutes, XVI-196 pp., 1937.
110. MORIARTY, REV. EUGENE JAMES, J.C.D., Oaths in Ecclesiastical Courts, X-115 pp., 1937.
111. RAINER, REV. ELIGIUS GEORGE, C.SS.R., J.C.D., Suspension of Clerics, XVII-249 pp., 1937.
112. REILLY, REV. THOMAS F., C.SS.R., J.C.L., Visitation of Religious.
113. MORIARTY, REV. FRANCIS E., C.SS.R., J.C.L., The Extraordinary Absolution from Censures.

114. CONNOLLY, REV. NICHOLAS P., J.C.L., The Canonical Erection of Parishes.
115. DONOVAN, REV. JAMES JOSEPH, J.C.L., The Pastor's Obligation in Prenuptial Investigation.
116. HARRIGAN, REV. ROBERT J., M.A., S.T.B., J.C.L., The Radical Sanation of Invalid Marriages.

www.ingramcontent.com/pod-product-compliance
Lightning Source LLC
LaVergne TN
LVHW050259080826
844660LV00012B/658
* 9 7 8 0 8 1 3 2 2 3 0 2 5 *